D0653621

# THE PRACTICAL GARDENER

INCORPORATING

## Flower Gardening

Sean McCann

## Vegetable Gardening

David Toyne

## Greenhouse Gardening

Sue Phillips

TED SMART

# FLOWER GARDENING

Sean McCann

This edition published in 1991 by
Paul Hamlyn Publishing, part of Reed International
Books Limited
Michelin House
81 Fulham Road
London SW3 6RB



ISBN 0600 572 900

Produced by Mandarin Offset
Printed in Hong Kong

# CONTENTS

# INTRODUCTION

By using just a small packet of annual seeds or cuttings donated by a friend you can create a spectacularly colourful garden, packed with a wide variety of plants, including drifts of daffodils in spring, dazzling begonias, scented roses, waves of gypsophila, and the sweetly scented, old-fashioned wallflower.

Such plants, and scores of others, are very easily raised, which is one of the reasons why they are all so popular. But not only are they a delight in themselves, they are also an excellent way of transforming even the drabbest patch of ground. What might currently be a garden more noted for heaps of builders' rubble or three years of neglect and weeds can, after the ground has been cleared, actively be seen to come alive and take shape. As the spring sun warms the soil, so new flower beds will eventually begin bristling with shoots, so that by mid summer your eye will be attracted first to one patch of colour, then to another group of plants, in such a way that your garden immediately seems larger, dramatically richer, and infinitely more interesting.

However, to get things right you have got to plan ahead. You may not achieve the best associations straight away. Few people, even the owners of the greatest gardens in the country, never have to make any changes. After all, a garden should mirror your own loves and favourite combinations of plants, so don't be afraid to experiment or to rearrange if the result does not please first time. Flower gardening is a continuing experiment, that is part of its fun.

One thing that people tend to forget when creating a new garden, or rethinking their existing one, is that once you have done your work you will immediately be able to survey a new, brilliantly colourful world. Remember that it will take a season or two for your new plants to fill the spaces you have left them. Try not to think of your garden as *the* flower garden, which will be filled with every conceivable plant. That just isn't possible, even in the largest gardens. However, if that sounds depressing, consider that it also means you will have to be highly thoughtful and creative. What is the best plant for that one patch of damp, shady ground?

Why not devote that whole side of the garden to plants with foliage in one particular shade of grey-green, perhaps leading to a cluster of white plants at the far end? Colour themes in a garden give a spectacular result.

The more you think about your garden, no matter what its size or situation, the more you'll be aware of the fantastic range of possibilities. Planning ahead isn't that different from establishing the colour scheme and look of a favourite room. It should be a delight to enter, and excitingly different from anything your friends have designed. Colourful, magical – a sign of your creativeness, and an unrivalled opportunity to explore the different kinds of beauty possessed by the many hundreds of different plants that can be grown in our climate.

Right: A dazzling display of marigolds (*Calendula*) formally edged with bedding plants. These include begonias, lobelia, pansies and calceolaria.

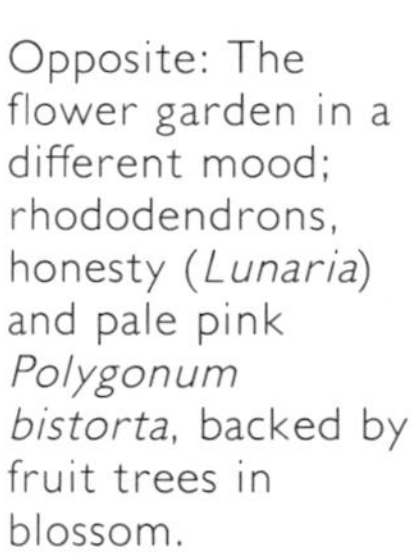

Opposite: The flower garden in a different mood; rhododendrons, honesty (*Lunaria*) and pale pink *Polygonum bistorta*, backed by fruit trees in blossom.

# CREATING A FLOWER GARDEN

There is no doubt in my mind that gardens are for flowers of every kind, from crocus to chrysanthemum, from snowdrop to cyclamen, from rose to simple pansy. Whether they are bulbous, annual, perennial or herbaceous, shrub or tree – there should always be something to keep colour in our lives no matter how drab our surroundings may be. Flowers give us colour as well as a very special excitement and pleasure. Flowers are for everyone and everywhere, whether it be in a garden of a great country house or a small cottage, in a window box on a busy street, or just a tumbling mass of lobelia in a small pot outside a doorway – flowers bring joy. The wonderful thing about them is that they can be grown with just a little care and attention. Provided you give them food, water, light and air – and a little bit of love you will have the makings of a marvellous garden. You do not have to be an expert to have plants in flower the whole year through.

Window boxes provide you with a great opportunity to experiment. After all, when you consider that in effect they allow you to select your soil, and that you can place them in full light or partial shade, it immediately becomes clear that they provide a fine opportunity for growing a wide range of colourful plants from early spring right through to Christmas. By changing the plants once or twice a year it is possible to try out new exciting plant colour schemes to keep the neighbours in constant wonder. Remember, even during the winter months small evergreens such as spotted laurel and variegated ivies will provide interest. They also form an attractive background, for example, for winter-flowering pansies or a variety of spring bulbs.

Another advantage for the modern gardener is that buying plants today is so much easier than in the past. There are more varieties now on offer, and there are few excuses for failing to raise them successfully, provided you buy first-rate plants and prepare the soil thoroughly. If

*Tradescantia virginiana*, the common spiderwort, named in honor of John Tradescant.

*Fuchsia* owes its name to Dr Fuchs; this is the popular cultivar 'Mrs Popple'.

you want immediate results, and are prepared to pay for them, you can even create an instant garden, complete with shed, lawn, paths, patio, beds of flowers in full bloom, and trees, all within a few days – just think of the Chelsea Flower Show!

## THE OLD AND THE NEW

It isn't just the ease of gardening that has made flower gardens so attractive, for plant breeders are continuously breaking through new barriers creating new types of flowers, new colours, hardier varieties of previously tender plants, and miniatures of just about everything. Yet while today's gardening catalogue may be a wonderland of plants and colour, remember that not everything in it is new – the old flowers are still there, particularly the old style hollyhocks, snapdragons, and the sweet pea with its unmistakeable fragrance. So don't get too distracted by the new kinds of plants that are proclaimed at the Chelsea Flower Show each year – the older plants are available and should always be considered.

They are also an excellent reminder of the exciting early years when the Europeans were introduced to new flowers. For example tradescantia (perhaps better known as spiderwort) took its name from John Tradescant (1570/5–1638) the famous plant explorer, and fuchsia owes its name to Dr L Fuchs (1501–1566), the German botanist and herbalist. Incidentally, other plants were named in different ways. The delphinium is from the Greek for 'dolphin'; dianthus is from the Greek word *dius*, meaning 'God', and *anthos* meaning 'flower'; and it's possible tulip may have come from the Turkish *tulnana*, meaning a 'turban'. The names of many other plants are concerned with ancient myths and legends.

One problem for the amateur gardener is that some plant names seem difficult and forbidding. If so, take comfort from the fact that most have common names, which we shall use wherever possible.

## GARDEN PLANTS

Over a century ago William Robinson (1838–1935), the eminent and influential Irish gardener and garden writer, wrote that '. . . a flower garden should be a thing of varied life.' He also offered the following advice to gardeners: 'Choose some beautiful class of plants and select a place that will suit them, even as to their effect in the garden landscape.' In that comment Robinson gives the key to what should be the great attraction of a garden. The plants should not only be carefully chosen, but carefully arranged. So, if you want to hide an ugly view, select tall growing plants that will eventually banish that eyesore; and if you want to emphasize a part of the garden or create a vista, then again consider your plants as part of an architectural plan.

The gardener must learn to view the garden from those parts that are most commonly used. Pick out what you would like to see when standing there, checking whether light colours will be best, whether you need height, or whether a specimen plant will be a winner. Yet this is not so much design in the flower garden, as taking an artist's view to produce something that will resemble a good painting. But don't forget, it will always be a 'painting' that you can reject or modify if you are unhappy with it, moving the various elements around and incorporating new ones where appropriate.

Low growing plants in full flower. White arabis, aubrieta and polyanthus associate well together and provide plenty of colour throughout the spring.

An annual border in summer with red salvias, begonias, tagetes, and lobelia. All can be raised from seed. The silver foliage of *Senecio cinerea* is an excellent foil to the hot colours of the flowers.

## FIRST CONSIDERATIONS

The first problem facing the gardener is deciding which sort of plants are needed. Making this decision involves answering a whole series of questions.

Do you want a permanent display, or will you be happy with a temporary arrangement, which can be changed next year or even next month if it doesn't look attractive? Note that your plants will have to be arranged around and between larger, more expensive, and probably permanent elements such as shrubs and trees. They are the 'main frame' of the garden. So too are the hardy perennials, which die down each winter but produce strong new growth the following year. Incidentally, some annuals behave in the same way, self-seeding and reappearing the following year, although you should not depend on that happening all the time and with every type.

The next question is, do you want to make the garden easy to look after? If you do then your choice will lean towards those plants that need little maintenance but provide long-term colour – many trees and shrubs obviously come into this grouping, but not all of these will fill a garden with that rich a diversity of plant form.

Roses, however, are a group of shrubs that will provide a marvellous array of colours, and provide long-term blooming, but remember they will require some attention for the best results.

Herbaceous borders can be equally colourful. They require a thorough preparation of the soil and careful planting, but once established they will need only routine weeding and dividing every three or four years for a wonderful return. In other words, there is no answer which does not require some input from you. And the greater your care and attention, the better will be the result.

Next, you must establish what size and shape plants you require. The biggest mistake made by gardeners is to plant a hedge that will grow and grow, needing cutting twice a year at least. That same hedge can also be a disaster if planted at the back of a flower border, for its enormous appetite 'eats' up the plant nutrients long before the flowers have had a chance to benefit from them. Permanent features, such as hedges and trees, should therefore be planted with great care, and in places where they will be easy to maintain by clipping and pruning.

Primulas and grape hyacinths (*Muscari*) provide interest in spring when the branches are bare.

## SELECTING GARDEN FLOWERS

The flower garden should be an amalgam of several elements. First, there are hedges and shrubs, which should be carefully chosen and very carefully placed. Then come the bulbs, many of which can be left in the ground until they need lifting because of overcrowding. The perennials, such as the delightful primula, will live for years in the herbaceous border or the rock garden, while annuals are planted, flower and die all within one season. Fourth are plants such as the sweet pea, border carnation, dahlia, chrysanthemum and fuchsia, many of which have cult followings, turning people who bought them, perhaps out of curiosity, into fanatics. Finally there are the roses – no garden would be complete without their wonderful blooms which they provide from May to December.

There can be little doubt that the annu-

*Helipterum roseum*, also known as acroclinium.

Bells of Ireland (*Molucella laevis*) is excellent for drying.

White tulips and lush green foliage provide a soothing colour association. The variegated foliage of euonymus continues the theme.

als and biennials provide the gardener with the widest range of plants, colour and fragrances for the least amount of money, but they do require some effort when it comes to seed planting, pricking out, weeding, watering, and dead-heading. Yet for variety and colour they are well worth the effort, as is immediately obvious on seeing a garden filled with the ever tolerant candytuft (*Iberis*), the massed colour of busy Lizzies (*Impatiens*), and the showy gazania. The flowering period for most of these plants is from June to October.

### Plant categories

The dividing line between annuals, half-hardy annuals and biennials is very fine. Basically, the half-hardy annuals can be sown outside in May for late flowering, but they may need to be planted under glass and then pricked out if needed earlier. Some annuals can also be treated this way, but most are better sown directly into the ground where they will be left to grow on. Biennials seeds are sown this year to provide flowering plants the next year.

Most of the bedding plants that are sold by the million every summer belong to these categories, and they all provide excellent material for extensive bedding schemes, brightening dull corners, adding spots of colour to the rockery, and filling gaps in more permanent beds or borders. Of course, they can be spectacularly successful in hanging baskets, tubs and window boxes. To get the best results from most of these flowers give them a sunny position, well-cultivated ground, and plenty of light and air.

### Drying flowers

In addition to providing garden colour, many annuals and biennials also provide delightful flowers for home decoration. However, do not try to emulate those ladies in the old Victorian garden prints who took flower cuttings and then placed them into large flat baskets. Flowers should be placed in water immediately on being cut, while those with woody stems will survive much better if the stem is cut *under* the water to avoid any risk of air-locks which will result in early wilting.

Bedding plants, such as the helichrysum (often called the straw flower), acroclinium (its proper Latin name is *Helipterum*, and its common name the everlasting flower), and *Molucella* (known as bells of Ireland because of the large green, bell-like calyx) also provide flowers which are excellent for drying. For the best results, take cuttings just before the flowers open.

Annual and biennial varieties of these flowers are extremely useful when you are brightening up very small areas with summer colour. Patio tubs, hanging baskets and window boxes all benefit greatly from them, but no-one would ever devote an entire garden, or even large sections of it, to annuals or biennials because the colour spread would not be good enough. These plants should be regarded as wonderful *additions* to the flower garden, growing side by side with the huge range of perennials in either the border or rockery.

### Perennials

The perennials give a sense of permanence and beauty to borders and rockeries, and can be landscaped, unlike annuals, which are passing beauties being the 'chorus' to the main 'players' in the garden. A well planted bed or border of perennials will last for years, requiring very little work yet providing a marvellous display. While most of the plants will die down in winter, others will withstand the cold leaving your garden not entirely devoid of leaf and colour.

The most sensible place to grow perennials is in the herbaceous and mixed borders where the majority of plants will flower year after year, only needing to be worked on when they become too big for their allotted place, and are possibly deteriorating. They should then be lifted and divided into several clumps, the new outside growth being used to ensure a future supply of colour.

The problem with perennials grown from seed is that they can be quite slow to start, which means that the herbaceous beds or borders take a couple of years to reach their full potential. For a more immediate effect buy the larger plants that are available. The other problem is that there is a bewildering range of these plants from which to choose – from the tiny ground-hugging plants, that are called alpines or rockery perennials, to those that grow 30 cm (1 ft) or more high and are classed as border perennials.

For the ordinary gardener these plants will be best used in a mixed border or, if the space is available, as an island bed where the plants can be seen from all sides. Although roses and other woody type plants make a successful mix, the perennials are at their best when used as groups rather than single specimens. If you later find there are unwelcome spaces between the taller plants, they can always be filled with various annuals.

### Bulbs

In addition to annuals, roses, and other shrubby types, there is always a place in the flower garden for bulbs, whether they be planted as separate subjects or within the various beds and borders. Although the word 'bulb' has a precise horticultural meaning, this is often overlooked and most people also include it to mean corms, tubers and some rhizomes (fleshy stems that creep below the surface producing plants such as the iris) in this category.

There is an extraordinary range of bulbs, with few other plant categories being able to provide the same amount of colour all the year round. Those more discerning gardeners who look beyond the familiar yellow daffodil and bedding tulip for something more unusual will find an even wider, excellent selection of new varieties of iris, gladioli, narcissus and daffodils, and tulips. Once you have selected your bulbs, you will need a well-drained, humus-rich soil which is, after all, the perfect garden soil.

## THE SOIL

Every garden, every bed, every border, even the smallest rockery, is only as good as its soil. Afterwards come the imagination, dedication, seeds and plants that will make your dreams come true. But for the time being unless the soil is right for your chosen plants, you can expect no help from nature.

Fortunately garden soil can be improved beyond recognition within a short period of time, though many gardeners mistakenly find this an awesome subject. Your first task is to decide whether a particular site is composed of good, bad or average soil?

Let us begin by looking at the ideal soil. It should be medium textured, with small and medium-sized particles containing few stones, the sort of soil that is generally called loam. It will be crumbly to the touch, and will drain well holding some water but not becoming waterlogged during heavy rains. It should also be high in organic material, have sufficient lime to stop any sign of sourness, and have sufficient plant nutrients to make sure that plants reach their full flowering potential. In other words, you will generally find good loam soil in a garden that has been cared for over a number of years. Most of this soil will be contained near the surface, the depth of which will vary from area to area – from 5 cm (2 in) to 60 cm (2 ft). This top-soil can be distinguished from the sub-soil by the fact that it looks more alive and fresh, whereas the sub-soil is generally a lighter (often sickly) colour and looks inert. The trick is never to mix the two – keep the top-soil to itself by placing it aside when you have to dig deeply. Replace it when the bottom layer has been dealt with.

However, not everyone can be blessed by the perfect soil, so most gardeners have to work at improving their plots. The basic types of soil that will be encountered are:

### Chalk soils

They have a white chalk (lime) sub-soil. The main problem is that since the land generally drains very quickly it needs generous amounts of manure and/ or compost to be dug in. And because of the quick drainage there is frequent leaching of the soil, which means that extra general fertilizer should be added, as well as iron and manganese, which will probably be needed once a year.

### Clay soils

These are cold, wet and heavy in the winter, and therefore of little use for early crops. But if you are a rose grower you will see a lot of value in clay although you still need to add compost, moss peat, or stable manure to improve the texture and open up the solidly packed soil and allow it to be become aerated. Worked well with lots of organic material, especially moss peat, the clay soil can become much sought after loam.

### Peat soils

These speak for themselves, being spongy and darkish grey or brown, and will be a delight for the grower of azaleas, rhododendrons and heathers. If you want to grow additional plants then you will have to investigate just how much liming is necessary to make the soil acceptable. While peaty soil can be very acidic and drains poorly, it is usually very fertile for adaptable plants.

### Sandy soils

Another quick draining soil, being gritty and fast drying so that again a lot of compost, moss peat and organic material is required to improve its condition.

### Stony soils

The back breaker – if you attempt to remove the stones! But once you realize that you will never achieve this without a complete transferance of new soil to the site, you need only remove the larger stones for a well aerated and reasonably productive garden.

## WEEDS AND OTHER GROWTH

These will also be a good indicator of the type of soil present – moss or a green slimy surface indicates that the drainage is bad; docks, buttercups or heathers usually reveal that it is an acid soil suitable for any plants that are listed later in this book. Good clover cover is an indication of alkaline soil, which means you will have problems growing good heather or azaleas. And, even though you will not welcome their presence, chickweed, nettles and groundsel indicate a productive, fertile soil. If you still require assistance in evaluating your soil type you can buy an inexpensive soil testing kit that will provide immediate answers. If you want even

Azaleas, here backed by *Magnolia* x *soulangiana*, flourish in a lime-free soil rich in peat.

more accurate help, approach a local gardening club where you will find information and help always at hand, or from a trained horticulturist.

The gardener who works with his soil and not against it is the one who will have most success, and who will get far more enjoyment from his garden. The main point to consider is that each type of soil is good for certain plants, so concentrate on growing them. First you must establish what soil is in your garden, or your new roses will not grow to their full potential, and your heather bed will be a source of dreams, not real enjoyment.

## DRAINAGE, WATERING, AND FEEDING

Drainage is also a very important aspect of good gardening. Even if you have a moist, soggy garden which cannot be improved do not despair because there are many exciting plants that you can grow. Chinese loosestrife (*Lysimachia clethroides*) bears long spikes of tiny white flowers almost like a buddleia; the marsh marigold (*Caltha palustris* 'Flore Pleno') with its spring flowering golden heads can only survive in these moist conditions, while the hybrid astilbes with their long feathery plumes will be wasted anywhere else. However, in the well-drained garden your choice will never be restricted – the lists of flowers that will do well in these conditions would fill a book on their own.

Making the soil fertile by drainage, compost and/or fertilizer is the gardener's main responsibility. If you remember that soils can be upset and unbalanced by cultivation, it is obvious that a little help will be needed to restore things to their normal condition. This can be done by replacing three major soil losses, nitrogen, phosphorus and potassium, on a regular and well-planned schedule. When you have decided on your fertilizer read the instructions and use accordingly. You will soon be able to spot those gardens and plants that are undernourished. However, the real gardener does not wait for these signs but sets out with a calendar for feeding right through the year.

Most long-lasting flowers or plants will need some help at least once a month during their growing season (my own plan is to nominate the last day of every month as feeding day). Fertilizing large areas is much easier than tackling small patches when the fertilizer must be kept off the plants lest it scorches the foliage. The way to ensure this does not happen is to measure out the quantity as recommended by the maker and put it into a small container. A matchbox may be ideal, but an old salt shaker is also very handy for distributing fertilizer among plants (make sure that from now on you restrict that salt shaker to the gardening box). Treat the ground around the plants uniformly.

The double marsh marigold (*Caltha palustris* 'Flore Pleno') needs a permanently moist soil. It thrives in the shallow margins of a pool.

However, feeding is not the main guarantor of success. Watering is just as vital being far more important than we imagine in these often wet summers. Some plants, such as roses and fuchsias, if growing on fairly well-drained land still need prodigious amounts of water and should never be allowed to dry out. Mature roses on a well-drained site will take up to 9.1 litre (2 gl) of water a day. Of course you don't have to molly-coddle them to that extent, but by watering them more frequently than most of us do they will be far healthier.

To ensure that plants get well watered and fed it is a good idea to use liquid or soluble fertilizers applied through a watering can or hose-end diluter. Liquid fertilizers are the answer where a quick result is needed because the necessary nutrients are immediately available to the plant. If you are watering frequently, increase the dilution by half or more. There is nothing that will rival a well-maintained garden, whose plants have been fed and watered regularly.

A diluter, easily attached to a hose end, will combine watering and feeding.

# PLANTS FROM SEEDS AND CUTTINGS

You do not need to be an expert to raise plants from seeds. If you stop and think about it this is exactly the way the plants do it themselves, and if left to their own devices many would propagate without any help from the gardener. In addition, most perennials produce their own new plantlets each year, while daffodils and other bulbs will increase, if left undisturbed for a number of years, even though the increase in quantity can mean a decrease in quality.

However, this does not mean that when you have bought packets of seeds of annuals, half annuals or biennials, you can sow and forget about them. They will require some basic attention, but once they have been given moisture, oxygen, a reasonably high temperature and, eventually, a food supply, they will develop without any problems. Another bonus of sowing seeds is that this is an inexpensive way of providing new flowers every year, while providing the extra thrill of knowing that the plants are entirely your own work.

These plants traditionally raised from seed not only provide a good display in the garden but also a supply of flowers for cutting and drying. Note too, that seeds of half-hardy annuals, annuals and biennials must be treated in different ways.

## HALF-HARDY ANNUALS

These are probably the most expensive types of seed to raise because they often need more care than annuals. Most would have originally come from the tropics and therefore cannot be planted out until the prospect of frost is over. They should also be raised under cover. The technique for planting them applies to many annuals that are to be planted out in heavy, wet, cold ground, and for some that are needed for early flowering.

The time to plant is generally in spring from March to April, and has to be done under the protection of glass, which may be an outside cold frame, a greenhouse, or even a sunny windowsill. The seeds not only need protection from frost but also a high temperature to start them growing.

The seeds can be planted in almost any clean container – a seed tray, seed pan or ordinary shallow flower pot will suffice. Whatever you use, do make sure that there are holes or cracks in the container for the water to drain away, and pebbles or stones in the compost to ensure the water drains away quickly. There are many seed composts available, the peat based ones generally being favoured because they are lighter to handle and provide good germination.

Firm the compost into the container with your fists or a small piece of board. At this stage the compost should be moist but not wet. Scatter the seeds thinly and then cover them with a very fine layer of compost. You will soon discover that there are many different types of seeds and that they need slightly different sowing methods. For instance, very fine seeds do not need to be covered at all – when handling them be sure that they do not stick to the firming board. (A good guide is to sow at twice the diameter of the size of the seed.)

Once you have sown your seeds you will need to cover the tray with a sheet of glass and put some dark brown paper or layers of newspaper on top. Keep the seeds warm, at a steady 16°C (60°F) to 21°C (70°F), and wipe and turn the glass daily.

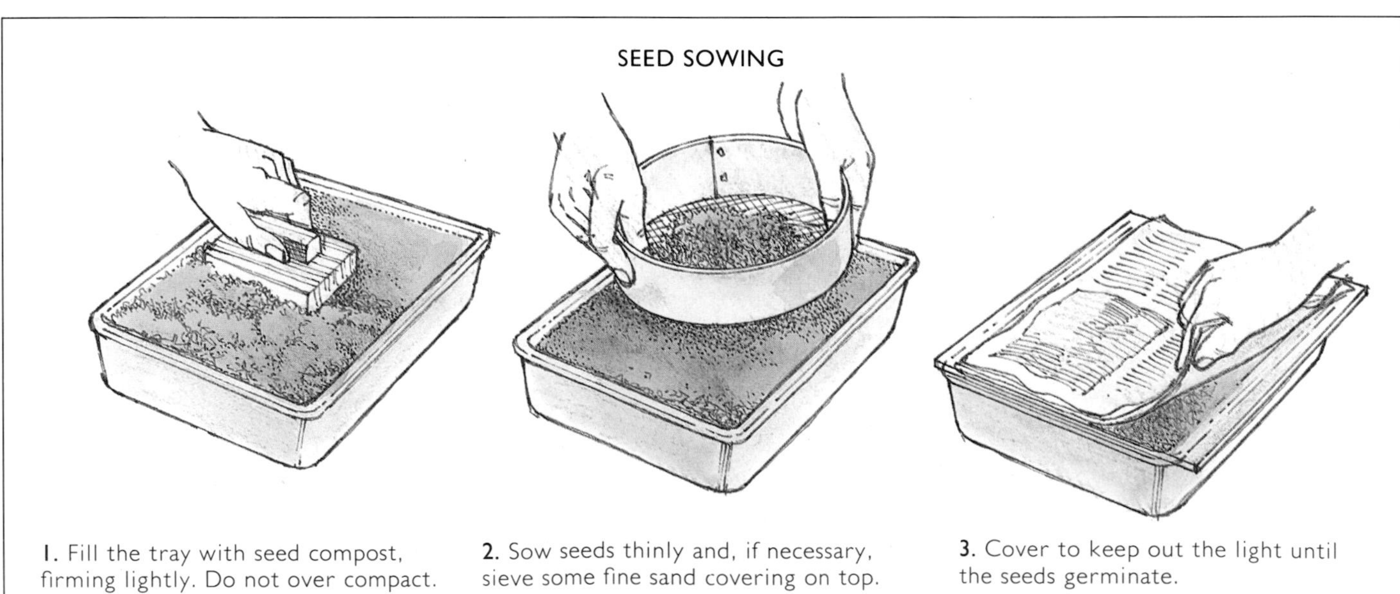


1. Fill the tray with seed compost, firming lightly. Do not over compact.

2. Sow seeds thinly and, if necessary, sieve some fine sand covering on top.

3. Cover to keep out the light until the seeds germinate.

Once the seeds have started to germinate the seedlings will need light, so take away the paper, and prop up the glass at one end allowing in air. After a couple of days it can be removed altogether. The tray should also be gradually moved into full light, while the compost must be kept moist (but not wet).

PRICKING OUT SEEDLINGS

Lift seedlings using a dibber. Transfer to trays of potting compost and gently firm in.

When the first true leaves have developed you can prick out the seedlings and place them in other containers filled with potting compost. Lift the seedlings gently by the leaves, and not by the stems which can be very easily damaged. The young plants should be given room to develop and left in the shade until they have settled into their new containers.

The next stage involves hardening them off. The container should be moved to a cooler room or a garden frame where the seedlings can gradually acclimatize to the outside temperature. Later, transfer them outdoors for a few hours during daylight. And finally, one week before you need to plant them out, leave the seedlings outdoors all the time.

While such instructions might seem complicated and fussy, raising seeds is actually an enormously simple task. Nor should you be worried if you do not have a greenhouse or cold frame, for a windowsill is a perfectly acceptable substitute. However, when raising seeds in this way slightly after your technique. Sow the seeds in a container and then cover with a transparent polythene bag which can be fixed round the pot with a rubber band, and supported above the compost by a section of wire coat hanger bent into a loop, the two ends sticking into the soil. Keep the pot in a shady part of the window until the seedlings begin to appear. The plastic covering can then be removed. Again, make sure that the compost is kept moist but never soaking wet. Using this technique your seedlings will develop on the windowsill with as much vigour as those in the greenhouse.

Some of the most interesting half-hardy annuals include:

**Ageratum** (floss flower) Neat, powder puff heads, free flowering and long lasting. Needs lots of water. Keep sheltered if possible. Best known for its blue flowers, but there are other colours worth considering.

**Amaranthus** (love-lies-bleeding) Long tassles of tiny booms. Not all are red, there is also a *A. viridis* which carries green tassles. Thrives in full sun and does not need a very rich soil.

**Antirrhinum** (snapdragon) The old-fashioned snapdragon is *A. majus*, but there are many different types now available both in shape, range of colour (reds, yellows and pinks) and height. Often troubled by rust (for remedy, see page 92). It likes a well-drained, medium soil in a sunny position.

**Arctotis** (African daisy) Long stemmed, showy flower in all shades of yellow and orange which closes in the evening. Full sun, no soil preferences. Pinch out to encourage bushiness. Needs support. Remove the dead flower heads.

**Calceolaria** (slipper flower) The bedding calceolaria, as opposed to the larger version sold as a pot plant, is an old-fashioned, almost forgotten flower available in various colours. It is very good for growing in pots, tubs or window boxes. Enjoys full sun.

**Celosia** (cock's comb) A tender, delightful plant with plumes or crested heads in brilliant shades of red, yellow and orange. Lightish soil in a warm, sunny position is best. Excellent for cutting.

**Cleome** (spider plant) Scented with an exotic flower that resembles a spider or fisherman's fly. Comes in shades of pink and mauve. Needs good soil and a sunny position. Grows to 90 cm–1.2 m (3–4 ft).

It is easy to see how *Cleome spinosa* acquired its familiar name of spider plant.

**Cosmos** (cosmea) Has fern-like foliage, flowers like single dahlias in white, crimson and all shades of pink. Good for cutting and for long-lasting garden display for which it should be dead-headed regularly. May need staking. Light soil, sunny spot.

**Gazania** (treasure flower) For the front of a bed, border or rockery. Daisy-like, showy, and a tendency to sprawl. The gold, bronze or apricot flowers close in the evenings. Sunny spot, light soil. Good for seaside gardens.

**Heliotropium** (heliotrope or cherry pie) An old flower retained for its heavy fragrance. Blooms are tiny. Must have a sunny spot and good soil. Look for the dark blue and purple cultivars.

**Impatiens** (busy Lizzie) Grows anywhere, and not just as a summer house plant. Can be grown in a shady, damp spot in the garden, but will also succeed in a dappled or sunny position. Available in a wide range of colours.

**Limonium** (statice or sea lavender) One of the everlasting flowers. Tiny, papery petalled flowers in every colour. Needs a light soil, sunny spot.

**Lobelia** One of the favourite edging plants. The royal blue variety is widely available, but it also comes in other colours, pale blue and carmine. Needs a rich, moist soil, and can grow well in shade.

**Mesembryanthemum** (Livingstone daisy) When it is given a light soil and full sun it will spread marvellously, almost flat on the ground. In less than full sun it will not do so well.

**Mimulus** (monkey flower) If you want a plant for a damp, shady spot, this is it. Available in orange, yellow and red, though there are also mixed colour cultivars. Must not be allowed to dry out.

**Nemesia** Multicoloured, easy to grow and quick to flower. Give it a sunny spot, lime-free soil is best; pinch out for bushiness and don't let it dry out. Cut back for a second bloom.

**Nicotiana** (tobacco plant) Grown for its fragrance. Modern cultivars produce the best flowers in shades of crimson, pink, purple, 'lime green' and white. Well-drained land with sun or dappled shade.

**Petunia** Among the most colourful (reds, pinks, mauves, yellow, white and bicolors) and dazzling plants for a sunny site, ideal for window boxes, tubs or hanging baskets. They will be very unhappy in prolonged wet or windy conditions. However, the Resisto strain will stand up to the rain.

**Phlox** Another plant that needs full sun if its tightly packed flower heads are to be seen to perfection. Great variety of colours – one of the best collections is 'Beauty Mixed' which includes white and shades of violet, pink and scarlet. 'Twinkle Star' is also a good choice. For rock garden, bed, window box. Beware of slugs.

**Portulaca** (sun plant) One of the half-hardies that do not like root disturbance. Plant outdoors where it will flower in a sunny and sandy spot. The blooms close up on dull days. They come in a wide range of colours including white, pink, yellow and orange.

*Phlox* 'Twinkle Star Mixed' needs a sunny spot for its flowers to give of their best. It is seen here with tagetes, royal blue lobelia and white arabis.

A good example of a one-colour border including petunias and lobelia, all in shades of mauve.

**Rudbeckia** (cone flower) A welcome late-flowering plant with lots of brilliant blooms in large daisy-like style. Available in shades of orange, yellow and deep red. Well-drained land, sunny or semi-sunny spot required.

**Salpiglossis** (painted tongue) If you can grow tender plants, here is an exotic addition with velvety, funnel-shaped flowers that are veined in strange mixtures of gold on purple, red on yellow, and yellow on red. Requires support, and pinching out. Well-drained, sheltered and sunny spot needed.

**Tagetes** (African marigold, French marigold) Not as popular as it once was, but still one of the most used bedding flowers where shades of yellow and orange are needed. Grows well anywhere. Deadhead to keep the display going through the summer.

**Verbena** Low growing, primrose-like, fragrant flowers usually available in shades of mauve, lilac and pink. Needs a good soil and a sunny spot. Pinch out young plants and deadhead regularly.

**Zinnia** Needs a fertile soil to produce its showy many coloured (white and shades of pink, mauve, yellow and red), daisy-like flowers. Also does best in a sunny position. A good cutting flower.

## HARDY ANNUALS

These seeds are sown directly into the ground for the best results. The time to plant is when the soil is warm and dry, which will probably be in April. The warmth is needed for germination, and the soil needs to be on the dry side so that a good seed bed can be made.

The most important gardening tip is do not rush; the plants will always catch up if you have to delay planting by a few weeks because of adverse weather conditions. I once knew an old gardener who always insisted that June was the vital month – slowing down those plants that had developed too early, and speeding up the late arrivals. He also insisted that when you saw the first annual weeds developing you should plant annual flower seeds.

However, not all annuals need to be planted in the spring. Many will be much happier if planted in September and they will, of course, be earlier flowering than the April seeds. To achieve success with annuals follow these basic rules:

- The bed should be in a good sunny position and be well drained.
- The soil must be thoroughly prepared so that it comes up after raking with as fine a tilth as you can possibly achieve.
- Drills should be watered gently *before* sowing, not after the seed has been planted otherwise they might be washed so deep into the soil that they won't develop.
- The easiest but least effective planting method is just to scatter the seeds over the ground. However, it will be hard to distinguish the early growth from the weeds, and create problems when weeding and thinning. It is therefore better to prepare drills, in which the tinier seeds will need far less covering than the larger ones.
- Sow the seeds thinly – the small ones can be mixed with fine sand to ensure equal distribution.
- To ensure equal germination all seeds need to be in close contact with the soil, so the drills should be firmed down with the back of the rake or a spade.
- Drills should not mean straight lines. Each kind of seed could have its own shape – horizontal, curved or diagonal.
- Seeds will need protection from birds, so cover the surface with twigs or stretch black thread across the beds.
- Mark each area with the name of the seed planted. Don't impale the packet on a piece of wood at the end of a row. It will quickly get blown away. Instead, either

SOWING HARDY ANNUALS

1. Rake the soil finely.

2. Mark out the areas for each different type of seed.

3. Sow seeds very thinly in drills.

4. Cover them carefully and firm in with the back of a rake.

make a proper label or place the packet in a plastic bag before fixing it securely to a small stake.

- Thin out the seeds on a gradual basis – but do begin early and keep them to about 5 cm (2 in) apart. About 10–14 days later carry out the final thinning to the distance recommended on the seed label.
- Since most of these plants set their own seeds it is possible to raise these seedlings. Collect seedheads and thoroughly dry, before labelling and storing them in an airtight tin for use next spring. Although these seeds won't necessarily provide you with exactly the same plant as the parent, it is still an excellent and enjoyable way of raising plants.

Some interesting annuals to try out in your garden are:

**Althaea** (hollyhock) Best grown as an annual. Likes a sunny, sheltered spot. May need staking. Single and double flowered forms come in all colours except blue. Can fall victim to rust.

**Alyssum** Dwarf cushions, usually of tiny white flowers but there are other colours available. Will grow anywhere in the garden. If you have the patience to trim off dead blooms it will go on flowering for a long time. Will also re-seed itself if the old flowers are left.

**Centaurea** (cornflower) Once dismissed as a weed, now appreciated as a valuable annual for flowering and cutting. There are pink, red-purple, and blue and white cultivars. The soil should be well drained. May need staking and should be deadheaded regularly.

**Clarkia** Easy to grow, upright, needs a lightish soil, slightly acid. Does not like to be disturbed. The flowers, available in white, pinks and mauves are good for cutting, but remove bottom leaves before putting them in the water.

**Dimorphotheca** (Cape marigold or star of the Veldt) This is in fact perennial although it is nearly always treated as an annual. Responds best in full sun, producing lovely daisy-like, usually orange flowers all summer. Don't disturb, but do cut and remove dead heads.

Clarkia is a reliable hardy annual in the border and lasts well as a cut flower.

**Eschscholzia** (Californian poppy) Full sun is essential, and a well-drained spot. The brilliant orange individual flowers do not last, but the plant flowers from June to September. It will also self-seed.

**Godetia** Bright, free-flowering favourites in mauves, pinks and white are colourful in the garden and good for

Godetia will give a lasting display in a summer border.

cutting. Does best on light land in a sunny spot, and needs watering in dry conditions.

**Helichrysum** (straw flower) A very popular 'everlasting' flower in pink, yellow, red and rust. Full sun required. Cuttings should be taken just before the flowers fully open.

**Iberis** (candytuft) If you want a flower that can grow in any conditions, this is it. Excellent as edging for footpaths, or in the front of a border. Perfumed flowers in red, pink or white.

**Limnanthes** (poached-egg flower) Makes a colourful, two-toned front for the border. Fern-like foliage and a flower which lives up to its common name, being white edged with a yellow centre. Likes the sun, and it will re-seed forever!

**Malcolmia** (Virginia stock) It will grow quickly anywhere, and blooms for weeks. The mauve, pink or white flowers smell delicious, especially in the evening.

**Nemophila** (baby blue eyes) Low growing, feathery, and attractive blue flower (other colours available) for the front of a border. Don't disturb and keep watering in dry weather.

**Nigella** (love-in-a-mist) Once it was just misty blue but now it is multicoloured. The cornflower blue is the loveliest ('Miss Jekyll' is a popular choice). Seed pods dry well. Needs good soil.

**Salvia** There isn't a park in the country that doesn't have some brilliant red spikes of salvia (often called the scarlet sage) among its bedding plants. Other colours available besides red. Not too fussy about soil conditions.

**Tropaeolum** (nasturtium) This climbing, clambering, trailing plant goes on and on, demanding little from the garden. It has orange, yellow and red flowers. It does not need feeding and loves a poor sandy soil. Dwarf varieties growing to about 30 cm (1 ft) are available.

**Viola** (pansy) The dividing line between a viola and garden pansy is very narrow. The viola is harder to grow and the flowers are smaller. Useful for bedding, edging, window boxes, and hanging baskets. Water well. Deadhead regularly. Protect from slugs.

Left: Pansies add a special charm to any garden.

Opposite: *Limnanthes douglasii* is aptly called the poached-egg flower.

Below: Candytuft (*Iberis*) in shades of pink.

## BIENNIALS AND PERENNIALS

Biennials are plants which you will sow this year for flowering in 12 months time. Many of the plants will re-seed and go on repeating themselves for years. They should be planted outdoors in a special nursery bed from May to July. The procedure for preparing the bed and the seed drills is just the same as for the annuals. However these plants differ in that they are planted out in the autumn in their final growing positions.

Lift the seedlings carefully and plant them in their flowering position, which should have been thoroughly prepared, and well watered. Make sure they never dry out. Among the best of the biennials are Canterbury bells (*Campanula*), forget-me-not, hollyhock, honesty, pansy, sweet William and wallflower, which will give a profusion of colour from spring through to autumn. Many of these can also be planted as annuals.

Perennials are treated in the same way, except that when the seeds germinate and the plants have been thinned and grown on, they are then planted individually into pots in the autumn. The main problem is that many perennials take years to reach a good flowering size, so unless you have extra patience and dedication ignore these plants or instead of raising from seed, buy plants already part grown. The dedicated gardener who ignores this warning will benefit from such marvellous plants as the primulas and polyanthus, lupin, delphinium, and geum, all of which grow well from seed.

Biennial plants which haven't been mentioned in the list of annuals, and which are well worth considering include:

**Bellis** (daisy) There are many varieties of *Bellis perennis* in white, pink and red,

Low-growing *Campanula portenschlagiana* is suitable for the front of a border or rock garden.

that make ideal edging plants or for growing in rockeries. Easily grown.

**Campanula** (Canterbury bells) These are produced in many shades of blue, pink and white. Protect from slugs, stake, and deadhead when the flowers fade.

**Cheiranthus** (wallflowers) The fragrant flower, synonymous with spring, comes in red, pink, yellow, purple, white and cream. Sunny spot required; and pinch out the young plants before planting.

**Digitalis** (foxglove) Tall spikes in a great range of colours as well as the traditional purple. Needs lots of water and is happy in a moist, shaded spot.

**Lunaria** (honesty) Although you will see most of these in shades of purple, white and pink are also available. The seed pods dry well for winter arrangements.

**Myosotis** (forget-me-not) You can buy it in other colours, but the blue is still the most popular with most of us. Will grow well in light shade, but do not let it dry out.

Perennials, as pointed out earlier, are generally better purchased as plants and then propagated as cuttings or root divisions. However, there are some that are successfully and easily raised from seed. Many are mentioned in the chapter, *Flowers for Cutting*. The primula and the geum are special cases.

**Primula** (primrose, polyanthus) No garden would be complete without them. The dividing line between the huge variety of flowers in this group is not really clear. Some need bog-like conditions, others are almost alpine in their size and treatment, and the old garden strains ask few favours and provide a wide range of sizes and colours. But don't despair – from a packet of seeds you can get a wonderful selection. In particular try the Pacific or the Goldlace strains. Since primulas are not long-lasting plants, it is better to grow replacements from seed every year. However, if you have a particularly delightful plant propagate by careful division. In the garden the plants thrive in partial shade.

**Geum** (avens) If you want a dense, weed-smothering plant for the summer this has few rivals. The flowers are bright, and come in shades of red, orange and yellow. A rich soil is vital to its success, and staking will later be necessary. Clumps should be cut back to the ground once flowering has finished, and like the primula the plant is not long lasting. Clumps can be divided every few years.

## CUTTINGS

Taking a cutting from a favourite plant and watching it grow, is one of the gardener's greatest joys. To the true enthusiast a cutting is just about anything – a tiny snip from the tip of a fuchsia or a geranium; a shoot from the base of a delphinium or peony; or a heel cutting taken from any medium hard-wood plant. All can be encouraged to grow, you will have more successes than failures.

There are four kinds of cutting. The *tip* cuttings are very short pieces of wood that have not yet flowered, and which are soft at the top and quite firm at the base.

Primulas come in a wide range of colours. The old-fashioned Goldlace types seen here are becoming increasingly popular.

*Basal* cuttings are taken from the base of the plant – they are usually young shoots which can be pulled or cut away.

*Heel* cuttings are obtained by removing a side shoot from the main stem in such a way that a piece of wood remains at the bottom, which is called a 'heel'.

*Hardwood* cuttings of shrubs are taken in autumn and planted outdoors. Choose well ripened shoots and trim to about 25 cm (10 in). Provided you take the appropriate cutting from the relevant plant and treat it correctly, you will have few problems. The planting stage should be handled as follows.

Having taken the cutting, remove the bottom sets of leaves which would otherwise be in danger of being buried under the soil. You must leave sufficient leaves above the soil for the plant to breathe. Next, dip the base of the cutting into a rooting hormone compound, shaking off the excess if powder is used. You should then make a suitable hole with a dibber or a pencil in a firmed, sterile potting medium, and gently ease in the cutting. If there is an interval between the cutting being taken and planted it should be kept in water, but you ought to avoid this.

The cutting must be kept in a humid atmosphere which can be created by covering it with a plastic bag (half a plastic soft drink bottle makes a good cover for smaller pots). Don't be tempted to look too soon for a root since cuttings don't like being tampered with. Leave the cutting for some weeks and if the new growth has appeared then a gentle tug will let you know whether it has rooted. Any leaves that turn yellow, fall off or start to rot should be quickly removed.

The cutting will grow on quite happily for some weeks, and when it has rooted sufficiently it should be potted on into a suitably sized container – probably a 7.5 cm (3 in) pot – filled with potting compost. If you have a number of cuttings consider raising them in a rooting bag or cold frame. If you intend taking a lot of cuttings then it will be worthwhile buying a propagator.

TAKING TIP CUTTINGS

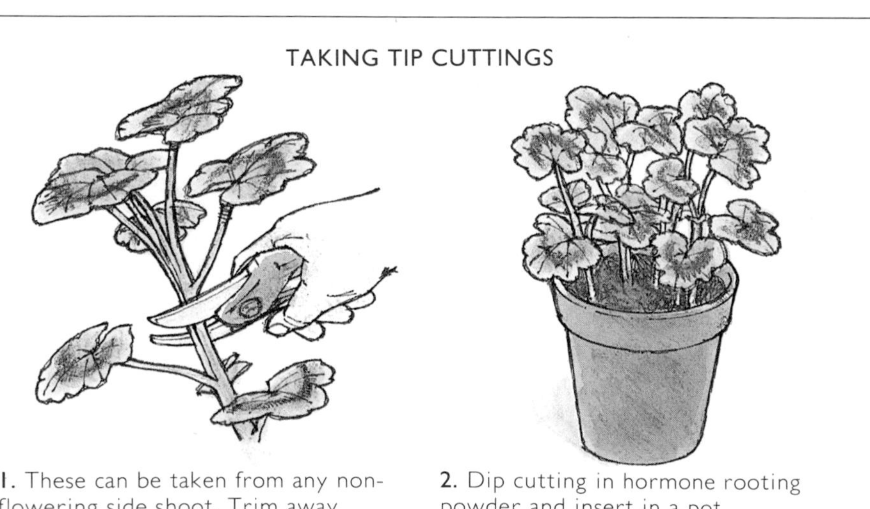

1. These can be taken from any non-flowering side shoot. Trim away lower leaves that would otherwise be under the soil.

2. Dip cutting in hormone rooting powder and insert in a pot immediately. You can plant on four or five cuttings in a small pot.

BASAL CUTTINGS

1. Young cuttings at the base of the plant can be pulled away carefully or trimmed with a knife.

2. Trim across the base and remove leaves from lower half of cuttings.

3. Insert in a hole close to the edge of the pot and water in very gently.

Probably the most successful cuttings can be taken for the flower garden from many of the plants mentioned later in the book (see Chaper 5), but the most popular, fuchsia and pelargonium, deserve special attention here.

**Fuchsia**

Fuchsias are such attractive plants and come in such a wide variety of colours and shapes that they are the subject of many specialist books. They have a large following of enthusiasts and are universally popular for planting in hanging baskets and containers, either on their own or in combination with other plants, to give a display which continues throughout the summer.

The major drawback, however, is that some fuchsias are so tender that they must be sheltered even in the summer. And most hybrid plants will need protection in the winter or be taken under cover. However, in warmer parts of the country and in mild winters some of the special outdoor varieties survive quite well.

There are hundreds of different fuchsias which can be grown as trailing plants, or trained to form bushes, pyramids or standards, and their classification is complex. One nursery which specializes in fuchsias actually lists 487 cultivars, and the number is still growing! However, it is enough to be aware of the delightful white, red, mauve, violet, pink, cream, rose, and bicolors that are available, mixing grace with a distinctiveness unrivalled by any other flower.

**Propagation** Propagating the fuchsia is almost child's play, and involves taking either soft tip cuttings about 8 cm (3 in) long in early summer or harder wood later in the year. In the case of the tips use non-flowered wood which can be planted outdoors in pots or at the foot of the mother plant. A cold frame or a propagator is, of course, better, but if you do not have one it is easy to improvise. The plants will usually root within three weeks. With hardwood cuttings, which can be taken after pruning, trim them to about 12 cm (5 in) dip them in rooting hormone and place them in a propagator. They need to be kept at a temperature of about 7°C (45°F).

If you want to begin collecting fuchsia you should not find any trouble purchasing several different varieties, recently well rooted, at a reasonable price. Some of the interesting varieties that the beginner could try include miniatures such as 'Lady Thumb' (sepals reddish carmine, with corolla white veined with carmine), and 'Papoose' (sepals bright red, with corolla very dark purple); or prizewinners such as

HEEL CUTTINGS

Break off cutting with a heel of older wood, trim neatly and plant.

HARDWOOD CUTTINGS

Trim cuttings to 25 cm (10 in) and insert in V shaped trench in sheltered border.

'Mieke Meursing' (red sepals, corolla pale pink), and 'Display' (sepals rose pink, corolla deep pink); or the very new and exciting 'Pink La Campanella' (a mixture of pale and dark carmine sepals, with white markings and a bright magenta corolla); or a hardy variety such as 'Garden News' (pink sepals, majenta corolla).

All you need to remember is that there are different types – outdoor, bedding and greenhouse. The outdoors are generally hardy in most of Great Britain. They should be left to die down of their own volition rather than being cut down in the autumn. Bedding varieties need to be taken indoors in the winter and transferred to pots. Store in a shed with plenty of light, do not feed and water very sparingly. They can be planted out again in the spring. The greenhouse varieties are best treated as indoor plants, but in a really good summer they can be placed outdoors on a warm patio.

**Pelargoniums**

Nearly everyone uses the term geranium to cover this wide range of plants, although the enthusiast would be much happier if its proper name was used. For the present, I will call them all geraniums. Botanically there is a slight distinction between the pelargonium and the geranium – the former has five stamens, irregular petals and a tube for nectar; the geranium does not have the tube, and has six or more stamens with a more regular shaped leaf. But some of these distinctions are now being blurred by the arrival of many new cultivars. Cultivar is the word denoting a cultivated variety, but the various hybrids and cultivars are still widely referred to as varieties.

Whatever name you call it by, the geranium is a wonderful flower. For many it is *the* flower of the windowsill (often being planted in a lovely old Victorian style pot), the essential blaze of colour in large bedding schemes, the long-lasting trailing flower in hanging baskets and tubs, and the provider of subtle foliage in the border. For all of these situations there is a different type – bedding geraniums, fancyleaf geraniums, regal perlargoniums and ivy-leaf perlargoniums, each with its own characteristic that will become obvious to the gardener as the plants begin to grow and flower.

The only problem with these plants is that they need a frost-free environment, which means that at the end of the summer and before the first frosts they must be moved indoors. From now on they should be given just a minute amount of watering until late spring, when the threat of frost has passed. A bright spot in a shed or under the staging in a greenhouse with good wrapping is usually good enough.

For growing geraniums you need a sandy, rich loam, good sunshine, and miserly watering. To keep it in top condition don't allow the aphids and whitefly to settle on it, and give the roots an occasional feeding with a soluble or liquid fertilizer to give the plant a boost.

This is another plant which is easily raised from cuttings – either stem cuttings (any time after flowering) or non-flowered tips, usually in the early summer. By using one of these methods you can have new plants developing from May to September.

These red geraniums (or pelargoniums) have attractively 'zoned' foliage, and are seen here with white alyssum.

**Propagation** Take a cutting about 7.5 cm (3 in) long in spring or early summer. I have always found that non-flowering tip cuttings are best because the growth is active and therefore encourages rooting. However, flowered cuttings will provide you with a good plant, though in a slower time. In either case trim stem to just below a leaf base and remove the lower leaves. These cuttings are among the easiest plants in the world to root, and even the top rose growers constantly express the hope that one day they will produce roses that can root as easily as a geranium.

## BULBS, CORMS, TUBERS AND RHIZOMES

The majority of bulbs and corms spread to form clumps, which will eventually require lifting and dividing every few years. The best time to do this is after flowering, when the foliage has died down. Lift the clumps carefully and divide the bulbs. Replant the biggest to provide next year's flowers. The small bulblets or cormlets, which are attached to the main bulbs, should be detached; these can be planted elsewhere in the garden where they can be allowed to grow in their own time. It may take two to three years for them to reach the flowering stage, and when they in turn are lifted the same process can again be adopted.

Rhizomes are underground stems which produce shoots and roots, and they can be increased, usually in the summer, by dividing and cutting. Trim away any rotten or diseased parts and then divide the rhizome into sections, each one containing roots and foliage or buds. Then plant the sections at the same depth as the original plant. Bearded irises can be increased this way. The easiest plant in this group to divide and propagate is the lily of the valley.

Probably the best known tuberous plants are the dahlias (see page 66) and the tuberous begonias (as opposed to the half-hardy annual, the bedding begonia).

### Begonias

These give a wonderful display of colour all summer long – provided that you can be sure they have a super rich soil, plenty of sunshine, and constant root watering when they are flowering. They make magnificent bedding plants with large rose-like blooms in just about every summer colour. *B. pendula* with its long, drooping stems is ideal for window boxes and hanging baskets.

The tubers can be divided when the young growth is beginning. Take pieces from the sides of the main tuber very carefully, and plant them separately in potting compost. Keep them under cover until all risk of frost has passed. Then they can be planted out where they will need a liquid fertilizer. Remove stems when foliage has died down, lift tubers and store away from frost over winter.

### PRESERVING FLOWERS

As well as the flowers that bear the name 'everlasting' – acroclinium, helichrysum and limonium or statice – there are many others that can be used for drying for winter decoration and in dried flower arrangements. They include larkspur, love-lies-bleeding, achillea, delphiniums, molucella, astilbes, sedums, ballota, even rosebuds.

The flowers should be picked just as the blooms are opening and before they reach maturity. Tie them in small bunches and hang them upside down in a dry dark cupboard, shed or attic where there is a good circulation of air; darkness prevents the colours from fading. Leave them alone if you can until they are needed for decoration. Grasses are particularly useful when dried in this way, and they provide graceful backgrounds for arrangements of other dried material.

Many people use the pressing method to preserve ferns, ivy, bracken, large leaves of trees or shrubs. The leaves should be laid flat between sheets of newspaper, making sure they are not overlapping. Weigh them down with equal pressure all over, and leave until completely dry. Leaves of trees, and shrubs and herbaceous plants can be placed between sheets of newspaper and then ironed. Treat hosta leaves in this manner. You will find that because drying with an iron is quicker, the leaf colour will be well preserved. The leaves can then be mounted on florists' wire and used in arrangements.

Tuberous begonias are truly magnificent summer bedders. Here they are interplanted with silver-foliaged Senecio and spider plants (*Chlorophytum*).

PROPAGATING BULBS, CORMS AND RHIZOMES

In the summer after flowering, gently lift rhizomes. Divide into sections with a sharp knife so that each section has some roots below and growth above. Replant at the same depth as original plant.

The small cormlets around the base of a gladiolus corm can be detached and, if grown on, will flower within two years.

Bulbs are easily propagated. Lift the bulb cluster after the foliage has died down and break off the side bulbs. Tinier bulblets can be planted in an out-of-the-way spot where they can grow on for two or three years.

# PLANTS IN CONTAINERS

This type of gardening is ideal if you have only a small amount of space as just about any plant, from a tiny alpine to a large standard rose, can be grown in a container and often plants will take on a different persona when displayed in this way. Perhaps they become more noticeable because they are rather more isolated from their immediate surroundings than when they are planted in a bed or border. In this way the true beauty of each flower can be appreciated in all its detail.

For instance, a large day lily (*Hemerocallis*) growing tall among the trailing foliage of a ground covering plant will prove a real eye-catcher. You can easily pick your own colour schemes and make your container plants match or tone in with the surrounding plants. Fuchsias come in a wonderful range of pinks, reds and mauves and are particularly suited to planting in tubs, pots and window boxes. The floribunda roses are also ideal for displaying in containers and 'Trumpeter' (red) and 'Korresia' (yellow) are specially recommended.

Hydrangeas in blue or pink, mophead or lacecap, will bloom for a long period while all the summer-flowering bedding plants are suitable. Particular favourites include ageratums, begonias, geraniums (pelargoniums), nasturtiums, pansies, petunias and Sweet Williams. Bulbs of all types can be used to give a good display and are invaluable for filling tubs with colour in the spring.

## SELECTING A CONTAINER

There are many types of containers available in all manner of styles and materials including wood, plastic, stone and terracotta. The plastic and glassfibre containers, although frequently despised for not being traditional, are often good value and preferable where ease of movement is required as they are very light. This makes them ideal for use in roof gardens or other places where heavier containers could cause problems. They are also available in many different shapes, including reproductions of the period vases and urns that decorate the great gardens. Always remember that when they are planted up they will look quite different with foliage softening their contours. The classical stone and terra-cotta containers are always beautiful but more expensive. Concrete containers can be used as substitutes with success as these now come in a range of attractive designs. Wooden containers provide a good natural and often neutral accompaniment to plants on a patio. Remember it is your choice, so select those you like and that suit your purse – but do check the range first before coming to a decision.

## PLANTING A CONTAINER

When planting up a container, be it tub, windowbox or pot, it is essential to ensure adequate drainage, so in addition to the drainage holes it is advisable to put a layer of broken crocks or pebbles in the bottom. Then fill the container with compost to suit the needs of the particular plants – lime-free or ericaceous compost for heathers, rhododendrons or camellias, for example. John Innes potting compost No 3 or an equivalent is best for roses or shrubs that are going to remain in the same pot for years, whereas John Innes potting compost No 2 or an equivalent will be adequate for bedding plants that are changed annually. A soilless compost will dry out quicker but is lighter, so more suited for hanging baskets, window boxes or in containers that will be moved about (taken indoors or into the greenhouse for winter). Once the plant is in position it is important to keep it adequately watered as the compost will dry out faster than the soil in a bed or border. A soluble fertilizer should also be applied according to the manufacturers' instructions to give the plants a boost in the growing season.

Each spring the top couple of centimetres (1 in) of compost in a container should be removed and replaced by fresh potting compost. Remember, too, that many shrubs and roses will outgrow their container and need moving on into something larger after a few years.

## POSITIONING THE CONTAINER

It is very important to find the best place for your containers. Try to place them where they will get at least some sunshine most days, but not where the plants will be scorched by the direct summer sun all day long. Remember that in a hot summer any container will dry out quickly and therefore will need a great deal of watering, so check the compost every day. Make sure that your containers harmonize with the rest of the garden whether they stand alone as a focal point or are grouped together, and that, if you need to move them frequently, they are easy to handle.

## HANGING BASKETS

Bright summer flowers, that will generally be viewed from below, can provide lovely spot colour against a stone, brick or concrete wall. Don't plant sparingly. When you think you have enough in the basket put in one more! As a general rule of thumb, plant trailing subjects around the edge and more upright plants in the centre. Make sure you hang the baskets where you can reach them for watering as they dry out very quickly indeed and may need watering more than once a day in hot summer weather.

Among the plants that do well in hanging baskets are trailing geraniums (pelargoniums) and pendulous fuchsias, both of which will tumble their flowers over the side of the basket and provide longlasting colour. Other plants that give great value include lobelias, creeping Jenny (*Lysimachia nummularia*), petunias, and trailing nasturtiums.

Fuchsias, petunias and trailing lobelia provide a show of summer colour in this window box.

## WINDOW BOXES

The deciding factor in planting up a window box is the amount of sun it will get. For best effect place it on a south-facing sill but for a less than sunny spot or even for a north-facing wall look for plants like Busy Lizzies, Californian poppies (*Eschscholzia*) and nasturtiums that will thrive in shade.

Window boxes can be produced with a lovely seasonal effect by using low growing tulips or daffodils in the spring and then changing to summer-flowering plants.

There are many lovely plants to choose from for summer effect in a sunny spot. Geraniums are, of course, one of the favourites but try tightly planted miniature roses ('Rise 'n' Shine' is a yellow variety that does very well) on their own. Other flowering plants that will brighten any window box include ageratums, begonias, trailing campanulas, fuchsias, heliotrope and petunias.

In autumn heathers (winter-flowering *Erica herbacea* cultivars) and winter cherry (*Solanum capsicastrum*) provide colour and an interplanting of variegated ivy or ivy-leaf pelargoniums will trail attractively and add interest throughout the year.

### PLANTING A HANGING BASKET

1. Line the basket with a generous layer of sphagnum moss or perforated black polythene before filling with a lightweight potting compost.

2. Plant trailing plants, such as lobelia, through the sides of the basket so they will cover the basket and hang down attractively.

3. Finally plant the top of the basket with some more upright subjects to give height. Plant closely and generously, and soak well before hanging up.

# CREATING A BORDER

The wonderful thing about gardening is that you are free to create as you wish. Lovers of shrubs can establish a shrub border; wonderful spot beds can be made from annuals; and roses can be spectacular when grouped together. But surely the most interesting sight of all must be the border that provides a little bit of everything – annuals, perennials, shrubs, bulbs, and roses. Most call it the mixed border, although 'versatile' might be a far better word because it suggests both colourful flowers and attractive foliage right through the year. Certainly the mixed border must rank as the most rewarding feature of the small to average sized garden. The possibilities are enormous. Just consider growing campanulas side by side with an elegant group of regal lilies, or having dramatic large-flowered delphiniums towering over old fashioned pinks, all close beside the soft coloured bearded iris.

A border of mixed or herbaceous plants will provide flowers and foliage for cutting, and plants that can be left in position for a number of years. Apart from pruning and dividing, they demand little work. However, it has to be said that these benefits will only be reaped by those who put the initial work into the planning, designing and preparing. That might sound horrifying to the new gardener, but remember it can be a pleasure.

Such a border can be planted anywhere, even in open lawn, although where it can be viewed from each side there will be more restrictions on the types of plants to be used. Most usually a background wall, fence or hedge will provide the necessary frame, and will also provide a windbreak which is important when taller plants are being grown.

## POINTS TO REMEMBER

The first point to remember about any wall, hedge or fence is that room should be left between the back of your border and the 'frame' should you need to walk along there when making repairs. You may need to paint a wall or fence, or clip a hedge. Also remember that hedges have hungry roots which can deprive the border plants of vital nutrients. The ideal gap between the two should be 45 cm (18 in), and if you can lay slabs, stones or any type of path

An herbaceous border should be a source of flowers and foliage for cutting through much of the year. This border is given height by rambler roses ('American Pillar') trained up rustic tripods.

Lilac provides fragrant flowers in late spring and early summer. This is the single 'Souvenir de Louis Spaeth'.

then access will be that much easier.

Another important point to remember about any border, whether it be shrub, mixed or herbaceous, is that it needs sun, so a south facing position is best. If this is impossible do not worry, for good borders can be created just about anywhere. The basic requirement is that the border is placed in the sunniest part of the garden. It also needs a certain amount of space to be effective. The minimum requirements are 1.2 × 3.7 m (4 × 12 ft). If the border is any smaller than this you should restrict the number of plants used to six or seven different types, ensuring they provide a good mix of flowers and foliage over a long period.

If you have more space it is possible to create one of a wide range of borders, incorporating varying widths and curves, which will be far more interesting than a border of straight lines. As I have already mentioned, one of the great advantages of a mixed or herbaceous border is that you can change it from year to year. And, as you become more adventurous and knowledgeable, it will be possible to create bolder and ever more spectacular displays.

There are, of course, many variations of borders apart from the herbaceous and mixed. The dedicated planner can devise a highly scented garden or a border devoted to one type of plant (such as the rose), or one-colour – delphiniums, dahlias, chrysanthemums and roses, among those that immediately come to mind, but there are so many others that the gardener can be spoilt for choice.

A scented garden has its own obvious pleasures, and despite the cries that scent is being lost by modern flower breeders there are many, many different types of flowers that can be used effectively in this way. The heady scent of wallflowers, the lovely mignonette and, of course night-scented-stock, are all excellent choices. But there are many more which can be appreciated from spring to winter, and they include the white *Nicotiana* (tobacco plant) and many forms of lilac, lavender, lily of the valley, the old fashioned border carnations, honeysuckle, viburnum, sweet peas, and jasmine.

*Nicotiana* 'Lime Green', like other tobacco plants, is at its most fragrant in the evening.

Some of the rules for creating a mixed border are:

- Careful soil preparation is vital. There is nothing to beat a well dug and fertilized bed.
- Soggy land or a sunless position are the two great handicaps. Try for good drainage and full sun.
- When selecting plants make sure that you have allowed space for those that are rampant growers and which, after a time, may well suffocate slower growing plants placed near them.
- Place taller growing plants (such as weigela or fuchsia) at the back of the border, with the lower ones in front. The middle area is reserved for the iris, lupin, stocks and other colourful average size flowers.
- Try to keep the ground between plants open by hoeing and weeding.
- A mulch of organic material – peat or well-rotted compost for instance – will keep down weeds and also conserve water. On the edges of beds a mulch of small forest bark can be very effective and looks quite good too. Certainly it can save a lot of hoeing.
- When cutting flowers for house decoration go very easy on new plants. The loss of stems and greenery can harm next year's growth. This will be obvious on perennials and even newly planted roses. If you want a flower from a first-year plant, then cut it with as little stem as possible and do not remove any leaves.
- Remove flower heads once they have faded, which will give the plants a chance of repeat flowering later in the season. Do not break them off – use a sharp scissors or better still shears or secateurs.
- Do not remove any foliage until it has died down.
- If you wish to move a plant in the border wait until autumn, but in the meantime identify it and make a note on the label of where you intend to place it.
- Wear gloves. There may be times when they will be awkward but for safety's sake it is much better to wear them constantly.

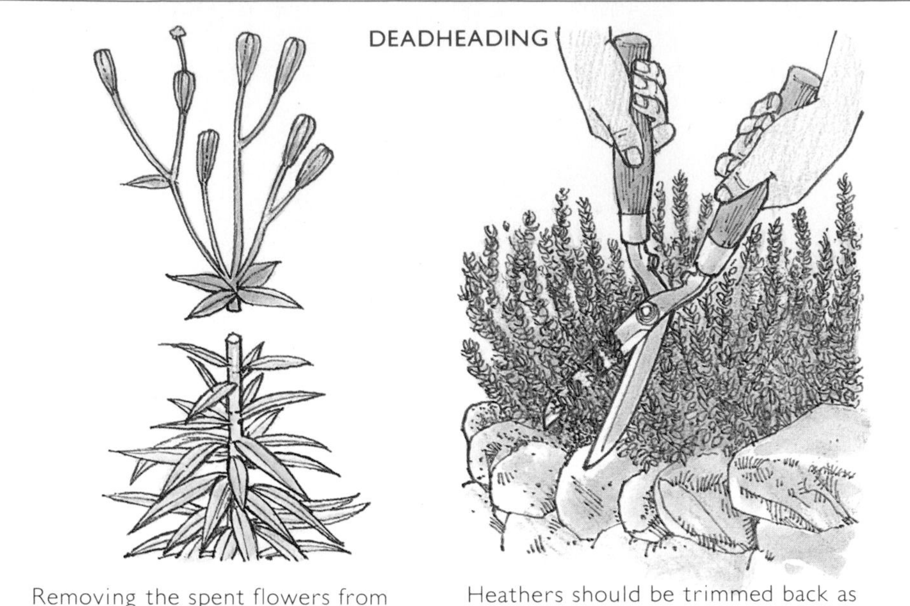


Removing the spent flowers from most plants will encourage another flush of bloom. Cut just below the flowerhead.

Heathers should be trimmed back as soon as their flowers have faded. Prune back any straggly shoots but do not cut into old wood.

Left: A traditional display of annuals brings brilliant colour to the garden in summer.

Opposite: One of the best-known borders with a colour theme – the red border at Hidcote, Gloucestershire.

## THE ANNUAL BORDER

Annuals are superb for bringing colour into a developing area, such as a shrub or herbaceous border. In order to make them truly effective they need to be spread boldly and in drifts, so that their colour isn't diluted in dribs and drabs. The rigid planning of tall flowers at the back and low ones in the front need not be adhered to in this instance – annuals of different heights, planted perhaps by colour and not by scale look far more interesting, natural and informal.

What has to be remembered is that making a border exclusively from annuals can be something of a chore and will not, of course, last beyond one season. But in a new and developing garden the annual is vital in providing almost instant colour. A box of hardened-off annuals can be transferred into the garden to give good colour and cover for quite a long period through the summer and autumn. If the faded flower heads are snipped off many plants will rebloom.

## BEDDING OPTIONS

With these flowers or shrubs the gardener is not restricted to a long line that most people call a border, whether it be one for herbaceous or mixed plants. The same sort of flowers can be used in an island bed, except that here the taller plants will be used in the middle and they must be selected with some care so that they do not throw other plants into their shade. A smaller bed may be prepared for annuals, and these too will be viewed from all sides.

Raised beds can be very effective where a line has to be broken or where the gardener finds that bending or stooping is difficult. The raised bed can be created using a retaining wall, the area being filled in with a well mixed soil suitable for whatever plants are to be grown. For instance, peat beds are very useful for growing lime-hating plants, and if they consist of peat blocks they will also provide slots into which small heathers or ferns can be placed effectively.

Rock gardens are a very specialized part of a garden and their success depends on the amount of work that is put into them (see pages 81 to 88).

## USING BULBS

There is a wide range of bulbous plants that fits into all these planting situations, from the stately hybridized gladioli to the daintier and highly fragrant autumn flowering *Acidanthera* (in fact, now classified as *Gladiolus callianthus*). Make sure that you know the eventual height that the flower will reach before planting it – some quite small bulbs can still produce tall plants.

It is a mistake to believe that all bulbs are trouble free, for they need good soil preparation and some care through the years. For instance, gladioli bulbs need lifting before winter sets in, while the others do need careful planting, good soil and feeding, just like other plants.

There are some bulbous plants that fit into a border more easily than others. The gladioli, for instance, does not always mix happily with border flowers although the interesting range of butterfly gladioli are much happier in this situation. And for a real eye-catcher there is the crown imperial, *Fritillaria imperialis*, not unlike its dainty cousins in the same genus. With its yellow or deep orange bell-like flowers circling the top of each 90 cm (3 ft) tall and quite thick stem, it is a plant that needs careful placing, but you can be sure it will create interest especially if you plant a small group of about six or seven together.

Freesias are always a delight because of their fragrance, and the outdoor variety presents a lovely display in the late summer and autumn. They require a dry, warm spot, and like most of these bulbous plants need to be kept watered. But the same message must be repeated – avoid constantly waterlogged soil. The well-drained, fertile piece of ground is where bulbous plants will grow best.

One of the most stately of bulbous flowering plants is the crown imperial, *Fritillaria imperialis* 'Lutea'.

## SHRUBS IN THE BORDER

Some of the most remarkable gardens are devoted exclusively to one or two colours – the red border at Hidcote, the white garden at Sissinghurst are just two very famous examples.

Beverly Nichols once had part of his garden planted with grey or bluish silver roses and another part devoted to white flowers.

Here are just a few ideas that you may care to adopt. Divided up into red, yellow, pink and violet, blue and mauve, and white flowered shrubs, you should be able to pick out easily the plants for your own favourite colour scheme.

The emphasis has been placed on flowering shrubs because they will provide a permanent framework in the garden and a setting for bulbs, herbaceous perennials and annuals with their more flamboyant flowers. Flowering shrubs can be also used alone for a more subtle effect. Many of these will provide additional year-round interest with fruits following flowers, silver or evergreen foliage and fiery autumn colour.

Of course there are a number of plants which come in a wide range of colours, particularly the roses (covered in detail in their own chapter – pages 51 to 63) and the rhododendron hybrids. No garden would be complete without a few shrubs, so here are some favourites that have proven themselves over the years and which will make ideal additions to the mixed border in any garden.

## RED FLOWERED SHRUBS

**Azaleas** These are now included in the genus *Rhododendron* but are still widely sold under their old name. These are, on the whole, much daintier plants and more suited to growing in small gardens. The evergreen or Japanese azaleas are low growing and quite adaptable, producing masses of flowers in May.

Look out for 'Addy Werry', 'Mother's Day' or the orange-red 'Orange Beauty'. The deciduous types are taller growing and include the triumphant 'Koster's Brilliant Red' among them. They need a lime-free soil, a sheltered site, light shade and plenty of moisture as they are shallow rooting. Propagate from seed or from layering low-growing stems.

**Chaenomeles** Better known as japonica, this early spring flowering shrub is perfect for training against a fence or wall. The best red-flowering variety is 'Knap Hill Scarlet' which flowers from March to May with golden fruits in autumn, but there are many to choose from of this hue. It does well in partial shade but is at its best in full sun. Trim back in summer after flowering Propagate from suckers or from heeled cuttings taken in summer.

**Enkianthus** The pagoda bush is renowned for its brilliant red and yellow flowers late in spring and also for its glorious autumn colour. *E. campanulatus* grows to about 2.4 m (8 ft) high. It needs a lime-free soil and light shade. The only pruning necessary is to cut away any old or damaged wood. Propagate from heeled cuttings in summer.

**Escallonia** (see page 41) 'Crimson Spire' is a good red form.

**Potentilla** (see page 40) 'Gibson's Scarlet' is an excellent red-flowered cultivar.

**Rhododendron** Like the azaleas they come in nearly every colour imaginable. There are many to choose from in various shades of red. The hardy hybrids are evergreen and need little in the way of pruning. Among the best red hybrids are 'Britannia', 'Cynthia' – vigorous and dark red, scarlet 'Doncaster', 'John Walter' and crimson 'Lord Roberts'. Among the dwarf growers to look out for is the dark red 'Elizabeth' which reaches between 90 and 120 cm (3–4 ft) and carries large trumpet-like flowers in April. They need a good acid soil and benefit from a spring mulch to conserve soil moisture in summer. Plant in a sheltered position, preferably in light shade.

**Ribes** (flowering currant) Search out some of the named varieties, rather than the species, *R. sanguineum*, the red 'Pulborough Scarlet' or the deep crimson, 'King Edward VII' are among the best. These are quick to establish and grow well in most soils reaching 1.8 m (6 ft) in height. Prune back after flowering and cut out any old, unproductive wood. To propagate take hardwood cuttings, about 30 cm (1 ft) long, and plant out in open ground in autumn.

**Rosa** (see pages 51 to 63)

**Weigela** This is a useful shrub for the border that comes in a wide range of colours including red. 'Bristol Ruby' is perhaps the best of the reds, flowering as it does in spring, summer and often again in autumn. It likes a humus-rich soil and a sunny or lightly shaded position. It may reach over 1.8 m (6 ft), but is very tolerant of clipping. In fact it makes an attractive informal hedge. Propagate from heeled cuttings in summer or from hardwood cuttings taken at the end of autumn.

## BUYING PLANTS

### Container grown plants

There is a difference between container grown plants, and container stuffed plants. Container grown plants should be just that – the plant should have been raised from a seed or a cutting, and then potted on to reach its final destination in the garden centre or store as a developing young plant. Stuffed plants have been lifted from the ground and then placed in containers when already fully grown. Obviously the shock of such a transfer can damage the plant enormously, so always look for plants that seem happy in their containers.

The good plant will be healthy looking with bright foliage – it will be well labelled and will look as though it has been growing successfully in the container. If there are signs of moss or small weeds in it don't worry, they will be a further indication that it is a container-grown plant. Wilted or yellowing leaves, signs of pests, dried out compost or a split or broken container are all signs that this is a poor plant, and best avoided.

### Pre-packed plants

Pre-packed plants are now widely available. These are bare rooted plants, packed in a plastic covering, with some moist peat or compost covering the roots. The main problem when considering them is that the packaging makes it very hard to see what you are buying, and the plant could be in a poor state from the warm conditions on the sales bench. Good stores will make sure that they only carry fresh stock. If you can see the plant, and there are signs of premature growth, shrivelled stems or small white roots, then reject it. The best plant is one that is completely dormant and looks healthy and strong.

### Trays of plants

These trays are commonplace, and vary in quality enormously. Seedlings may be dried out and dying, they may be thin and spindly, have yellowing leaves, or be so far advanced that the roots are growing out through the base of the tray. What the gardener needs are sturdy, compact little plants that are growing evenly. Many of these plants will also be seen offered in bunches and wrapped in paper. You should only buy them if you know they are absolutely fresh, and you can plant them immediately. Always select a full tray or a section of a tray, rather than loosely wrapped plants.

### Seeds

The great value of buying seeds is that you can get a far greater range of annuals and biennials than if you are depending on the purchase of pre-grown bedding plants. But make sure that you will be using the seeds fairly soon. Read the instructions thoroughly and make sure that the plant is for you. Many people believe that in purchasing seeds the plants will flower in a short time. This is not true. Many of the more beautiful plants that you can grow from seeds need a whole year, in which they must be transferred from their initial growing place into containers, before being planted out in their flowering positions the following year.

## YELLOW FLOWERED SHRUBS

**Berberis** (barberry) These shrubs carry yellow to orange flowers in late spring and summer. They also carry very sharp prickles, so beware! There are many different kinds to choose from and all are easy to grow in most garden soils. *B. darwinii* is evergreen and one of the best for flowers, followed in autumn by almost black berries. It grows to 1.8 m (6 ft) or more.

*B. wilsoniae* is lower growing and deciduous with translucent pink to red berries in autumn.

No regular pruning is necessary but every few years they benefit from thinning out and removing the old wood. Propagate species from seed or cuttings taken in summer.

**Buddleia** *B. globosa* has small ball-like heads of fragrant yellow-orange flowers in June. This shrub can grow to 4.5 m (15 ft). Lightly prune after flowering to keep in shape and prevent straggly growth forming. It thrives in most garden soils but prefers full sun. Propagate from seed or from hardwood cuttings.

**Chimonanthus** A deciduous shrub that is known as winter-sweet. This is a very good name because it tells you that the plant will produce very fragrant flowers, yellow with purple centres in winter. It may take some time for the plant to become established, so be patient. It will eventually reach 3 m (10 ft) and needs a sunny, well-drained spot. Best grown from seed.

**Corylus** (hazel) *C. avellana* 'Contorta' grows into a small tree about 3 m (10 ft) high although it may reach double that. If you want an unusual plant this is the one for you! Its branches are so contorted that it was once described as Harry Lauder's walking stick. The yellow catkins are a welcome arrival in the garden in January and February, just before the arrival of the daffodils. *C. avellana* 'Aurea' has yellow foliage and a more shrub-like habit. Hazels will grow in most places including open, windy or partially shaded sites. Propagate from suckers. Pruning is a simple task; just cut away old, exhausted branches in early spring to encourage new shoots.

Left: *Berberis darwinii*, evergreen in flower. It carries nearly black berries in autumn.

Opposite: 'Goldsworth Yellow' is a particularly hardy rhododendron hybrid.

**Enkianthus** (see page 37) This shrub comes with yellow flowers as well as red.

**Forsythia** Sometimes this is called golden bells or the leafless tree. Both these descriptions are apt at some time during its seasonal cycle. Certainly the yellow flowers on the leafless branches brighten up every spring at just the time when colour is sorely needed. Don't over-prune. Cut back stems that have produced flowers and, if heavier pruning is needed, shorten some of the stems. It usually reaches about 2.4 m (8 ft) and is easily raised from cuttings taken after flowering.

**Hippophae** (sea buckthorn) *H. rhamnoides* is a spiny shrub with silver foliage. It is perfect for hedging or screening in windy places, especially by the sea. It has insignificant yellow flowers and is grown for its orange berries. To ensure a good crop you must grow at least one male and one female plant although one male to three females gives a better show. The great advantage of this shrub is that the berries remain untouched right through the late autumn and winter. It grows well in most soils and tolerates sun or shade. An occasional trimming back is the only pruning necessary. It can be grown from seed in autumn.

**Hypericum** An attractive group of shrubs with golden yellow flowers in summer and early autumn. They range from the invasive and ground covering rose of Sharon to 'Hidcote' which can top 1.5 m (5 ft). *H. inodorum* 'Elstead' reaches about 1 m (3 ft) and forms lustrous red berries after flowering. Hypericums suit most well-drained soils and grow well in sun or light shade. Prune back in spring and propagate from heeled cuttings.

**Lonicera** (honeysuckle) Fragrant flowered climbing plants, suitable for training over walls and fences or up tripods or pillars in the border. They grow well in most soils but prefer a sunny spot. *L. japonica* 'Halliana' is a vigorous evergreen with yellow and white flowers; *L. periclymenum* 'Belgica' and 'Serotina' are the early and late flowering Dutch honeysuckles with pink and yellow flowers. The winter honeysuckle, *L.* ×*purpusii* bears pale yellow flowers in winter and spring. Propagate from hardwood cuttings in autumn.

**Mahonia** These shrubs grow well in most places and are easy to care for. They have good evergreen foliage and bright yellow, fragrant flowers followed by dark blue fruits. Plant in shady sites, under trees or in full sun – they look good all the year round. *M. aquifolium* (often called the Oregon grape) is small and bushy, reaching about 1 m (3 ft), with foliage that turns bronze in autumn. *M. japonica* is taller and

*Hypericum* 'Hidcote' produces large golden flowers through summer into autumn.

more upright, growing to 1.8 m (6 ft) with flowers from mid-winter into spring. 'Charity' is a very good upright shrub reaching 2.4 m (8 ft) with very large sprays of flowers. Mahonias require little in the way of pruning. Species can be raised from seed.

**Phlomis** Attractive grey-green foliage and abundant yellow pea-like flowers in June, *P. fruticosa* needs a sheltered spot away from danger of hard frosts. It is wide spreading and generally reaches about 90 cm (3 ft) high. It fits well into most borders, especially in association with other silver-leaved plants. It is ideal for dry places and looks good tumbling over a wall. Cut back old or damaged wood in spring. Propagate from cuttings taken in early summer and rooted under cover.

**Rosa** (see pages 51 to 63)

**Santolina** (cotton lavender) A sunny well-drained site is essential for this shrub that carries silver-grey foliage and, in summer, yellow button-like flowers. As it grows low keep it to the front of the border. *S. chamaecyparissus* grows to about 60 cm (2 ft) while one of its hybrids, 'Nana', is lower. Pruning means trimming back after flowering. Cut hard back every few years to keep the plant bushy. Propagate by cuttings in summer.

**Senecio** A tough shrub, especially tolerant of wind and sea-salt breezes. However it does need a sunny-sheltered spot away from all danger of heavy frosts. The two most likely plants that you will find are *S. greyi* or *S. laxifolus*; but these are more correctly called *Senecio* 'Sunshine'. They grow to about 90 cm (3 ft) high. For pruning you simply need to tidy up any straggly branches in spring. They make an attractive informal hedge and can be propagated from cuttings in summer.

**Potentilla** The shrubby potentillas come in a range of yellows from lemon to gold to 'Tangerine'. They flower from summer into autumn. 'Elizabeth' is buttercup yellow. Give them a sunny position and a light, well-drained soil and they will make a rounded bush about 60 cm (2 ft) tall. Take heeled cuttings in early autumn and raise in a cold frame.

PLANTING A CONTAINER GROWN SHRUB

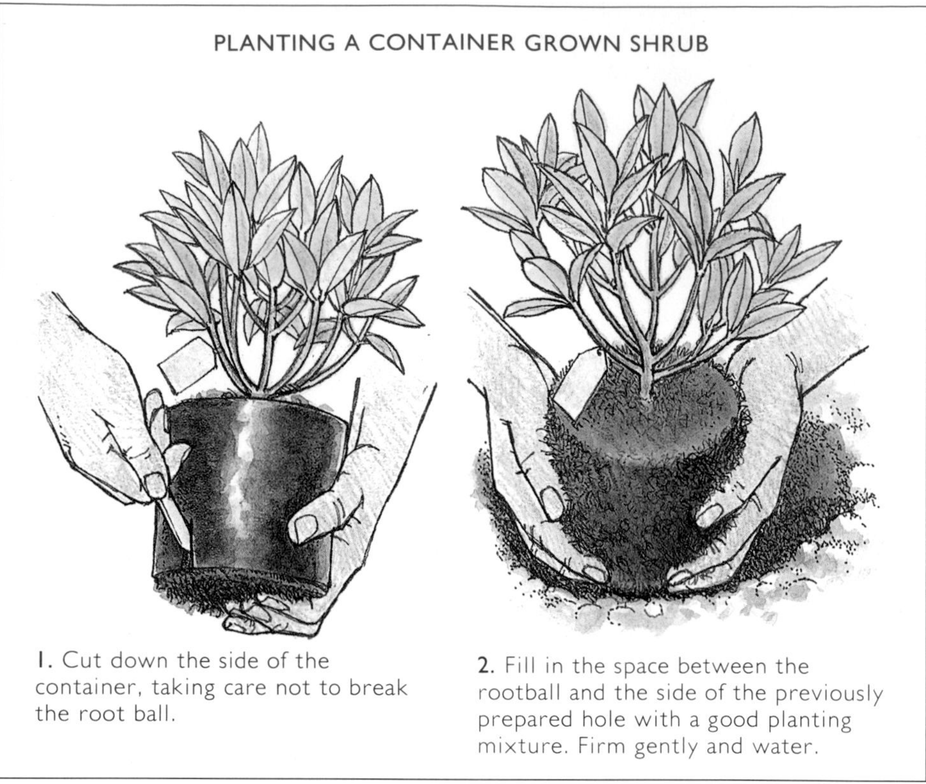

1. Cut down the side of the container, taking care not to break the root ball.

2. Fill in the space between the rootball and the side of the previously prepared hole with a good planting mixture. Firm gently and water.

**Rhododendron** (see page 37) *R. lutea* has fragrant yellow flowers; *R. wardii* has pale yellow, bell-like flowers and grows to 1.5 m (5 ft); try the evergreen hybrids 'Bo-Peep' and 'Goldsworth Yellow'.

## PINK AND VIOLET FLOWERED SHRUBS

**Buddleia** The lovely butterfly bush grows best in a sunny, well-drained spot and deserves more care than it is usually given. Its varieties come in shades of pink and mauve, lavender and purple, growing to about 2.4 m (8 ft). Plants can easily become leggy, so hard prune back to old wood in March. 'African Queen' is deep purple; 'Black Knight' deep purple-red; 'Empire Blue' is violet-blue; 'Ile de France' rich blue-mauve; and 'Royal Red' deep pink-purple. Propagate from cuttings in the autumn.

*B. alternifolia* has soft purple flowers on arching branches. It will form a large dome-like shrub, up to 4.5 m (15 ft). Take heeled cuttings in late spring.

**Camellia** The only real problem with this beautiful shrub is that it needs to be grown in a sheltered spot, away from the wind and in lime-free soil. The more moss peat you can dig in when planting the better your camellia will grow. It likes light dappled shade. The foliage is dark glossy green and flowers in shades of pink and white appear from March to May.

Some varieties have striped petals, others double or semi-double flowers. Choose from the *C. japonica* range; 'Elegans' is pink flecked with white, 'Lady Clare' is semi-double and deep pink. *C.* × *williamsii* hybrids are hardier and freer flowering. 'Donation' is the most famous. Propagate from leaf cuttings – they may take many months to root.

**Daphne** These shrubs produce fragrant flowers in a wide range of colours from white to shades of purplish pink. *D. mezereum* is widely available and produces purplish red flowers from March to April. It grows to about 1.2 m (4 ft). *D.* × *burkwoodii* reaches about 90 cm (3 ft) with pink flowers, while *D. cneorum* is only about 30 cm (1 ft) tall with rose pink flowers. Daphnes need sun or a lightly shaded position and humus rich soil. Little pruning is necessary. Raise from cuttings in summer. The attractive scarlet berries are highly poisonous.

**Deutzia** This shrub is covered in flowers in June in colours that range from white to light purple. Many carry flowers of more than one colour. *D. rosea* is a smaller variety carrying pink flowers while some of the hybrids like D. 'Mont Rose' has rose pink flowers and 'Contrasta' has lilac-purple blooms. It is an unfussy plant which grows to between 1.2 m and 1.8 m (4–6 ft) tall. After flowering cut back shoots that have bloomed and also cut away any damaged, old, unwanted wood. Take cuttings in autumn.

**Erica** There are many heathers to choose from ranging in colour from pale pink to deep purple. Summer flowering *E. cinerea* 'Pink Ice' is pale pink and grows to about 15 cm (6 in). *E. herbacea* has many cultivars; two of the best are 'King George', rose pink, and 'Vivellii', a bright carmine. Both flower from winter into spring and make a bushy ground cover. Plant with conifers for a classic combination. Although *E. herbacea* will tolerate some lime, most heathers prefer an acid soil and a position in the sun. Propagate from heeled cuttings in early autumn.

**Escallonia** For hedge or border there is always a place for this pink, white or red flowered shrub with it honey scented flowers from June to early autumn. It will grow to about 1.8 m (6 ft). There is a wide range of hybrids available, among them 'Edinensis' – showy, bright pink, 1.8 m–2.4 m (6–8 ft); 'Glory of Donard' – pink reaching much the same height, and 'Apple Blossom' which is pink and white. Escallonia thrives in most soils but in colder areas give it the protection of a wall. Prune back flowered shoots. Propagate from cuttings in summer.

**Fuchsia** (see page 26) Many to choose from in all shades of pink and mauve.

**Hebe** (see page 44) 'Pink Wand' is a good pink hybrid.

**Hibiscus** This shrub needs full sun, some shelter and a good rich soil to do well. *H. syriacus* grows to 2.4 m (8 ft) and comes in a wide range of colours with both single and double flowers which bloom from July to October. Look out for the violet 'Blue Bird', 'Woodbridge' which is rose pink

*Camelia* x *williamsii* 'Donation' is one of the most beautiful of all flowering shrubs and is surprisingly hardy.

*Daphne* x *burkwoodii* is smothered with fragrant pink flowers in early summer.

with a darker eye, and the double magenta 'Duc de Brabant'. Prune long shoots back lightly in spring.

**Hydrangea** There is a very wide selection of these late summer flowering plants. They thrive in a rich, well-drained but moisture-retentive soil and a sunny position, although they will tolerate shade. The colour depends on the soil. If it is acid, flowers are blue, but in neutral or alkaline soil they become pink unless a blueing powder is used every seven to fourteen days. Among the Mopheads (more correctly known as Hortensias) 'Deutschland', 'Hamburg' and 'La France' are recommended. The more graceful Lacecaps include 'Blue Wave' and 'Veitchii'. They will all grow to about 1.5 by 1.5 m (5 ft by 5 ft) and look splendid in a tub. Dead head in March, not autumn. Propagate in summer from soft tip cuttings.

**Rosa** (see pages 51 to 63)

**Spiraea** (see also page 47) *S.* × *bumalda* is a good pink. Its variety 'Anthony Waterer' has attractive foliage often tipped with pink and white.

**Weigela** (see page 37) *W. florida* 'Follis Purpureis' has pink flowers and, as its name suggests, purple foliage. 'Variegata' has pale pink flowers and attractive variegated foliage.

*Weigela florida* 'Variegata' has two attractions – its pink flowers and variegated foliage.

*Ceanothus* 'Delight' is one of the hardier of the evergreen Californian lilacs.

## BLUE AND MAUVE FLOWERED SHRUBS

**Caryopteris** The lovely blue spiraea flowers in August and September. *C.* × *clandonensis*, growing to about 60 cm (2 ft), is the one that is generally available and within its grouping there are a number of hybrids such as 'Blue Heaven' and 'Kew Blue'. It likes a chalky soil but most good garden soils will prove suitable, provided it can have a position in full sun. It may prove tender in heavy frosts but growth is quick to re-establish itself. Prune back in spring. Short cuttings about 7.5 cm (3 in) grow easily when taken in summer.

**Ceanothus** Californian lilac comes in as wide a range of blues as you can find. It can grow from 1.8 m to 3 m (6 ft to 10 ft). There are two groups. The evergreens

## CLEMATIS

For many years now clematis has been known as the lace maker of the garden, and there is hardly a better description. Here is a plant that will clothe the ugliest fence, the barest tree stem and cover any barrier with a furnishing of flowers and foliage that are the equal of any other garden plant.

*C. montana*, with its masses of small white flowers in May and June will climb to any height, cascade its way over a shed or fill the wall at the front of the house. All it will ask in return is that its roots are kept in shade and its head in the sun. This is surely the great climber of the garden, although it should be stressed that it needs a little support. This may be a trellis, wires or the stem of a tree, but without some help it may well flop to the ground. It also has pink flowered forms, 'Elizabeth' and *C. montana* var. *rubens*, which are equally vigorous.

Clematis are no different from most other plants, with many different species and varieties available to choose from. There are those that will race to get head high in the sun, others that will tumble around the ground to give a mass of ground cover, and some that make free standing border plants. In flower shape too they are quite different, ranging from 'Nellie Moser' with large flat, pink petals barred with carmine red to *C. viticella* with its masses of small purple flowers, and *C. tangutica* and *C. orientalis* with their yellow, lantern-like flowers in late summer and autumn. The colour range runs through all the blues and the purples to white, yellow, red, pink and cream, many of these with contrasting bars.

Clematis climb quite differently from other climbers, which may rely on tendrils or sucker roots or even thorns. They hang on by their foliage stems or petioles which wrap themselves around the support and become almost tendril like. They really are at their best when climbing trees or mixed in with the branches of a shrub and can be the perfect companions to a climbing rose.

**Planting and general care**

Since clematis do not like being disturbed, plant them out between autumn and spring where you intend to grow them. To keep the roots moist and shaded, stones can be placed over the soil and other plants used as base cover. Tie in the young growth.

Pruning is generally dictated by the amount of space needed. If you can, allow clematis the run of its support and then leave it alone; if some pruning is needed take out old and weak stems and shorten long ones by up to a third, cutting just above a strong bud. Young plants should be pruned back to 20–23 cm (8–9 in) from the ground in early spring, but after that they will only need minimal pruning.

The following are some of the many hybrids that can be recommended:

**Blue and purple** 'Blue Gem' (sky blue); 'Lady Betty Balfour' (rich purple with cream stamens); 'Perle d'Azur' (pale blue); 'The President' (deep purple-blue with red stamens); and, most popular of all, 'Jackmanii Superba' (deep violet-purple).

**Red** 'Ernest Markham' (rich red); 'Ville de Lyon' (small and bright); 'Niobe' (ruby-red).

**Pink** 'Bees Jubilee' (pale pink with deeper bar); 'Hagley Hybrid' (shell pink, brown stamens); 'Nelly Moser' (pale pink with carmine red bar and at its best growing on a north facing wall).

**White** 'Duchess of Edinburgh'; 'Mme le Coultre (white, yellow stamens).

*Clematis montana* var. *rubra*

'Ville de Lyon'

'Nelly Moser' keeps her colour best against a north wall.

have small leaves, small clusters of tiny flowers and they need sun. The deciduous plants are hardier and with more open flowers. They can suffer damage in severe winter but there are varieties such as 'Delight', that are hardier than others. Make sure ceanothus are planted in the spring, in a warm soil and a sheltered position. If exposed to cold, wet windy weather they are in trouble right from the start. Try the deciduous 'Gloire de Versailles' with its powder blue panicles of flowers in summer and autumn and growing up to 2.1 m (7 ft). The deeper blue flowers of 'Chester' (deciduous) or the evergreen 'Autumn Blue' are also recommended. Little pruning is needed for the evergreens while the deciduous varieties require their flowered shoots to be cut back to about 90 cm (3 ft) in March. Propagate from cuttings in summer. Ideal for training against a sheltered wall or fence, or at the back of a border.

**Ceratostigma** The hardy plumbago is usually represented by *C. willmottianum*. It makes a very pretty shrub growing to about 90 cm (3 ft). It needs a dry, warm, sunny spot and thrives on chalky soil with its bright blue flowers appearing late in summer and autumn. It makes a delightful partner for Michaelmas daisies. Pruning means cutting back to about ground level every April. Propagation is by division of roots or summer cuttings.

**Hebe** Once known as veronica, these come in many shapes and sizes, and colours too, so decide where you are going to plant it before making your purchase. For the blue border the violet-blue flowers of 'Autumn Glory' are a dominating brilliance from June to November and are accompanied by evergreen foliage of green and purple. 'Veitchii' is bright blue, 'Midsummer Beauty' lavender, but there are many others to choose from in shades of mauve, pink, lavender and white. The shiny foliage of these bushy plants make them a great attraction in the garden but remember that they can be tender especially in very cold areas. Very little pruning is needed and they will easily strike from short sideshoots taken in summer.

**Hydrangea** (see page 42)

Left: *Hebe* 'Midsummer Beauty' is evergreen, like all hebes, and suitable for seaside planting.

Opposite: Wisteria in full flower is one of the loveliest sights in early summer.

**Lavandula** For a fragrant edging that flowers between mid summer and early autumn, lavender is unsurpassed. *L. vera* is pale blue. While *L. spica* is the old English lavender. They like a limy soil, well drained, and good sun. Take away flowers as they fade (they are used the world over for pot-pourri) and then trim back in March. Do not cut into the hard wood when pruning. Summer cuttings will provide new plants.

**Rhododendron** (see page 37) 'Blue Tit' grows to about 90 cm (3 ft) and is lavender blue. Suitable for the rock garden.

**Syringa** Lilac is one of the most prolific shrubs and is found in many gardens where it forms a graceful small tree. You may think of it clothed in fragrant trusses of lilac or purple flowers but there is a special beauty in those lovely white cultivars. Unfortunately the flowering period lasts only a few short weeks early in summer. Lilacs do well in most soils and only need pruning after flowering when any thin unproductive wood should be cut away. 'Charles Joly' has double purple flowers; 'Souvenir de Louis Spaeth' is single and purple, and *S. velutina* has mauve flowers and forms an attractive rounded bush reaching 1.8 m (6 ft). Generally speaking all cultivars are grafted so propagation is not recommended, however some of the species can be grown from heeled cuttings taken in summer.

**Wisteria** Lilac-blue flowers hang in long trusses in May and June. This vigorous climber can top 6 m (20 ft). It looks at its best trained over a pergola or against a sunny wall in a humus-rich soil. Cut back side shoots in summer and long growths in winter. It is propagated from eye cuttings, small pieces of stem containing a bud. These are pressed into a pot containing a peat/sand mixture. Cover with clingfilm until signs of growth show.

## WHITE FLOWERED SHRUBS

**Buddleia** (see page 40) 'White Cloud' and 'White Bouquet', both hybrids of *B. davidii*, are ideal for the white garden.

**Camellia** (see page 40) The single white *C. japonica* 'Alba Simplex' is to be highly recommended.

**Carpenteria** Fragrant white flowers appear in mid summer. This shrub needs to be given full sun and as frost free a situation as possible. It will grow tall, up to 3 m (10 ft). Choose *C. californica* 'Ladham's Variety' which needs tipping back and a light pruning in spring. Propagate from cuttings in summer.

**Chaenomeles** (see page 37) 'Nivalis' is a fine white variety of *C. speciosa*.

**Choisya** The Mexican orange blossom is one of the neatest of garden shrubs forming a dome of glossy green trifoliate evergreen leaves. Only one species is available – *C. ternata* – and this grows to about 1.8 m (6 ft) over a period of six years. The flowers that are produced in May resemble orange blossom and the leaves

*Carpenteria californica* needs a sheltered spot and is best grown against a south- or west-facing wall.

Left: Mexican orange blossom (*Choisya ternata*) has attractive evergreen foliage.

Opposite: Lucky white heather, *Erica herbacea* 'Springwood White', providing attractive ground cover with ivy.

when crushed are fragrant. Plant in a sunny position or in partial shade in a well-drained, even a chalky soil. It needs little pruning but may be damaged by frost, in which case any dead or damaged wood should be cut out. Propagate from cuttings in summer; these should root with ease.

**Cotoneaster** These range from low ground-hugging plants to elegant trees, but all have small white flowers, often tinged with pink in June. One of the most popular is the wall-hugging *C. horizontalis* which grows from 60 cm to 1.2 m (2 to 4 ft). Often called the fishbone cotoneaster because of its distinctive branching pattern, it is deciduous with showy red berries in autumn. For orange berries try the graceful *C. franchetti; C.* 'Rothschildianus' has yellow berries and both will grow to 1.8 m (6 ft). Cotoneasters grow well in most soils but prefer a sunny position. Trim back into shape in spring if necessary.

**Deutzia** (see page 41) The excellent white *D. scabra* 'Plena' carries double white flowers which are light purple on the reverse of the petals.

**Erica** (see page 41) Everyone wants to grow lucky white heather. 'Springwood White' is low growing, reliable, and quite the best white variety. It flowers in winter.

**Hydrangea** (see page 42) *H. paniculata* 'Grandiflora' carries large heads of white flowers in late summer, turning pink with age. A spreading shrub reaching 1.5 m (5 ft). 'Lanarth White' is a lacecap from the *H. macrophylla* group.

**Magnolia** Not quite as difficult to grow as many believe. It does need a little tender, loving care in both planting and in the selection of a well dug, humus-rich, sunny site. A moisture-retentive soil is essential and to this end place plenty of good rotted compost around the roots and as a mulch. There are some magnolias which eventually form trees like *M. grandiflora* which is most spectacular and grows to 6m (20 ft) with large flowers from July to the end of September.

'Alba Superba' is one of the popular *M.* × *soulangiana* hybrids and grows to about 3 m (10 ft) high, while *M. stellata* is bush like and only half that size with dainty, star-like flowers in March and April. *M.* × *highdownensis* is a beautiful hybrid of the purest white which flowers late in spring.

**Olearia** (the daisy bush) Huge heads of white daisies appear on *O.* × *haastii* between July and September. This evergreen bush grows to 1.8 m (6 ft). It needs sunshine and a well-drained soil. Although it cannot stand frost it copes well with wind. Remove faded blooms after flowering and then prune out any dead or damaged shoots in April. If it grows too tall it can be kept down by hard pruning after flowering. Propagate from cuttings in summer.

**Philadelphus** The mock orange forms an elegant shrub covered with very fragrant white flowers in June or July. 'Belle Etoile' is a wonderful single-flowered shrub and 'Manteau d'Hermine' has double flowers; these are just two of many good cultivars there are to choose from. They grow to just over 1.8 m (6 ft) in most garden soils and like a sunny position or one of light shade. Propagate from hardwood cuttings in autumn.

*Philadelphus*, mock orange, brings fragrance to the garden in summer.

**Pyracantha** The firethorn is best known for its masses of red berries in autumn and winter. In cold spells, these provide a popular source of food for birds. However this spiny, evergreen shrub also is smothered in tiny white flowers early in summer. It is generally grown as a wall shrub but it can be used within a border where it can reach to 1.8 m (6 ft) high. Prune back unwanted shoots. Propagate from seed or from summer cuttings.

**Rhododendron** (see page 37) 'Sappho' is a beautiful white-flowered hardy hybrid, but may grow over 4 m (13 ft) high.

**Romneya** The tree poppy grows to 1.8 m (6 ft) high. Large white fragrant flowers with a yellow eye are borne from July to October on *R. coulteri* or until the first frost kills them. Frost may kill the plant back too but it usually grows again well enough in spring. Give it full sun, some shelter and a warm soil. It rarely survives transplanting. In March prune it to within a few centimetres of the ground. Propagate by cutting the thick roots into pieces and planting them, right way up, in a pot containing a peat/sand mixture.

*Romneya coulteri*, the tree poppy.

**Rosa** (see pages 51 to 63)

**Spiraea** Easy to grow and quick to establish. There are several different types to choose from. The spring flowering ones

*Spiraea* × *arguta* in full flower lives up to its familiar name of bridal wreath.

The spreading branches of *Viburnum plicatum* 'Mariesii' bear masses of flower heads in early summer.

generally produce white flowers. They are carried in many different ways – spikes, domes and even flat heads. The pure white heads of *Spiraea × arguta*, also known as bridal wreath or foam of May, are a wonderful sight. This shrub grows to about 1.8 m (6 ft).

Summer flowering spiraeas tend to be pink to purple. For something really unusual, try *S. japonica* 'Shirobana', 60 cm (2 ft) high, with a mixture of deep pink, crimson and white flowers during the summer months. These deciduous shrubs prefer a sunny position and a humus-rich soil. They can be raised in a frame from cuttings taken in summer.

**Syringa** (lilac – see page 44) 'Madame Lemoine' has glorious panicles of double white flowers.

**Viburnum** A varied group of shrubs with white or pink-tinged flowers; several also have attractive berries late in the year. *V. × carlesii* is a rounded shrub with fragrant white flowers in spring. It grows to about 1.5 m (5 ft). *V. plicatum* 'Mariesii' has large flat flowerheads. *V. farreri* carries sweet scented flowers in winter on bare branches. *V. opulus* 'Sterile' is known as the snowball tree because of its huge balls of sterile florets carried in summer; its foliage colours well in autumn too. The evergreen *V. tinus* is greatly under-rated. This winter flowering shrub makes an excellent hedge and provides a fine background for spring-flowering bulbs. Viburnums need little in the way of pruning and most can be propagated from cuttings taken in summer and raised in a heated propagating frame.

**Weigela** (see page 37) 'Mont Blanc' has fragrant white flowers. Another good white variety is *W. florida* 'Alba'.

## PLANT CARE

Even the best planned and best planted garden can be taken over completely by nature in a matter of months if left uncared for. But such care does not necessarily mean hard work, but it does mean keeping a constant lookout for aphids, caterpillars, emerging weeds, flowers that have died off, and those that are suffering from lack of water. On pages 89 to 92 we look in detail at the pests and diseases that you have to watch out for, so here I shall concentrate on some of the remaining key things you have to do to keep your garden in top notch.

*Viburnum farreri* is winter flowering.

## Watering

Before starting any planting session you must water the soil, and thereafter ensure your plant or shrub does not dry out and wilt. Even in what seems a wet season there are often plants in a closely planted bed or border that will get very little rain simply because the larger foliage is acting as an umbrella, so never assume that nature has given your plants sufficient water. Keep a close eye on them through the year, but never going to the opposite extreme of keeping your beds soaking wet all the time. Also, every plant needs time to absorb the water in the soil so you must allow for a drying-out spell.

When you bed-out new plants they will need to be well watered immediately (it is best if the soil is already wet). For the following few weeks, until they have become established, they will most likely need more watering, especially if there is a dry period in spring or early summer. When they become established they will be quite happy to go for longer periods without watering, but in drought conditions or in a period of warm, windy weather they will need attention. As soon as the top couple of inches of soil becomes dry or the foliage begins to look dull, that is the time to water.

Also ensure that you water thoroughly. A dribble around each plant does more harm than good. Ideally use a hose to water the immediate root area until it is well soaked, and then move on to the next plant. A watering can is quite effective in a small area, but the constant filling can make it a terrible chore.

## Feeding

All plants will suffer hunger pangs and look 'demoralized' if they are not occasionally fed. Although different plants have different feeding patterns, so often in a garden the miniature plants get the same amount as the large, hungrier ones, with the result that the little ones are over-fed and the large plants are left at almost starvation point. (There are a few plants that grow better if they are left without food, but they are so few that they need not concern us here.)

Feeding begins when a planting spot is being prepared. The inclusion of bone meal or a general fertilizer is vital to get the plant off to a good start. After that a fertilizer can be sprinkled around the roots, while a soluble or liquid fertilizer is very effective for the large leafed plants. The purpose of feeding is to build up a plant's resources, as much as to help it to give its best immediately, and for this reason annuals do not need feeding to the same extent as perennials.

Remember that all powder or granular fertilizers should be used only when the ground is moist, that they should be kept off foliage and away from the stems. After spreading they should be raked into the top couple of inches of soil. Foliar feeding is a very acceptable method of fertilizing, especially when you want instant results, for example when a plant needs to recover from an insect or disease attack, or after a particularly wet or windy spell when the plant has been under stress. A dilutor or hoser on the end of a hose pipe will do the job effectively and quickly.

## Hoeing and weeding

Weeds may look lovely in the countryside but they rarely enhance anyone's garden. Indeed, if they are given the freedom to grow then they can undo all the good work you have put into your garden. They compete for space, food, water, look unsightly, and eventually take over the whole area.

The best way to keep them down is with

DIVIDING HERBACEOUS PERENNIALS

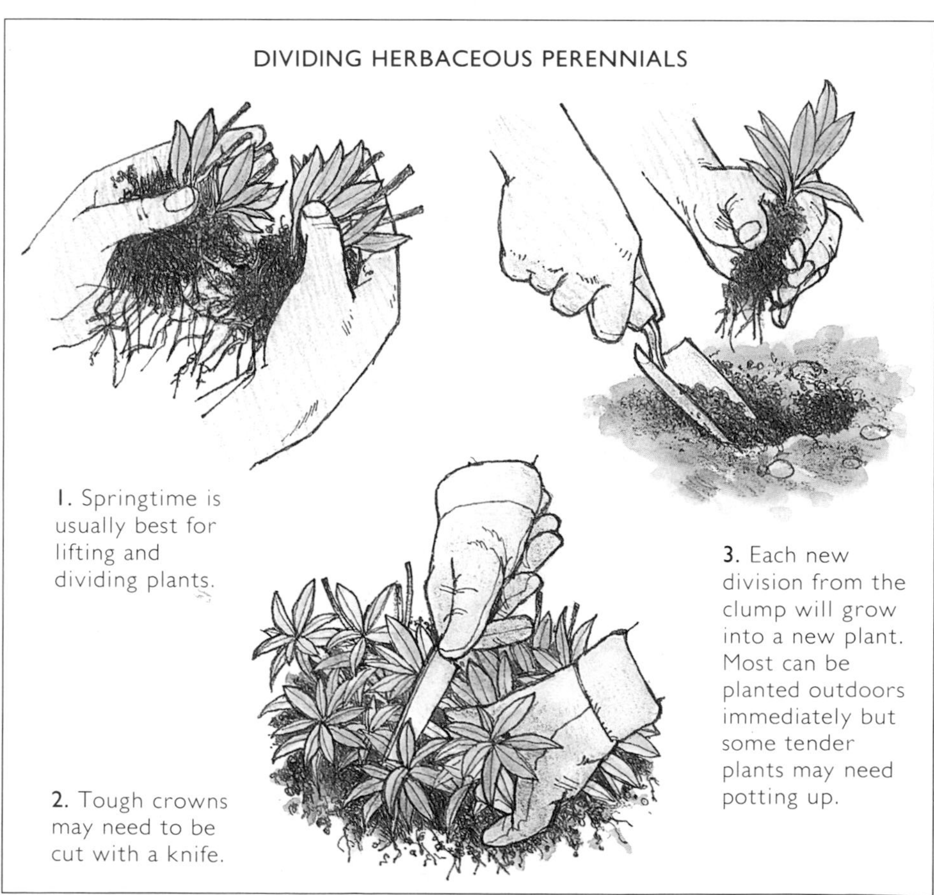

1. Springtime is usually best for lifting and dividing plants.

2. Tough crowns may need to be cut with a knife.

3. Each new division from the clump will grow into a new plant. Most can be planted outdoors immediately but some tender plants may need potting up.

a hoe. Regular hoeing as soon as seedling weeds appear should ensure control. However, if you do intend to use a chemical please follow the rules on the label precisely and keep it safely locked away. Never leave any trace of a weedkiller in a container that a child might drink from. If you do use a watering can for a weedkiller, label it, and do not use it again for any other gardening task.

Many weed problems will be stopped at source if roots and pieces of root are removed. But it does not matter how thorough you have been, some will reappear from time to time. Hoeing these weeds when they are tiny and before they get a chance to reseed the ground is vital. Hoe gently and with care, never going any deeper than is absolutely necessary. If there are any deep-rooted weeds, such as dandelion, dock, nettle or thistle, dig them out by hand.

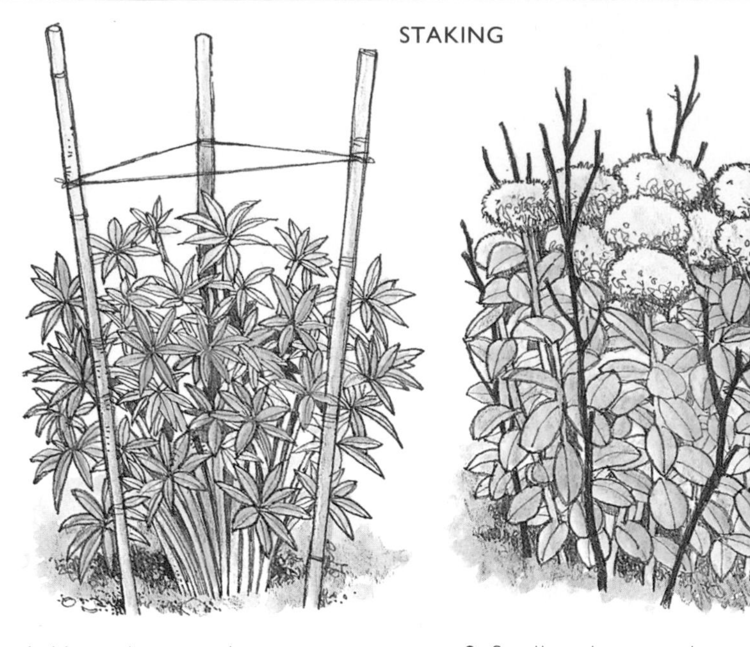


1. Many plants need support, especially in the herbaceous border. Put stakes in early. Place three or four canes around the stems, keeping growth tidy by means of string tied around the canes.

2. Smaller plants can be easily kept in place with small twiggy sticks. Do not just tie stems to a single cane.

### Staking

Staking in a garden can often look ugly, but it is necessary for many plants that are weak stemmed or for tall ones that are growing on exposed sites. There is nothing worse than finding plants that have been caught by an overnight wind and damaged, almost beyond repair.

Once you know the plants that need staking – those that are tall, large-headed, spindly or climbers – then you can tie them while they are still quite small. There is no point waiting until the weather becomes windy, for once a plant has collapsed, perhaps from its own weight, it will never recover, cannot be repaired and will only be fit for the compost heap.

For most plants ordinary pea sticks will suffice – just push them into the soil when the plant is about 30 cm (12 in) tall. With plants that need higher staking use bamboo canes, but don't clump too many stems together. Instead, set three or four canes about 23 cm (9 in) apart, at the corners of an imaginary triangle or square. Tie gardening string round the canes, creating a 'cage'. This holds in the plants but also gives them some freedom, and plenty of air and light. With some specialist plants like dahlias, chrysanthemums, sweet pea or standard roses, the stakes should be put in before planting so as not to damage the roots or tubers, in the case of dahlias, in any way.

### Pruning and cutting back

There is surprisingly little pruning or cutting back needed in the flower garden. The removal of spent blooms in the summer or cutting back of growth when a plant becomes overcrowded, is all that is involved. Among the spring-flowering plants in the rockery many will put out ugly foliage in the summer, and this can be cut back without affecting the plant – often some cutting back will bring the bonus of a second set of flowers.

The same message applies to winter and spring pruning. The majority of plants die down by themselves. Annuals will, of course, die off; the remnants can go on the compost heap. The only other job for the gardener is to cut down and clear away the dead foliage and begin to make plans for the following year's flowers. There may be some plants such as border roses, which will need pruning, and this is dealt with later in the book. Many fuchsias die back naturally – if they don't they can be hard pruned right to the ground, but not before March. However, if you live in a very mild area you may find that fuchsias retain their foliage right through the winter.

### Winter tasks

For a great number of plants winter means rest, but there are some, like the half-hardy perennials, that will need lifting and storing until it is time for planting again in the spring. If you wish to take a chance you could leave the plants in the ground, covering the crowns with peat moss, twigs, and leafmould to keep them frost free, until the following spring. But, having said that, it should be added that the gardener ought to make his own investigations about his plants so that their winter care requirements are known. Evergreens and winter-flowering plants should, of course, be left alone.

A very light dig with a fork is all that is needed to clear up the beds and borders, which also gives you a chance to take out any perennial weeds that have escaped attention earlier in the year. It should be stressed that this is a careful operation, and that roots should not be disturbed unless a plant is to be lifted and divided. If you have delicate alpines they will need protection from the rain. You can either construct a small plastic housing, or cover them with a sheet of glass.

# THE ROSE GARDEN

Since medieval times the rose has been called the flower of flowers. And it still reigns supreme as the most adaptable of plants, a symbol of absolute beauty, purity, peace and joy. Undoubtedly a great deal of its popularity has been built on a certain mystique, but this is allied to the fact that the rose can be grown just about anywhere, in a mixed border, its own special bed, in rockeries and on large banks, in containers, and window boxes, and in warm greenhouses and conservatories.

There is hardly a large or small, public or private garden in Great Britain today without a rose of some kind. And every year more and more new rose varieties are being developed to add to the thousands already on sale, increasing the range of colours, fragrances, shapes and styles. Many of the new varieties echo the old roses, but bring with them the best of the modern varieties. Miniature roses, which really only became popular 50 years ago, are now almost a cult on their own. Today there are so many roses for every type of garden, and for every position within these gardens, that it is no wonder new gardeners are bewildered by the enormity of the choice.

The nature of the rose has changed in just over a century. Before the late 1800s it was expected to flower for only a short time in the early summer months but, even for this period, the beauty of the rose was such that it would have been churlish to have expected more from the Damasks, Musks Bourbons, Albas, and others. Today, with the arrival of hybrid teas (large flowered), floribundas (cluster flowered), miniatures and climbers, that provide flowers from May until December, the rose has had adaptability allied to old fashioned beauty.

Rose lovers now find that even the smallest garden can be turned into a true rose garden with plants that are scaled-down versions of the delightful old style varieties. If you prefer the older roses, then provided you have a medium size garden there shouldn't be any problem. When deciding which kind of rose to buy, also consider the most recent innovations, the English roses, which bring together the flowers of the old roses with the almost constant flowering possibilities of modern varieties. Finally, there are the patio roses, small and compact, with medium sized flowers, being far more versatile than the name suggests.

It's very tempting, when deciding where to plant a rose, to give it too much prominence. Instead, you should consider mixing them. So a yellow climber such as 'Golden Showers', or a shrub such as 'Mountbatten' will excel when interlaced with the blue *Clematis* 'Countess of Lovelace' or 'Perle d'Azur'. Roses really mix superbly well with herbaceous flowers, although many people believe this is sacrilege. To prove the point, just imagine a border with roses mixed with hollyhocks, delphiniums, foxgloves and a carpet of pinks at their feet. Nor are violas, and the grey tints of catmint and lavender, Canterbury bells (*Campanula*) and perlargoniums out of place with the rose. Similarly,

Hybrid tea rose 'Just Joey' has ruffled petals and superb colour.

in shrub borders, the rose is invaluable and mixes well with forsythia, lilac and flowering currants (*Ribes*).

Underplanting, other than in mixed borders, can be a problem when the rose bed needs mulching and feeding, the process being hindered by the presence of other smaller plants. But that does not apply to spring bulbs, while violas, primulas and auriculas, if used with care, can be a lovely foil. In all cases the shrubs, perennials and low-growing plants and bulbs can bring colour to the garden when the rose is out of flower, and at other times will create an exciting foreground or backdrop, as with delphiniums which make ideal bed-mates for roses.

## HYBRID TEAS

Probably the ultimate in the rose breeder's skills is shown in the hybrid teas (also described as large-flowered bush roses) that produce the largest and most beautifully formed blooms of all. The colour range only lacks the true blue and the deep black. They are also the most highly scented group of the modern roses, but their greatest glory comes from their ability to produce continuous crops of flowers from early summer to mid-winter.

Where they are grown in the garden is best decided by you. Ignore such advice that demands hybrid teas are grown in beds of one type. Siting the rose is an artistic decision, partly influenced by the shape, height and colour of its companion plants. You should have few problems in making a decision, particularly when planting such splendid roses as the lovely big 'Solitaire' with its yellow touched red blooms, the copper of 'Just Joey', the soft apricot of 'Helen Traubel', the red and almost cabbage sized 'Alec's Red', and the yellow-pink and orange of 'Lincoln Cathedral'. They all have their place when well-grown, and will show they are robust enough to grow in a group of their own or among the plants in a mixed border.

Every year hybrid teas are improved. In recent times the greatest changes have been brought by the Scottish-bred 'Silver Jubilee' (a soft confection of pink and cream) which has passed on its great foliage, well-shaped blooms and good, even bush growth to many new varieties. Another recent rose, the vermillion, tall-growing 'Alexander', is also the herald of strong growth and flower power in tomorrow's roses.

Among the hybrid teas there are many cultivars which are grown only by exhibitors who are prepared to cover them so that rain does not harm the blooms. Unfortunately many of these roses find their way into the ordinary garden because they have been seen in full beauty at a flower show and assumed to be a typical rose. The best place for the non-exhibitor to see roses is therefore in a garden or a rose grower's field. Tempting though it is to buy roses on the basis of reading a marvellous description, you should remember that nothing beats seeing roses 'in the flesh', when you will instinctively know whether they are your kind of flowers and which varieties you prefer.

## FLORIBUNDAS

It always seems much easier to place floribundas in mixed borders and beds because of the clusters of blooms that they carry, with an informality that is often lacking among the hybrid teas. It is this characteristic which gives them their alternative classification as cluster-flowered bush roses. Unfortunately the floribundas are not the greatest possessors of fragrance, although a little searching will reveal that there are quite a number of pleasantly scented varieties available, including 'Margaret Merril', 'English Miss', 'Arthur Bell', 'Korresia', and 'Fragrant Delight'.

Floribundas can be seen at their best in beds of one variety, but this should not stop anyone using them with groups of other plants. The flower type is extremely varied, ranging from the hybrid tea perfection of shape, to the old fashioned quartered and loose petalled flowers. The colour range is also extremely wide, with some beautiful types of blooms that have not been repeated as successfully in the hybrid teas. The mauves, purples and lilacs are very well represented, with superb cultivars such as 'Escapade' (light lilac) the much deeper 'Lilac Charm', and the beetroot-purple 'News'. The distinctive pink of 'Elizabeth of Glamis' is matched with a lovely fragrance, but this one can be difficult to grow, not always being sufficiently hardy in a severe winter. And one of the most famous floribundas is 'Queen Elizabeth', justly revered for its enormous quantities of blooms. It is also tough, and does not demand much attention other than heavy pruning in the spring.

The range of floribundas available to British gardeners is second to none, and the type of roses available is extraordinary. There are even some excellent low growers, including the scented 'Amber Queen', 'Korresia (the best of the yellows), 'Trumpeter' (the best of the reds), the white 'Iceberg', and the lovely pink, 'Sexy Rexy' (which will triumph despite, or possibly because of its name).

## SHRUBS

The way roses are being bred today you could grow just about any rose as a shrub whether it be a hybrid tea, floribunda or an old garden rose. However, there is a special classification for shrubs, which is broken down between old and modern varieties. They embrace a huge range of roses some of which grow like climbers, others that need huge spaces, and some that flower right through from spring to late autumn. They also have a wide range of flowers, from those with five petals, to others numbering almost 100. In bush form, some are lax and others upright; some will make an enormous bush, while others stay well within the normal range of 60 cm–1.2 m (2 ft–4 ft) high. Such a diversity should immediately convey the old but still highly valid message 'Let the buyer beware', because no matter how pretty the sales pictures and descriptions may be, one of your first considerations must be select a rose for the space you have available.

Choosing a shrub is obviously a very personal matter, but I feel that the new English roses will prove to be very popular. They are a mixture of the old roses and the newer types, and combine flowers in the form and in the style of old roses (mostly big, heavy-petalled, and perfumed) with the repeat flowering of the modern varieties. They are available in wonderful colours, though the bush form may still need a little improvement. Nonetheless, it is a fine addition for the borders.

Placing shrubs at the back of the border will give a great framework and a long-flowering period, from a form that blends easily with the herbaceous and perennials.

The rose garden at the Royal Horticultural Society's Garden at Wisley in Surrey.

Left: 'Ballerina' is a delightful shrub rose suitable for growing in a tub as well as in the open garden.

Opposite: The deservedly popular miniature rose 'Baby Masquerade'.

But do make sure that the size is what you want. When it comes to colour you will find few yellows among the old roses, but two new ones – 'Graham Thomas' from the English roses, and 'Mountbatten' – are worth seeking out. They ensure there's no excuse for omitting a shrub rose from your garden, whether it be large or small.

## MINIATURES

These roses are usually half the size (or even smaller) of those already mentioned, and twice the value. They can be grown in the front of a border, in a pocket of a rockery, or along the top of a wall or bank that has sufficient soil. They are also ideal for window boxes, tubs, the greenhouse, and even the conservatory. In fact they are the most versatile of all small plants. And the colour range too is everything you could ask for, ranging from lavender to green, from whites to pure reds, and from pink to apricot, with others in bicolors. Miniatures are so popular that in some parts of the world they sell in greater numbers than all the other types of roses combined. Yet 10 years ago they were widely being dismissed as 'toy roses'.

What exactly is a miniature rose? To most people it is a small plant, no more than about 30 cm (12 in) high, with small flowers and small foliage. But that isn't necessarily so, for miniatures today come in sizes varying from 7.5–10 cm (3–4 in) high, to shrubs and climbers which grow to 1.2–1.5 m (4–5 ft) high carrying masses of tiny blooms. But bloom size too can vary, from the very small to about 4 cm (1½ in) across when fully open.

The world's number one miniature has existed since the 1960s. It is the French-bred orange-red called 'Starina' that carries perfectly shaped blooms on a well-shaped bush. But it is now being closely rivalled by the newer varieties. My own nomination as the best of the miniatures for garden growing is the coral-pink 'Angela Rippon', which is widely available.

Most of the top new miniatures have been bred in America where there is an astonishing boom in their sales, though they are only now beginning to arrive in Great Britain. However, widely available throughout the country are small potted roses ('Sunblaze' and 'Rosamini' are but two) from French and Dutch breeders. These are generally sold in flower, and once they have bloomed in the house they can be transferred to the garden. Indeed, these purchases can often prove very good value for the pots generally have three or four little plants that have been struck from cuttings, which can be separated and planted out individually in the garden or into pots or a window box.

One of the great benefits of the miniatures is that they are very simple to grow from cuttings. In fact, one American writer says that they grow so easily from cuttings that 'they spread like gossip'. Certainly they are easy to propagate and very easy to fall in love with. An additional bonus of taking these cuttings is that the plants will often be far more dainty than those that have been produced by the more traditional method of budding or grafting.

## CLIMBERS AND RAMBLERS

Calling roses ramblers and climbers is, in a way, giving a false impression because they will not climb or ramble without some help from the gardener or from nature by way of support. This support may have to be wires, tying, or help to find a way through an old tree. Once that help is provided, and if you have objects to cover, such as an archway or tree stump, then the results should be spectacular.

Ramblers and climbers are quite distinct. The ramblers have been with us for generations, their huge trusses carrying hundreds of generally small blooms. They provide a mass of colour all through the summer, but there is only one flush of blooms. Their main use nowadays is where a rampant grower is needed to provide colour and foliage high up in old trees. But later they can be quite troublesome, needing attention if their condition deteriorates, and cutting back after their summer flowering. Among the best of them are 'Albertine' (pale pink and very fragrant), 'American Pillar' (deep pink, white eye), and 'Crimson Shower' (crimson with a light fragrance), while the giant and tree topping *Rosa filipes* 'Kiftsgate' will cover anything where it can grow rampantly and without hindrance.

Climbers are quite a different proposition. Their stems are stiff, with flowers ranging from the small to those as large as on the hybrid teas. Many are also tough and fairly disease resistant, while new ones are being hybridized all the time. The latter have the added bonus of being repeat flowering – for perfection look to 'Handel',

An archway wreathed in roses.

*Rosa filipes* 'Kiftsgate' will cover the branches of the tallest tree; give it plenty of space.

'Albertine' is one of the most popular and vigorous of the ramblers. Its copper-pink buds open early in summer.

which has cream with rosy-pink edgings to the flower, the apricot-pink 'Compassion', or the deep red 'Dublin Bay'. In one respect these modern climbers are quite different to the older ones, like some of the climbing Bourbons (such as the lovely 'Zephirine Drouhin') because they do not grow with the same vigour – some will only reach 3 m (10 ft) high, and only then after quite a struggle.

Also widely available are climbing versions (called sports) of many bush roses. Unfortunately these climbing roses usually put all their energy into producing the first batch of flowers, which means that you get very little of the repeat flowering benefits of the bush form. But when they bloom they can be spectacular, with 'Cl. Shot Silk', 'Cl. Mrs Sam McGredy' and 'Cl. Ena Harkness' being among the best available.

More than any other group of roses the climbers need careful choosing. Check their potential for repeat flowering, their expected height, size of flower, fragrance, and disease resistance before purchase.

## BUYING

The best time to see roses and to make your selection is during the summer when the full effects of weathering can be seen on the blooms. Roses make wonderful pictures in catalogues, but the compilers often fail to show or mention the growth habit, the amount of thorns, the real colour, the height, whether it is bushy, upright, open, or spreading, and the amount of rain resistance there is in the flower. The ideal bedding roses, in my opinion, are 'Silver Jubilee' (peachy cream), 'Trumpeter' (orange-red), 'Korresia' (yellow), 'The Times' (dark red), 'Just Joey' (fragrant, coppery orange) and 'Iceberg' (white), but there are hundreds of others that are worth considering.

The sooner you order in the summer the better your chance of getting top-class bushes. The roses will generally be sent to you bare-rooted from November onwards. Huge numbers of gardeners also buy prepackaged roses which are bare rooted but they may suffer by having only a little peat moss or compost around the roots to keep them moist. You can also buy container grown roses, which are the ideal kind to plant during the growing season.

With all these roses you are looking for a good strong bush that looks healthy. Anything less is not worth buying – there is no such thing as a bargain rose. Stems should be green and without the wrinkles that point to wilting, and they should be well ripened (most bronze type foliage or stems will be unripe). There should be, at the very least, two good stems, and the roots system should have some fibrous growth. The buds should be dormant in all prepackaged and bare root purchases.

## PLANNING

There are no rules as to where you should plant a rose or how they should be planted. Although it is advantageous to remember that beds are better planted with only one kind, and that borders can be multipurpose, these rules can be ignored if the roses are properly placed within their confines. There is nothing worse than a huge bed or front garden of roses thrown together like a handful of smarties – different colours but no overall shape. While I do not believe that plant colours ever clash, I do feel that some control is needed. Without it you will have a chaotic mass of tall stems and buried blooms entangled in an unsightly mess. Another general point worth considering is that hybrid teas are best kept in a batch on their own where the individual blooms can be admired, while floribundas are the roses for big splashes of colour.

### Key planning points

- With bedding roses plant the taller varieties in the centre.
- Stagger the planting within a bed.
- Keep the roses at least 45 cm (18 in) from the outside edges of the beds to avoid problems when trimming the grass.
- Don't make the bed any deeper than 1.5 m (5 ft), otherwise you will have difficulty reaching and cutting off dead heads.
- The same points apply to borders and to beds, except that as the roses are not being seen from all sides the tallest (like 'Queen Elizabeth' and 'Alexander') should be at the back, medium-sized growers in the centre, and low growers (such as the miniatures and the patios) in the front row.
- Try to plant roses in batches of three to five to form a group of one colour.
- Some roses make good hedges, but do check the height and colour before you place your order. There is a huge range of roses available in this category, providing a superb all the year round flowering screen to just about any height.
- There are many roses, such as the new patio types 'Sweet Dreams', 'Sweet Magic' and 'Cider Cup', and the older 'Ballerina' with its five petalled blooms of light pink and white eye which are ideal for planting in tubs and urns.

## PLANTING

There is no such thing as a successful, shaded rose garden. The rose, even more than other flowers, needs sunshine galore as well as plenty of water, food, air and light. It is improved by being sheltered from cold winds.

The planting time lasts from late October to late March. There is no doubt that the sooner you can get the bushes in the ground the better chance they have of settling down quickly, and the better their growth and flowering will be during their first season.

Most of what has been said about soil for flowers also applies to roses. The best kind is a medium loam that isn't waterlogged, and which has a pH of around 6.5. However if your soil needs attention, then use peat to increase acidity, and nitrochalk to increase alkalinity. The finest thing you can do for the rose bed is to add manure or other humus. You should prepare the soil so that there will be time for it to settle before the arrival of the bushes. When the bushes do arrive, waste no time in planting them. With bare root or root-wrapped roses it is better to get them heeled into the ground in a protected spot if the soil is unsuitable for planting. This involves covering the roots and lower parts of the stems with soil, and leaving them until conditions have improved.

PLANTING A ROSE BUSH

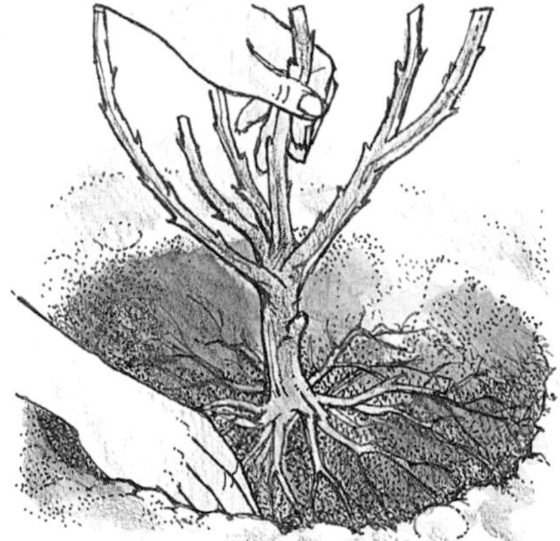

1. Fit and spread the roots snugly into the hole after pruning the rose.

2. Replace the soil and firm in gently with the foot.

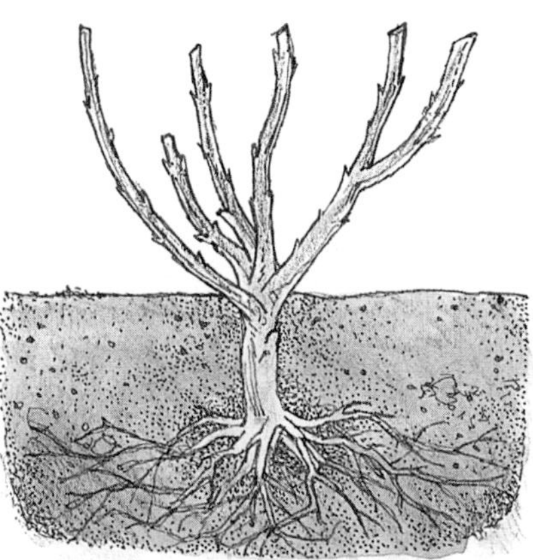

3. The bud union should be slightly below ground level when planted so that it will level off as soil settles. Insert label in the soil by the bush.

When you unpack your roses, whether they be in a grower's bag or are pre-packaged from the store, place them into a full bucket of water and give them a good soaking. Then cut away all the broken, decayed or spindly shoots, and cut back any very long shoots to about 30 cm (1 ft) from the base. The next task involves creating the planting mixture in a wheelbarrow. Use one part soil, one part moist peat, and four (gloved) handfulls of bone meal. Mix thoroughly.

Once a good size hole has been dug, spread out the roots in it, particularly if they are all growing in one direction. Now cover the roots with the planting mix, keeping the bud union (the knot-like portion where the roots meet the top growth) about 2–3 cm (1 in) below the soil level.

Use the same technique to transplant older roses, but note that it will require more watering. You should also beware of planting new bushes in soil where roses have been previously grown. They will not thrive. If you must use the same place then make sure that you remove an area at least 60 × 60 cm (2 × 2 ft).

## PRUNING

Nothing frightens the new gardener more than the thought of pruning, yet it is quite a simple task, once you know the rules. They involve:

- Pruning from mid March in the south of the country, to early April in the north. Pruning too early means that premature growth can be killed off by winter frosts. Pruning too late means that a lot of important early growth is wasted.
- Using the best secateurs. They are costly but definitely worth the extra money. No matter what kind you use, make sure they are always kept clean and sharp.
- Trimming back long growth to about half the length of the stem. Follow this by cutting out entirely all dead wood and any stems that are diseased or damaged. If the pith is not pure white keep cutting until it is; this is the sign of healthy growth.
- Cutting out all thin stems and those that rub against each other. Unripe growth must also be removed.
- Producing a clean, ripe, strong and healthy bush with an open centre.

PRUNING A ROSE

1. First remove old, dead or broken wood.

2. Take out all twiggy growth and thin out the centre of the bush.

3. Hybrid teas may be pruned hard to five or six eyes from the base but bushes should be pruned to suit the garden.

Note: Ramblers are pruned in late summer or autumn as soon as flowering has finished.

Climbers need little pruning, but do cut away any old, damaged wood, and leave the climber at the length and height and spread dictated by the needs of its position and your garden.

## GENERAL MAINTENANCE

This involves three principal tasks:

**Mulching** This operation keeps the ground moist, eliminates many weeds, and improves the soil structure. If manure is used it provides some food for the roses.

**Watering** Roses need more water than most plants, but that does not mean that they like to be kept standing in mud. Young and newly planted or transplanted bushes need water regularly in a dry spell. A little soluble fertilizer in the water never does any harm. Roses can take up to 9.1 lt (2 gl) each, every couple of days.

**Feeding** A small handfull of fertilizer should be applied to every bush in the spring when the soil is moist. If this is repeated every month until the end of July there will be a wonderful response from the plant. Foliar feeding is also very useful – wet the leaves thoroughly and spray using a diluter or hoser on the end of a hosepipe.

## PROBLEMS

It is not possible to eliminate all the troubles from a rose garden, but by tackling problems before they appear the gardener should always be the winner. The major problems are three diseases known as **black spot, mildew** and **rust**, all of which live up to their names and are easy to spot.

Spray with a recommended fungicide immediately after pruning, so that any leftover spores are eliminated. After that, spray once a month to prevent these diseases from taking hold. Most chemical treatments are designed to prevent rather than cure, although some of the newer ones do have curative qualities.

When spraying, follow these tips. Do not spray in sunny or windy weather, but when the foliage is dry, preferably in the evening. Spray the top and bottom of the foliage until the liquid drips from it. You should wear clothes that cover and protect as much of your skin as possible. Also wear a mask and glasses. And finally, once you have finished, throw away empty chemical containers into the rubbish bin, and drain away any left over solution.

Other problems caused by aphids and the like should be handled individually. It is useless spraying with a multichemical if there is no need for an insecticide. However, when aphids do appear then a cocktail spray that includes an insecticide, fungicide and some foliar feeding is perfect for the roses.

Regular spraying against all bugs and these specific diseases will pay off, and even if you have only a couple of bushes far greater results will be achieved by constant care and attention. You should also watch out for caterpillars, slugworms, beatles, and so on.

## RECOMMENDED VARIETIES

This list contains a number of roses of proven ability which will go on flowering with normal care and attention for 15 to 20 years – and maybe longer.

### HYBRID TEAS

**'Alec's Red'** Crimson, globular and very fragrant. Vigorous growth. Needs watching for black spot.

**'Alexander'** Vermillion, medium sized with a slight fragrance. Brilliant colouring and a tall grower. Cut flowers when they are young.

**'Blessings'** Coral pink, medium sized, fragrant. The ideal bedding rose with wonderful flower producing abilities. (See page 60.)

**'Double Delight'** Creamy white, edged raspberry red, large and very fragrant. Exquisite in a warm, sunny, dry summer, but falls victim to mildew easily. Blooms also 'ball' in the rain.

**'Fragrant Cloud'** Geranium red, large, very fragrant. Excellent for bedding but does need watching for signs of mildew and rust.

**'Grandpa Dickson'** Lemon yellow, large, slightly fragrant. An upright grower, needing to be well fed and watered to get it to its best.

**'Harry Wheatcroft'** Scarlet, striped yellow, large, slight fragrance. Flamboyant and named after one of the rose world's greatest characters.

**'Helen Traubel'** Apricot, large and fragrant. A lovely rose that blooms heavily but often has weak stems. Waterproof.

Hybrid tea 'Blessings' is ideal for bedding with its splendid flower producing abilities.

**'Just Joey'** Coppery orange, medium sized, fragrant. Its ruffled petals give it great style. These, together with its wonderful colour, make it one of the most sought after roses of recent times.

**'Lincoln Cathedral'** Orange, pink, yellow, large, slightly fragrant. A new rose that has won national acclaim; may need some rain protection.

**'National Trust'** Crimson, medium-sized, little fragrance. A great bedding rose, lowish growing, strong stems, great for cutting.

**'Rose Gaujard'** Deep red, silver reverse, large, slightly fragrant. A tall and strong grower, and an ideal choice for bedding.

**'Silver Jubilee'** Peachy, pink, salmon and cream, with a large, fragrant rose that is the best of the recent varieties. Superb for bedding.

**'Solitaire'** Yellow with a touch of red on the tips, large, fragrant. Vigorous grower, almost rainproof, superb blooms for cutting.

**'Troika'** Orange-bronze, shaded red, large, fragrant. Very healthy, excellent bedding and cutting rose with good disease and rain resistance.

### FLORIBUNDAS

**'Amber Queen'** Saffron yellow, fragrant. Low growing. Although new is a worldwide favourite. Healthy, dark foliage.

**'Ainsley Dickson'** Salmon pink with tones of red, slightly fragrant. Winner of the top prize of the Royal National Rose Society. Ideal for cutting and bedding.

**'Anne Cocker'** Vermillion, little fragrance. A good variety for bedding and cutting. Late flowering.

**'English Miss'** Silvery pink, very fragrant. Healthy with a flower in the style of a camellia. Free flowering with good repeat performance.

**'Escapade'** Soft rosy violet with white eye; fragrant. Unique and a great producer of blooms. Perfect as an individual bush or in a bed of its own.

**'Fragrant Delight'** Coppery salmon, very fragrant. Vigorous and upright with flowers that are almost hybrid tea shape. Very good bedding rose.

**'Iceberg'** White, medium size and slightly fragrant. One of the great roses in growth and flower production. Watch for black spot.

**'Korresia'** Yellow, fragrant, probably the best of all the yellow bedding roses with trusses of blooms that do not fade.

**'Margaret Merril'** Pearly white and very fragrant. High centered flowers, produced in plenty but they can develop spots in the rain.

**'Matangi'** Vermillion, white-eye, reverse of petals silver. Well-shaped buds and a very vigorous bush that can be kept lowish, but it will also grow tall if left with light pruning.

**'Memento'** Salmon vermillion, slightly fragrant. If you want a bright bedding rose this is it – compact with a great record of flower production.

**'Queen Elizabeth'** Pink, large blooms and slightly fragrant. One of the world's great roses – tall, stately and needing heavy pruning to be kept to a reasonable size.

**'Sexy Rexy'** Rose pink, slightly fragrant. Wonderful plant for bedding and cutting. Bushy grower and fine flower production.

**'Southampton'** Apricot-orange, slightly fragrant. Very vigorous and upright. A wonderful flower for cutting.

**'Trumpeter'** Orange red, slightly fragrant, probably the best of the red bedding roses, producing flowers right into winter. Great disease resistance.

## MINIATURE ROSES

**'Angela Rippon'** Coral pink, bushy, healthy and a great flower producer.

**'Baby Darling'** Orange and pink blend and very popular.

**'Baby Masquerade'** Changes colour from yellow to pink to red. Very good.

**'Darling Flame'** Orange vermillion with golden reverse. Healthy, bushy.

**'Rise 'n' Shine'** Lovely yellow, lots of flowers. Also known as 'Golden Sunblaze'.

**'Red Ace'** Deep red and bushy grower that gives lots of flowers.

**'Starina'** Bright vermillion, the star of the miniatures.

*Note:* Other low-growing roses are often catalogued as patio roses, but they are very good in all parts of the garden. They are also quite new but contain some wonderful roses such as 'Sweet Dream' (peach-apricot rosette type), 'Sweet Magic' (orange with golden tints), 'Wee Jock' (deep crimson), 'Little Woman' (rose pink), 'Rosabell' (rose pink, quartered blooms), 'Gentle Touch' (light pink), 'Red Rascal' (scarlet-crimson) and 'Rugul' (yellow).

This list will go out of date as more and more of the American bred roses arrive on the market. Not included are the many little plants that are sold over the counter in numerous stores today. All can easily be increased by cuttings.

## SHRUB ROSES

There is such a wide range of shrub roses in many different forms that it is impossible to give anything approaching a full range. The list that follows is therefore built round the roses recommended to the members of the Royal National Rose Society in its annual review, with the addition of a few personal favourites. They are all repeat flowering, unless specified.

**'Aloha'** Rosy salmon pink, slightly fragrant. Often named as a climber but does better when controlled by pruning and grown as a shrub.

**'Anna Zinkeisen'** Creamy white, fragrant. Vigorous shrub, growing to 1.2 m (4 ft) and a constant producer of lovely open flowers.

**'Ballerina'** Pink, white eye, little fragrance. Full heads of tiny white and pink flowers. Wonderful garden or tub variety. Perfect for mixed borders.

'Canary Bird' is a shrub rose with clear yellow flowers.

**'Buff Beauty'** Apricot to yellow, fragrant. Marvellous flowers in quantity. Perfect for single or group planting or in a mixed border.

**'Canary Bird'** Yellow, slightly fragrant. Arching stems of beauty. Needs plenty of room since it can grow to a large size.

**'Cardinal Hume'** Purple, slightly fragrant. Very unusual modern shrub that is good for hedging, in a group, or as a specimen bush.

**'Chinatown'** Yellow, touched pink, fragrant. Healthy, and disease and rain resistant. Bushy and tallish – good for the back of a border.

**'Eyeopener'** Red with yellow centre, slightly fragrant. Praised for flower and foliage pleasing to 'fastidious garden planners'.

**'Felicia'** Light pink, fragrant. Carries fine trusses of bloom on a handsome plant and can be planted in a group, as a hedge, or individually within a border.

**'Fred Loads'** Vermillion, fragrant. The five-petalled flowers are carried in great trusses on strong stems. The plant can grow very tall.

**'Fountain'** Bright red, fragrant. Reliable – disease and rain resistant – although the stems can be a little thin and may break in heavy rain or strong winds.

**'Frühlingsgold'** Creamy yellow, fragrant. Although it is only a summer blooming variety it is one of the great roses with arching branches of large flowers.

'Nevada', a fine shrub rose with creamy white flowers.

**'Joseph's Coat'** Yellow to pink to red, slightly fragrant, medium-sized flowers. This if often regarded as a climber, but pruned back makes a good shrub for individual planting or in a border group.

**'Mary Rose'** Deep pink, slightly fragrant. One of the new English Roses. Shrubby with spreading plants and pretty cupped, petal filled flowers.

**'Sally Holmes'** Creamy white, slightly fragrant. Huge shoots, often with massive trusses of bloom held well above the foliage. Best in a close group of three or as a hedge for full effect.

*Note:* The range of shrubs could also be complemented by others of proven ability such as 'Nevada' (flowers in June with some repeat flowers in late autumn), 'Marguerite Hilling' (a pink sport of 'Nevada' and identical in all but colour), 'Pearl Drift' (a low, wide plant), 'Penelope' (light pearly pink, noted for its free blooms), 'Rosarie de l'Hay' (wine red, fragrant, tough), and 'The Fairy' (pink, spreading, and a wonderful low-growing rose).

## CLIMBERS AND RAMBLERS

No climbing sports of bush roses are mentioned here, but a number of them are worth considering (see climbers in earlier part of this chapter). All are repeat flowering, unless specified.

**'Albertine'** Pale pink, very fragrant. Great early summer flowering rambler.

**'American Piller'** Pink, white eye, little fragrance. Rambler. Needs lots of care.

**'Breath of Life'** Apricot to apricot pink, slightly fragrant. Full hybrid tea type flowers.

**'Compassion'** Salmon pink to apricot, fragrant. Strong and stiff growth with big hybrid tea type flowers.

**'Danse du Feu'** Orange scarlet, little fragrance. Vivid colour, medium-sized blooms and a generous grower.

'Frühlingsgold' is a superb shrub rose with arching branches.

The lovely flowers of 'Handel', one of the best climbing roses of all time.

**'Dublin Bay'** Rich blood red, little fragrance. Slow to establish growth and can be used as a shrub as well as a climber. Superb flowers.

**'Golden Showers'** Bright to light yellow, fragrant. Dependable with good flower production rate.

**'Gloire de Dijon'** Buff yellow, fragrant. Big flowers of Victorian shape. Watch for mildew.

**'Handel'** Cream, edged rosy pink, slightly fragrant. The number one climber for growth, disease and rain resistance, and flowers that look lovely and cut well. Not rampant.

**'Kiftsgate'** White, fragrant. Extensive rambler. Flowers mid summer. It can be grown up a tree as it will tackle any height; and when it does it is generally impossible to prune. Best in large gardens where there is plenty of room.

**'Maigold'** Yellow, fragrant. Blooms only once and very early, but still a great favourite.

**'Mme Grégoire Staechelin'** Rosy carmine, very fragrant. Early summer flowering but the most generous of roses. Vigorous.

**'Morning Jewel'** Bright pink, slightly fragrant. A real eye-catcher with glowing colour and a good health record. Highly recommended.

**'New Dawn'** Shell pink, fragrant. Lovely clusters of bloom all summer long with some repeat flowers. Easy to grow, even from cuttings.

**'Pink Perpetue'** Rose pink, slightly fragrant. Free flowering with a pretty cupped flower in good trusses. Watch for signs of rust under the leaves.

**'Rosy Mantle'** Deep pink, fragrant. Large flowers with glossy foliage. A vigorous climber.

**'Veilchenblau'** Violet, fading to slate grey, fragrant. The most unusual of all roses. A spectacular rose in mid summer.

**'Zéphirine Drouhin'** Carmine pink, very fragrant. Pretty. Also known as the thornless rose. Must be watched for disease (black spot and mildew).

# FLOWERS FOR CUTTING

It always seems an anomaly to talk about flowers for cutting. Shouldn't all flowers be for cutting? True, but many are better than others. Nasturtiums, for instance, make a wonderful display in the garden but they do not make good cut flowers; dahlias do. So too do sweet peas, chrysanthemums and dozens of others that can take you in an alphabetical list from *Achillea* to *Zauschneria californicia*.

In this chapter we look at the best methods of cultivation and some of the special types of flowers that make the finest decoration. There will be many more plants that you can use from annuals to bulbs, and most will be successful, but this is a list of the tried and trusted types of flowers, from the popular spring-time narcissus, to the end of the year chrysanthemums.

When it comes to cutting flowers it must be remembered that the sooner flowers are put into water the better they will be. The best time to take blooms is early morning or late evening. Give them some hours in deep water and then set about arranging them quickly but with care. With the thicker type of flower stem it is always effective to cut it under water, and to cut at an angle so that the stems will not sit on the bottom of the vase and so fail to take up water. If flowers begin to wilt they can often be brought back to life by placing them in warm water for a few minutes or, if the stems are woody, like roses, by holding them in boiling water for about a minute.

Here are the details of some of the more popular flowers for cutting. This is followed by a general list of some of the more unusual types that are worth trying, and with the appropriate methods of cultivation.

'Tête à Tête', a variety of *Narcissus cyclamineus*

## MAKING A SELECTION

### Narcissus

The flower that everyone knows, everyone can grow, everyone cuts, and is the herald of spring (it is actually called a daffodil when the centre trumpet is as long or longer than the petals). There is an exciting range of types now available in colours from pure white to delicate pink, and in blends of these colours. They grow from a few centimetres up to 60 cm (2 ft).

Choose a well-drained and sunny position to get the best from them. Plant from August to September, the earlier the better. Give them a generous hole (recommended depth is three times the size of the bulbs) in a well-cultivated piece of land. Generally they can be left undisturbed for a number of years, but when the clumps get too big and provide more foliage than flowers they should be lifted and divided. Many growers do this each year when the leaves have died down. Remove the smaller bulbs from the parent – if they are placed in an out of the way part of the garden or a nursery bed they will grow to flowering size in a year or two. Bulbs can be given some soluble fertilizer when the flowers have died down, which will build them up for the following year. The foliage should only be cut away when it has died down completely. In a dry summer the ground where the bulbs are resting should be watered deeply.

Red tulips underplanted with wallflowers make a cheering display in spring.

Narcissi are ideal companions among rhododendrons, their colouring contrasting well with the pink, red and purple flowers of the bushes. Look and see the wide range available each autumn; as well as the old favourites the gardener will find a wealth of new types that deserve a chance. However, the newer varieties can be quite costly.

Here is a selection to choose from.

**Trumpet narcissi** (daffodils) 'King Alfred' (yellow), 'Beersheba' (white) and 'Newcastle' (bicolour).

**Large-cupped narcissi** 'Carlton' (yellow), 'Silver Lining' (white), 'Fortune' (bicolour).

**Small-cupped narcissi** 'Frigid' (white), 'Mahmoud' (bicolour) and 'La Rianta' (bicolour).

**Double narcissi** These have more than one ring of petals, which are identical to the cup – 'Golden Ducat' (yellow), 'Snowball' (white), 'Texas' (bicolour).

**Triandrus narcissi** There are usually several flowers per stem. 'Liberty' (yellow), 'Thalia' (white) and 'Dawn' (bicolour)

**Cyclamineus narcissi** These can include many of the low-growing varieties. 'Peeping Tom' (yellow), 'Tête-à-Tête' (bicolour).

**Jonquilla narcissi** These have several flowers per stem, often known as jonquils, which are fragrant. 'Sweetness' (yellow), 'Golden Sceptre' (deep yellow), 'Bobbysoxer' (bicolour).

**Poeticus narcissi** Later flowering and very fragrant. 'Actaea' (yellow cup), 'Pheasant's Eye' (red cup).

**Tulip**

Like the narcissi the tulip is a fairly undemanding bulb that provides lovely flowers for cutting. It is planted slightly later (November or December) at a depth of about 15 cm (6 in), and in good soil. However, unlike narcissi, most tulip bulbs will improve with being lifted every year although some will continue to increase and bloom for a number of years if left alone. They should be lifted when the foliage has turned yellow. Store the dry bulbs in a frost-free place.

Every year there are new choices. Tulips are divided into a number of different groups, namely single early, double early, Triumph, Darwin, Lily-flowered, Rembrandt and Parrot, to mention just a few, all of which have their own cultivars within the groups. Probably the most popular are the Cottage Tulips, those old-fashioned tulips with the egg-shaped blooms that eventually open to about 13 cm (5 in) wide, and which come into flower from early May onwards. Although they are often as tall as 90 cm (3 ft) they have stout, strong stems that withstand all but the stormiest conditions. There is a wide

Left: *Tulipa greigii* has attractive foliage as well as shapely blooms.

Opposite: Dahlias are most effective when planted in a bed on their own.

range of colours available, from the strong red of 'Halcro', to the subtle light green, pink and purple softness of 'Artist'.

When mixed with forget-me-nots (*Mysotis*) and wallflowers (*Cheiranthus*) they can make a wonderful display in an island bed or border. There are so many combinations that work well with these flowers that the garden planner should never be at a loss, possibly turning to grape hyacinths (*Muscari*), white pansies (*Viola* × *wittrockiana*), or any of the grey-blue leafed plants such as catmint (*Nepeta*) or lavender.

The following list is compiled from popular kinds that are well proven.

***T. clusiana*** (lady tulip) One of the many beautiful species tulips – and probably the loveliest of all with its greyish, grass-like foliage and the slender flowers that are white, flushed or streaked, with pink. There are some within the group that have more brilliant colouring than the parent species.

***T. greigii*** A dwarf species with long-lasting flowers that are often mottled or streaked with purple-brown. Good for rock gardens and raised beds.

***T. kaufmanniana*** Dwarf; blooms in March with a star-like flower. Ideal for the rockery. Bulbs do not need lifting in the winter.

***T. fosteriana*** This species is known for its huge blooms which can reach 25 cm (10 in) when fully open. Species are creamy-white, but its hybrids are multi-coloured. 'Red Emperor', 'Easter Parade' (yellow), 'Stresa' (yellow with red band), 'Fritz Kreisler' (salmon pink) are the best known.

**Darwin tulips** Renowned for their brilliant colouring and strong stemmed robustness. 'Scarlett O'Hara' grows to 60 cm (2 ft) high; others to look for include 'Apeldoorn' (orange-red), 'Zwanenburg' (white), 'Jewel of Spring' (red, tipped yellow).

**Lily flowered tulips** Strong stemmed, weather resistant and very good for garden bedding. Long flowers have pointed petals that arch gracefully outwards. 'China Pink' (pink), 'West Point' (golden yellow), 'Arkadia' (buttercup yellow) and 'Queen of Sheba' (orange and red) are all to be recommended.

**Rembrandt tulips** So-called because they are flecked or streaked with another colour. They are often called Bizarre tulips, and with colours as in 'Victory' (yellow and brown) 'Gloire de Holland' (violet and white) or 'Absolon' (yellow and red) they can be quite a novelty in the garden.

**Parrot tulips** So-called because of their frilled petals. Unusual looking. Weak stem, many bicolours including 'Texas' (red, tipped yellow), 'Black Parrot' (blackish purple), and the pink and green 'Fantasy'.

*Note*: There are also many tulips that are sold as double-early, single-early, and double-late. There is a wide range to choose from, so with judicious selection the gardener can have tulips from early April until late May.

**Dahlias**

The dahlia is almost a specialist plant, taking such a hold on gardeners that they only want to raise these flowers, and nothing else. The first dahlia plants were sent from Mexico in the 18th century, and the generic name commemorates a Swedish botanist, Anders Dahl (1751–1787).

Over the years the dahlia has remained a constant favourite, adored for its late summer flowers, although different varieties have changed in popularity. Plant sizes vary enormously from about 30 cm (1 ft), to those that can reach almost 2.1 m (7 ft). The flowers too come in a wide range, from 2.5 cm (1 in), to a world-record size of over 53 cm (21 in).

Dahlia enthusiast go to great lengths to make sure that they have the perfect flower at the end of the summer, but for the ordinary gardener this isn't necessary. The plant requires very little help for a healthy display.

The plants can be grown from seeds, rooted cuttings or tubers. They should be started indoors in spring in gentle heat, being transplanted in late May or early June. They need a good soil which gets at least a few hours sunshine every day, thorough watering and a liquid feed during the growing period. The taller dahlias will require staking, which should be done before planting. To increase the plant's bushiness, the growing tips should be pinched out when they are about three weeks old. If you want long stemmed plants nip away any side shoots two weeks later. Finally, disbudding (removing some of the flower buds) to produce fewer and larger flowers should be done when the flower buds are pea sized.

Dahlias should really be grown in a bed or border on their own to be truly effective, but they can also provide late colour in a mixed border at a time when the herbaceous flowers have mostly died down. Taller varieties are available for the back of the border, with smaller plants, such as Lilliput, useful for the front, which will bloom from late July until the first frosts.

DAHLIA CUTTINGS

Plant tubers in moist compost in March. The young shoots will provide basal cuttings.

The flower heads are made up of miniature flowers, known as florets, and the type of floret is the key to identification.

There are many types of dahlias, from single-flowered, through collerette, to decorative and cactus. Here is a selection:

**Single-flowered** Made up of flowers of one ring of ray florets. Examples include 'Princess Marie Jose' (pink), 'Yellow Hammer' (yellow), 'Orangeade' (orange-red).

**Collerette** Very colourful, with an outer ring of flat ray florets, an inner ring of collar florets, and a central group of disc florets. Look out for 'La Giaconda' (scarlet and gold), 'Claire de Lune' (yellow and cream), and 'Chimborazo' (red and cream). For seed raising, try the Dandy strain, with its wide range of colours.

**Decorative** Full, double blooms on stems that grow between 90 cm (3 ft), and 1.5 m (5 ft). Try 'Jocondo' (purple, giant), 'Thames Valley' (yellow, large), 'Terpo' (red, medium), 'Gerrie Hoek' (pink, small), and 'David Howard' (orange, miniature).

**Pompon** Full, double, globe-shaped blooms, less than 5 cm (2 in) in size; the plant height is about 90 cm (3 ft). 'Hallmark' (lavender), 'Willo's Violet' (light purple), 'Noreen' (pink) are all good.

**Cactus** Full double blooms. Florets are narrow and pointing. Various sizes of blooms and plants. Consider 'Danny' (pink, giant), 'Irish Visit' (red, large), 'Appleblossom' (pale pink, medium), 'Doris Day' (red, small), 'Pirouette' (yellow, miniature).

*Note*: These are only a very small selection of the types of plant available. There are many varieties available to choose from. You could also contact the National Dahlia Society through the Royal Horticultural Society in London.

**Dianthus**

There are various forms of dianthus – sweet William (ideal as a cut flower and easy to grow as an annual or biennial), alpine pinks and annual carnations. The straightforward dianthus is well known to most gardeners as the old fashioned pink and few gardens would be without these or

*Dianthus* 'Doris' is one of the best of the modern pinks.

CUTTINGS OF PINKS OR BORDER CARNATIONS

Take cuttings or 'pipings' from side shoots in June. Strip foliage from the lower section of the cutting; make a suitable hole in sandy soil or compost with a dibber and firm in.

the modern pink. While they are better for garden flowering, many can still be well worth growing for cutting.

There are a few growing points that should be remembered. The plants do not do well with a damp mulch under them; they need full sun; and they only need water in exceptionally hot summers. Most of the plants lose their vigour after a few years, but nearly all can be grown on from non-flowering sideshoots in late summer. The flowering period is June to July in the warmer parts of the country.

The best of the modern pinks are 'Doris' (pale pink with salmon ring), 'Daphne' (pale pink, crimson eye), 'Cherry Ripe' (deep pink and double), 'Alice' (white, maroon eye), 'Haytor' (white), 'Robin' (scarlet), 'Valda Wyatt' (lavender double), 'Bovey Belle' (bright purple double). These are all quicker growing than the older pinks, and also provide good crops of autumn blooms.

**Delphinium**

The large flowered hybrids of modern delphiniums barely resemble their wild ancestors. The huge, tall spikes of stately beauty, with large flat flowers, often with a contrastingly coloured eye, have an extended colour range that goes through all shades of blue and purple to yellow, pink and red. Today the delphinium waves its own magic power over the borders in every type of garden. They are quite stupendous when grown in groups in a mixed border, when grown side by side with all the usual border plants, and at the back of a border of roses they are truly eye-catching. Their association with roses goes so deep that the Royal National Rose Society has recently planted many varieties in their beautiful gardens at St Albans.

They may not be the easiest plants to grow, but the dramatic effect they achieve in both the garden and as cut flowers is worth the trouble. They need a well-drained, fertile and sunny site, preferably with some shelter from strong winds. However, even with shelter they will need staking when the plants are quite young.

Plant in the early spring, giving protection from slugs, otherwise the young plants will disappear almost overnight. The flowering period is June and July, but if the plants are cut back there will be another flush of blooms in the autumn. At the end of autumn cut the plants to ground level. As many will deteriorate with age, the solution is to lift the clumps in spring and divide them, replanting the most vigorous parts. They may also be raised from basal cuttings.

It is possible to raise plants from seed which will last for a few years. The 'King Arthur' (purple with white eye) and the Pacific Giants group are well worth growing. The Belladonna types are also easy to raise from seed – a packet will produce many different plants in various tones of blue. The difference between these and the large-flowered hybrids is that they are much smaller, and not as unwieldy, but they lack the magnificence of the bigger plants. The flowers carried in branching heads are cupped, rather than flat, in form. Look for the strains Pink Sensation and Blue Bees. The best plants obtained from the seed should be selected and planted in the border where they will last for some years.

The delphinium is another flower that is constantly being improved by breeders who import added attraction to its stately beauty. Among the most recent introductions is one in true delphinium blue, bred by an amateur member of the British Delphinium Society. It grows to 1 m (3 ft 6 in), and is named 'Clack's Choice'.

Delphiniums, the traditional blue-flowered herbaceous perennial for the border.

Plant selections vary from one catalogue to another, but these are some of the most impressive. A check should be made on their eventual height as some varieties grow from 2.4–3 m (8–10 ft), while others stay at hip to shoulder height. 'Skyline' (sky blue with white and blue eye), 'Vespers' (blue mauve), 'Butterball (cream), 'Blue Tit' (blue), 'Galahad' (white), 'Black Knight' (rich purple with darker eye), 'Clifford Lass' (pink), and 'Gemma' (lavender and mid-blue).

### Sweet pea

Probably the most prolific plants for producing flowers for home decoration (and for your local show) are sweet peas (officially named *Lathyrus*). One spike alone can produce a bowl full of blooms. Plants can be raised from seed in a number of ways, either in a cold greenhouse from October onwards, in a garden frame or cloche from February to April, or outdoors in the flowering position from March to April.

Sweet peas have hard seeds, so to improve the rate of germination they benefit from being soaked in water overnight; if you find they are still very hard, they can be chipped with a sharp knife. Sow the seeds about 13 mm ($\frac{1}{2}$ in) deep in a humus rich soil in a sunny position, and keep them watered, particularly in dry weather. This is another case of the deeper prepared ground, that incorporates plenty of manure or compost, producing better flowers. The plants also require regular feeding – liquid feed applied every 10–12 days will prevent some of the troubles to which they can fall prey, such as bud fall. And finally, a good thick mulch of well-rotted manure or compost, applied in May, will conserve vital moisture for the plant, but do make sure that the mulch is kept away from the stems of the plant.

Young plants should be protected from slug damage, and be supported with twigs to encourage climbing. Approximately three to six weeks later the final, larger supports – 1.8 m (6 ft) high – should be put in place. They can be made of either canes or plastic netting. To achieve bushy plants nip out the top growth when the plants are about 10 cm (4 in) high.

You should take your cut flowers when the bottom bloom on each stem is in full colour. If the flowers are not cut they should be removed as soon as they fade to encourage new growth.

Your choice of sweet pea will be dictated by what the various seed companies offer. Those to look out for, by common consent, are the Spencer strain. A selection within this group include 'Air Warden' (orange-scarlet), 'Winston Churchill' (crimson), 'Leamington' (lavender), and 'White Ensign' (white). There are several dwarf varieties – look for 'Little Sweetheart', 'Snoopea', 'Peter Pan', and 'Bijou'. These are low growing and are mostly very fragrant. They also combine well with other annuals such as clarkia and candytuft, and the blue cornflowers.

Beginners should have few problems in growing good sweet peas; but if you can

Sweet peas provide an excellent source of flowers for cutting.

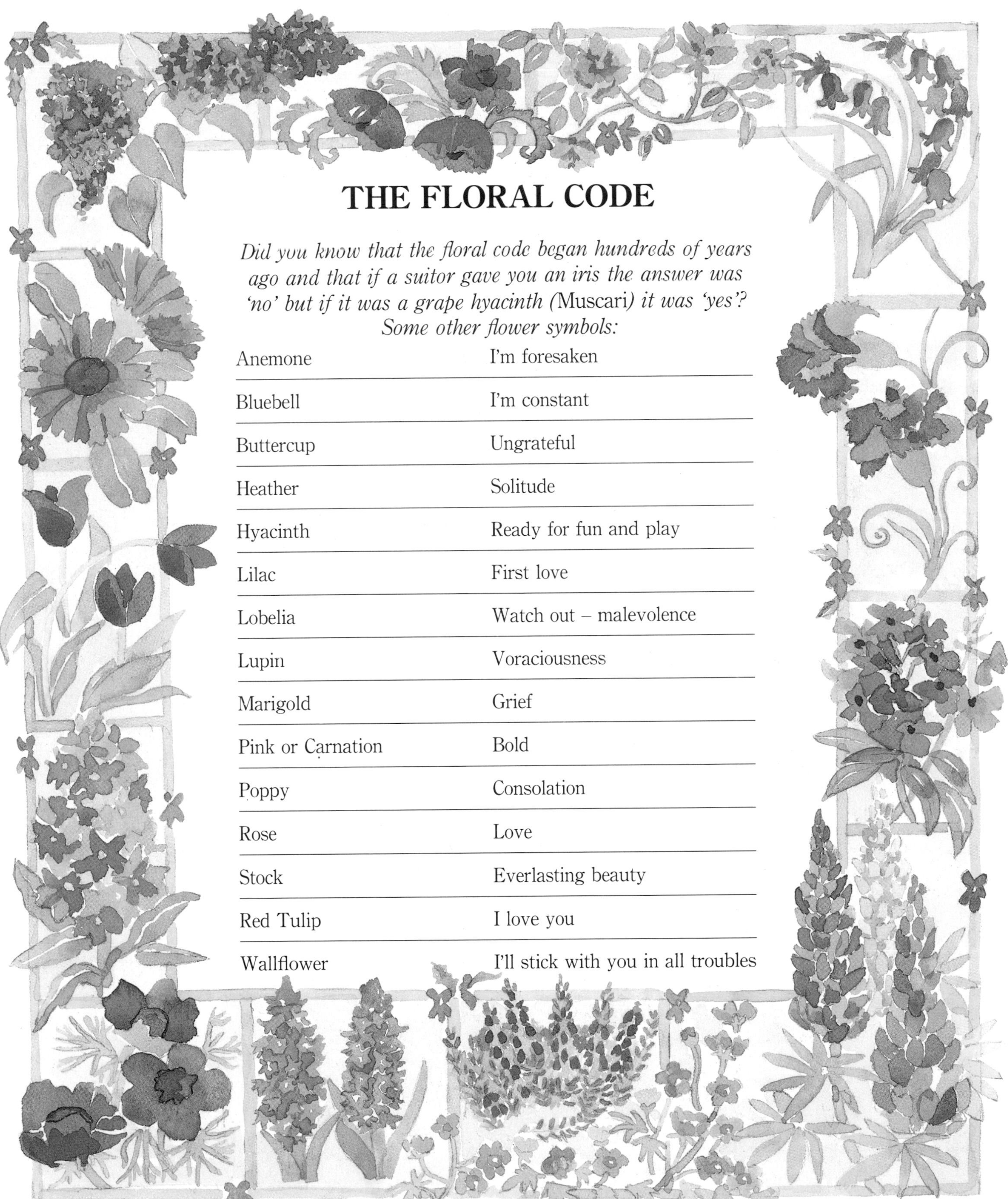

# THE FLORAL CODE

*Did you know that the floral code began hundreds of years ago and that if a suitor gave you an iris the answer was 'no' but if it was a grape hyacinth (*Muscari*) it was 'yes'? Some other flower symbols:*

| | |
|---|---|
| Anemone | I'm foresaken |
| Bluebell | I'm constant |
| Buttercup | Ungrateful |
| Heather | Solitude |
| Hyacinth | Ready for fun and play |
| Lilac | First love |
| Lobelia | Watch out – malevolence |
| Lupin | Voraciousness |
| Marigold | Grief |
| Pink or Carnation | Bold |
| Poppy | Consolation |
| Rose | Love |
| Stock | Everlasting beauty |
| Red Tulip | I love you |
| Wallflower | I'll stick with you in all troubles |

discuss your techniques with an expert at a local flower show, you should get even better results the following year.

**Chrysanthemum**
After the rose, the chrysanthemum is the most popular flower grown in Great Britain today. It's come a long way from its starting base in China, round about the year 500 BC.

The great glory of these plants is that they can be grown anywhere, from a rock garden to a window-box, and from a general border to a greenhouse. They come in annual form, being easily grown from seeds sown in February – for example, the Charm and Cascade kinds – or as herbaceous perennials – the Shasta daisy *(C. maximum), C. coccineum* (also known as *Pyrethrum roseum*), and the autumn flowering *C. rubellum*. Chrysanthemums also include many specialist perennials. This means that they can be grown outdoors from the summer, right through to October, and after that under cover. Within these groups they are sub-divided into many classes, sections and sub-sections. But for the real chrysanthemum lover, the growing season is from late summer to winter.

Chrysanthemums are easy to grow for the uninitiated. It is when enthusiasm rises above the ordinary garden level and the competitive edge takes over, that they really do become the ultimate challenge for the exhibitor. The flower gardener will be dealing mainly with the outdoor chrysanthemums which grow in the open ground without protection from summer until September.

STOPPING A CHRYSANTHEMUM

When plants are about 20 cm (8 in) tall the soft growing tip should be pinched out. This will increase the number of flower-bearing side shoots.

These include those with small flowers which can sit at the front of a border, and those with decorative sprays of blooms for garden display which may need staking. Certainly, if decoratives are to be used for cut flowers, they will need staking, some pinching out of the top growth when the plant is about 20 cm (8 in) high, and disbudding, in order to produce one specimen bloom on a stem. It may seem like a lot of work to produce these superb flowers, but in fact is relatively easy and any half-enthusiastic flower gardener will be prepared to put in this amount of work for the ample rewards. If you have a greenhouse the rewards can be even greater, for there is a large group of chrysanthemums, called late-flowering, which normally bloom between October and late December, and which also provide a fine display.

When deciding where to grow your chrysanthemums aim for a well-drained but moisture retentive soil, in an area that receives some hours of sun each day. The plants prefer slightly acid conditions with plenty of organic matter dug into the top spit. Later, they may be propagated by dividing the roots or as rooted cuttings. When dividing a plant the outer portions of the stools can be taken away, and they will make satisfactory plants, although the rooted cutting method produces the better plant quicker. To take cuttings the stools should be overwintered in a cold frame or greenhouse. From new shoots at the base of the plant (not the sides) take cuttings

Disbudding chrysanthemums allows large, specimen blooms to develop.

DISBUDDING A CHRYSANTHEMUM

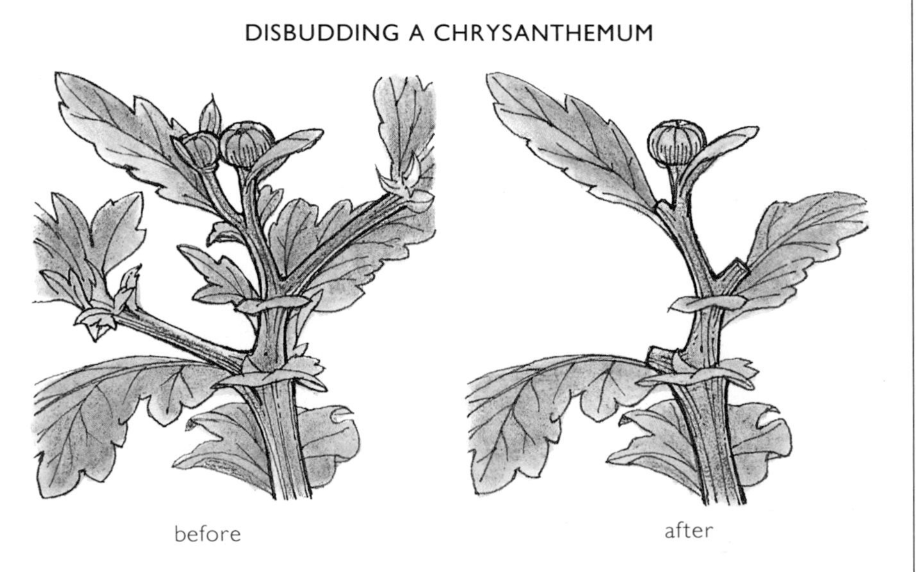


This is carried out to ensure the production of one superb bloom per stem. Leave the main bud untouched but take out each unwanted lateral shoot.

FLOWER TYPES OF CHRYSANTHEMUM

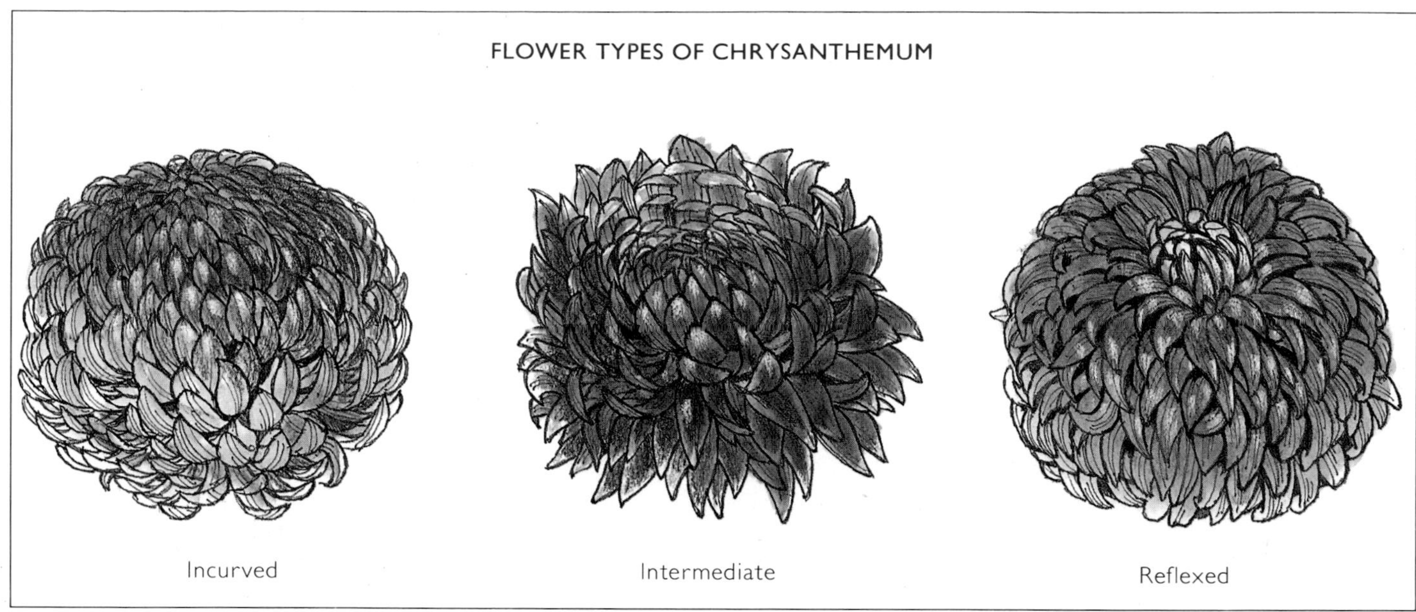

Incurved Intermediate Reflexed

which can be rooted in a heated propagator, and then transferred into pots where they should be regularly and thoroughly watered before being planted out in the border.

Watering in dry spells and feeding every 12 to 14 days with a soluble fertilizer is the way to bring the best out of the plants, which will also appreciate a mulch of peat or compost.

Slugs and birds can cause problems (see page 91), so act now before it is too late. The main trouble, however, is caused by the eelworm, which reveals itself in a blackening of the foliage. If it appears the plants *must* be destroyed to stop it spreading, and the ground should not be used for planting chrysanthemums again as this organism persists in the soil in a dormant form for many years.

Well-rooted cuttings of chrysanthemums can be purchased at a very reasonable price and provide an ideal way to get started. There are also numerous chrysanthemum societies throughout the country where the ordinary gardener is as welcome as the top exhibitors.

Because of the number of new cultivars being introduced each year and those being withdrawn there is a problem – as with most flowers – of giving a really up to date selection of plants.

In the meantime I will recommend one in particular – it is the decorative, incurved, large-flowered yellow called 'Derek Bircumshaw'. And in addition, here is a brief list of just a few of the likely winners for those who want to grow the decorative types.

### Incurved

The florets are turned towards the centre, the blooms forming a tight ball.
Medium-flowered – 'Martin Riley' (yellow), 'Nancy Matthews' (white).
Large-flowered – 'Derek Bircumshaw', 'Evelyn Bush' (white).

### Intermediate

This type of chrysanthemum has irregularly incurved and loosely held florets.
Medium-flowered – 'Cricket' (white), 'Claret Glow' (deep-pink).
Large-flowered – 'Keystone' (purple), 'Escort' (red).

### Reflexed

The florets are turned outwards and downwards from the centre.
Medium-flowered – 'Karen Rowe' (pink), 'Regalia' (rosy-purple).
Large-flowered – 'Tracy Waller' (pink), 'Abundance' (yellow).

For those who just want a good outdoor display, the following will give fine results. 'Allbright' (bright yellow, spiky reflex), 'Bessie Rowe' (large incurving white), 'Promise' (rose purple incurve), 'Lilian Hoek' (bright-orange, bronze, decorative spray) and 'Orangeade' (golden orange reflex).

### Other plants

As well as these very popular flowers there are numerous others that are superb for providing cut flowers. Many of these are annuals. (Look through pages 16 to 22 where you will find a rich collection.) Others include such wonderful flowers from corms, such as gladioli, and bearded and other kinds of iris, and perennials such as Russell Lupins.

Here is a brief outline of some of the needs and characteristics of these plants selected to keep your house full of flowers throughout the summer.

**Asters** (Michelmas daisy)

Pink and lavender coloured with a yellow centre, autumn flowering, and easy to grow is the usual description. But this isn't entirely true. Other colours are available, notably lavender-blue, red and mauve, for instance, and not all *Asters* are Michelmas daisies. Nor do they all grow in the late autumn – some of the *Asters* will bloom as early as July – *A.* × *frikartii* and *A. amellus* in particular.

*A. novae-angliae* and *A. novi-belgii* are the true Michaelmas daisies and they can be difficult to grow being prone to disease, particularly wilt and powdery mildew (see page 92). However, you should not let this deter you from growing them. One of their advantages is that there are a number of different varieties that can grow from dwarf plants to giants that reach to 1.2m (4ft) high. Good sun and a

Left: Sedum and Michaelmas daisies – the opening of their flowers marks the end of high summer.

Opposite: *Aster* x *frikartii*, rudbeckia and sedum in full flower.

Below: The star-like bracts of *Astrantia major*.

well-drained site are needed.

Propagate by dividing clumps in the autumn or spring.

**Astrantia**

Although this plant has its critics, the Astrantia major has still been a great garden favourite for hundreds of years. It is highly regarded as a cutting flower, with tall stems of 60–90 cm (2–3 ft) high flowers rising above clumps of coarse leaves consisting of three leaflets. The flowers are quite small, being a 2.5 cm (1 in) collection of tiny pink and white florets surrounded by green and white bracts or leaves that look like petals.

There are a number of different cultivars available, and they all grow well in ordinary garden soil that is kept free from slugs and provides dappled shade.

Propagate by division of clumps between late autumn and early spring. Seeds may also be sown under glass, but they will take at least 18 months to bring to flowering size.

**Gaillardia**

This is the fiery coloured daisy-like flower that can be seen in just about every border, where it lives up to its popular name of the blanket flower. Apart from the older *Gaillardia aristata* there are a number of dazzling cultivars in a variety of colour combinations. Flowers grow to about 60 cm (2 ft) high, and may need some staking as the weight of the flower can bend the stems. However, they are excellent for cutting.

To get them growing correctly they need a light, sandy soil and full sun. The stems must be cut to ground level when flowering has finished in September, and should be lifted and divided to avoid deterioration. They can be grown from seeds.

**Gladiolus**

Also known as the sword lily, this yields wonderful cut flowers. The one problem, however, is that the flowers have a short full-bloom life, and they are not quite right for mixing in a border. It is therefore better to place them in a special bed where they can be staked and cared for as individuals. The best way to tackle the brief flowering problem is to stagger the planting of the corms from March to May, which should result in flowering from July to September. They need a well-drained site, rich soil, and plenty of sunshine, as well as some protection from strong winds. Corms should be lifted at the end of October, checked for any sign of disease, dried and housed in frost-free conditions.

There are five main groups, ranging from the large-flowered hybrids – which will grow anything up to 1.2 m (4 ft) high – to the miniatures – which can be as small as 30 cm (12 in). Within these groups there are scores of different varieties.

**Gypsophila**

This plant is often called baby's breath and is the background for many flower arrangements. Its tiny flowers on thin stems with greyish green leaves are the ideal acompaniment to most floral decorations. Generally accepted as the best of the varieties outside the species, *G. paniculata* is the double flowered and pure white 'Bristol Fairy'. It needs a gritty, limey soil deeply cultivated in a good sunny position to grow well. Once it has become established it will not transplant well and should be propagated by seed, basal cuttings in spring or stem cuttings taken and grown on in a cold frame in the summer.

### Iris

The tall growers which are placed in the herbaceous border are grown from a rhizome, while the bulb types produce smaller varieties that can be planted at the front of a border. However, all are a delight to the flower arranger who is prepared to lavish attention on them, and who is not going to be too disappointed if some prove to be less than hardy.

The initial problem is one of too much choice – there is a different type of iris for just about every spot in the garden, so you must know which type you want. *Iris kaempferi*, for example, is a beautiful water-loving specimen that needs sun, warmth, and to grow in about 15 cm (6 in) of water. The valuable *I. pseudacoruus* (known widely as the yellow flag) also needs a moist spot – it is also commonly known as the *fleur-de-lys*, the emblem of the Kings of France and of the Boy Scout movement. *I. xiphioides* (the English iris), with shades of blue, violet and purple, and a central gold stripe, is excellent for group plantings, especially on account of its grey foliage. *I. xiphium* (Spanish iris) is more wide ranging in colour – blues, white, yellow, bronze and bicolored – and also looks good in single or mixed colours.

You can propagate the latter two irises by division, when the foliage has died down. *I. germanica*, the bearded iris, stately and interesting, will grow in just about any good soil, but if left in moist

Left: Tall growing bearded irises in a herbaceous border.

Opposite: An eye-catching combination of colours featuring Lilies and lady's mantle (*Alchemilla mollis*), with *Lysimachia punctata* in the background.

soggy land it can easily develop an infection.

Look out for the lovely frilled and ruffled 'Dancers' Veil' (blue and white) and 'Royal Torch' (violet with an unusual blue beard). You should also look for details of new varieties in the horticultural press; in the 1988 Royal Horticultural Society's Summer Show the sensation was a new golden yellow iris, with chocolate veining of excellent form, regarded as a great breakthrough. This has not been named at the time of writing, but it does show that there are new cultivars of most flowers that the inspired gardener ought to buy.

### Lilium

Within this genus there is a wonderland of types that can provide a magnificent diversity in the garden, and exceptional cut flowers. Once regarded as hard to grow, the modern hybrid lilies have spread the gospel of wonderful colours and wide-ranging fragrances (don't expect that they will all smell delightful – some are obnoxious!), at heights from 30 cm (12 in) to 1.8 m (6 ft).

Since bulbs must never be allowed to dry out, plant them immediately after purchase. October is the best month for planting, when the soil is still frost free. Plant them about 15 cm (6 in) deep in well-cared for soil that gets sun and some shelter. You should then be rewarded with the exciting sight of, for instance, clumps of *Lilium candidum* (Madonna lily) with its pure white, fragrant flowers that carry a golden centre. Another excellent lily is *L. regale* (regal lily) with unrivalled clusters of wine red flowers which, when they open in July, show the pure white interior with a deep yellow throat and golden stamens. All the bulb requires is a sheltered site on good soil. You should also think about planting the giant Bellingham Hybrids that require a shaded, moist spot in the garden for their light orange, crimson spotted flowers.

Some of these wonderful flowers may be attacked by botrytis disease (this applies especially to the Madonna lily which will require regular spraying. The message for the summer is therefore to keep the lilies watered, and occasionally to add a liquid or soluble fertilizer). Divide mature clumps in the autumn and replant straight away, although you may not get flowers the following year. Note that you can also grow some lilies from seed.

### Lupinus

This is the flower that everyone immediately associates with the cottage garden. Lupins are quick growing, tolerant of most conditions, and are available in a wide range of colours including pinks, blues, yellows and bicolours. The man who deservedly gets the credit for the great lupins of today is George Russell, who selected them from plants growing on his allotment in the 1930s, and who has given the world a range that bears his name.

Left: Russel lupins with the beauty bush (*Kolkwitzia amabilis*) – a perfect partnership for a pink border.

Opposite: Pink pyrethrum, more correctly called *Chrysanthemum coccineum*, growing with helenium in late summer.

Lupins grow with large, densely packed masses of bloom, and survive provided the slugs and mildew can be kept at bay. They prefer a slightly acid soil and can be grown from seed or from basal rooted cuttings. Generally the purchase is from a mixed selection of Russell Lupins, but single colours are also available.

The Woodfield Strain of new generation lupins are worth searching for, and are regarded as being the best of the modern selections for flowering from the bottom to the top of the spikes, and retaining their freshness over a long period. Since nearly all lupins reseed very easily, the seed heads should be taken off before this happens – the removal of the flower spikes will also lead to reflowering. Interestingly, as the result of a flood in a New Zealand nursery some years ago, Russell Lupins have been washed all over that country and are almost an environmental hazard!

**Matthiola**

Most gardeners will know this better as stock, that versatile and heavily scented flower that is now part of a wide range of plants that can be brought to flower from spring to autumn, and on through winter if you have a greenhouse. *Matthiola incana* is the general bedding type, while *M. bicornis* is night scented stock, but not nearly as interesting to look at as *M. incana*. These plants do not ask for much,

just a decent, not too acid soil in any bed, border or open garden. The only problem is getting them started! Seeds need to be watched and the instructions followed to the letter as some may be hardy annual, others half-hardy, and others biennial. Concentrate on those with double flowers, and handle the seedlings very carefully.

**Pyrethrum**

The flower arrangers' delight, now classified as *Chrysanthemum coccineum*, although the older name remains in popular use. It is also known as feverfew (as is *Matricaria*, a half-hardy annual which is also known as the mayweed and has a strange pungent smelling flower) because it was alleged to cure fever.

Pyrethrum has a long stem and good feathery foliage. Mainly pinks and reds, they like a lighter soil, well-drained and in full sun. They may need support, growing to about 90 cm (3 ft). The flowers should be cut as they fade. The prettiest are probably the singles – look for 'Bressingham Red' (crimson), 'E.M. Robinson' (pale pink), and 'Brenda' (deep pink).

The perennial rudbeckia makes a colourful addition to an autumn display.

**Rudbeckia**

You can have any coloured coneflower as long as it is in the yellow and orange range! The flower is also listed among the half-hardy annuals, which can be quite similar. The perennial has long-lasting, non-fading colour in August and September, and the flower, spiky petalled with a darker eye, is well clothed in foliage along the stem. They vary in height from about 60 cm (2 ft) upwards, and will grow without too much fuss in reasonable soil and in full sun or dappled shade. Divide the clumps every three years in autumn or spring, and stake the flowers, especially the larger ones. Keep the flowers dead headed and cut the foliage back to the ground in September. The giant varieties include 'Golden Glow'; the more compact 'Goldquelle' suits the front of the border.

**Scabiosa** The flower that really echoes summer when used in floral decorations. The blooms are perfect for arranging and come in all shades of blue, darker mauves, as well as some white. The flowers have such a coolness, cleanness and delicacy about their frilly edged blooms that they have been called the 'pincushion of the garden'. They have also been known as the mourning bride, possibly because of the darker shades, and the roughness of the leaves which were supposed to cure itchiness. It is a perennial and is best planted in the spring about 45 cm (18 in) apart. It also prefers a limey soil and full sunshine, and may need some twiggy support in exposed places. The flowers should be cut for use in arrangements, but if they are allowed to fade on the plant they should be cut off to allow for new growth. The flowers will be produced from June to the first frosts. Propagate by division in the spring, or by basal cuttings. One of the most popular is 'Clive Greaves' – medium-blue, large flowered, long stemmed, growing to about 90 cm (3 ft). 'Miss Willmott' is a good white, while 'Moerheim Blue' and 'Imperial Purple' are also well worth considering. The only danger is from slugs.

# THE ROCK GARDEN

Interest in growing rock plants has greatly increased in recent years. There are a number of reasons why this is so – in particular the introduction of new species and hybrids from their native habitats and the opening up of parts of China, Japan, other Asiatic countries and the Andes to botanists and the general public. It is now possible to obtain a wide selection of rock and alpine plants.

## SITING A ROCK GARDEN

With the fast rising cost of land, large gardens get fewer and fewer, for the tendency is to build the largest possible number of houses in any given space. Hence the attraction of rock plants, which, compared with most other plants, take up relatively little space. Even the smallest of gardens can be adapted to cultivate these small plants; the only drawback is where large, established trees are present. One often sees small mounds of soil planted with rock plants set among a few rocks placed almost up against tree trunks. No feature could be more doomed to failure, for in the matter of a year or so only the rocks will still be there – the plants will have disappeared.

Where possible, choose a site which is open and sunny and away from surface-rooting trees. The drip from these will rapidly cause a large number of plant fatalities. If the garden is small or surface-rooting or surface-suckering trees are already established there – poplars, silver birch, elms or limes, for example – it may be necessary to grow the plants in troughs and other containers, raised above the ground and sited as far as possible from the trees. If the garden is in half shade (the kind of dappled sunlight to be found in a woodland clearing – full shade is not suitable), it is still possible to grow many of the low growing ericaceous plants, such as the dwarf rhododendrons.

A well-stocked rock garden in summer, showing how much colour and interest can be packed into a relatively small space.

Creating a small rock garden in a trough (or even an old sink) allows you to give the plants exactly the right growing medium needed for healthy cultivation.

## DWARF RHODODENDRONS

There are many to choose from and the following are just a small selection. They will all tolerate light shade.

***R. calostrotum***
With its pink to purple flowers borne late in spring, it reaches 30 cm (1 ft) high.

***R.* 'Chikor'**
A good dwarf hybrid with clusters of lemon-yellow flowers in late spring.

***R. imperator***
Very low growing, reaching only a few inches high and spreading to about 30 cm (1 ft). It has funnel shaped flowers in deep rose-purple which appear in late spring.

***R. pemakoense***
Possibly the dwarfest of all the rhododendrons. It has pinkish purple flowers.

***R. radicans***
Barely reaching 2.5 cm (1 in) in height, this carries large – for the size of the plant – single flowers, which vary in colour from light mauve to deep purple and show in late spring.

There is also a range of small hybrids available which are suitable for growing in this way.

For rhododendrons it is necessary for the garden soil to be lime-free, but here again such plants can be grown in troughs or other containers in a compost of four parts leafmould and one part lime-free loam and sand, these proportions to be by bulk, not weight.

## RAISED BORDERS

In a small garden not large enough to accommodate a rock garden, it should be possible to build up border edges, especially if there is a small lawn. On a sloping site a small dry wall could be constructed, thus providing a two-level plot, which will enable a selection of trailing plants to be grown; for example, arabis, alyssum, the many colour forms of aubrieta, phlox, campanulas and helianthemums. These will give a wonderful display of colour starting in early spring and continuing through to summer. All these trailing plants can be underplanted with suitable dwarf bulbs, extending the flowering season over six months.

## SOIL

Although it is seldom possible to choose the soil of one's garden, much can be done to make existing soil suitable for rock plants. The best medium is a light open soil with very free drainage. If possible, a lime-free soil is preferable, for lime can be added where this is required. Rock plants which approve of lime do not demand it, but lime-hating plants will only grow – and this is normally for a short period only – in specially prepared pockets of lime-free soil. So if you have an alkaline soil it is best to avoid growing all lime-hating plants. A rich loamy soil can be made ideal for the vast majority of rock plants by adding really coarse sand or small gravel, and, for really sharp drainage, a graded horticultural Perlite (an expanded volcanic rock that improves drainage and water availability, and aerates the soil).

If the soil is a heavy clay, it will be necessary to approach the problem in a different way. No attempt should be made to lighten it by adding drainage materials, a task which would perhaps be too difficult anyway. However, if there is a natural slope it can be turned to good use by digging a pit at the base between 20–25 cm

(8–10 in) deep and filling it up with some coarse rubble and then a layer of upturned turves or other such roughage to prevent soil washing down and blocking the drainage. The rock garden is then built up by about 20 cm (8 in) using a light, open compost. At least one quarter of the bulk of the compost around the drainage pit should consist of either leafmould or peat. This will provide an ideal spot for plants that prefer a greater quantity of moisture, such as Asiatic primulas.

Whatever soil is used over the clay it should have all perennial weeds removed; if this very important task is neglected, it will result in many back breaking hours being spent in attempting to remove them after planting has been completed, or, in bad cases, dismantling the rock garden with dire consequences to the plants. Nothing is more upsetting, for instance, than finding bindweed coming up in the centre of a dainty alpine plant.

## CONSTRUCTING A ROCK GARDEN

It is difficult to give exact instructions on building a rock garden. A great deal depends on the available area and the type of rock employed. The actual construction must be left to the gardener's choice, and provided a few simple rules are followed the result should appear natural and aesthetically pleasing. Natural stone suitable for the rock garden is available in three types – limestone, sandstone and tufa. It makes sense to choose a source and type of rock which is reasonably near to hand, for rocks, expensive in themselves, are heavy and costly to transport.

First, the rock when positioned should have two exposed sides, one sunny, where plants can be placed which demand such a position to give of their best, the other in semi- or full shade for plants which require such conditions. Secondly, if the rock being used is limestone, which normally has distinctive strata, it should be placed almost horizontal to the surface, which gives it a natural look comparable to that of rocks in their natural surroundings. Lastly, do not overdo it, it is only necessary to have one or two outcrops in a small rock garden, which should be kept simple with the planting carried out round the highest point of the stone being used.

The next best rock to use (after limestone) is one of the local sandstones, which are found in many parts of the country; this is less costly and in many cases arrangements can be made to pick the stone up from the quarry, thus resulting in a considerable financial saving. Sandstone normally blends in better with the surroundings unless, of course, you live in a limestone area. If sandstone is used make sure that it is not composed of a large percentage of soft material, as this has a tendency to disintegrate after hard frosts.

Tufa is light to handle, extremely por-

Whatever rock you choose, remember that it must blend in well with its surroundings and should act as the perfect foil for the plants you wish to grow: this attractive ivy-leafed *Cyclamen hederifolium* stands out beautifully against the weathered rocks.

A cross section through a small rock garden showing the placement of the rocks and the way the plants have been positioned between them.

ous and easy to drill. A small chisel can also be used to make holes in it to take plants without causing too much root disturbance to those already planted. Place in the base of the hole a small amount of flaked leafmould and detritus removed from the piece of tufa when making the hole. When planting in tufa obtain small specimen plants, seedlings, or even rooted cuttings. Remove the plant from its container, taking care not to break too many roots, gently remove any loose soil, and insert the plant in the hole sideways, gently working the planting mixture around the roots and firming gently. Topdress with small pieces of tufa around the neck of the plant. This method of planting has been used successfully over many years, but tufa is costly. However, this is offset to a certain degree by its weight as it is much lighter than other mediums and easier to handle.

With a larger rock garden, it is a good idea to include a network of pathways in your design to allow access for planting, weeding and other maintenance.

## SCREE BEDS

Scree beds can be constructed as an edging to a lawn, flower border or path. With such features it is possible to grow a wide selection of dainty little plants without the use of a great deal of rockwork or even rocks at all. Wherever the beds are made they should be well clear of any trees, for the roots of the latter will quickly gain entry and exhaust the soil to the detriment of the rock plants. Scree borders should also be well away from the dense shade cast by buildings. Apart from these considerations, the actual aspect is not important, for there are many rock plants that can be cultivated in sun or semi-shade.

A scree bed is made by placing paving stones so that they form a box. Such a scree bed can be of any length to suit the site. The width should be at least 40 cm (16 in). The material to use in building up the 'shell' can be natural York stone, which is very expensive, broken paving stones or slabs of concrete. The paving stone should allow one to build a frame in which to grow a representative collection of rock plants. Once the size has been decided on, a base should be constructed to carry the walls. Depending on the width of the pieces of paving stone used, a layer of cement 6 cm ($2\frac{1}{4}$ in) deep should be laid under these to form the base for the stones. This concrete base should extend about a further 8 cm

A scree bed of colourful alpines makes an attractive edging for a gravel path in a sunny part of the garden.

(3 in) beyond the stones and be made smooth, thus forming a narrow path between the scree bed and the lawn. This will allow a lawn mower to be used right up to the wall of the scree bed.

When laying the base, holes for drainage must be made at regular intervals. To prevent pests such as slugs, woodlice and so on gaining entry, small pieces of perforated zinc should be placed over these holes.

Whatever stone is used, this should be fixed on the base by the use of a cement mix and the walls built to a minimum height of 20–24 cm (8–10 in). A few weeks after completion of the building the scree borders are prepared, as follows. First, a good layer of broken crocks or roughage is added, followed by a well-firmed layer of peat or leaf roughage to prevent the compost filtering down and blocking up the drainage. The border is then filled to the top with either of the following mixtures: for sun lovers and bulbs equal parts of loam, leaf-mould and sharp sand, and for plants that require half shade the same mixture with an equal quantity of peat added. In each case a small handful of bone meal is spread over the surface of the compost, well watered in and left to settle. After a week or so the scree border will be ready for planting.

A peat garden is perfect for a collection of rhododendrons.

### Planting

The chosen plants, which must not be pot-bound, should be carefully removed from their pots, the drainage material in the base removed and a few roots teased loose. Remove some of the old surface compost, plant in a prepared hole in the scree border and make firm. The surface should then be covered with stone chippings. Finally, a few decorative pieces of rock will put a finishing touch to the border.

## TROUGH GARDENS

Troughs are very popular today, but unfortunately the real thing is difficult to find and, if found, generally costly. However, any trough which is at least 12 cm (5 in) deep is suitable for growing a wide selection of rock plants. They can also be used to grow specimen plants or dwarf bulbs.

The compost required is similar to that used in the scree border, and the same method is used in preparing the trough. Make sure that a lime-free loam or ericaceous compost is used if lime-hating plants are grown. Watering is very important, especially during the re-establishment of the plants.

## THE PEAT GARDEN

A large number of plants requiring lime-free soil can be accommodated in this type of garden. The top 10 cm (4 in) of lime-free soil in a semi-shaded part of the garden should be dug over, all roots removed and plenty of well-rotted leafmould or peat mixed in. Peat blocks are used to construct the wall, and blocks measuring 24 by 12 cm and 8 cm (10 by $5\frac{1}{2}$ in and 3 in) deep are ideal. Make sure that they are moist. They should be laid as when building a brick wall and two layers are necessary. A compost of four parts leafmould or peat, one part fibrous, neutral loam and one part coarse sand is used like a cement mix, working it into all the cracks as the wall is being built. Fill the rest of the bed with the same mixture. After planting, topdress the bed with 3 cm ($1\frac{1}{4}$ in) of moss peat and water the plants in. This bed should be kept moist at all times to give of it best.

A peat garden needs a layer of rubble for good drainage. Moist peat blocks form the walls.

A peat garden is an ideal place for primulas and rhododendrons. Some gentians like *G. sino-ornata* flourish there too.

## DWARF SHRUBS

Mention should be made of the role of dwarf shrubs which can add shape, height and colour to the rock garden scree bed, trough garden or peat bed, and if evergreen kinds are mixed with deciduous ones this will provide interest during the winter months.

## PROPAGATION

There are two main methods of increasing rock plants, by seed or cuttings.

### Seed

John Innes seed compost is both a suitable and efficient germinating medium. A lime-free seed compost is also available. Seed of the normal types of rock plants is best sown in late February. This will provide the resulting plants with six months of growth during spring and summer so that they make sturdy specimens ready for planting out in early autumn. Seed should be sown thinly and covered with a fine dressing of sharp sand, and must be kept moist by immersing the seed pan in water, as necessary.

### Cuttings

These also provide a ready means of increase, and in the great majority of cases green cuttings will root quite easily. They are best taken from small pieces of new growth, placed in a pot containing a mixture of equal parts sharp sand and fine peat. Where possible, they should be between 2–3 cm ($\frac{3}{4}$–$1\frac{1}{4}$ in) in length, the lower third of the stem being left clear of leaves (these leaves should be removed by giving each one a gentle upward pull). Insert the cuttings around the edge of the pot to a depth where the bottom leaves touch the rooting medium. Water the cuttings in well. Place a plastic bag over the whole pot and make firm with a rubber band. Rooting should take place in a few weeks, and signs of new growth will be evidence of this. The small plantlets are then grown on in John Innes No 1 potting compost or an equivalent until ready to plant in their permanent positions in the rock garden.

## SELECTED PLANTS FOR THE ROCK GARDEN

The following selection should provide plenty of colour and interest. Look out for those that require a lime-free soil.

***Aethionema* 'Warley Rose'**
This sub-shrubby perennial has fleshy leaves. The pinkish-red clusters of flowers arise in summer. An easy plant to grow. Propagate by seed or cuttings taken during summer. This is one for a chalky or limy soil – 15 cm (6 in).

***Andromeda polifolia* 'Nana'**
This charming evergreen shrublet, with its narrow leathery leaves, silvery grey on the underside, is suited to both rock gardens and peat beds. Clusters of urn-shaped rose-pink flowers appear in May. It requires soil with a high humus content and can be increased by softwood cuttings planted in lime-free compost in summer – 5 cm ($2\frac{1}{2}$ in).

***Arabis caucasica* 'Rosa Bella'**
A summer flowering perennial with grey-green, slightly toothed leaves. Best planted in a sunny position, 'Rosa Bella' has attractive reddish-purple flowers. Readily propagated by division or by cuttings taken during the summer – 15 cm (6 in).

***Aster alpinus***
A spreading herbaceous perennial plant with solitary flower heads, in summer, consisting of white or pink ray florets surrounded by yellow tubular disk florets. Grows well in limy soil. Propagate by division in spring or autumn – 15 cm (6 in).

***Aubrieta***
A graceful compact evergreen plant with grey-green foliage. The showy, semi-double flowers appear in spring. They come in shades of purple and mauve and make an attractive display. Faded blooms should be removed. Propagate by cuttings taken during spring or division in late summer – 10 cm (4 in).

***Bellis perennis*** (double daisy)
This showy, neat, almost stemless herbaceous perennial plant has semi-double flowers in various shades of pink during the summer months. Young plants often flower better than old specimens and may be propagated by dividing the crowns after flowering – 10 cm (4 in).

***Berberis* × *stenophylla* 'Corallina Compacta'**
A charming evergreen shrub suitable for the trough garden or rock garden. The attractive and abundant yellow flowers in spring are followed by purple fruit covered by blueish bloom. Propagation is by layering or by cuttings taken with a heel during summer – 15 cm (6 in).

***Campanula*** (bellflower)
The massed display of flowers produced by *C. carpatica* is most attractive. Abundant, bright blue bell-shaped flowers ap-

The beautiful little gentian *Gentiana sino-ornata* is an excellent plant for the rock garden, provided you can give it lime-free soil.

pear over a long period during summer. Readily propagated by cuttings in spring or by division – 30 cm (12 in).

*C. cochlearifolia* is another summer-flowering perennial. This spreads by underground runners and sends up slender branched stems carrying the bell-shaped, blue flowers. The foliage is a fresh green. Can be increased by seed – 5 cm (2 in).

***Cyclamen hederifolium***
*(C. neapolitanum)*
The deep green leaves with silvery markings are most decorative; these persist well into the spring and appear after the dainty mauve flowers of autumn. A lovely cormous plant for naturalizing, which is usually long lived. New plants can be raised from seed – 10 cm (4 in).

***Daphne cneorum*** (garland flower)
Tiny, trailing evergreen shrub with narrow deep green leaves, grey on the underside. The fragrant, rose-red flowers are borne profusely in spring. New plants can be raised by seed, or by cuttings of the previous year's wood taken in summer – 15 cm (6 in).

***Dianthus***
*D. alpinus* is a mat-forming pink which makes loose cushions of bright green, narrow, strap-shaped leaves. The large and attractive flowers show in summer. They vary in colour from white to deep pink with dark purple spots at the base of the petals. An attractive plant for the rock garden or trough increased by seed or by softwood cuttings taken during summer – 5 cm (2 in).

*D.* 'La Bourboule' is a delectable little tufted perennial plant with narrow silvery leaves which, together with the most attractive bright pink flowers in summer, make it a much admired plant for rock garden or container. Plants may be increased by cuttings taken during summer – 8 cm (3 in).

***Erinus alpinus***
This delightful tufted plant forms cushions of foliage with small pink flowers arising in spring. Ideal for crevices and the wall of a raised bed. Plants may be propagated by seed sown during spring. Plants may also be increased by division after flowering – 15 cm (6 in).

A mixed planting of yellow and purple varieties of *Iris pumila* – this tiny member of the iris family requires full sun if it is to thrive.

***Gentiana*** (gentian)
*G. verna* is one of the most attractive of the many gentians available. The tufted perennial gives rise to delectable deep-blue solitary flowers in summer. Easily propagated by fresh seed sown in containers to remain out of doors during winter or by division – 10 cm (4 in).

*G. sino-ornata* is another beautiful little plant with prostrate stems ascending at the tips with deep blue, long funnel-shaped, terminal, solitary flowers in autumn. An excellent plant for ground cover on the rock garden and easily propagated by division or by sowing fresh seed. Needs an acid soil – 15 cm (6 in).

***Geranium cinereum*** **'Ballerina'**
This is one of the true hardy geraniums (not to be confused with the pelargoniums or bedding geraniums). An almost stemless herbaceous plant with attractively lobed leaves. The most attractive and abundant white flowers veined crimson arise in summer. Propagate by seed or by division in spring – 15 cm (6 in).

***Geum*** × ***borisii***
This herbaceous perennial forms a basal rosette of attractive leaves giving rise to bright orange flowers in summer. This is best increased by division in spring or autumn and is a lovely plant for the rock garden or raised bed – 30 cm (1 ft).

***Helianthemum nummularium***
**'Wisley Primrose'**
(rock rose or sun rose)
A spreading semi-shrubby evergreen much used to cascade over a dwarf wall and most attractive when planted at the edge of a raised bed. The attractive leaves are green on the upper surface and grey beneath covered with downy hairs. Abundant yellow flowers appear in summer. A useful plant which needs a sunny spot and should be trimmed back after flowering to avoid getting straggly. Propagate during summer by cuttings taken from non-flowering shoots – 30 cm (1 ft).

***Iberis sempervirens*** (candytuft)
A bushy, evergreen sub-shrub with fragrant white flowers in winter. Plants can be raised by sowing seed, by cuttings taken in June or the rootstock can be divided – 60 cm (2 ft).

***Iris pumila***
The small rhizome gives rise to stout tufts of green, sword-like leaves. Miniature bearded-iris flowers appear in spring and summer and come in a range of colours from white to purple. Plant in full sun. Propagate by division of rhizomes after flowers fade in June – 5 cm (2 in).

***Lamium maculatum*** (dead nettle)
A spreading evergreen perennial with underground stems giving rise to shoots with leaves attractively variegated in silver in the variety 'Beacon Silver'. The flowers are blue and carried in dense clusters. Readily increased by division or by striking softwood cuttings during summer – 38 cm (15 in).

*Pulsatilla vulgaris*, with its beautiful violet flowers, thrives in full sun and in alkaline soil, but does not like to be transplanted once it has been established.

***Linaria alpina***
An attractive, prostrate perennial with spurred, intense blue flowers with a deep yellow centre in summer and autumn. A most adaptable plant suitable for growing in a dry wall or rock garden. Propagate by division in spring, by seed or by softwood cuttings during mid-summer – 15 cm (6 in).

***Lithospermum diffusum* 'Heavenly Blue'**
Evergreen sub-shrub with trailing stems which give rise to beautiful and abundant deep blue flowers in summer. Cut back when flowers fade to avoid a straggly appearance. It needs a lime-free soil. Propagate by cuttings taken from previous year's growth – 20 cm (8 in).

***Lysimachia nummularia***
A creeping evergreen perennial with trailing stems bearing roundish leaves. The bright yellow flowers appear in summer, being ideal as ground cover in the rock garden. It is also suitable for growing in a hanging basket or container. 'Aurea' has yellow stems and foliage. Divide in autumn or spring – 10 cm (4 in).

***Oxalis adenophylla***
A roundish bulb-like base gives rise to abundant greyish or silvery-green leaflets on long thin stems. Large, solitary, pink, bell-shaped flowers open in summer. An interesting and adaptable plant for a trough or scree garden in a protected position. Increase from offsets from the bulb-like base – 15 cm (6 in).

***Papaver alpinum*** (alpine poppy)
A charming perennial with lobed leaves. The attractive white or yellow flowers appear in summer. Propagate by division in spring – 15 cm (6 in).

***Primula***
*P.* × *juliae* 'Wanda' is a charming early-flowering primula with bright purple-red flowers in spring standing clear of the dense mat of coarsely toothed, cordate leaves. Propagate by sowing fresh seed, the subsequent seedlings being potted firmly in well-drained compost which should be kept moist when growth is active. Remove dead leaves – 10 cm (4 in).

*P. denticulata* is another favourite primula whose sharply toothed, mealy-covered leaves grow to 30 cm (1 ft) long provided the soil is not too dry. Rounded heads of flowers come in various colours including white and shades of mauve, with yellow centres. Self-sown seedlings should be weeded out to retain the choicest flowers and the best selections can be increased by division – 20 cm (8 in).

***Pulsatilla vulgaris*** (Pasque flower)
An almost black, fibrous rootstock gives rise to most attractive pinnate foliage. Beautiful violet flowers with yellow stamens terminate the long hairy stems. Fresh seed germinates readily and plants can also be increased by root cuttings taken in July – 15 cm (6 in).

***Saponaria*** (soapwort)
A herbaceous perennial for the rock garden readily increased by cuttings with a heel in July. This choice little plant is slow growing and produces abundant pink flowers in summer. Best in a sunny position – 5 cm (2 in).

***Saxifraga burseriana***
A much admired little cushion-forming perennial. The dainty reddish stems arise through silver-grey leaves to produce reddish flower buds which open to display glistening white or pinkish petals in spring. Readily propagated by division and easily grown on in a raised bed or rock garden – 5 cm (2 in).

***Sedum spathulifolium* 'Capablanca'**
Evergreen plant forming a dense cushion-like clump producing runners from the base. Leaves form a silver-white rosette, those on the erect flower stem are scattered, club shaped and spreading. Yellow flowers in summer provide a bonus to the attractive leaves. Propagate by division – 13 cm (5 in).

***Sempervivum*** (houseleek)
A rosette-forming perennial up to 5 cm (2 in) across and composed of densely packed fleshy leaves with reddish or green tips. In the case of *S. arachnoideum* these are connected with cobweb-like hairs. Bright red flowers terminate an erect stem in summer. An easy plant to grow and multiply by division – 5 cm (2 in).

***Thymus citriodorus*** (lemon thyme)
A lemon-scented evergreen shrub with attractive pale lilac flowers in summer. Plant in full sun and propagate by cuttings during late summer – 30 cm (1 ft).

***Veronica spicata*** 'Incana'
This evergreen perennial is one of many useful plants within the genus. The leaves are toothed and the blue flowers appear in summer. Best in full sun. Increase by cuttings in summer – 20 cm (8 in).

***Viola cornuta***
The creeping stems give rise to large flowers with a slender spur. 'Alba' has white flowers. A prolific flowering plant and easily propagated by division or by seed – 30 cm (1 ft).

# PESTS AND DISEASES

Troubles? Diseases? Pests? No matter what you call them, fortunately there is a remedy for all complaints. All you have to do is accurately identify the problem, and act promptly.

However, before we turn to specific problems, note that many are caused by ignorance of plants' needs. Remember frost is a problem to tender plants, and that an abundance or lack of water, too much sun or no sun, and poor feeding must be generally thought about. To thrive, plants must be healthy. If they are not healthy, they will not withstand the problems that are bound to afflict them at some point in their lives. But there are two main reasons for a lot of troubles, and these can't be stressed often enough, waterlogged ground and lack of hygiene. If the gardener can tackle these early on then many of the problems mentioned in this chapter will fail to materialize.

Here is a 10–point trouble-shooter's guide that will put you on the right path.

**1.** Buy the best plants available and make sure you know their likes and dislikes.
**2.** Before you think of planting, clean-up the garden. Get rid of weeds, old plants that will never be any good, and rubbish that may harbour pests.
**3.** Prepare the ground thoroughly. You will notice that the majority of plants named in this book need a well-drained soil. Never forget that.
**4.** Make sure that the soil and the planting time is right for your new plants. Most summer flowers should wait until the likelihood of hard frost is over. Water the soil first so that the plant is going to get immediate help to grow on. A plant that wilts is in trouble straight away.
**5.** Too many gardens show signs of plant starvation. Keep them regularly fed. A small amount of regular liquid feeding will do the plants a power of good. Applications of general fertilizer in powder or granular form should be done very carefully as it can scorch if it falls on the foliage. An absence of fertilizer results in bad plants, poor flowers and general disabilities. On the other hand too much feeding can result in too much foliage, and few flowers. Find the happy medium.
**6.** Foliar feeding is the way to help a plant immediately, overcoming a pest or disease attack. Spray on the leaves during a dry evening, never in full sun.
**7.** The man who wrote that you are nearer to God in your garden was very accurate – but you will be closer still if you are on your knees! Yes, by getting close to your plants you will soon spot the defects, the first pests, and the first signs that something is going wrong.
**8.** You do not always have to use chemi-

Keep your plants healthy and your garden full of flowers by following the trouble-shooter's guide (above).

Inspect chrysanthemums regularly as they may be troubled by several pests and diseases.

cals to overcome problems. Caterpillars can be picked off by hand. Keep an eye open for all ugly bugs! And if a plant dies in the garden immediately lift it and look for the reason – were the roots eaten away, does it look dry, are there bugs on it, or on the roots? Close inspection will provide the answer.

**9.** Slugs can be one of the worst marauders in the garden. They eat away young plants almost overnight, and once the foliage has been attacked there is no remedy. Put down chemical bait, or consult a local gardener to see how he or she tackles the problem.

**10.** Spray with care. Chemicals can be dangerous to you, your family, your neighbours, your pets and your plants. Never spray on a windy day, for even the slightest breeze will carry the chemical to nearby plants. A weedkiller can easily destroy other plants.

You should wear eye protection, even sunglasses are better than nothing, and gloves. Check that the chemical is right for your plants – some used on roses can kill fuchsias. Also, keep the spray off blooms if you can possibly manage it. Never store any chemical in a bottle or other container. And finally, make sure they are well out of the way of children who are naturally inquisitive.

Let us now look individually at some of the more likely trouble spots. I will not give details of the possible sprays you should use, but any reasonable plant store or garden centre will have a good range to choose from.

## FOLIAGE TROUBLE MAKERS

### Aphids

Don't just call them greenfly – they come in multicoloured hordes of green, white, black, pink, and yellow flies, and they sap the life from a plant. Spray thoroughly. There are two main insecticides – **contact** (which will kill off the living aphids but not the eggs that will hatch the next brood), and **systemic** (which gets into the plant so the next aphid that sucks the plant will pay the penalty). Don't believe the soapy water theory. It washes them off, but then they shake themselves dry and climb back on board again. They will ruin plants if not killed.

### Caterpillars

They attack with a lack of discrimination. You can identify them by the irregular and often large holes eaten in the foliage. They are an early season invader. Pick them off if you can, but if not use a spray.

### Earwigs

They are the curse to dahlias, chrysanthemums and roses in particular. They hide in the plants by day when you may be able to shake them out. If you put little bundles of straw on top of canes among the flowers they will nest there, so making it easy to dispose of them. Spray or dust to keep them at bay between May and October.

Make an earwig trap by filling a pot with straw and putting it on a stick among the flowers.

### Slugs and snails

The major contenders as the real nasties. They too leave irregular holes in plant leaves and can also be spotted by their trails of slime, particulary over shady, poorly drained land. Avoid leaving them any hiding places in decaying rubbish. There are slug traps for anyone who doesn't want to lay down chemicals in the form of pellets or liquid slug bait. The slugs will fall in and drown in a saucer of beer. But clean and well-cultivated land is the best deterrent.

### Capsid bugs

These attack many plants, such as dahlias and chrysanthemums. Tattered holes appear in the bottom leaves, and the foliage becomes spotted, puckered and distorted. Again, the message is be hygienic – rubbish and weeds will give the bug a hiding place, so clear all these away or burn them. Spray with a suitable chemical when the first signs are spotted.

### Woodlice

These are to be found just about every where, and are night eaters that hide by day. Again, hygiene is the main method of prevention, although there are some very effective powders for eliminating the nests that expand quickly and easily in damp rubbish, or under wood or pots.

## ROOT TROUBLES

These are unfortunately not seen until it is almost too late. But when any plant dies a check should be carried out on the soil for any of these bugs.

### Vine weevil

Probably the 'new' curse for the gardener. It has long existed, but in recent years has increased enormously, attacking plant roots through their grubs. The adult is black, nasty looking and slow moving, and lives on the foliage, eating small irregular notches into the leaves during the night. The young turn into the nastiest attackers – wrinkled, creamy coloured, brown-headed grubs that exist in good peaty type soil. A plant will suddenly die and when examined will be found to have no roots. Search the soil and destroy.

The worst affected plants are primula, fuchsia, rock plants, pot plants of all sorts, and just about any plant with a tender root. There are various sprays and powders available for tackling this disaster, but the best way is to hunt them down and destroy. Also, clean up any hiding places and spray any wild ivy growing on walls and such like, where they are likely to be hiding.

### Chafer grubs

These are similar to the vine weevil, but bigger. Curved, creamy, brown-head, with a silver tail, they live on the roots of herbaceous plants as well as dahlias and chrysanthemums. Sprinkle chemicals on the ground.

### Millepedes

Black, brown and spotted, they tend to curl up when disturbed. They cause root damage but can be stopped in their tracks by one of the special slug-type chemicals that are also recommended for this root predator.

### Leatherjackets

Pests that cause most trouble on heavy, wet soil, and early in a spring that follows a wet winter. Troublesome among the herbaceous plants. Treat as for millepede.

### Cutworms

When a plant dies because the stem has been nibbled away this is the culprit. Once the problem is spotted look for a 5 cm (2 in) brown, greenish or grey sluggish insect and destroy.

## ROOT DISEASES

### Black root rot

This probably is most prevalent in the flower garden. It can be found attacking sweet pea, begonias, geraniums and others. The leaves turn yellow and the root will die and turn black. It most often occurs where the same type of plants have been repeatedly grown in the same area. Rotate plantings to avoid attack.

### Club root

A serious disease that can affect flowers, although it will be mainly found in the vegetable garden. The roots become swollen and plants will be undersized and die when young. Improve the drainage, adding lime for possible control, but it might be necessary to sterilize the soil.

### Other root diseases

There are some other root diseases that are specific to particular plants and areas, but the above mentioned are the commonest. Of course root troubles often begin above ground too, and a plant attacked by a fungus or disease such as rust will eventually stop growing, and the root growth will therefore be affected.

### Storage rots

Various rots can set in through bad storage (this allows fungal attacks), or through the bulbs being grown on in waterlogged conditions. Daffodil bulbs can be affected with the narcissus fly – if bulbs are soft when lifted or show distress when growing, they are probably being attacked by the maggot of this fly. Control is not easy, but soft bulbs should be destroyed and the ground cleaned up around the dying foliage. Any soft bulbs, corms, tubers, or rhizomes should be destroyed.

Tubers of the dahlia can be affected by fungal rot. To prevent this stand the tubers upside down when lifted, and allow them to dry out thoroughly. There are sprays that can be used, and again the tubers must be left to dry before being stored. Any badly diseased parts can be cut away and destroyed.

## STEM AND LEAF TROUBLES

Many will be caused by some of the pests already mentioned, the aphids being the main source of the problem. However, other troubles will be caused by diseases such as mildew and rust that must be controlled immediately. The commonest disease is mildew, with either powdery or downy symptoms.

### Powdery mildew

This can be seen in gardens where there has been a lot of rain, and even in gardens where the roots have been allowed to dry out. It appears like a white mould on the leaves, eventually distorting the foliage.

The great thing is that it can be easily controlled by a number of very good systemic sprays. The initial spraying should be followed up by another within 10 days, and if the instructions with the product are followed the damage can be minimized. Roses, delphiniums and daisies all fall prey to the powdery mildew.

Powdery mildew on a rose.

### Downy mildew

In damp weather some flowers are also likely to fall prey to downy mildew. Yellowing patches on the leaves, followed by a greyish growth of mould under the leaf, will give the warning, and unless tackled immediately plants can be ruined. A different spray is needed here, so specify your problems before purchasing any chemical treatment.

### Rust

A real killer, especially of roses, but also geraniums, carnations, chrysanthemums. It often appears in just one section of a garden, and will not spread, even to similar varieties of the affected plant. It is easy to identify, for it creates foliage spots which are a bright, rusty colour. If allowed to develop the rust spots gather until they have covered the surface, and then become black and fall off like rust from metal. Spraying must be repeated regularly.

### Botrytis

This is a grey mould that destroys plants by attacking foliage and stems. Remove the leaves, and if a stem is affected cut below the mould and destroy the mouldy material. Systemic fungicides are the only answer.

### Stem rots

There are other types of stem rot in which parts of the stem decays. This is most common in herbaceous plants. It can be recognized by black raisin-like growths inside the stem. The only solution is to lift the plants and destroy them.

### Foot rot

This will be spotted by the blackening of the stem base, and from then on it will be the herald of a number of diseases known by names of the plants affected – geranium blackleg, pansy sickness, various crown rots, and so on. It is often caused by waterlogged ground. Destroy the affected plants and water the ground with one of the special compounds.

Many plants have specific diseases that affect their growth and cause wilting, bulb damage and rot. The gardener cannot know them all, but by keeping a keen eye on his flower beds and borders he shall spot the first sign of trouble, and be able to act quickly and efficiently.

Foxgloves and pyrethrum make a charming combination.

# INDEX

*Page numbers in italics indicate captions to illustrations*

# ACKNOWLEDGEMENTS

The Publishers wish to thank the following for providing photographs in this book:
Eric Crichton 53, 82, 83, 84, 85, 86, 87, 88; The Garden Picture Library/Brian Carter 29; Insight Picture Library/Linda Burgess 31, 35; Andrew Lawson 56; Harry Smith Collection 60, 55b, 57.
The following photographs were taken specially for the Octopus Publishing Group Picture Library:
34, 51, 92; M Boys 2, 8t, 10, 11t, 11br, 22t, 33b, 38, 39b, 41t, 42t, 43tl & tr, 44, 45, 47t, c & bl, 62, 63l & r, 81, 93; Constance Spry & Cordon Bleu Group/Steve Lyne 28; W F Davidson 9 18, 22b, 23, 24, 46, 48, 79; J Harpur 6, 7, 8b, 11bl, 15, 17, 19, 21, 25, 33t, 36, 39t, 41b, 45, 47br, 55t, 64, 68, 72, 75, 77, 78, 90; N Holmes 42b, 65, 66; A Martin 54; G Wright 9, 14, 22c, 27, 32, 43b, 49, 61, 67, 69, 70, 74, 76, 80, 89.
Illustrations by Jim Robins.

# VEGETABLE GARDENING

# VEGETABLE GARDENING

David Toyne

# CONTENTS

With clever planning and the use of modern cultivation methods, it is possible to grow an impressive selection of vegetables in a modest-sized garden.

# INTRODUCTION

While it is true to say that your local greengrocer or supermarket can provide all the vegetables you need and, often, tropical varieties flown in as well, there are good reasons for growing your own.

First, there is something very special about the taste of a vegetable picked just before it goes into the pot – however good transport and storage facilities are, shop-bought produce just cannot match it. Second, you can grow varieties that are not available from the retail trade, with better and different flavours. Third, the fresh air and exercise obtained while working on the plot is highly therapeutic. And finally, you will also be saving money.

It was reckoned that the traditional allotment plot of 27·5 m × 9 m (90 ft × 30 ft) would provide a family of four with vegetables for a whole year. The development of heavier cropping varieties and new techniques in cultivation, however, now make it possible to grow a sufficient quantity of vegetables in the much smaller area you are likely to be able to set aside in today's more modest gardens.

## CHOOSING THE SITE

The ideal place for a vegetable garden is an open but not exposed site, sheltered by walls to the north and east. It also has a slight slope towards the south without a restricting wall on that side to trap cold air in winter, so forming a frost pocket. We would all like the opportunity of picking such a site, but usually we are faced with the garden we have. It is therefore comforting to know that, provided the site is not too over-shadowed or exposed, good crops of most vegetables can be grown without too much difficulty.

As few vegetables will tolerate shade to any degree, a good deal of sunlight is preferable, so your plot should be kept away from the shade cast by houses or large trees. Also, remember that the spreading roots of trees steal water and food from your crops.

Vegetables grown in rows have a formality which may not fit in with the rest of the garden and it is generally accepted that they are best grown in a separate plot, hidden behind a screen or hedge, along with a compost heap and a cold frame. However, there has been a recent revival of the geometrically designed vegetable plot with square, rectangular or diamond-shaped beds intersected by brick or paving-slab paths, much like the traditional herb garden. These feature gardens may even take the place of the main ornamental garden.

Combining vegetables with ornamental plants is also becoming popular in small gardens. Walls or fences can support runner beans and peas, and small beds – perhaps with courgettes or sweet corn – can be integrated with the flower garden. The more unruly vegetables, like cabbages and broad beans are, however, still kept discreetly tucked away in the traditional plot.

Undoubtedly, if you are able to start from scratch either with a virgin garden or by moving an existing vegetable plot, it is easier to meet more of the ideal requirements and to ensure that the rows of vegetables run north to south to avoid one row shading another.

## DECIDING WHAT TO GROW

Whether your aim is to supply your family with vegetables for the whole year or just to grow a few special varieties, several factors must be taken into account.

### CLIMATE

Local climatic conditions can vary within a relatively short distance, and although varieties have been specially bred for the colder conditions of the north, certain crops may still not be successful in those areas, in higher places, or even in normally favourable areas if the garden has the wrong aspect and is exposed to a prevailing wind. To help you make the right choice the A–Z of Vegetables (see pages 37 to 75) gives details of suitable vatieties and their hardiness.

Despite these restrictions, vegetable gardening is full of surprises and it may be worth trying a crop that is theoretically unsuitable, especially if you can first raise strong plants in a greenhouse and provide protection in the garden with cloches.

### SPACE

The amount of space you have is an important factor in deciding what to grow. With an area 18 m × 6 m (60 ft × 20 ft) it is certainly possible for today's average family to have fresh vegetables all the year. By using intensive cropping methods (see Managing the Plot) the area required for self-sufficiency can be considerably reduced.

With only a small space available, however, it would be better to grow the rarer, more expensive crops, like asparagus, or varieties of ordinary vegetables with lower yields but superb flavour, such as the potato 'Epicure'.

If you are lucky enough to have space for a full-sized plot, long-term storage, thanks to the introduction of the domestic deep-freeze, is no longer a problem.

Potatoes and onions can be stored for several months in a frost-free shed. If you bury carrots or beetroot in boxes of peat or sand they will also keep for some time.

### TIME

Another limiting factor, although less tangible than the others, is the time you can spare for the necessary operations. Beginners will take much longer than experienced gardeners to carry out the same tasks, and some crops need more attention than others – celery, for example. Because the plot size and intensiveness of cropping are variable, it is difficult to be specific, but an hour a day, or its equivalent each week, will certainly produce satisfactory results in all but the largest vegetable plot.

# PREPARING THE PLOT

The area chosen for the vegetable garden is often grassed over – either as old pasture in the case of a new estate, or as a lawn in an established garden. The former will contain perennial weeds, and both will have pests that must be dealt with.

An established lawn that has been regularly mown is the basis of that legendary material called loam and, provided it is relatively free of deep-rooted perennial weeds, you can use it for making your own seed or potting compost. This is done by skimming about 2·5 cm (1 in) of the turf off your proposed plot with a spade and stacking it upside down in neat layers in a sheltered corner of the garden. After decaying for two or three years, it will have become rich fibrous loam.

## DIGGING THE PLOT

If you do not wish to make use of the turf in this way, mark out the plot and skim off one spade's width and set it aside. Next, remove the soil to make a trench the depth of a spade blade and also set this aside. Then skim off the turf from the next spade width and turn it in the previous trench before covering it with the soil from the second trench. Proceed in this

Garden spades and forks come in a variety of sizes so use ones suited to both your strength and your height. When not in use, try to keep them clean and wipe the metal parts with an oily rag once a year.

SINGLE DIGGING

1. After marking out the plot, skim off a strip of turf, one spade wide. Set the turf aside to place in the final trench.

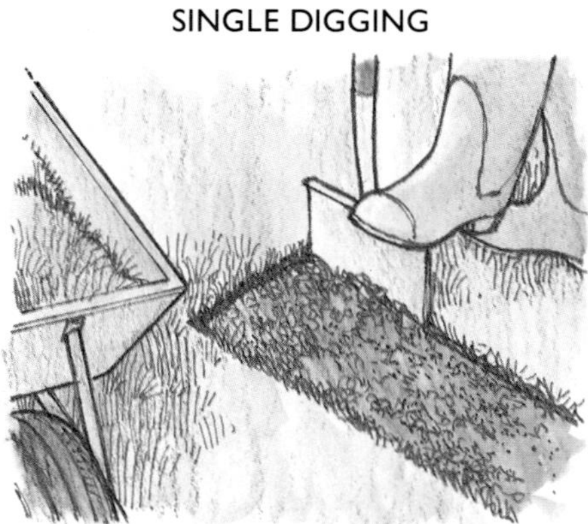

2. Dig out the soil to one spade's depth and place it in a wheelbarrow – it will be used at the end of the job in the final trench.

3. Make a second trench, turning the turf and soil from it into the initial trench. Repeat, and fill final trench with topsoil from wheelbarrow.

HOW TO DIG CORRECTLY

1. First, chop at right angles to the trench, marking out only a small bite at a time.

2. Holding the spade vertically, and placing one foot on the tread, cut down parallel to the trench.

3. Slipping one hand down to the base of the handle, turn the clod over into the previous trench.

Double digging is only necessary once every ten years or so on compacted soils. After making a trench to one blade's depth, loosen the soil at the bottom with a fork.

manner until you have dug the last trench, and fill it with the turf and soil you originally put aside. This is called single digging.

On very compacted soils double digging is necessary, perhaps just once in several years. This involves loosening the soil at the bottom of the trench to a further spade's depth, before turning in soil from the next trench.

If you are making your plot from pasture or an old lawn that is full of perennial weeds it is best to spray the area first with a safe, total weedkiller. Such a weedkiller is taken up by the foliage and transported through the plant, but is inactivated by the soil and therefore leaves no harmful residues.

**CHOOSING IMPLEMENTS AND DIGGING TECHNIQUES**

A good, sharp spade is the usual implement, although a fork may be better for clay or stony soil and is essential for loosening the bottom of trenches and for double digging. Spades and forks vary in length and weight so you should choose one tool with the combination that suits you and the job best.

Digging is probably the most strenuous work there is in the garden. If you are out of practice, take it easy for the first couple of days until your back and muscles get used to it. Take a small 'bite' at a time with the spade or fork, chopping at right angles to the trench before cutting down parallel to it with the spade's blade or fork's tines held vertically. Then turn the squarish clod forwards and over into the previously made trench. You will soon find how much soil you can comfortably handle, and which of the implements is more suitable for your soil. As the days go by you will find that you can do more and more digging at a time.

**WHEN TO DIG**

Autumn or early winter are usually regarded as the best times for this operation so that ensuing frosts can break down the rough clods. This is really only true on heavy soils; the lighter ones are often best dug in spring. Heavy winter rains 'puddle' the surface and when this dries out a hard 'cap' may be formed. This prevents weed seedling emergence, and vigorous raking will soon break it up to form a seed bed ready for sowing.

By incorporating manure into the soil, you improve its fertility and its structure. Dig it in, either in autumn or winter.

## FEEDING THE SOIL

Growing plants take a lot of goodness from the soil which must be replaced, especially in the vegetable garden where most of the produce is harvested and therefore unavailable for composting.

### MANURE, COMPOST AND FERTILIZERS

The value to the soil of manure or compost is two-fold. First, it physically improves all types of soils – from light, free-draining, chalky or sandy soils to heavy, wet, sticky clay. It holds together light free-draining soils, giving them more substance, and opens up heavy soils to provide better drainage. It also introduces air spaces and absorbent reservoirs which hold water and nutrients in readiness for the plants.

Second, manure or compost provides a fertile breeding ground for micro-organisms, such as beneficial bacteria and fungi, and larger creatures like worms. All of these play their part in digesting the organic material to release its nutrients, and forming humus which improves the soil's texture and workability. However, for the best yields of top quality produce, you must add more nutrients than are provided by manure or compost alone. A combination of compost or manure and fertilizer is ideal.

The nutrients vital for all plants are divided into three groups: major, intermediate, and trace elements.

### MAJOR NUTRIENTS

There are three major nutrients:

*Nitrogen* Often called 'the leaf maker', this is vital for all green parts of the plant.

*Phosphate* Known as 'the root maker', this nutrient is also essential for converting the energy of sunlight into plant growth.

*Potash* This – 'the flower and fruit maker' – is principally needed for its role in carbohydrate (starch and sugar) production which gives fruit and vegetables their flavour, promotes ripeness, hardiness, and drought and disease resistance.

These three, often abbreviated to NPK, are used in quite large quantities. Note, however, that unlike nitrogen, which can be used 'straight' by plants, phosphate is given to plants as $P_2O_5$ (phosphorus pentoxide) and potash as $K_2O$ (potassium oxide). It is these formulae that you will see printed on the bags of fertilizer sold to amateur gardeners.

**Intermediate nutrients** These – magnesium, calcium and sulphur – are used in smaller amounts. They are not normally lacking in soils, but magnesium, in particular, is essential to soils already rich in potash. It is also necessary if you are growing tomatoes, for example, which require extra large amounts.

**Trace elements** These include iron, manganese, boron, zinc and copper, of which only minute amounts of each are required by plants. Soils in this country do not generally suffer from deficiencies of trace elements, but if they do, it is usually manganese, which is always worth providing. Usually manure or compost can provide virtually all the trace elements needed by vegetables.

### APPLYING FERTILIZERS

Fertilizers are sold as 'straights', like sulphate of ammonia, which contains only one major nutrient (in this case, nitrogen) or as 'compounds', which contain two or more major nutrients and sometimes various combinations of intermediate nutrients and trace elements. Unless you suspect that one of the major nutrients is missing from your soil, it is easier to use

APPLYING FERTILIZER

**Base dressing:** before sowing or planting rake a dry base dressing into the soil. For application rates, follow the manufacturer's instructions carefully.

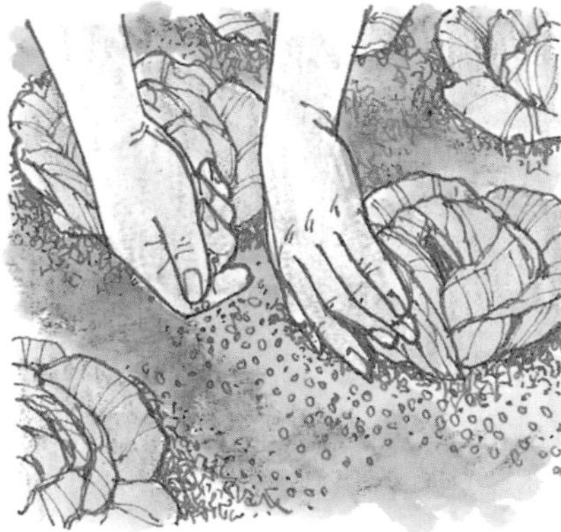

**Dry top dressing:** this is sprinkled around the plants once they are growing. If it does not rain for a few days after applying, water it in.

**Liquid top dressing:** dilute liquid fertilizers before use, according to quantities given by the manufacturer. Apply around the base of the plant, using a watering can.

the compound types, which are readily available and cheap. This particularly applies to the soluble fertilizers which, being concentrated, are even greater value for money.

Whether the source of a fertilizer is inorganic (naturally occurring or manufactured minerals) or organic (derived from animal or plant materials) its constituents, when in the soil, become solutions of inorganic salts, which is the only form that can be absorbed by the plant.

There are two ways of applying fertilizers: as a base dressing or as a top dressing. A base dressing is applied to the soil before planting or sowing, and is usually either raked or forked in. Top dressings are subsequent applications of fertilizers, either dry or liquid, given to growing plants.

To help you make a choice of fertilizer, the chart below compares the major nutrient and trace elements content, and speed of action – fast, medium, slow or very slow – of several popular and readily available fertilizers.

**BASE DRESSING – WHICH AND HOW MUCH?**

The type and quantity of fertilizer depends on the answers to three questions:

- Have you dug your plot from previously grass-covered land?
- What type of soil do you have?
- What crops do you wish to grow?

**Previously grass covered** If the answer to the first question is 'Yes', this is a special case. Because grass is an efficient remover of potash from the soil, old lawns or pasture will be more deficient in this nutrient the older they are, so when your plot is cultivated for the first time, a heavy dressing of potash is essential for raising

PLANT FOODS IN GROWMORE AND ORGANIC FERTILIZERS

| Fertilizer | Major nutrients (percentage) | | | Other nutrients | Acting rate |
|---|---|---|---|---|---|
| | N | $P_2O_5$ | $K_2O$ | | |
| Growmore | 7 | 7 | 7 | none | fast |
| Mushroom compost | 0·5 | 0·3 | 0·6 | calcium, magnesium | slow |
| Garden compost | 0·4 | 0·2 | 0·5 | soil improving qualities | slow |
| A tomato fertilizer | 4 | 4·5 | 8 | magnesium | slow |
| A general purpose organic fertilizer | 7·3 | 5 | 5·2 | calcium, sulphur, trace elements | slow |
| Dried blood | 12 | 2 | 1 | trace elements | fast |
| Blood, fish and bone | 5 | 8 | 6 | trace elements | medium |
| Hoof and horn | 12 | 1 | 0 | calcium, sulphur | medium |
| Seaweed meal | 1·5 | 0·5 | 2 | magnesium, calcium, sulphur, iodine, trace elements | medium |
| Bone meal | 4 | 20 | 0 | Up to 23% calcium, and magnesium, sulphur, trace elements | very slow |

good crops. The simplest remedy is to use a ready-made compound fertilizer containing all three major nutrients but one in which there is a high level of potash. Such a base dressing will not cause an imbalance and can be applied over the whole area in addition to and before any other treatments.

**Soil type** If your soil is light chalk or sand, a heavy dressing of well rotted garden compost or farmyard manure should be dug in when making the plot, before applying the base dressing. If, however, your plot has been cut from grassland on a light soil the base dressing could be dug in at the same time as the compost or manure.

**What crops?** This brings us to the important matter of lime and soil pH. All rain is slightly acid and slowly dissolves the calcium (an essential nutrient) in the soil, making it more available for plants but also washing it away. Manures and some fertilizers also make calcium more available to plants so they are able to take up more of it. But heavy cropping will reduce the quantity of calcium available making the soil more acid.

For this reason vegetable gardens have, traditionally, been given an annual dressing of garden lime, ground chalk or limestone. But the extent to which soil loses calcium is often exaggerated and comparatively few soils in this country are deficient in lime (even the brassica family, which is lime-loving, does not like extremely alkaline soil). The message, therefore, is not to lime the vegetable garden every year as a matter of course.

Soil acidity or alkalinity is measured on a pH scale of 1 to 14 – pH 1 is very acid, like sulphuric acid, and pH 14 is very alkaline, like caustic soda; the middle point, pH 7, is neutral. Discovering the pH of your soil is simple with one of the pH test kits readily available. Test several areas, because the pH can change dramatically within quite a short distance.

Most soils fall between pH 4·5 and pH 7·5, although peaty soils may be lower than this and those on chalk will be higher. The chart opposite will help you to determine if lime is needed in the soil, and how much. The pH should be raised gradually by annual dressing so the recommended yearly amount is given as well as the total amount required.

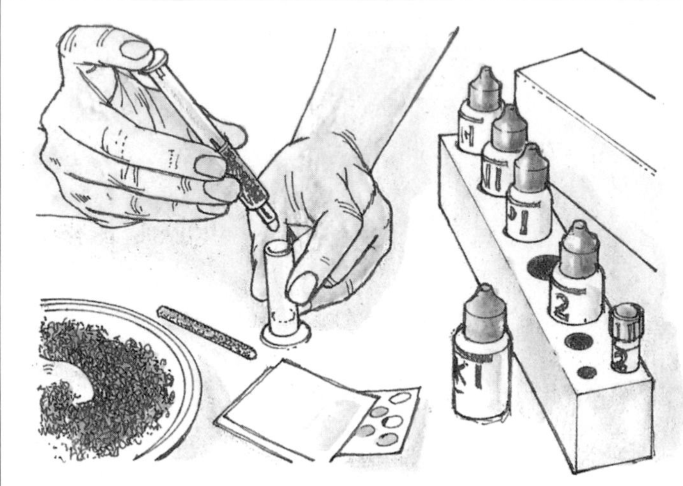

Simple kits for testing the pH of your soil are readily available.

Opposite: Green manure is a quick-growing crop of alfalfa, mustard or rape which is dug into the soil just before flowering, so introducing valuable nutrients to the soil.

Very acid, sandy, and peaty soils may be naturally low in trace elements and liming them might induce deficiencies of these trace elements and reduce crops.

## WHEN TO LIME

The most convenient time to apply lime is in autumn, but as manure and fertilizer do not mix with lime this would depend on when these other two are used. The simple rule is to lime only the cabbage patch, which, if the standard crop rotation is used (see pages 25 to 28), will mean each area of the plot will be limed once in three years. The manure and fertilizer can then be dug in during the following spring when the lime has been weathered into the soil.

## ORGANIC MANURES

In natural conditions plants die down or shed their leaves. All this material decomposes and returns valuable nutrients to the soil. In the garden we interfere with this natural process by clearing everything away – in the case of vegetables by harvesting them. In the vegetable plot, then, it is doubly important to return as much organic matter as you possibly can to the soil.

Adding organic matter, such as well rotted manure and garden compost helps to hold together light soils and breaks up heavy clay. It also encourages organisms to multiply, releasing valuable plant nutrients from the organic material and from the soil. As it decays, it leaves a residue of essential humus which continues to

Scatter lime on the surface of the soil, preferably in autumn. The rain will then wash it into the ground. Never dig it in, as this would leave the soil near the surface untouched.

conserve water and the nutrients from fertilizers which may be added to the soil later on.

Not all the bulky organic materials added to the soil are equally beneficial. The term 'organic matter' includes, for example, peat and mushroom compost, both of which are widely available, but they do not have the same properties as manure or compost. Here are the benefits and shortcomings of the various types available to the gardener.

**Green manure** Specially sown, quick-growing crops which are dug into the soil while still growing and 'green'. Examples are mustard, rape, alfalfa, sweet clover, and Italian rye grass. Sow at about 38 g/sq m (1 oz/sq yd) and rake into the levelled soil's surface. They are grown for six to eight weeks and then dug in, usually before flowering and certainly before setting seed. Sow from March to about July, although quicker-growing mustard can be sown as late as September.

*Soil-texture improvement* Soft green plants decay rapidly, so green manuring must be repeated annually.

*Plant-food content* It provides nitrogen, especially alfalfa and sweet clover, which accumulate this element in their root nodules. These then rapidly decay to release it again. It also traps any nitrogen from a previous fertilizer dressing and prevents it being washed or leached out of the soil. As green manure consists of immature plants, it is not a valuable source of trace elements.

**Leafmould** This consists of rotted-down autumn leaves. Tree and shrub leaves (especially those with large amounts of natural preservative, like plane, beech, horse chestnut and all evergreens) are slow to decay, taking more than a year to produce crumbly leafmould. Gathering them into piles or putting them in bins speeds up the process only slightly. Small quantities, however, can be successfully composted in polythene sacks – in these it is easier to ensure the leaves are thoroughly wetted before closing the top and you can store them somewhere reasonably well protected from extreme cold. A high nitrogen fertilizer, one of the straight nitrogen fertilizers – urea or ammonium sulphate – or rich organic matter, like cow manure, will produce much quicker results than leafmould.

During a warm autumn and from spring onwards stir or water the rotting leaves (according to type) into the heap or bin, but cover them well to keep out the rain, which could make the leaves excessively wet and reduce the speed at which they will decay.

*Soil-texture improvement* Leafmould is essentially a soil improver, valuable because it is slow to decay completely, rich in humus and conserves the nutrients from fertilizers. Add it to the soil at about 3 kg per sq m (5 lb per sq yd). It is almost weed-free, making it an excellent mulch for between and around vegetables.

*Plant-food content* One of the reasons why leaves fall from trees in the autumn is that they have returned most of their essential nutrients to the plant and can no longer sustain themselves. Thus, when made into leafmould, they have no real food value. Those from broad-leaved trees growing on alklaine soil contain a considerable amount of calcium which is beneficial to the cabbage family.

**Peat** This is the remains of plants which have decomposed under airless conditions in bogs and, consequently, their remains are very durable.

The durability of its contents depends on the age of the peat – some of the younger, less-decomposed ones, such as many of the Scandinavian peats available, begin to decay again quite rapidly after being added to the soil.

| AMOUNT OF LIME NEEDED TO RAISE SOIL pH TO 6·6 | | | | | | |
|---|---|---|---|---|---|---|
| Original pH | Clay or peat soil | | Average loam soil | | Light sandy soil | |
| | kg per sq m | lb per sq yd | kg per sq m | lb per sq yd | kg per sq m | lb per sq yd |
| 4·0 | 2·7 | 5 | 1·7 | 4½ | 2 | 3¾ |
| 4·5 | 2·2 | 4 | 1·9 | 3½ | 1·6 | 3 |
| 5·0 | 1·8 | 3¾ | 1·5 | 2¾ | 1·2 | 2¼ |
| 5·5 | 1·2 | 2¼ | 1·1 | 2 | 0·8 | 1½ |
| 6·0 | 0·8 | ¾ | 0·5 | 1 | 0·4 | |
| Annual rate | 0·27 | ½ | 0·54 | 1 | 0·81 | 1½ |

*Soil-texture improvement* All peats are excellent and relatively long-lasting soil improvers, but only a little humus is left by the time they are completely decayed. Also, because they are light, quite large quantities are required to achieve real improvement – up to 5 kg per sq m (10 lb per sq yd) may be necessary before any benefit is felt. Peat is weed-free and sterile, making it a good mulch.

*Plant-food content* Major and minor plant foods are almost totally lacking in peat and most peats are quite acid, so additional lime will be necessary when they are used on acid soils with crops requiring a higher pH value.

**Bark** A by-product of forestry and timber production, this is sold in composted and pulverized or chipped forms. Only the finer grades of composted bark should be used in the soil. The chipped forms are only advisable as a mulch where crops are to be grown.

*Soil-texture improvement* Composted bark is even slower to decay than peat and, as it is an equally excellent soil improver, it is theoretically the better of the two. It is more expensive – although less is needed and a little more humus is eventually formed. Both composted and chipped barks are weed-free and good for mulching, but bear in mind chipped raw bark contains resins which inhibit seed germination so it is best used only around established plants. A 2·5 cm (1 in) layer of composted bark is recommended for digging in and a 5 cm (2 in) layer for mulching.

*Plant-food content* Bark provides a small quantity of trace elements, when thoroughly composted.

**Farmyard manure** Often abbreviated to FYM, the original cow, pig or horse manure was a mixture of dung and straw bedding. It had to be stacked and thoroughly composted before use, otherwise the tough straw content would decay in the soil using up any nitrogen present, as well as any added from fertilizers. FYM is still one of the most valuable forms of organic matter, but today wood shavings and other equally decay-resistant bedding materials are also used for animals. This means the rule to use only 'well rotted' manure is even more important.

Opposite: Always enclose the compost heap so you can make a high pile, and keep it looking neat and tidy.

Left: As peat is virtually free of weed seeds, it makes an excellent mulch. It is one of the more expensive choices, however.

Left: Composted bark makes an effective and attractive mulch for mature plants.

Marrows must be grown in soil which is rich in organic matter.

*Soil-texture improvement* FYM is not a long lived soil improver – about 80 per cent is used up within the first year or so, but during that time it is an excellent and rapid soil conditioner and source of humus.

*Plant-food content* Many factors affect its food value but, on average, two bucketfuls of FYM will provide up to 60 g per sq m (2 oz per sq yd) of nitrogen, 30 g per sq m (1 oz per sq yd) of phosphate, and 60 g per sq m (2 oz per sq yd) of potash, which is quite substantial compared with other organic materials. The same amount will also provide all the necessary trace elements for up to five years' cropping.

**Garden compost** The variety of ingredients used and their original condition means that garden compost is much more variable in content and in the time it takes to rot down than farmyard manure – that is where the difference ends. Well-made garden compost is just as good for the soil in every other way – moreover, to everyone with a garden it is free.

## MAKING GARDEN COMPOST

Composting garden and household waste is quite simple as, left to its own devices, all plant and animal remains will eventually rot down. In the garden the idea is to speed up this process and, barring disasters, the end result is bound to be reasonable compost even if the waste is just piled up and left.

### BASIC RULES

There are just six basic rules for making good garden compost:

- Enclose the area to make a tidy and manageable pile and always add a good depth of fresh material.
- Make the heap dimensions as big as practicable – 1 sq m (3 sq ft) is about the minimum practical size.
- Construct a container with materials having good insulation properties. Contrary to popular belief, if the compost heap is properly constructed inside the container, extra aeration, through or under its walls, is not required.
- Use any fresh or cooked plant or vegetable waste, but avoid hard woody waste unless you can shred it or smash it up with a hammer. To avoid attracting vermin do not include animal waste other than eggshells, and do not include newspapers unless they are used to provide some of the insulation.
- Mix the waste when it is added, especially if there are large quantities of one type, like lawn mowings or leaves. This will give an even blend of soft and hard, wet and dry, small and larger pieces. Mixing also keeps the heap well aerated, supplying oxygen to the micro-organisms responsible for composting.
- Cover the heap to keep out rain – water it when more moisture is required.

Following these rules will produce good

compost in six to nine months, depending on the time of the year and the temperature – cold weather prolongs the process considerably.

**WEED-FREE COMPOST**

There is nothing more annoying than an attractive, dark brown, crumbly layer of compost spread between vegetables turning into a forest of chickweed or annual meadow grass before your eyes. It is reasonably easy to keep a high proportion of weed seeds out of the heap by pulling out weeds from your beds and borders before they flower. To be on the safe side, remove weeds as soon as they appear. Lawn mowings may also have annual grass seeds in them – mowing more frequently should reduce the likelihood of these becoming a problem as well.

Keep out all perennial weeds – docks, dandelions, couch grass – unless they can be spread out in the sun for several days so you are quite sure they are dead and will not revive in the ideal conditions of the compost heap.

Dealing with any weed seeds that remain in the heap means cooking them to a temperature of at least 40°C (104°F) for two days or more. This can be achieved only by providing efficient insulation in a small heap; in a large heap the same effect is produced by its sheer size – about 1·8 m (6 ft) square and high appears adequate. In the latter case the outer layer, which provides the insulation, will not heat up enough. Chop it off at the end of the composting process and use it to start a new heap, using only the well rotted, weed-free centre of the heap in the garden.

THREE PART COMPOST BIN

Where space permits, it is best to have a compost heap with three compartments: one for filling with recent waste; one for the compost in the process of decomposing; and the last for the compost ready for using in the garden. Forking the compost from one bin to another has the advantage of aerating it. The heap can be built on either soil or concrete.

**MAKING THE HEAPS**

Invariably, there is insufficient material from a small garden to construct a heap all in one go. Waste added a little at a time will be in a fair state of decomposition by the time the enclosure or bin is filled, without having heated greatly during the process (heating is an essential part of the decomposition process). To overcome this, it may be better to accumulate the waste separately and then mix and stack it in one operation when there is enough. The mixing adds extra air and restarts the composting process, giving a better end-product. Clearly, if you can spare the time and energy to turn and mix the heap even once after its first heating and cooling cycle it will pay dividends.

The ideal system is to have three 1·8 m (6 ft) square bins – constructed of wooden planks or lined with thick expanded polystyrene blocks for insulation – one filled, one to turn the freshly filled one into and allow it to mature, and a third for the mature compost currently being dug out for use.

Both experiment and experience have shown that there are no obvious benefits from constructing the heap on soil and no drawbacks to having it on solid surfaces, like brick or concrete, although asphalt seems to inhibit decay in the lower layers. Little benefit is derived from digging the soil beneath the heap, or from providing aeration at its base.

The heap should be sited in a shaded, sheltered spot.

**ADDITIVES**

In an evenly mixed heap it is unlikely that additives will speed up the process or make compost with better soil improving qualities. Watering on or mixing in a compost-maker or fertilizer is beneficial where large quantities of decay-resistant waste, like straw, prunings or evergreen leaves are included and mixing with the softer waste was not possible. The additives, of course, do increase the plant food value of the finished compost.

Nevertheless, although compost heaps regulate their own acidity producing roughly mature compost, in industrial areas it may be beneficial to use a compost maker, or to dust the surface of the heap with garden lime during its construction after every 15–23 cm (6–9 in) layer. This treatment is also a good idea if the waste is excessively wet or you find that the compost produced tends to be sticky or difficult to separate.

# VEGETABLE GARDENING EQUIPMENT

There are several useful items which you should prepare in advance of the growing season. They will make your gardening much easier later on when you will be fully occupied sowing, planting, tending and harvesting your crops. None are particularly expensive to buy and some can be made simply.

## SUPPORTS

Runner beans, climbing French beans and, to a lesser extent, peas are all popular crops which require some form of support.

### PEA SUPPORTS

For the garden pea grower, twiggy sticks saved from hedge, tree and shrub prunings are traditional supports and still are considered to be the best way of controlling these sprawling plants (even the dwarf varieties tend to sprawl). Pea sticks are becoming more difficult to obtain, but several brands of durable, inexpensive plastic netting are available. When attached to canes or simple sticks pushed into the soil, they serve the same purpose most effectively.

Fencing in peas with a low wall of netting or polythene each side of a row can also be effective, but picking may be awkward. If using polythene, you should make sure a gap exists between the polythene and soil so there is plenty of air movement. Otherwise, mildew and botrytis (grey mould) may be a problem.

### BEAN SUPPORTS

The main thing to remember about supporting runner beans is the weight of the plants and the wind resistance they offer when fully grown, particularly after heavy rain. Your bean poles – good bamboo

Twiggy pea sticks make the most attractive and effective support for peas, but they are becoming more and more difficult to obtain. Netting stretched between canes is a useful substitute.

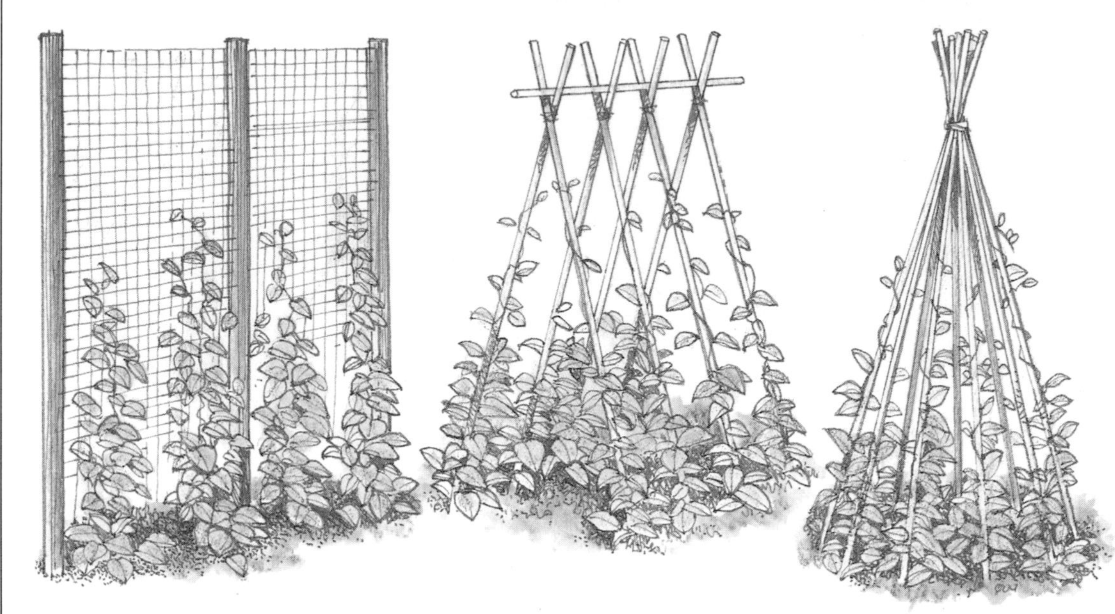

**BEAN SUPPORTS**
Stretch plastic netting across a wooden frame and have it free-standing. Otherwise, mount it against a wall.

Drive two rows of bamboo canes into the ground at a slight angle so they meet and cross near the top. Place poles in the V-channel and tie with string.

Arrange bamboo canes in a wigwam shape securing them at the top with string.

canes are best – must be well anchored in the soil and to each other.

The usual arrangement is to have double rows of poles about 23 cm (9 in) apart and 45 cm (18 in) between the rows, pushed at least 30 cm (12 in) into the soil – preferably more – at an angle so that the ends of the poles cross a short distance down from their tops (tie them together where they cross). Additional poles should be placed in the V-channel formed where the uprights cross, and also tied in position. To save on poles, stout strings can be substituted for some of them, but do make sure that you leave sufficient poles to provide good support for your crop.

Alternatively, the poles can be arranged in a wigwam shape, either tied at the top or pushed through flexible plastic discs specially designed for the job. Metal poles, rather like clothes-posts, to which strings or wires are attached to form a bell tent-like structure, are also available. These are easier to use and move, and take up much less space in the garden and when stored.

Improvised wooden frames with wire, string or plastic netting stretched across them can be used in various ways to support runner beans. Mount them vertically on walls and fences; in lean-to fashion against them; or they could be free-standing with supports. The strength of plastic netting is good enough for it to be used just suspended or supported between canes or poles in a single row.

A wooden frame is more expensive than an aluminium frame, but is better at conserving heat. The glass lights usually slide open on runners, making it easy to regulate the ventilation.

CLOCHES

A plastic tunnel cloche, made with wire hoops and plastic sheeting, covers a large area of ground cheaply.

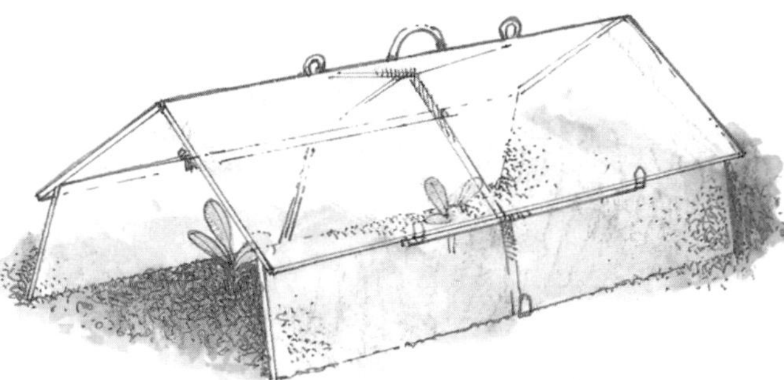

A barn cloche, made from panes of glass held together by a wire frame, is costly but excellent for large plants.

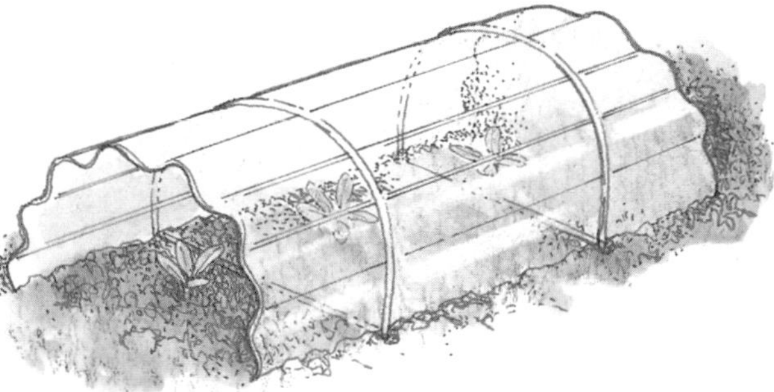

A corrugated PVC cloche, held in position with wire hoops, is long-lasting, and serves many uses. Being light, it is easy to move.

An improvised cloche, made by leaning some spare window panes against a wall.

Two different types of frame: the kind in the centre of the picture is made from corrugated PVC secured by wire hoops; the nearer one consists of panes of glass held in wire frames. When the plants inside are sufficiently sturdy to withstand the cold, the frames can be removed.

## TRANSPARENT PROTECTION

Lights (the detachable lid of a frame) and cloches made from glass or acrylic, polycarbonate or polythene sheet are useful for protecting seedlings and plants from cold and wet. They also give a much longer growing season and, therefore, enable you to grow earlier and later crops outdoors.

Cloches are also useful for hardening off. This is when seedlings which were germinated indoors are placed in a frame and gradually exposed more and more to outdoor temperatures before being finally transplanted to the plot. To harden off plants, remove the cloches from each row in the daytime when the weather is not too cold; replace them in the evening.

When propped against walls and fences, several pairs of frames can be used together to form a row of large cloches over early broad beans or salad crops, like winter lettuces. Smaller pieces of the rigid

Tent-like cloches, made from rigid glazing materials and secured at the top with strong clips. This type of cloche, which is easily assembled, has the advantage of being compact to store.

glazing materials can also be made into instant tent-like cloches with the help of wire frames.

You can also make polythene sheeting into tunnel cloches with the aid of wire hoops and string. The hoops can be bought ready-made, but soft galvanized wire is easily bent to form them or, even cheaper, use the wire clothes hangers from dry-cleaners. Remember, too, that mini-cloches can be fashioned from the multitude of transparent plastic containers that are given away – giant lemonade bottles and jerry cans, to name just two. The advantage of plastic cloches is that the larger ones are easier to carry than the glass ones of equivalent size. You can grow up to two or three rows of vegetables to maturity in the larger ones. Heavy-duty polythene will last for up to three or four years. Take into account, as well, the size of crops you will be growing before choosing your cloche. As a general rule of thumb, choose a cloche which is approximately twice as high and one-and-a-half times as wide as the nearly matured vegetables. Clean the glass, polythene or plastic when it gets dirty, in order to continue to allow light in.

You do not need to remove cloches before you water vegetables or fruit. Simply water on top of the cloche, and the water will run down the sides and into the soil beside the plants. Watch for sudden changes in weather. On warm days, open up cloches to keep the temperature down. Close them again about an hour before nightfall. On frosty nights, cover the cloches with sheets of newspaper.

Breakages add to the cost of using glass cloches. Bear in mind, however, that transparent plastic materials, particularly polythene sheeting, do not have the same heat-retention properties as glass – under plastic cloches with their ends on, for example, the temperature can be lower than that found outside. Also, because humidity tends to be higher inside than out, and as wet cold is more damaging to plants than dry cold, it is advisable to provide some ventilation to correct this situation, and to prevent the onset of the fungal diseases which are likely to develop rapidly in humid conditions.

# MANAGING THE PLOT

Growing vegetables successfully depends on a range of factors: making the best use of your ground, knowing when to sow and plant, when to feed and water, and so on, but first you must decide what to grow.

A well planned plot in which every available space is occupied by healthy vegetables.

## PLANNING WHAT TO GROW

Putting on paper your crop preferences and making notes on the timing of the various operations will help you to formulate an overall plan.

A mixture of staple and favourite vegetables is most likely to be your starting point. It pays to be a little over-cautious at first, until the mysteries and benefits of successional sowing, catch cropping, intercropping, intersowing, close spacing, optimum spacing and bed systems are all revealed (see pages 22 to 25).

Keep your plan simple and first learn how to become efficient at growing just a few crops. Try not to be tempted into growing crops or varieties of dubious reliability or hardiness in your part of the country.

In cold years, outdoor cucumbers, tomatoes, probably sweetcorn and even kidney and runner beans can be disappointing. So it's a good idea to look at established vegetable plots in your vicinity, see which crops are being grown, and ask your neighbours and local allotment gardeners to recommend varieties they have found to be reliable.

In recent years plant breeders have been putting great efforts into developing earlier, more hardy varieties for growing from seed. Together with your own observations and the knowledge of local gardeners, these varieties will almost guarantee a good crop wherever you live.

The availability of a freezer, and space or facilities for storing onions and root vegetables will influence your plan, as will the price of vegetables in the shops. Winter brassicas, for instance, can be expensive and may be well worth growing for their economic value. Since other crops will have to be omitted to make room for such a crop, the plan may have to be amended. This, in turn, may make it more difficult to give a roughly equal area of ground to the three main types of vegetables – the cabbage family, the root crops and the legumes (peas and beans), plus the remaining crops. The significance of this is covered in the section on crop rotation (see pages 25 to 28).

In order to take account of these many factors, your plan will need to be flexible. The A–Z of Vegetables chapter, which gives approximate sowing dates, planting-out times and the length of time the crop is in the ground before harvesting, will be helpful.

## MAXIMIZING YOUR CROPS

Ways to increase the quantity of vegetables which can be harvested from the same amount of ground have always been sought by gardeners. One method is to

SUCCESSIONAL SOWING
Sow quick growing crops, like lettuces, at frequent intervals to give you a steady supply of fresh produce.

CATCH CROPPING
As the broccoli and cauliflower are harvested, the ground they occupied is used for quick growing crops.

Sweet corn makes an effective and decorative windbreak in this garden, where vegetables and pretty flowering annuals grow side by side.

protect seeds, seedlings and young plants with cloches and cold frames, or to raise seed in a greenhouse or on a windowsill before planting out in more clement conditions. In this way the growing season is extended, thus increasing the crop.

Making the best possible use of the ground available is another way.

## ORNAMENTAL VEGETABLES

In small gardens, where lack of space may prevent you setting aside a plot solely for vegetables, it's worth considering growing ornamental crops in flower borders.

With their scarlet flowers and climbing habit, runner beans look most effective trained up a wall or even over an arch or pergola. A row of sweet corn makes an attractive windbreak and fennel is a wonderful foliage backdrop.

## SUCCESSIONAL SOWING

It makes sense to sow quick growing crops, such as radishes, and vegetables that do not keep well, at frequent intervals during the year so that there is always a fresh crop coming on. Successional sowing, as it is called, can be applied to beetroot, carrots, lettuce, spring onions, spinach and even dwarf beans. Two or three sowings of dwarf beans – one under cloches in March or April, one at the usual May/June time and one during July – will provide pickings well into autumn, especially under cloches. Sow only short rows of the salad types, about 1 m (3 ft) at a time.

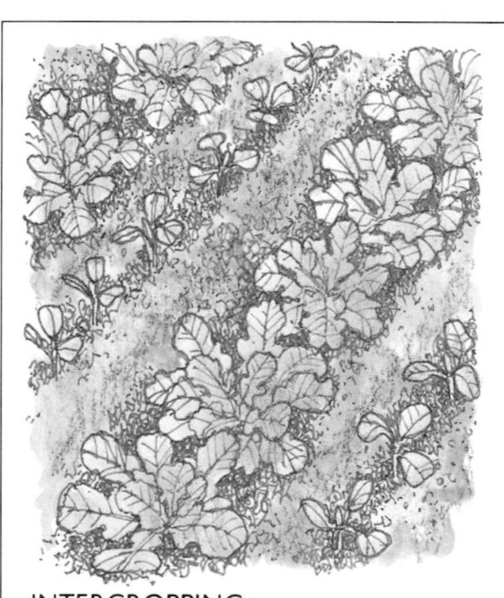

INTERCROPPING
While long-term crops are still young, use the ground in between for quick growing crops.

The bed system divides a plot up into small square rectangular beds with paths in between.

Notice how the space left between the runner bean poles has been filled with 'Salad Bowl' lettuces. These particular varieties have great ornamental value, as the leaves are picked off the plants, just a few at a time – the plants remain in the ground until the end of the season.

OPTIMUM SPAC
When vegetables
unstaggered row
space, and also de

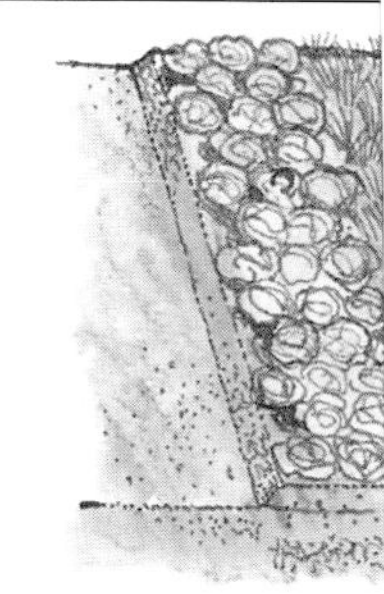

A BED SYSTEM
A bed system con
small beds, no mo
(4–5 ft) wide, with
between. It should

## CATCH CROPPING

Whenever an area of soil becomes vacant between crops, or even when a single plant or row fails unexpectedly, put in a catch crop. Any of those vegetables used for successional sowing will usually be satisfactory, perhaps with the exception of dwarf beans which may take a little too long, although in the broccoli plot they would be an ideal catch crop from the end of May onwards.

## INTERCROPPING

The same principle as catch cropping applies, but this method makes use of the soil between rows of long-term crops, like Brussels sprouts, before they get too big and spread out across the rows, cutting off the light from the soil below. It can be used for growing salad crops or for raising seedlings of other brassicas for transplanting later.

When the maincrop plants are young and there appear to be acres of bare soil between the rows, it is all too easy to be over enthusiastic with intercropping. Beware of ending up with a shorter crop which is planted too thickly, swamped by the maincrop which deprives it of light and air, and makes it impossible to get between the plants to weed, spray, or pick.

A row of lettuces has been planted in between these runner beans to make use of available space and light, before the beans grow taller – a practice known as catch cropping.

With extra p
water and foo
thorough wate
dry top dressin

**INTERSOWI**
Mixing two o
sowing in the s
nique. It make
plot, and also h
a quick germin
marks out the
with a slower
makes hoeing d
The quick-grov
long before the
Sowing sprir
another possibi
ively proven, th
the onion smell
(especially whe
thinned or pul
carrot fly in its
Vegetables wi
at different time
dates for interso
crop for this tre
varieties of Br
gettes is also av

**CLOSE SPACI**
Growing plants
than recommen
crops like carrots
are made as the r
as an early, tend
ing between ro
(using two rows
between every pa
sive use of space.

INTERSOWING
Mix and then sov
of seed together
Onions and carro
risk of carrot fly.





CROP ROTATION PLAN

**PLOT B**
Legumes and salad vegetables need rich soil which has been recently manured.

**PLOT D**
This can be reserved for permanent vegetables, speciality crops and your collection of herbs.

**PLOT A**
Root crops should not be given a plot which has been freshly manured. Grow them on a plot where manure has not been incorporated for two years.

**PLOT C**
Brassicas thrive in alkaline or neutral soil. The plot which has just been limed is best for them.

YEAR 1
B
A
D
C

YEAR 2
A
D
C
B

YEAR 3
C
D
B
A

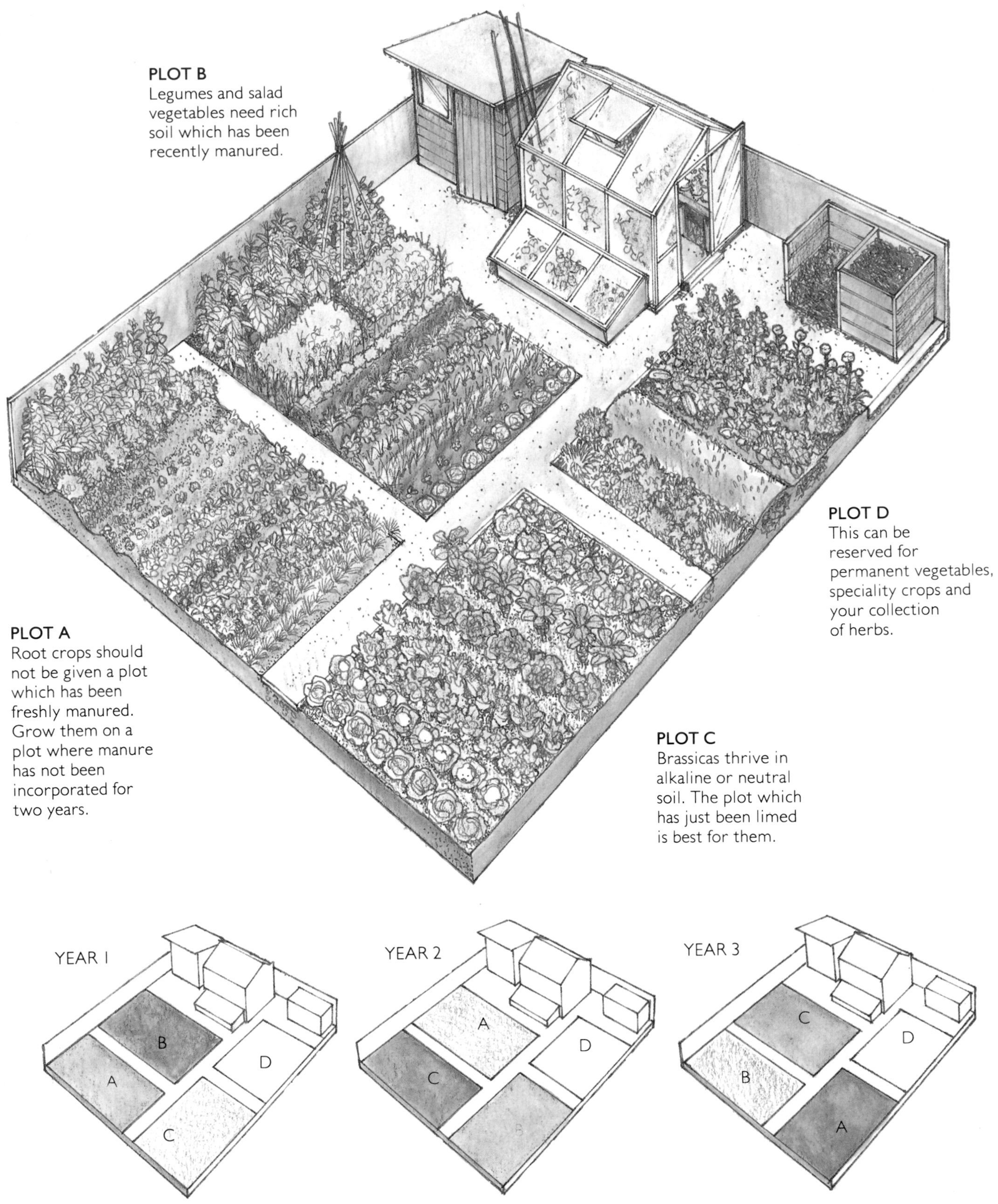

transfer of pests and diseases attracted to a particular type of plant, it would help to grow all vegetables on fresh soil every year. On smaller plots this is impossible, so a system was devised to ensure that crops are grown on the same ground as infrequently as possible.

Above: Legumes like peas and beans should be grown in rich soil where plenty of manure has been incorporated.

Right: Root crops such as carrots should not be grown on freshly manured soil.

Dividing the area available into sections and growing a different group on each area every year – 'rotating' them – is the solution. The Victorians used a seven-year rotation but nowadays, when gardens and allotments are much smaller, the three-year rotation is virtually the only system widely used.

Unfortunately, moving crops a few yards from year to year will not deter above-ground pests to any great extent, except where other preventative measures are taken (see the chapter on Pests and Diseases). Below-ground pests, also, will only be deterred if they are specific to one particular crop and move about in the soil very little, like the minute eelworms which affect potatoes and cabbages.

The occurrence of plant diseases (most of which are caused by fungus attacks), however, is reduced by crop rotation. Fungi grow from minute spores, ever present in the air and soil. Dividing the plot into three roughly equal areas and allowing a gap of at least two years before growing the same group of crops on the same soil is therefore an extremely worthwhile measure.

The order in which the vegetable groups follow each other on the same soil is important because, although the main benefit is disease control, the regular additions of fertilizers contribute greatly to soil

| VEGETABLE GROUPS FOR CROP ROTATION | | | |
|---|---|---|---|
| Root crops | Brassicas | Legumes and salad vegetables | Permanent and specialist vegetables |
| beetroot<br>carrot<br>chicory<br>Jerusalem artichoke<br>parsnip<br>potato<br>swede<br>turnip | broccoli<br>Brussels sprout<br>cabbage<br>calabrese<br>cauliflower<br>kale<br>kohl rabi<br>radish | asparagus pea<br>beans, broad, kidney and runner<br>celeriac<br>celery<br>endive<br>leek<br>lettuce<br>onion and shallot<br>pea<br>spinach, spinach beet<br>and leaf beet<br>sweet corn | asparagus<br>aubergine<br>capsicum<br>cucumber<br>Florence fennel<br>globe artichoke<br>herbs<br>marrow, courgette, pumpkin<br>and squash<br>tomato |

fertility. Legumes (peas and beans), onions, beet and salad crops need plenty of rich manure so this is dug in for them. Root crops, however, must not have fresh manure so they are kept away from the manured section, arriving there two years after it has been manured, by which time the manure has largely rotted away leaving only a fertile residue of humus.

Left: Brassicas prefer neutral or slightly alkaline conditions. Grow them on a plot which has just been limed.

## PLANTS, SEEDS, SEED BEDS AND SOWING

### PLANTS

Always buy vegetable plants from a reliable source. You can then be sure that the plants have been grown from seed in clean, sterile compost. The cabbages will not start with club root and will have been protected from cabbage rootfly attack; tomatoes and cucumbers will not be affected by viruses. Also, all the plants will be correctly labelled.

The best plant sources will insist on these rules being stringently observed by their suppliers and they will only sell the plants at the right time of the year. It is no use, for example, having marrow plants on display in April when they should not be planted out until June. You should be able to plant your specimens in the garden soon after buying them, so make sure that you can cope with the quantities you buy.

Generally, good clean, green and healthy plants are their own advertisement. Always avoid plants with yellowing, eaten or mildew-powdered leaves. The compost should be evenly moist and not shrunken away from the sides of the pot or tray, and large roots should not be protruding from the bottom of the container, a sign of starvation. You can carefully tap out pot-grown plants to examine the root system, which should be white. If a plant is healthy and not pot bound or too old, some unused compost should be showing between the roots.

Florence fennel can be grown in the fourth bed of a rotation scheme.

### SEEDS

Growing vegetables from seed is still the most popular way and, for most kinds, the only possible method. It is also cheaper than buying plants, and raising them under controlled conditions will ensure a healthy stock.

Although vegetable seeds must comply with extremely strict laws on reliability of germination, cleanliness and purity, they can still vary considerably, depending on their source and how they were treated since harvesting. There is no point in skimping – for good crops you must buy the best quality seed, preferably sold in air-tight foil envelopes; these can help keep them fresher for much longer.

Pelleted seeds are single seeds coated in a soft, dry clay, which makes the tiny ones easier to sow individually. The work of thinning and transplanting is greatly reduced and there is less waste, but it is still advisable to sow two or three pellets at each position in case some do not germinate. Pelleted seed is, of course, more expensive and thorough watering is essential to ensure that the coating is dissolved, allowing the seed to take up water for its germination.

What used to be referred to as a seed variety – indicating some variation and advantage over other varieties of the same crop – is now often called a cultivar, the term being derived from the words 'cultivated variety'. This means that the

Vegetable seeds raised in trays or pots should be sown in the best John Innes seed compost. Make sure it is free of lumps.

variety has been specifically chosen or bred for garden cultivation.

'F1' cultivars are varieties that have been bred for a particular set of qualities, such as early cropping, sweet flavour, or even – in the case of the pea 'Bikini' – almost leaflessness. The qualities are selected in parent plants and pure lines of these are bred through many generations before they are finally crossed or mated with each other to produce the F1 seed. This is extremely pure, resulting in plants which are almost identical and which produce uniform, and usually much heavier, crops. Obviously, this expertise has to be paid for, so F1 seed is relatively expensive. Its reliability usually makes up for this, however, and its more precise cropping period makes the produce ideal for storing in the deep freeze.

**Seed beds and sowing** Whether you are sowing in boxes, pots or the open ground, the ideal conditions are the same – the soil must have a fine, crumb-like consistency, a firm level surface and be evenly moist, but not wet.

In a seed tray or pot this is achieved by using the best John Innes seed compost or a peat-based compost, which will be free of lumps. Over-fill the seed tray or pot and

PRICKING OUT SEEDLINGS

1. When the young seedlings are large enough to handle, loosen their roots with a stick, and prick them out holding by the leaf, not the stem.

2. Fill new trays with John Innes potting compost No. 1 and, making holes large enough to take the seedling roots, plant them up to their necks.

3. Place a fine rose on the watering can and gently water in the seedlings. Make sure that you keep them out of direct sunlight for a few days.

carefully push the compost into the corners before levelling off and firming with a flat piece of wood to about 6 mm ($\frac{1}{4}$ in) below the rim.

Outdoors, if you dig medium to heavy soils in winter, leaving rough clods, you will get a 'frost mould' or finely crumbled surface by spring. Don't walk on this when it is wet, but once it is dry enough not to stick to your boots, firming with your heels and raking to a fine tilth (often described as wheat-sized grains of soil) will produce an ideal seed bed.

Lighter soils usually dry out more quickly and can be dug in spring, but the seed bed is made in the same way. Covering any soil with cloches or polythene (see pages 19 to 20) will warm it and dry it quickly for an earlier start.

Approximate sowing depths and distances for each crop are given in the A–Z of Vegetables chapter, but the general rules are:

- Sow at the right time. A little variation, to make allowances for the weather and growing conditions, will always be necessary, but try to resist sowing too early – this is one of the commonest causes of failure.
- Sow at the right depth. Many seeds will not germinate if they are sown too deeply or the soil is firmed over them too severely, especially if it is cold and wet.
- Sow thinly. Sowing too many seeds is wasteful and means that more time is needed for thinning out and tending the seedlings. They will also be more prone to collapsing from damping-off or other plant diseases.

These rules apply to seeds in trays, pots and in the open soil, but the sowing techniques vary. In trays and pots, covering smaller seeds with a shallow layer of moist vermiculite is, perhaps, an easier method than using a precise depth of sifted seed compost. In the case of tomatoes, though, sharp sand is better because it helps to remove any sticky seed coats as the tiny seedlings emerge.

On the plot, sowing in drills (shallow grooves) made with a hoe, the back of a rake or even a stick, is still the most common method, even where a bed system is being used. Use a garden line (low-priced polypropylene string will last indefinitely) to make straight, neat rows. If the string is stretched and the end stake pushed in at an angle away from the end of

SOWING SEED OUTDOORS

1. Rake ground which was previously dug over, working it to a fine tilth. If necessary, add a base dressing (see page 11) at the same time.

2. Stretch a line down the rows and make straight, shallow drills or grooves, using a pointed stick or a draw hoe.

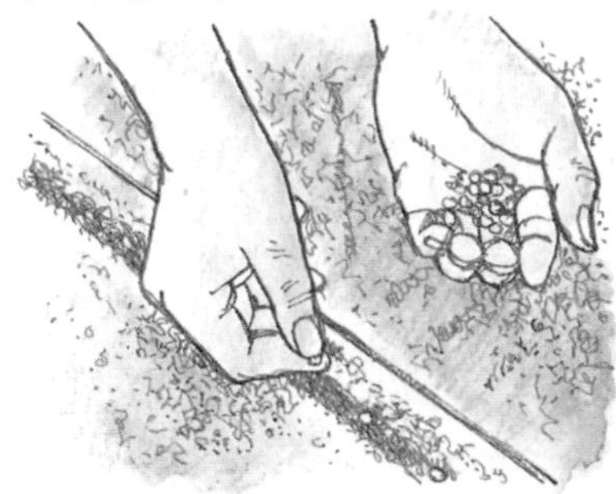

3. Water the drill lightly. Sow the seeds as evenly and thinly as possible to prevent wastage and reduce the need for thinning out later on.

4. Cover the seeds by shuffling along the rows, pushing the soil back over the drill. Write labels to indicate crop name and sowing date.

Sow the seed in shallow grooves, taking care not to scatter it too deeply.

# VEGETABLE SOWING CALENDAR

| VEGETABLE | SITE | TIME |
|---|---|---|
| ASPARAGUS | outdoors | April |
| ASPARAGUS PEA | under glass<br>outdoors | early April<br>May |
| AUBERGINE | peat pots under glass | March |
| BEANS, BROAD | cloche<br>outdoors<br>outdoors, mild areas | Jan–March<br>Feb–May<br>Oct–Dec |
| BEANS, KIDNEY | under glass<br>outdoors | Mar–April<br>May–July |
| BEANS, RUNNER | under glass<br>outdoors | mid Mar–April<br>mid May–July |
| BEETROOT | peat pots under glass or cloches<br>outdoors | late Feb<br>early April–July |
| BROCCOLI | outdoors | April–May |
| BRUSSELS SPROUTS | under glass<br>outdoors | late Feb–early March<br>mid March–April |
| CABBAGE, | | |
| spring | outdoors | July–Aug |
| summer | under glass<br>outdoors | Feb–March<br>March–early May |
| winter | outdoors | April–May |
| savoy | outdoors | April–May |
| CALABRESE | outdoors | April–July |
| CAPSICUM | peat pots under glass | March |
| CARROTS, | | |
| short | cloches<br>outdoors | Feb–March<br>March–July |
| intermediate and long | outdoors | April–June |
| CAULIFLOWER | outdoors | mid March–May |
| CELERIAC | peat pots under glass | Feb–March |
| CELERY | under glass | Mar–April |
| CHICORY, | | |
| forcing | outdoors | May–June |
| non-forcing | outdoors | June–July |
| CUCUMBER | peat pots under glass | April |

| VEGETABLE | SITE | TIME |
|---|---|---|
| ENDIVE, | | |
| curly | outdoors | March–Aug |
| Batavian | outdoors | July–Sept |
| FLORENCE FENNEL | outdoors | April |
| KALE | outdoors | April–May |
| KOHL RABI | outdoors | April–Aug |
| LEEK | under glass<br>outdoors | Feb–March<br>March–early June |
| LETTUCE | under glass<br>outdoors | Feb–March<br>March–Aug |
| MARROW, COURGETTE, PUMPKIN, SQUASH | under glass<br>outdoors | April<br>early June |
| ONION, SHALLOT | under glass<br>outdoors | Dec–Jan<br>Feb–March or Aug |
| PARSNIP | outdoors | late Feb–April |
| PEAS | cloches in mild areas<br>cloches in cold areas<br>outdoors | Oct–Nov<br>Feb–March<br>April–June |
| RADISH, | | |
| summer | cloches<br>outdoors | Jan–Feb<br>March–May and Aug–Sept |
| winter | outdoors | July–Aug |
| SPINACH, | | |
| summer | outdoors | March–May |
| winter | outdoors | Aug–Sept |
| New Zealand | outdoors | May |
| leaf beet | outdoors | April |
| SWEDE | outdoors | April–June |
| SWEETCORN | peat pots under glass<br>outdoors | April<br>June |
| TOMATO | under glass | April |
| TURNIP, | | |
| earlies | cloches<br>outdoors | Feb<br>March–April |
| spring greens | outdoors | July–Aug |

the row, it will remain taut when the drill is drawn.

After sowing the seed, shuffle along the row, using your feet to push in the soil and cover the seeds from each side. Or use a rake – always from the side, never along the row, otherwise all the seed could finish up at one end of the plot.

Fluid drilling, a new technique, sometimes used by commercial vegetable growers, is worthy of mention. This involves sowing pre-germinated seed. Sow ordinary seed from a packet on moist tissue paper, taking care not to flood it and keep at the temperature recommended for germination on the packet. When the majority of seeds have just produced their first shoot or root, carefully mix them with thin wallpaper paste (one without a fungicide) in a large polythene bag. Once the seed drill is prepared, cut off a small bottom corner of the bag and squeeze out the seedling/paste mixture, as if icing a cake, along the drill. Cover with soil and tend the crop as usual. With fluid drilling it is important to observe the normal seed-sowing timing – the pre-germinated seedlings are very tender and adverse weather conditions can give them an even greater set-back if you are not careful.

Hoe between the rows of vegetables to keep weeds down – catch the weeds when they are still seedlings.

## WEEDING

Like all plants, weeds need space, air, light, food and water. They will deprive the vegetables of this, so reducing the potential harvest. They will also harbour pests and diseases.

There are many types of weeds in the garden but, for the purposes of getting rid of them, they can be divided into two groups. Annuals are plants which grow, flower and seed at least once in a year; while perennials keep going for many years.

The distinctions between the two different groups are important because they determine the way in which the weeds are treated and controlled.

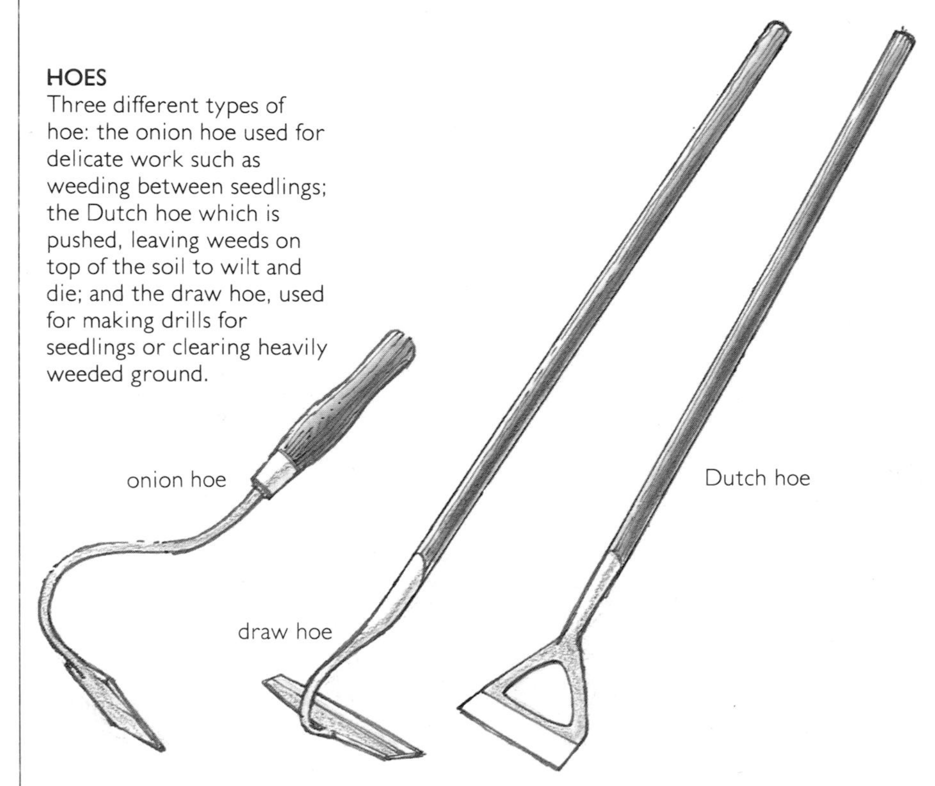


HOES
Three different types of hoe: the onion hoe used for delicate work such as weeding between seedlings; the Dutch hoe which is pushed, leaving weeds on top of the soil to wilt and die; and the draw hoe, used for making drills for seedlings or clearing heavily weeded ground.

### HOEING

Among growing vegetables, annuals and small seedlings, perennial weeds are best removed by hand or by hoeing. Hoeing has the additional advantage of loosening the soil surface to form a weed-free, moisture-retentive layer or mulch. Hoe only during dry weather so that the uprooted and decapitated weeds shrivel and die before they get a chance to re-root. Use a hoe which is suited both to the job in question and your personal requirements – your height and strength for example.

**Onion hoe** This is suitable for delicate work amongst seedlings. It keeps the soil loose and open and the surface dry, discouraging further weed seeds from germinating and preventing the evaporation of valuable water from the ground by acting as a mulch.

**Draw hoe** As its name suggests, the draw hoe is drawn towards the gardener, cutting off the weeds with its backward facing edge. This action makes it easy to avoid the plants.

**Dutch hoe** This is often D-shaped, with the cutting edge on the straight bar; it is pushed away from the user. It is easier to damage plants with this type if you're not careful, but it has the advantage of being much easier on the back and arms.

When choosing either the Dutch or the draw hoe, make certain that the handle is long enough; it needs to reach at least the shoulder when it being used at the correct angle. Also make sure that the blade is at the right angle to the shaft: in use it should be almost parallel to the ground. Finally, keep the cutting edge sharp by frequently filing it or using a sharpening stone. Hoes, like all gardening tools, should be cleaned and wiped over with an oily rag before putting them away.

### STALE SEED BED METHOD

Launching an attack on annual and perennial weeds before they even appear is the essence of the 'stale seed bed' method, most valuable for the clean start it gives. After preparing the seed bed, it is left for some days until the majority of the weed seeds disturbed or exposed by the digging and preparation have germinated and emerged as seedlings. These are then burnt off, either with a paraffin-fired flame gun, or chemically with a contact weedkiller like paraquat. With a little luck and by making an effort to disturb the bed as infrequently as possible afterwards, the soil can often remain free of weeds for almost the whole season.

### DIGGING

Perennial weeds, like bindweed, ground elder and dandelion or the narrow-leaved couch grass, must be thoroughly removed when digging as they all have the ability to sprout and grow again from the tiniest piece of root left in the ground. Just hoeing off their tops is ineffective.

Turning young annual weeds into the bottom of the trench when digging is effective if you can be absolutely certain that there are no perennials larger than seedlings present.

### MULCHING

As mentioned previously, loosening the soil surface when hoeing forms a weed-free moisture-retentive layer or mulch. Covering the soil with another layer of material will have the same effect and give extra benefits like reducing weed growth.

A good mulch should be thick enough to prevent weed seeds germinating and stop water evaporating from the soil, while allowing rain or irrigation water through without hindrance. Rotted manure, garden compost, peat or spent mushroom compost are much the best materials: a 5 cm (2 in) layer effectively prevents many weed seeds from germinating, but also makes any perennial weeds that come through a great deal easier to pull out. It also encourages worms, whose soil-moving activities aerate the soil and slowly decay the organic mulch, to add humus and trace elements to it.

### WEEDKILLERS

It is important to understand the effects of various weedkillers before applying them.

**Contact weedkillers,** like paraquat, kill the green parts of all types of plants above the ground. They are useful for clearing ground of annual weeds before sowing or planting.

**Residual weedkillers,** like simazine, are applied to the soil and prevent weed seeds from germinating and young seedlings from growing.

**Translocated weedkillers** are taken up by the leaves and roots to kill the whole plant. They are used for clearing land of established perennials when making a new vegetable plot, or for specific kinds of weed problem, like bindweed in the sweetcorn, or grass weeds in the cabbage patch. The most useful types, they are further divided into three groups according to the plants they kill.

*Total weedkillers,* like glyphosphate, which kill virtually all annual and perennial, broad-leaved and grass-type weeds.

*Broad-leaved weedkillers*, like '2, 4D' which kill only dicotyledons (non-grass weeds).

*Grass weedkillers,* like alloxydim sodium, which kill some annual grasses but mainly persistent perennial species, especially couch grass (*Agropyron repens*), a particularly stubborn weed.

**Applying weedkillers** Always use weedkillers carefully. They are not as poisonous these days, compared with the arsenic and mercury compounds used in the past, but they are still dangerous, especially in concentrated form.

Keep clearly marked, separate sprayers from watering cans, and apply only in still, cool weather. Drifting spray can cause severe damage in the garden, and in warm weather the vapour, even from a lawn weedkiller being used some distance away, can affect plants: tomatoes for instance acquire an unpleasant taste resembling disinfectant.

A layer of thick black polythene acts as an effective mulch for preventing loss of moisture from the soil in summer.

## FEEDING

The original organic manure, lime and fertilizer base dressing used on the plot to recondition impoverished soil, to prepare for planting and to feed the crops as they become established (see pages 10 to 15), will not be sufficient for most vegetables for a whole season. The soil will not be impoverished and the plants will not starve, but there is a point at which insufficient plant nutrients are available to produce the best crop in quality or quantity. So, after some weeks (exact timing depends on the vegetable), the crop will need extra feeding in the form of a top dressing.

The same fertilizer given as a base dressing may be used, but liquid feeding with a fortified seaweed or a soluble plant food will give the most efficient and quickest response. The easy-to-remember rule is to use as much solution, at the recommended strength, as you would for a thorough watering. This could be as little as 300 ml ($\frac{1}{2}$ pint) for young tomato plants or as much as 9 litres (2 gallons) for plants heavy with several trusses of fruit. The beauty of this simple feeding rule is that it does away with the complicated instructions necessary to cater for every stage of every crop in different soils, in differing climates, and at varying times of the year.

Where there is a variation from this rule or additional feeding is considered to be important, it is noted under the individual crop in the chapter on A–Z of Vegetables.

FEEDING METHODS

When only small amounts of liquid feed are required for a crop, it is simplest to dilute the plant food in the watering can, and then pour it around the base of the plants.

For large volumes of liquid feed, use a hose-end dilutor. Place a special fertilizer block in the dissolver canister attached to the end of the hose pipe.

Large volumes of liquid feed take a surprisingly long time to water on and a hose-end dilutor, which uses water directly from the tap to dilute a concentrated solution, makes the task much easier. There are small 568 ml (1 pint) or 1136 ml (2 pint)-bottle versions, but take care to select one that produces a large volume of coarse spray which will apply enough liquid to feed all the plants adequately and in a reasonable time as well.

Do not choose the fine-spray types, suitable for pesticides or foliar feeding, because they do not apply a large enough volume to root-feed efficiently. There is a large-volume coarse-spray type which attaches to a watering can rather than a small bottle and therefore has the added advantage of supplying a lot more liquid feed from just one filling of the concentrate, so consider one of these.

Digging plenty of well rotted manure into the soil will help conserve water, thus reducing your summer tasks.

## WATERING

In the majority of years, even the wettest ones, there is almost invariably a time when the soil becomes too dry to give the best possible crop. Leaving watering until the soil becomes noticeably dry will not only reduce the quantity but also the quality of the crop by inducing woodiness in carrots and beets, and toughness in beans. Also, as roots and fruits suddenly find themselves with abundant water after a period of drought, they expand and may eventually split.

Digging in plenty of organic manure on plots other than those with root vegetables (see Crop rotation pages 25 to 28), and mulching in spring, after the wettest part of the year, will conserve water, but more will almost certainly be needed.

### HOW MUCH WATER?

Water thoroughly and carefully. It is most important to give enough to suit the crop and the circumstances. Soil loses water by evaporation and plants literally suck it out, to the extent that 1 sq m (1 sq yd) of ground may lose up to 20 litres ($4\frac{1}{2}$ gallons) in just one week of dry weather. There is, therefore, no point in just sprinkling water around plants. It will do little good and could be harmful, inducing plants to make roots close to the soil's surface in an attempt to get at the small amount of water available. The resulting roots will then be even more susceptible to drought as evaporation dries out the soil on the surface.

For overall watering never use less than 5 litres per sq m (1 gallon per sq yd) and preferably 10 litres per sq m (2 gallons per sq yd). Seedlings may need less volume at each watering, but it will be required more often. Because the plants develop rapidly and use more and more water, the total amount applied for seedlings may well be the same.

### WATERING METHODS

In larger vegetable gardens a hosepipe is all but essential in dry weather. Turning down the flow to a trickle for careful watering alongside each plant is the ideal way of watering seedlings and young transplants until they are sturdier and better able to withstand overhead watering by hand or automatic sprinkler.

Measuring the amount of water applied is simple with the various types of overhead sprinkler, using a row of jars or tins across the width of the spray. These will indicate when 2·5 cm (1 in) of water has been applied, as well as showing clearly any variation over the area so that the sprinkler can be moved to compensate.

You can also measure the amount of water applied by using a perforated flat hose. This gives an ultra-fine upward spray, although it will naturally take a lot longer. The 'weeping' or 'seeping' type of hose, however, is made of porous plastic or it has a stitched row of perforations down the edge which allows water just to seep or drip out. Consequently, these kinds will moisten soil directly. To calculate the amount they have used, the flow rate from the tap must be multiplied by the length of time they are left running. These are the gentlest of all and are unlikely to cause any damage to the plants or soil unless left on for a very long time.

Finally, there are hose-end dilutors. These can be used for feeding and for watering (see page 11), applying water at the same time as the root and foliar feed.

## HARVESTING

One of the most important reasons for growing your own vegetables is that they can be enjoyed at the peak of perfection. Precisely when this is will depend on a number of things. Not all vegetables are harvested when they are ripe. Beetroot, for instance, are delectable when young and no bigger than a golf ball, so they need not all be grown on as a main crop and pickled or stored for the winter. Carrots are another example: sowing them more thickly than recommended will provide a succulent crop of tender young roots, thinner than a finger, which have a distinctly different, but equally pleasant flavour compared with their mature roots.

Courgettes are only small marrows: at that stage they are quite different from the mature vegetable and picking them encourages more to develop, with the result that you can have courgettes followed by marrows. Cut the courgettes when they are no longer than 7·5–10 cm (3–4 in).

Beans need to be picked relatively young if the pods are not to become tough or stringy – unless, of course, the dried seed is wanted for red kidney or haricot beans to be used through the winter.

Some vegetables must be grown on until mature or they will not keep: marrows and the large onions are examples, although there is nothing to stop you picking or pulling any crops for immediate use throughout the summer.

For details on when and how to harvest specific vegetables see the A–Z of Vegetables chapter.

### HOW TO HARVEST

There are several points to bear in mind when harvesting your crops:

- They must be firm, thoroughly ripened, well dried and free from rots or other plant diseases.
- With root vegetables, take great care in lifting the below-ground parts. The underground spread of many crops grows deeply and is not easy to see, and they are all too easily speared. Keep the fork well back from the line of the leaves to avoid damaging them and causing consequent rotting in store.
- Do not damage either the vegetables themselves or the plants from which they are picked. Do not tear peas or beans from their vines, since stems damaged in this way seldom recover fully. Cut the leaves of leaf crops cleanly wherever possible – beetroot leaves, however, should be twisted off.
- A few vegetables do not deteriorate with age – within reason, of course. Jerusalem artichokes can be left in the ground throughout the winter, provided slugs are

Water seedlings and young transplants with a hosepipe. Make sure you turn the flow down to a steady trickle. Only when the plants are sturdier should you use automatic watering.

A perforated flat hose, the upper surface of which has thousands of minute holes, gives a fine upward spray of water. Lay it along the ground between rows of vegetables.

A basket of home-grown produce, picked when the vegetables are at the peak of perfection.

Radishes are best picked when they are still quite small. Left in the soil for too long they may become woody and even hollow.

Below: Gently lift out leeks with a fork, when they are still fairly young. The flavour deteriorates as they grow larger.

not a problem. Parsnips are said to improve in flavour if left in the ground until after a frost. In mild parts of the country, celeriac can stay in the ground – hard northern winters, however, tend to be a little too severe.

Although celery probably improves with age fairly consistently, it is not all that hardy. The trench varieties which have the benefit of added protection from earthing-up, can be left in the ground, however.

# A–Z OF VEGETABLES

Where possible, the information on each vegetable crop has been standardized under a sequence of headings to make it easier to find what you want to know. However, as with every aspect of gardening, there are a hundred ways of doing every job, all perfectly satisfactory in their own right, so do not be afraid to experiment or feel bound to follow all the recommendations here.

When planning and cultivating a vegetable garden the rule is to be flexible. Remember that it is quite difficult to do anything drastically wrong – in fact, it is far more likely that you will develop new methods which are ideally suited to your own location and growing conditions.

Before launching into the A–Z here are a few general remarks on the information included under some of the headings in this chapter.

Globe artichokes are harvested in June and July. Pick when they are still tightly wrapped, using a pair of secateurs and leave some of the stem attached.

**VARIETIES**

Generally each crop has a large number of varieties and they have so many pros and cons that choosing is difficult even for the expert. Only the most popular and reliable ones, in order of preference, have been included here.

**GROWING TIME**

Because local and seasonal variations can be important factors, the figures given can only be an average indication of the length of time a particular crop will take up space, and how long you will have to wait before you can eat it. The figures will help you to determine whether the crop concerned is worth trying.

**SOWING AND PLANTING**

Sowing dates cannot be hard and fast because there may be snow or frost on the day you intend, for example, to prepare the parsnip bed. During a cold late spring, it may also pay to delay sowing by a week or two. Indoor sowing, of course, will not be affected by the weather. Where sowing under glass is recommended, this can also be taken to mean windowsill sowing.

Slightly closer or wider spacing may be more convenient or practical in some circumstances. Pot sizes are given where applicable, but don't worry if the right-sized one is not to hand; make do with the next size.

Broad dates are given for crops which require transplanting or planting out rather than being sown *in situ*. Useful tips, such as whether firm planting or extra fertilizer is advisable at planting time, are also given.

Often, the average width of a mature plant gives an indication of the space the whole crop will take up in the plot. In recent years, however, growing schemes other than the normal row system have become popular, so the number of plants accommodated in 1 sq m (1 sq yd) of soil has been given.

**POSSIBLE PROBLEMS**

These include pests, diseases, nutritional disorders and other hazards peculiar to the vegetable concerned. Tips are given on how to deal with them.

## ARTICHOKE, GLOBE

A thistle-like perennial of the daisy family, grown for its edible petals and the flower heart or 'fond' under the hairy seed 'choke'. Its delicate flavour is highly thought of by gourmets, but it is a large plant, up to 1·5 m (5 ft) tall, and takes up a lot of space for a comparatively small yield over a relatively short season. Only grow it if you are passionate about the vegetable or you own a large plot of land.

**Soil** Medium to light, rich soil with good drainage is best, but any fertile soil will produce some results. Any amount of well rotted manure, compost or peat incorporated into the soil will be appreciated by the plants.

**Planting** In spring – late March or April – plant strong rooted offsets (basal shoots growing from a parent plant) at least 25 cm (10 in) high, 90 cm (3 ft) apart in the row and between rows. Ensure the rooted base is planted firmly to just above the old soil line on the stem, and at least 5 cm (2 in) deep. Water in well and keep watered until new growth has begun.

Allow one plant per sq m (sq yd).

**Cultivation** In dry weather water copiously. Mulch when established and every spring thereafter.

Hoe around young plants regularly. Like all permanent residents of a plot, artichokes attract perennial weeds – bindweed and couch grass can be carefully treated with glyphosphate gel and alloxydim sodium, respectively.

Feed regularly: top dress in spring each year and liquid feed with a concentrated soluble food regularly in summer.

Protect the crowns from frost in the winter. Cover with their own leaves as they die down, and bracken, straw or peat.

**Possible problems** Almost trouble-free. Blackfly and slugs may require treatment.

**Growing time** Planting to cropping, 18–24 months.

**Harvesting** Cut off all flower buds as soon as they form in the first year. Cut for eating from the second year; remove the large centre bud first and progress to the side buds as they develop. Pick when the bud is fat and green but before the petals begin to open. Cutting may last for three months from late June in some years, but normally finishes a little earlier.

**Special points** Beautiful, tall, silvery foliaged plants that would grace any herbaceous border if the space is not available in the vegetable plot. Every spring, remove and plant rooted suckers from established plants, which are relatively short-lived, to obtain a succession.

**Varieties** 'Biarritz': the largest amount of edible flesh and best flavour, but is not reliably hardy except in the south. 'Vert de Laon': a good second choice.

Jerusalem artichokes reach up to 2·4 m (8 ft) tall so they need some form of support. Drive a stake into the ground at the end of the rows and then run strong cord between the stakes.

## ARTICHOKE, JERUSALEM

A tall tuberous-rooted perennial of the daisy family, more closely related to sunflowers than to thistles. It reaches 2·4 m (8 ft) or more, and its knobbly root tubers have a flavour similar to the flowers of the globe artichoke. The quantity of tubers, their nutritional value and ease of cultivation make this crop more worth growing than the globe artichoke.

**Soil** Any soil will do with the exception, perhaps, of acid sands and peats. Manure from the previous crop is ideal – the number of tubers is less and slug damage worse if fresh manure is used.

**Planting** Plant small to medium tubers in February or March, 45 cm (18 in) apart and 15 cm (6 in) deep, with the pointed nose of the tuber upwards. One row, used as a screen or windbreak, will probably be enough, but if not, space other rows 90 cm (3 ft) apart. Unlike almost any other vegetables bought at supermarkets for eating, its tubers can be used for planting. Named varieties, of course, should be better.

Allow three plants per sq m (sq yd).

**Cultivation** Extra watering is unlikely to be necessary, although drought may reduce the number and size of the crop.

Ridge the soil around the stem bases as

they grow. They will root into this and give themselves valuable extra support for later in the year when they are top heavy and offer a great deal of wind resistance. Knock in a robust stake at each end of the row, and run strong rope each side of the row about halfway up the plants to help stabilize them.

**Possible problems** A remarkably trouble-free crop, other than from slugs; the sweet, starch-free tubers seem to attract them from miles around. Plant with slug pellets or slug tape and water with a liquid slug killer, based on metaldehyde or the less noxious copper sulphate.

**Growing time** From planting to digging 10–12 months.

**Harvesting** The odd plant can be dug up for a summer meal of small tubers, but the majority do not reach maximum size until about October, or even later in northern districts. The tubers are hardy and can be left in the ground until wanted. Cut down the stems to about 30 cm (12 in) to lower wind resistance. Slugs may be a problem on tubers left in the soil, so some can be lifted, packed in boxes of moist sand or peat and stored in a cold, dry and frost-free place.

**Special points** Rotation of such large plants may pose a problem and it is fortunate that they do not seem to deteriorate appreciably when grown in the same soil for several years.

**Varieties** There is nothing to choose between the few that are available but 'Fuseau' has the edge because its tuber is a little smoother skinned than that of the other varieties.

Asparagus spears should be cut when they are about 10 cm (4 in) above the ground. Make your cut 7·5 cm (3 in) below the soil surface.

## ASPARAGUS

An unlikely member of the lily family, grown for its new leaf stem shoots or spears which are cut as they appear through the ground in the spring. A sought-after gourmet delicacy, but can only be considered if you have a large garden because it occupies a lot of land for a long time.

**Soil** Completely weed-free and well drained soil is more important than fertility. Digging and preparing the trench the previous autumn, incorporating a good dressing of organic manure in the bottom spit is ideal, but the standard soil preparation for a vegetable plot will produce a perfectly satisfactory crop.

**Sowing and planting** 'Connover's Colossal' can be raised from seed, but it will be three years from sowing to the first cut. Sow in April in a standard seed bed, 13 mm ($\frac{1}{2}$ in) deep; thin seedlings to 15 cm (6 in) apart and grow on until the following spring.

In April, plant the one-year 'crowns' 30–45 cm (12–18 in) apart in a prepared trench 30 cm (12 in) wide and 20 cm (8 in) deep, with the roots spread evenly over a central mound or ridge. Cover the crowns with about 5 cm (2 in) of soil and gradually fill the remainder of the trench as the plants grow, until it is level with the surrounding soil.

Allow six to nine asparagus plants per sq m (sq yd).

**Cultivation** Humus in the soil and an annual mulch of manure in autumn will retain water in all but the driest weather, when the plants must be well watered.

Weed the bed regularly by hand and use a selective weedkiller. Any garden weedkiller containing '2,4-D' will kill weeds without harming asparagus, although it always pays to follow the instructions carefully. However, do not spray the plants deliberately.

Around established beds, posts and wires should be used to support the floppy ferny growth of the mature plants.

**Possible problems** Rarely, violet root rot can virtually destroy a whole asparagus bed; plants wilt and die and the roots

Pick asparagus peas when they are still small or they will become stringy. The pods are eaten whole and have a flavour reminiscent of asparagus, hence the name.

turn mouldy and purple. There is no cure – make a new bed in another part of the garden and do not use the affected area for at least three years.

The little black and orange asparagus beetle and its grub may severely damage leaves and stems which are stripped. Spray with permethrin, derris or a special insecticidal liquid soft soap in the evening.

**Growing time** From planting to first cropping, 24 months.

**Harvesting** New plants are left to settle in and enlarge their crowns for two whole seasons after planting. It is only in their third season, 24 months or so after planting, that a few spears can be cut from each plant. From this time onwards all the spears can be cut when they are 10 cm (4 in) above ground. Cut the spears about 7·5 cm (3 in) below ground with a sharp knife. Cutting can continue until about mid June when the plants must be allowed to grow and build up crowns for the next year's crop.

**Special points** Once planted, an asparagus bed will not crop until its third year, but it could then go on cropping for 20 years. So thorough preparation, additional spring mulching and top dressing, and liquid feeding in summer after cutting has finished, will pay dividends.

**Varieties** 'Connover's Colossal': a safe, reliable, heavy cropper if conditions are right. 'Lucullus': seems set to take over as the favourite; it has all the advantages of the former variety and it is an all-male variety, the significance of this being that there will be no self-sown seedlings to adulterate the crop or berrying females of reduced vigour.

## ASPARAGUS PEA

This legume is not a true pea, but a type of annual vetch, grown for its curiously shaped pods, which are eaten whole like a mangetout pea. The pods have a slight flavour of asparagus, so it can best be described as a novelty vegetable.

**Soil** As for the garden pea (see page 68).

**Sowing and planting** Rows, 38 cm (15 in) apart. Sow seed 7·5 cm (3 in) apart, 5 cm (2 in) deep. Thin seedlings to 30 cm (12 in) apart. Under glass: in early April in pots for planting out in early June (it is not frost hardy). Outdoors: during May. The indoor sowings should be planted out when about 2·5 cm (1 in) high.

**Cultivation** Similar to ordinary garden peas in its requirements and it, too, needs pea sticks for support.

**Possible problems** It tends to crop far less than peas but, by way of compensation, has fewer ailments.

**Growing time** 70 days.

**Harvesting** Pick frequently as soon as the pods are 2·5 cm (1 in) long, before they become stringy from June to August.

**Varieties** Only the species, *Tetragonolobus purpureus*, is available.

## AUBERGINE

Widely known as the egg plant, this is an annual member of the tomato family. Because of its tenderness, it can only be grown in a sunny sheltered site in mild gardens or in a greenhouse. Aubergines make small bushes up to 75 cm (30 in) high; their fruits are of a less distinct flavour than the tomato. Most varieties are black-skinned but you can also grow white-skinned ones.

**Soil** Like the tomato, the aubergine is a heavy feeder and adequate fertilizer is more important than rich soil, although it is best to have good drainage and, in the greenhouse, to use sterile seed and potting composts. Growing bags are excellent for aubergines.

**Sowing and planting** In a temperature of at least 18·5°C (65°F), sow two seeds in a peat pot of soilless compost, in February for a greenhouse crop and in March for an outdoor crop. Take out the weaker seedling when the first true leaves are visible and grow on until they have six to eight leaves before planting, complete with pot, in April in the greenhouse and May under cloches. Harden off outdoor plants, and plant 60 cm (2 ft) apart in rows. Water in well.

**Cultivation** When the plants reach 30 cm (12 in) high pinch out the growing tips to make them produce more fruiting side shoots. Put in canes for support and, as the plants grow, tie the stems to the canes with string.

**Possible problems** Aubergines are not prey to most of the troubles of tomatoes, but they can be badly affected by red spider mite, whitefly and aphids, all of which are very persistent. Control these pests with a spray programme using a plant extract or refined pure soap insecticide.

Feed regularly, preferably at every watering once the first fruit has begun to swell. Use a high-potash, soluble tomato feed which, usefully, contains extra magnesium and calcium.

**Growing time** 140 days.

**Harvesting** Picking extends over about two-and-a-half months between July and October, although outdoors this could end by September. Choose firm, ripe fruit 10–15 cm (4–6 in), and pick while still glossy. Older fruit can be tough and tart. Cut the fruit stems to avoid damaging the plant with secateurs rather than tearing them off.

**Special points** Keeping the air humid, but buoyant, and misting over the plants with clean soft water will encourage the fruit to set, as well as discouraging red spider mite.

**Varieties** 'Black Enorma': produces the largest aubergines of all. 'Black Prince': an F1 hybrid; heavier cropper than the reliable old favourite 'Long Purple'. 'Easter Egg': a white-skinned egg-shaped novelty with a milder flavour than most.

Aubergines will only thrive and produce ripe fruit outdoors in the mildest parts of the country. They must be grown in a warm, sunny and sheltered corner.

Allow 100–120 days between sowing and harvesting broad beans. After the crop has been harvested, dig the plants into the ground as a green manure.

## BEAN, BROAD

The hardiest of the beans; standard types are up to 1 m (3 ft) high, dwarf types 30–45 cm (12–18 in). Spring sown only; autumn sowing is only considered worthwhile by experienced growers, except possibly in mild areas.

**Soil** Any good soil, preferably free-draining and not too acid; apply manure or compost in autumn or winter and fertilizer a week before sowing or planting out.

**Sowing and planting** Double rows, 20 cm (8 in) apart and 60 cm (2 ft) between each pair of rows. Seeds 20 cm (8 in) apart and 5 cm (2 in) deep. Outdoors: February to May, except in the south where October to December is possible. Under cloches, in a cold frame or cold greenhouse, January to March. Plants from seed sown indoors can be hardened off and planted out from March onwards.

Allow five plants per sq m (sq yd).

**Cultivation** In an average year watering should not be necessary until the pods begin to swell, then water thoroughly in dry weather.

Young plants are easily swamped by weeds; frequent hoeing is probably the easiest way of keeping these down. Staking large plants may be necessary, especially in windy weather – a cane at each corner of the growing area with string encircling the crop is an alternative and wise precaution. Pinch out the top shoots of each plant when the first flowers have set pods – this gives an earlier crop and deters blackfly which are attracted to the softer green growth.

**Possible problems** Blackfly on young shoots are best picked off. Chocolate spot is a fungus disease that looks just as it sounds; feed well with a high potash fertilizer to prevent it.

**Growing time** 100–120 days.

**Harvesting** June to September; pick as often as possible; small, young beans are more tender and tastier, so pick when no more than 7·5 cm (3 in) long to encourage the maximum crop. Mature beans for winter use should be picked when the pods begin to shrink (but before they actually shrivel) and the shape of the seeds can be clearly seen.

**Special points** Dig in the whole plant after picking is finished as a green manure, or cut off the stems and leave the roots to decay and return the nitrogen fertilizer from their root nodules to the soil.

**Varieties** 'Aquadulce Claudia': a large white-beaned long pod variety, very hardy and reliable cropper. 'Masterpiece': early cropping, green-beaned long pod variety; strong flavour, suitable for freezing. 'The Sutton': dwarf, white-beaned, short podded variety; good for early sowing and cropping under cloches.

## BEAN, KIDNEY (FRENCH)

These are frost tender. They have rounder but smaller pods than runner beans. Most types produce small bushy plants up to 45 cm (18 in) high. One or two climbing varieties reach up to 1·5 m (5 ft). Well worth growing.

**Soil** They dislike acid soil and prefer it not too heavy. Use manure or compost the previous autumn and lime, if acid, three or four weeks before sowing.

**Sowing and planting** Rows 45 cm (18 in) apart. Seeds 10 cm (4 in) apart, 5 cm (2 in) deep. Under glass: March to April. Outdoors: May to July, two or three successional sowings, about three weeks apart, will prolong cropping.

Although usually sown *in situ*, a few seeds sown in pots or boxes will provide replacements for the inevitable losses in early sowings.

Allow nine plants per sq m (sq yd).

**Cultivation** Soak thoroughly in dry weather when flowering or picking.

Weeds may swamp young plants; hoe carefully, for they are very easily chopped off at ground level. Pea sticks prevent floppy plants falling over.

**Possible problems** Blackfly and, especially on the dwarf varieties, slugs may damage the pods.

**Growing time** 60–90 days.

**Harvesting** Late June to early November if early sowings and late crops are protected under cloches. Pick several times a week to keep the young beans coming. Small pods that snap easily and which have no sign of the beans showing through the skin are the tastiest and least stringy. Leaving pods on the plant until yellowing, before final drying and shelling indoors, will provide a supply of haricot beans for winter use.

**Special points** Liquid feeding is especially beneficial and after the main picking will encourage a second, although smaller, flush of pods.

**Varieties** 'Masterpiece': an early, but heavy cropper. 'Canadian Wonder': heavy crop, good flavour but often difficult to find. 'Remus': crisp and sweet, beans held above leaves for convenience and protection from mud splashes. 'Blue Lake': heavy cropping climber. 'Blue Coco': purple-podded climber, very good flavour, attractive plants.

## BEAN, RUNNER

A perennial, usually grown as an annual. The most vigorous bean, climbing up to 3·7 m (12 ft) and making a useful screen as well as a most acceptable vegetable. It makes an attractive plant grown up walls or even an arch.

**Soil** Rich, light, well drained, non-acid soil produces the best crops. Dig a traditional bean trench in autumn, with a good deep layer of well rotted manure or compost at the bottom before refilling. Leave for the winter and earth over with fresh soil from the sides; lime only if soil is very acid and top dress with fertilizer a week or two before sowing or planting out.

**Sowing and planting** Rows 45 cm (18 in) apart. Sow 20 cm (8 in) apart, 5 cm (2 in) deep. Under glass: mid March to late April. Outdoors: mid May to July.

Plant seedlings raised under glass in late May to early June. Outside, take care to harden seedlings off gradually or protect with cloches for the first week or so.

Allow nine plants per sq m (sq yd).

**Cultivation** Water regularly and very thoroughly in dry weather. Mulching is useful with such thirsty plants to discourage evaporation from the soil.

Hoe regularly and watch for bindweed hiding in the twining bean stems. Liquid feeding is appreciated and foliar feeding is very effective. Pinch out the shoot tips at the tops of the supports.

**Possible problems** Large colonies of blackfly can stunt growth and cause distorted pods. Look out for them in summer.

**Growing time** 90 days.

**Harvesting** Mid July to late October or early November, depending on season and locality. It is important to keep picking young beans to prevent the plants ceasing production. Such high yields and cropping rates mean that, at some point, there is bound to be a surfeit; so a deep freeze is a priceless asset.

**Special points** Watering with lime water, a handful of garden lime in a 9 litre (2 gallon) watering can, may be effective in poor set years. Spraying with water or sugar solution does not improve 'set'. Pinching out the growing points as soon as the seedling stems begin to twine will

Pick the runner beans when the pods reach 15–20 cm (6–8 in) long. This will encourage the plants to continue producing a healthy crop for at least two months.

With their scarlet flowers and rambling habit, runner beans make attractive plants for training up arches and arbours. This releases ground in the vegetable patch for growing other crops.

produce shorter plants and earlier, but smaller, crops.

**Varieties** 'Achievement', 'Enorma' and 'Streamline': all for sheer quantity. 'Kelvedon Marvel' and 'Kelvedon Wonder': shorter, earlier and substantial croppers. 'Red Knight': a good freezer, with excellent flavour and stringless.

## BEETROOT

A biennial root crop with more or less round or cylindrical roots projecting above soil level. Dark red varieties have always been preferred in this country; there are white and golden types as well. Grown for salads and for winter storage.

**Soil** Deep, light or sandy soils produce the best beetroot. Deep digging will make most soils suitable, but only use land that has not been freshly manured for at least a year; fresh manure or compost produces 'fanging' or forked roots. On very light, poor soils you will find an extra dressing of a soluble tomato food or any of the high-potash fertilizers will increase the results dramatically.

**Sowing and planting** Rows 30 cm (12 in) apart. Sow seeds 10 cm (4 in) apart, 2·5 cm (1 in) deep. Seeds appear to be relatively large but in reality are small capsules containing more than one seed. Sow two capsules at each position and pull out all but the strongest seedling when about 2·5 cm (1 in) high.

Under glass (cloches): sow seeds from late February. Outdoors: sow seeds from early April to July.

Beetroots, like other root crops, tend to produce split or forked roots if transplanted, but this does not happen if seed is sown in peat pots and these are planted out without disturbing the young roots from late April.

Allow 35 plants per sq m (sq yd).

**Cultivation** Lack of water causes toughness while excess water can cause the roots to split; evenly moist soil is the answer and regular moderate watering the safeguard.

With such a relatively low growing crop, weeding is vital. Weedkillers can be most useful if applied correctly and carefully – it is easy to damage seedlings and young, swelling roots by carelessly wielding the hoe.

**Possible problems** Susceptible to trace element deficiencies. Lack of boron causes dark, soft areas on the skin and heart rot. Shortage of manganese shows as curled, yellow leaves. Both will be prevented by using plenty of manure in previous years (see crop rotation, pages 25 to 28). Foliar feeding with a soluble plant food may help reduce the symptoms, which are aggravated by liming the soil.

**Growing time** 90–120 days.

For the best beetroot, grow on a light or sandy soil which has been dug deeply, but not manured for at least one year.

## BRASSICAS

Brassicas are members of the cabbage family, a group that includes broccoli, Brussels sprouts, cabbage, cauliflower, calabrese and kale – all leaf crops – as well as kohl rabi (or turnip-rooted cabbage), swede and turnip.

Because of their close relationship they like the same soils and cultural conditions. In order to save repetition, their common requirements are given here, while the special needs of a particular crop are reserved for their individual entries.

**Soil** Although brassicas have a reputation for liking lime, they do not thrive in very limy or chalky soil. In fact, they prefer slightly acid conditions and only very acid soils will need liming (see page 12). They require a deep, fertile soil – one of the commonest reasons for failure is a lack of organic manure and fertilizer. A good dressing of manure, no later than the previous autumn, will pay dividends, but this must be dug in long enough before planting to allow the soil to settle again thoroughly; the manuring for the previous year's crop may be sufficient if it was heavy enough. Strangely, for such strong growing, deep rooted vegetables, loosening the soil is not advisable since they must have firm foundations to grow into. Just light hoeing and raking to remove surface weeds is recommended.

**Planting** The timing of planting out varies with the type and variety concerned, but all should be planted very firmly. Try to keep a good root system with plenty of soil attached, and make the planting holes with a dibber and not a trowel. Make the hole about 10 cm (4 in) deep and 'puddle-in' the plants by pouring water into the hole before covering the roots. Then make another hole alongside the first and lever the dibber towards the plant to compress the soil around its roots. Tread the soil firmly around each plant and fill the hollow you make with water. Keep the transplants watered and shaded for the next two or three weeks.

Newly planted 'Hispi', a variety of spring cabbage grown for its delicious flavour. Medium-sized, compact and quick maturing, this is an excellent choice for a small plot.

Protect your brassicas from the ravages of pigeons by stretching nylon netting over the plants, making sure they are completely covered. Pigeons can destroy an entire crop by eating the soft parts of the leaves.

**Cultivation** Never let brassicas go short of water. Unless the weather is constantly wet, keep the soil deeply and evenly moist, especially for seedlings and new transplants. Up to 20 litres per sq m (4 gallons per sq yd) will not be excessive for a strongly growing established crop.

Extra top dressing with fertilizer will be needed in mid summer or, alternatively, regular liquid feeding will produce more succulent plants, particularly in drier years. The taller brassicas – Brussels sprouts and broccoli – may need staking in case there are winter gales. Earthing-up the stems and, firming the soil also helps.

**Possible problems** Brassicas can be prey to a wide range of pests and diseases, but most are quickly recognized and easily dealt with by the methods outlined in the chapter on Pests and Diseases. Of these, pigeons, slugs and caterpillars are the most common; others are comparatively rare. There are three problems that require special attention.

*Club root:* this fungus disease, also known as 'finger and toe' disease, causes club-like swollen roots and dramatically reduces the crop yield. The disease cannot be effectively removed from the soil, where it lies dormant for many years, so brassicas should be grown on the patch as infrequently as possible.

Liming discourages it and in recent years this treatment has been preferred to the application of mercurous chloride, benomyl or thiophanate-methyl club root dips. The latter can be used to puddle-in the transplants by making a thin watery paste and dipping the roots in it before planting them out. Perhaps the most satisfactory way of overcoming the problem is to grow your own plants from seeds sown in sterile seed compost, potting on into 12·5 cm (5 in) pots of sterile potting compost and planting out with their undisturbed root ball.

*Cabbage root fly:* grubs from eggs laid in the soil bore into the stem at ground level and cause the plant to wilt easily and perhaps die. Raising seedlings and potting them on in sterile compost allows bromophos or diazinon to be incorporated with the compost at the same time.

*Cabbage mealy aphid:* this aphid is particularly difficult to deal with as it always hides under the leaves and its mealy, waxy coating prevents sprays from wetting it thoroughly, with the result that insecticides are ineffective. The new refined and safer soap sprays, with their combined insecticidal and wetting properties, are better.

Red cabbages are sown outdoors in spring and harvested in the autumn. If you cut them in late autumn they can be stored over the winter.

Sow winter cabbage outdoors in May for cutting from November onwards. Cook them immediately after harvesting.

Broccoli is not the easiest of brassicas to grow but your efforts will be rewarded with a delicious crop. It is harvested by cutting a few shoots from each plant at a time. You should expect another picking six to eight weeks later.

**Harvesting** May to October with those to be stored for winter mainly pulled in July to September. Thin out small roots, up to 4 cm ($1\frac{1}{2}$ in) in diameter, by pulling every other plant – use these for cooking. Always pull before the roots become large and woody, showing white rings inside. Always twist off the foliage to discourage bleeding. Store mature crops pulled in September and October in boxes of peat. Lift carefully and do not break or bruise the skins or rot will set in during storage.

**Special points** Use netting to protect seedlings from birds. Single seeded varieties like 'Monopoly' and pelleted seeds are available which, sown singly, do away with the need to thin or 'single' plants.

**Varieties** 'Boltardy': a bolt resistant type as its name suggests – i.e. it does not easily run to seed before producing a good root. 'Avonearly': an equally popular red beetroot. 'Burpee's Golden' and 'Snowhite': yellow and white varieties respectively, the former being particularly interesting because it does not bleed.

## BROCCOLI

A hardy flowering brassica, with flower spikes similar to small cauliflowers, but with a more delicate flavour. It makes a delectable vegetable, but does take up a great deal of space and time. Calabrese, a half-hardy continental type, is dealt with separately (see page 51). Consult brassicas (pages 46 to 47) for cultivation.

**Soil** Good drainage is preferred and is more essential than for some brassicas.

**Sowing and planting** Rows 15 cm (6 in) apart. Seeds 13 mm ($\frac{1}{2}$ in) deep and no less then 13 mm ($\frac{1}{2}$ in) apart. Remove the weakest seedlings to leave about 7·5 cm (3 in) between plants at transplanting time. Sow in mid April and May. If club root is a problem sow in sterile compost in a cold frame. Lift seedlings carefully and plant firmly from early June to early August.

Allow two plants per sq m (sq yd).

**Possible problems** To prevent wind rock, earth up; refirm by treading and restake if necessary.

**Growing time** 300 days.

**Harvesting** Early varieties are usually ready for cutting between February and March, late ones in late March to mid May. Cut frequently, while in tight bud, taking a few shoots at a time and cutting the central spike first. Plants will then re-crop over six to eight weeks. A good freezer vegetable – blanch for three minutes after soaking in salt water for fifteen minutes.

**Special points** These are not the easiest brassica to grow.

**Varieties** 'Early' and 'Late Purple Sprouting': very hardy and useful for winter vegetables in cold areas. 'White Sprouting': also has early and late varieties, but tastes more like a cauliflower, and may be a little less hardy in severe winters.

## BRUSSELS SPROUTS

The tallest brassica and one of the hardiest. Larger varieties grow 1·2 m (4 ft) tall. All reliable winter croppers. Takes up a lot of time and space, but such a reliable and popular winter vegetable is indispensable. (See brassicas, pages 46 to 47 for cultivation details.)

**Soil** Brussels sprouts need the firmest soil of all brassicas. Leave the soil for several months before planting; do not dig, and firm thoroughly by treading around young plants, repeating this frequently as they establish.

**Sowing and planting** Rows 15 cm (6 in) apart. Seeds 13 mm ($\frac{1}{2}$ in) deep and no less than 13 mm ($\frac{1}{2}$ in) apart. Under glass: late February to early March. Outdoors: mid March to mid April. Remove the weakest seedlings to leave about 7·5 cm (3 in) between plants at transplanting time. Lift plants carefully with as little damage to roots as possible and replant very firmly between late April (indoor sown) and late June (outdoor sown).

Allow two to four plants per sq m (sq yd).

**Possible problems** Buttons 'blown' or opening, usually caused by poor infertile soil, loose planting or insufficient water. Wind rock can be severe; earth-up, refirm by stamping in, and stake the plants if it is necessary.

**Growing time** 200–250 days, depending on variety.

**Harvesting** Picking on individual

plants can be over two or three months, especially with the selected varieties, and runs from mid to later September through to about April in an average year. Pick progressively from the bottom up, a few sprouts at a time. F1 varieties tend to have even buttons so pick these when they appear at their best. Delaying the start of picking until after the first frost is claimed to improve the flavour.

'Widgeon' is an F1 hybrid Brussels sprout.

Cabbages do take up a large amount of space, so they are best grown only in fairly extensive plots.

**Special points** Do not skimp on the fertilizer base dressing and give extra liquid top dressing in the summer, but do not give any nitrogen fertilizer after August as this may produce a slightly bitter flavour.

**Varieties** 'Peer Gynt' and 'Citadel': early and main season F1 hybrids producing well flavoured, uniform buttons. 'Roodnerf-Seven Hills' with long lasting tight sprouts, 'Bedford Fillbasket' with large sprouts and 'Rubine', red sprout of unique flavour, are not F1 hybrids so need picking carefully as they reach their peak.

PICKING BRUSSELS SPROUTS

1. As the plants grow, pick off any yellow leaves or loose-leaved sprouts from the bottom of the stem. This will create better air circulation.

2. When the sprouts are ready to harvest – they should be small and compact – pick from the base upwards. There is an old saying, that they taste better after a slight frost.

## CABBAGE

A hardy, single-headed brassica which includes some of the fastest and longest growing green vegetables. Four types make cabbage the longest cropping vegetable by far. There should not be a month when they are not available – they may be scarcer in June or July, but with a little practice these months can easily be covered, too. The long cutting season and ease of cultivation make cabbages desirable vegetables, although they do take up a large amount of space and time considering that most provide only one picking, and the spring types use valuable summer vegetable space.

**Soil** Not quite so dependent on firm soil as other brassicas.

**Sowing and planting** Rows 15 cm (6 in) apart. Seeds, 13 mm ($\frac{1}{2}$ in) deep, not less than 13 mm ($\frac{1}{2}$ in) apart. Remove the weakest seedlings to leave about 7·5 mm (3 in) between the plants at transplanting time. Sow spring cabbage outdoors, July in cold or northern areas, August in warm southern areas. Summer cabbages: under glass, February and March; outdoors, March to early May. Winter cabbages: outdoors April and May. Savoy cabbages: outdoors, April and May.

Allow seedlings to establish well with six or more leaves before transplanting. Plant spring cabbages early, 12 cm (5 in) apart to give greens from the thinnings. The others, 30–45 cm (12–18 in) apart depending on type and variety. Follow any instructions on the seed packets.

Allow for up to five plants per sq m (sq yd) for winter, summer and Savoy types and ten to eleven for spring types.

**Cultivation** Keep well watered as heads reach maturity, and liquid feed with high-potash fertilizer. (See brassicas, pages 46 to 47, for cultivation.)

**Possible problems** Some varieties are prone to splitting in cold weather.

**Growing time** Summer varieties: 120–200 days; winter and Savoy varieties: 150–240 days; spring varieties: 240 days.

**Harvesting** Spring types, April to August; summer types, July to November; winter types, October to March. Spring cabbage planted extra thickly can be cut as spring greens from March onwards until the remaining plants are 30–45 cm (12–18 in) apart. Store cut winter cabbages in straw after trimming off outer leaves and roots. Winter variety 'Jupiter' will store hanging up by its roots. Early cabbages can be induced to produce several more smaller heads if a cross cut is made in the flat surface of the remaining plant stem.

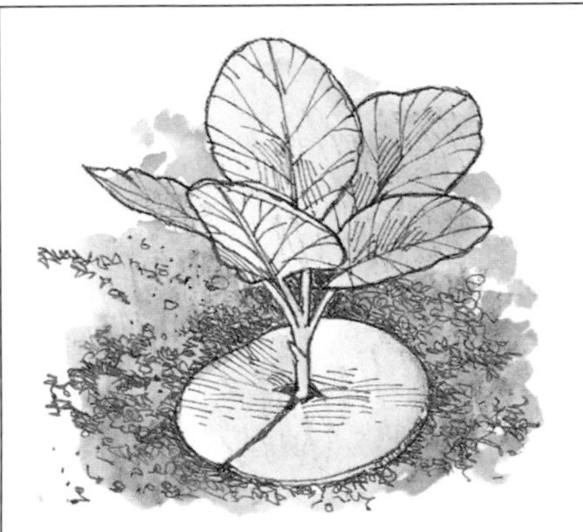

CABBAGE PROTECTION
Brassica collars can be put around the stems of cabbages, after transplanting to prevent cabbage root fly (a common brassica pest) damaging the root systems.

Cabbages are not the best brassicas to freeze, but very firm heads which are blanched for one minute are reasonably satisfactory.

**Varieties** Spring cabbages: 'Spring Hero': a very solid medium to heavy weight F1 round-headed variety; 'Durham Early': a pointed-head type which produces darker spring greens. Summer cabbages: 'Hispi' and 'Spitfire' are both fast growing pointed-head F 1 varieties. 'Hispi' is a little earlier and 'Golden Acre', a solid round-head, cuts about the same time. Red cabbages: not great favourites, but just as tasty and even more attractive raw in salads, a late summer type – a small but reliable, solid plant. Winter cabbages: the new 'Celtic' F1 is the best variety, split-free even in the hardest weather; the F1 'Jupiter' keeps well when stored whole in a shed or outhouse. Savoy cabbages are crinkle-leaved winter cabbages: 'Savoy King' is an F1 which has all the best features of this type – a gentler, less peppery taste, extreme hardiness and less demanding of good soil and fertilizer, which makes it an easy variety to grow.

Calabrese is not fully hardy, so it is grown outdoors in summer for picking before the arrival of winter.

## CALABRESE

A green, fast growing Italian version of our purple and white sprouting broccoli. Much smaller than either of these, it is usually under 60 cm (2 ft) high and not fully hardy in winter. Its short growing period, smaller size and delicate flavour make this a good vegetable to grow if you have space during summer, but it can be temperamental, like its brassica relative the cauliflower.

**Soil** Water conservation, especially in light soils, must be improved with adequate organic manure.

**Sowing and planting** Sowings *in situ:* rows, 30 cm (12 in) apart. Seeds 13 mm ($\frac{1}{2}$ in) deep, 15 cm (6 in) apart. Sow three seeds per position and pull out the two weakest when the first true leaves are formed. First sowings, April to May; successional sowings, two or three in June and July. For transplanting, sow into 7·5 cm (3 in) pots of sterile loam-based seed compost. Sow three seeds per pot and thin to leave the strongest seedling in each pot.

Almost alone amongst the brassicas, calabrese objects strongly to the upheaval caused by transplanting. For earlier crops and protection from club root or cabbage root fly, use the pot sowing method to plant out without disturbing the roots unnecessarily.

Allow 20 plants per sq m (sq yd).

**Cultivation** Keeping the soil evenly moist at all times is as important for calabrese as it is for the other flowering brassicas.

**Possible problems** Lack of water, especially at critical periods such as in the seed bed or when the flower spikes are forming, will cause bolting and produce small, inferior heads. Caterpillars can hide more easily in the open heads; soak the calabrese in salt water before cooking if this pest is suspected.

**Growing time** 90–150 days.

**Harvesting** The picking of calabrese usually starts about July but can be as early as June if pot grown transplants are used instead.

Capsicums (sweet peppers) can be grown outdoors in mild parts of the country, but raise the seeds under glass first. Outdoor plants usually reach only 60 cm (2 ft) high.

Cut the central spike first – this is often quite large, resembling a small green cauliflower. The side shoots on each plant will then develop over the next two or three weeks. Cut only a few spikes at a time when the flower buds are lightly closed.

## CAPSICUM

The sweet pepper is an annual member of the tomato family, but it has a more distinct flavour and crisper texture than either the tomato or the aubergine. A valuable greenhouse crop, it is also reliable outdoors in most years. Its light, sweet peppery taste and crisp, crunchy texture, lends itself perfectly to salads.

**Site and soil** Sun and shelter are necessary and the soil should be fertile, well-drained and with a general fertilizer added before planting.

**Sowing and planting** Treat capsicum seeds in exactly the same way as when sowing and planting aubergines (see pages 40 to 41), except that you should plant out the seedlings with 45 cm (18 in) gaps between plants and rows.

**Cultivation** The growing requirements are virtually identical to that of aubergines, with two important exceptions. First, the plants must not have a check to growth and need frequent repotting up to planting out size. Second, do not pinch out capsicums; they are naturally bushy plants.

**Possible problems** Capsicums have a tendency, like tomatoes, to blossom-end rot if they suffer from lack of water or calcium when the fruits are swelling. This condition appears up to two weeks after the shortage that caused it.

**Growing time** 120 days.

**Harvesting** Again the same as aubergines, between July and October, with the likelihood that picking will finish earlier outdoors. Cut the fruits off, starting when the first ones are fully grown but still green, to induce further flowering. Like tomatoes, sweet peppers will ripen off the plant – more quickly in a warm place than a cold one.

**Varieties** 'Canape': an F1 hybrid, a good variety for greenhouse and outdoor growing. 'Ace': possibly even more tolerant of cold summers.

Maincrop carrots are lifted between August and October. Loosen the ground with a fork first and then clean off the soil.

## CARROTS

The carrot is a biennial (it would flower in its second year), but it is harvested in the same year as sowing. An essential crop, the early, short types are considered to have the edge over the later, longer rooted varieties.

**Soil** Deep, light, and preferably sandy soil is best for carrots. Light but shallow soils may grow a good crop of 'Kundulus' or another short- or ball-rooted variety. Root crops always come at the end of the rotation cycle when there is the least organic manure in the soil.

**Sowing and planting** Rows 15 cm (6 in) apart. Sow seeds 13 mm ($\frac{1}{2}$ in) deep, very thinly along the drill. Under glass (cloches): short-rooted in late February to early March. Outdoors: short-rooted in March to July; successionally every two or three weeks for a constant supply of fresh carrots. Intermediate- and long-rooted in April to June for later, maincrop carrots.

Root crops, including carrots, do not generally stand transplanting because the inevitable damage to the single tap root causes distorted growth and often double roots. They can, however, be raised in peat pots and planted out, pot and all; this will produce show quality carrots. In the garden, the seedlings are grown *in situ* and thinned progressively (the thinnings can be eaten) until the remaining plants are about 3·5 cm ($1\frac{1}{2}$ in) apart.

Allow 80 intermediate- and long-rooted varieties and 144 short-rooted varieties per sq m (sq yd).

**Cultivation** Keep the soil moist by watering in dry periods, otherwise sudden heavy rainfall may cause root splitting.

Annual weeds are unlikely to be a problem in the row but keep an eye open for the odd perennial weed creeping in; between the rows, hoeing and hand pulling will be necessary.

**Possible problems** Carrot fly, specific to carrots and parsnips, is the only major pest, although wireworm also attack the roots in new gardens or on ground that was old grassland. Soil insecticide (bromophos or diazinon) in the seed drill and applied around the crowns of the plants once or twice while they are growing, is the most effective control. Screening the plants to prevent access to the flies, intersowing with a disguising crop (see page 24) and resettling by watering in after thinning out are the natural alternatives to using insecticides.

The maggots of carrot fly tunnel into the roots and may cause them to rot. They are more of a problem on dry soils.

Culturally, by sowing maincrop carrots at the end of May and always lifting earlies by the end of August, you will avoid the pests' main egg-laying periods and any ensuing problems.

**Growing time** 80 days for short-rooted and 130 days for intermediate- and long-rooted varieties.

**Harvesting** Pull early carrots from June, using a fork to lever them from the soil without damage. Lift the maincrop from August to October or, in milder areas on light soil, leave them in the ground for the winter protected by straw and polythene sheeting. Roots for storage in boxes of peat or sand are lifted between October and December. Only firm, undamaged crops should be stored and they must be examined regularly through the winter for signs of rot.

**Special points** Sowing sparsely reduces labour, reduces thinning, reduces the smell of bruised plants and thus their attraction to passing carrot flies. If thinning has to be done, choose a dull or wet evening, dispose of the thinnings in the dustbin or bonfire and firm and water in the remaining seedlings.

**Varieties** Short-rooted – 'Early Nantes': a slightly tapered, tender, early favourite. 'Kundulus': a small ball-rooted, fast growing, early cropper, with a shape and length that probably makes it the best for shallow soils. Intermediate-rooted – 'Nantes Tip Top': an evenly tapering, cylinder-shaped carrot; clean and core-free flesh, which makes it excellent for eating. 'Royal Chantenay': a selection of the popular 'Chantenay Red Cored'. Long-rooted – 'Autumn King': a very long-rooted but stumpy late variety good for storing over the winter.

To grow cauliflowers successfully, you must have deep rich soil, follow planting instructions carefully and water well. They can be tricky plants to cultivate.

## CAULIFLOWER

A hardy, single-flowering head type of brassica. Like cabbage, the different varieties give a long cropping season, but its scarce gap is usually mid winter. It can spread up to 1·2 m (4 ft) wide. The mid winter gap and the time and space taken, the difficulty and unpredictability of growing the crop, all reduce its value in a small garden.

**Soil** The soil must have adequate organic manure to help conserve water.

**Sowing and planting** Rows, 15 cm (6 in) apart. Seeds, 13 mm ($\frac{1}{2}$ in) deep, not less than 13 mm ($\frac{1}{2}$ in) apart. Remove the weakest seedlings as they grow to leave transplants about 7·5 cm (3 in) apart when ready for moving. Sow all types between mid March and May. Grow the seedlings on until they are quite large plants with at least six leaves before carefully transplanting with as large a root system and as much soil as possible. Plant firmly between June and July.

Allow one plant per sq m (sq yd).

**Cultivation** Keeping the soil moist at all times is the main secret of success.

Seedlings and mature plants forming curds are most susceptible to water shortage. Mulching helps a great deal. It is a hungry crop; liquid feeding at the roots, and foliar feeding until the curd forms, will both help to ensure a much better crop. Consult brassicas (see pages 46 to 47) for points on general cultivation.

**Possible problems** Premature formation of small curds is caused by lack of water and browning of the curds by either sun scorch or frost damage. Protect from both these problems by bending the outer leaves over the centre.

**Growing time** 150–350 days.

**Harvesting** Cut the heads progressively as required, while still tight and firm. Do not leave until the flower heads begin to separate. Plants pulled complete with roots and hung up will keep some weeks in a cool place.

**Varieties** Summer: 'All The Year Round' must be the first choice as it is

Celeriac is a good speciality vegetable to try, as it is fairly easy to grow. The edible root has a delicious nutty flavour.

probably the easiest; 'Snow Crown', an F1 hybrid produces firm, round, medium-weight heads. Autumn: 'Barrier Reef' is a newer variety recommended for its good leaf cover, which protects the curd (flower) from browning frost. Winter: the so-called winter varieties actually grow through the winter and are cut in the spring, so the name is a little misleading; they are not totally hardy and even the various strains of 'English Winter', such as 'St George', are really only possible in very mild areas.

## CELERIAC

Turnip-rooted celery is much less labour intensive and somewhat easier to grow than celery. It has an attractive and distinctive nutty flavour and it does not have the problem of stringiness as it ages. In spite of these assets, however, celeriac is still a rarity in the vegetable plot.

**Soil** Soil type and conditions preferred are rich and well prepared with lots of organic manure if possible.

**Sowing and planting** Sow two seeds to a peat pot, under glass no later than February or March. Remove the weaker seedling as soon as possible to avoid disturbing the remaining one. Grow seedlings on until they have about six leaves and harden off before planting out in late May or early June.

Plant 30 cm (12 in) apart in rows 45 cm (18 in) apart.

**Cultivation** Keep well-watered for maximum growth and final size, but dry conditions do not affect flavour or texture to any degree. Keep the 'bulb' sides free of leaves and shoots as the summer progresses. Earthing-up from September protects the roots in cold areas.

**Possible problems** One or two carrot or celery pests occasionally cause problems but, apart from slugs, celeriac is remarkably trouble-free.

**Growing time** 220 days.

**Harvesting** Lift at any time, but the roots increase in flavour with size, so they are normally grown on until October before harvesting begins. Not altogether hardy but it can stay in the ground with some protection in most areas. In cold, heavy soil lift and store in boxes of peat.

**Varieties** 'Claudia': the best as it combines the flavour and solid storage qualities of 'Marble Ball' with a less lumpy exterior – a considerable bonus.

## CELERY

A member of the carrot family and originally a native of marshland, celery is a biennial grown for harvesting in its first year. In spite of its value as both a cooked and raw vegetable, it is such a complicated and time-consuming crop that you will need to be keen in order to grow it. The self-blanching types are a little easier, however, and, luckily, most commercially grown celery is now self-blanching.

**Soil** Rich, well prepared soil with plenty of organic manure is preferred by both types of celery. The trench for trench varieties should be 30 cm (12 in) deep and 38 cm (15 in) wide. Dig over the bottom as in double digging and add a generous layer of manure or compost. Tread this down well before returning the top soil, firming to within about 7·5 cm (3 in) of the trench top. The remaining soil from the trench is ridged along the sides to be used later in earthing-up the plants as they grow.

If the plants are to be grown on the level, using blanching collars, prepare the trench in the same way but completely fill it with top soil.

**Sowing and planting** Sow thinly under glass in trays or pots, in early March in a heated greenhouse or propagator; April in a cold greenhouse or frame. Transplant into deeper trays when seedlings have two true leaves. Gradually harden off when seedlings have more than five leaves.

The self-blanching varieties should be planted in blocks of short rows at 23 cm (9 in) spacing in both directions. For details of the trench for those varieties requiring this, see below. Plant 23 cm (9 in) apart. Allow 10 plants per sq m (sq yd) for the trench varieties and 15 for the self-blanching ones.

**Cultivation** Lack of water for any length of time causes plants to bolt and makes their heart stems inedible. The manure in the trench will help to conserve water, but in dry weather 20 litres per sq m ($3\frac{3}{4}$ gallons per sq yd) will be needed to top up the soil water reserve.

When self-blanching plants are well established, it is best if straw or some similar material is pushed in around the sides to assist with blanching both the inner and outer stems. Trench celery will need its first earthing-up when it is about 30 cm (12 in) high. First, tie the stems loosely together and then, in three equal stages of about 7·5 cm (3 in) each at roughly three-week intervals, earth-up to the bottom of the leaves. Using blanching collars of paper, corrugated card or polythene avoids the necessity of earthing-up.

**Possible problems** The maggots of celery fly tunnel inside the leaves, causing blistering. Affected plants may die, but in any case the stems will be bitter tasting. Picking off affected leaves will be successful if caught early enough, but using unblistered plants and spraying, if necessary, with a short-lived systemic insecticide, like permethrin and heptenophos, is the only real answer.

Slugs are the biggest problem on both types of celery, particularly when they get inside the blanching collars. Slug tape, encircling each plant, is probably the best deterrent.

**Growing time** Self-blanching 150 days; trench 250 days.

**Harvesting** Cut self-blanching varieties as needed from mid to late July. Trench varieties are usually ready by November, but the pink types are slightly hardier and can be left until December or January. Freezing destroys the crispness of celery but it still maintains its flavour for cooking. Scrub and blanch for about three minutes.

**Special points** Older seeds are known to germinate better than fresh ones. To ensure that as many as possible grow, fluid drilling of pre-germinated seed (see page 32) is particularly valuable.

**Varieties** Self-blanching varieties – 'Latham Self-blanching': resistant to running to seed. 'Greensnap': stringless. Trench types – 'Hopkins Fenlander': excellent flavour and crispness, but not easy to grow well. 'Clayworth Prize Pink': naturally pale pink, but blanches easily.

## CHICORY

Belonging to the daisy family, chicory is

A row of trench-grown celery which has been earthed-up.

### TRENCH-GROWN CELERY

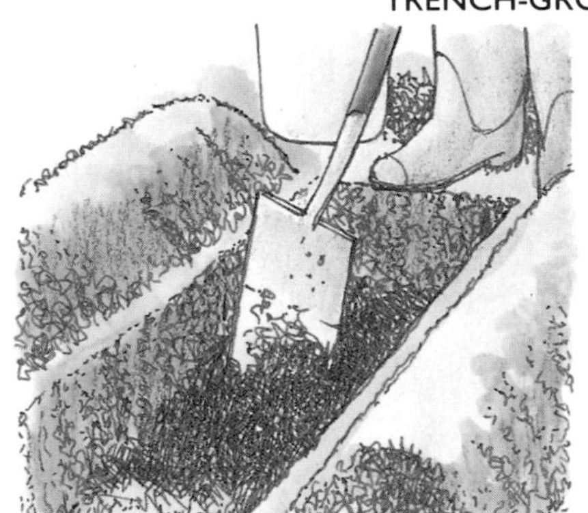

1. Dig a trench about 30 cm (12 in) deep and 38 cm (15 in) wide. Loosen the bottom of the trench to another spade's depth and add manure.

2. Tread down the trench bottom. Return the topsoil and firm to within 7·5 cm (3 in) of top. Ridge remaining soil along the trench edge.

3. When the celery reaches 30 cm (12 in) high, loosely tie black polythene or newspaper around the plants.

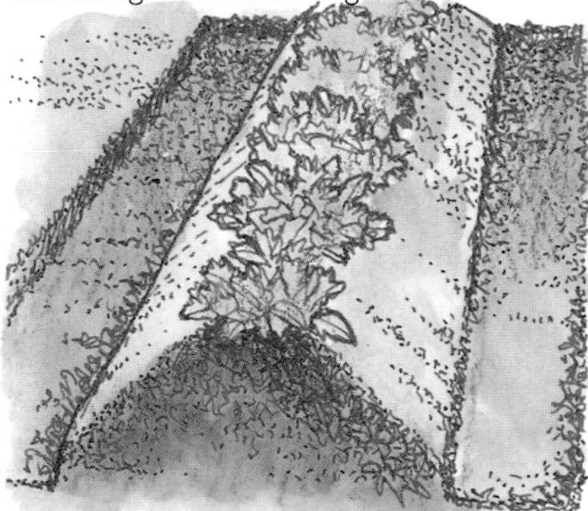

4. Earthing-up is done in three stages, at three weekly intervals. After last earthing-up, only leaves should be visible.

Two varieties of chicory: 'Normato' (left) and 'Sugar Loaf' (right).

grown for its lettuce-like leaves or, the forcing varieties for their blanched shoots or 'chicons'. It is more bitter than lettuce and not to everyone's taste, but the chicons are less bitter, much crisper and make a useful contribution to salads.

**Site and soil** Grow in any ordinary soil in an open, sunny place.

**Sowing and planting** Sow the seed of forcing varieties in May and June, the non-forcing varieties in June and July. Sow thinly 13 mm ($\frac{1}{2}$ in) deep in rows 30 cm (12 in) apart.

Thin out the seedlings to 15 cm (6 in) and then, for the non-forcing types only, to 30 cm (12 in).

**Cultivation** Keep down the weeds by hoeing, and water in dry conditions. Lift the thick roots of the forcing varieties in November, cut the leaves back to about 2.5 cm (1 in) and the roots to about 15 cm (6 in).

Pot them tightly in pots or boxes of peat or sand with the leaf crowns just showing, and keep them covered or in the dark. Also

FORCING CHICORY

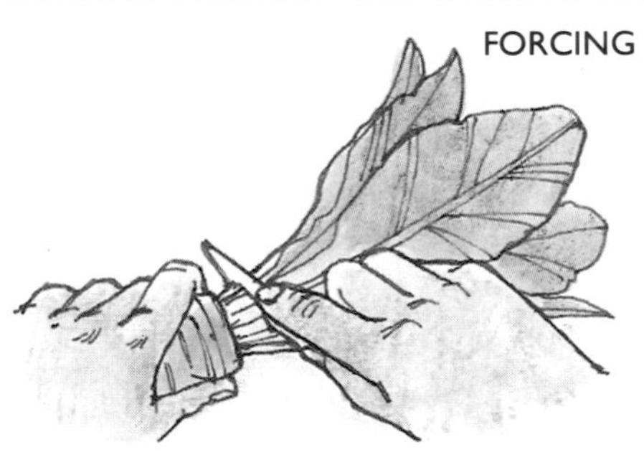

1. Lift forcing varieties of chicory in November. With a sharp knife, cut the leaves back to 2·5 cm (1 in) and the roots to about 15 cm (6 in).

2. Pot the chicory tightly in pots of sand or peat, so that their leaf crowns are just showing above the surface.

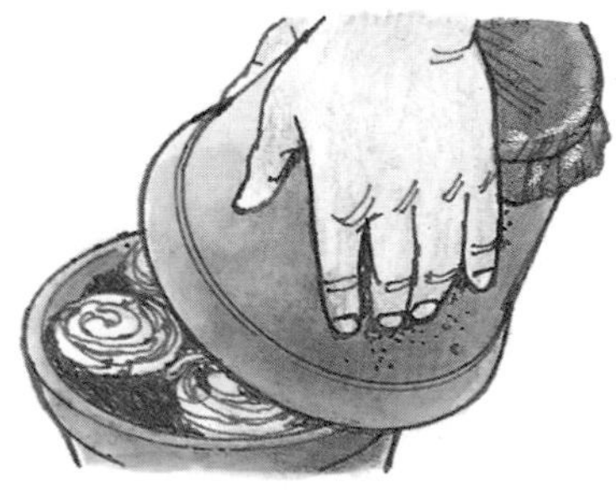

3. Place an empty pot, with its drainage holes covered by black plastic, over the chicory crowns to keep them in the dark.

4. Maintain a temperature of about 13°C (55°F) around the chicory. They are ready for cutting when they reach 15 cm (6 in) high.

its drainage holes with tiles or black plastic to exclude the light. Only blanch the plants you require for immediate use, for they soon rot once blanched.

**Special points** The winter-picked broad-leaved types will need the protection of cloches in very cold districts.

**Varieties** Curly-leaved – 'Green Curled': pretty, deeply cut, crisp leaves good for picking in late summer and autumn. 'Moss Curled': much the same. Broad-leaved – 'Batavian Green': for late autumn and winter picking. 'Golda': a newish compact variety with slightly upright leaves for easier blanching.

## FENNEL, FLORENCE

The ferny leaved fennel, a member of the carrot family, is usually grown as a herb, but the Florence form has a bulbous base which, like its foliage, has the flavour of aniseed. It can be eaten raw, boiled, steamed or braised.

**Site and soil** It requires a well drained, light, fertile soil and a sunny sheltered position if the bulb is to form.

**Sowing** Sow seed thinly in April, 13 mm ($\frac{1}{2}$ in) deep and in rows 45 cm (18 in) apart. Thin the seedlings to about 30 cm (12 in) apart.

**Cultivation** Keep well watered and feed regularly to ensure rapid and even growth. Ridge the soil around the base as it begins to swell in order to blanch the 'bulb', and continue this until it is fully swollen, about 10 cm (4 in) across.

Allow eight plants per sq m (sq yd).

**Possible problems** Running to seed or bolting will be caused by a check in growth due to insufficient watering. Watch out for slugs and snails.

**Growing time** 80 days.

**Harvesting** The bulbous base is ready for cutting through the summer and, in good years, through to early autumn if it is protected. Cut the bulb off just above ground level when it is the size of a tennis ball.

**Special points** Warm summers are needed for this crop so, in this country, an open south-facing position which receives plent of sun and is sheltered from cold wind, is essential.

**Varieties** 'Zefo Fino': is a popular bolt-resistant variety.

## KALE

Kale, a member of the cabbage family, is valuable for its hardiness and its winter-picking season. It is reasonably easy to grow and, picked young, the leaves, although stronger tasting than many brassicas, make an excellent vegetable.

**Soil** Kale will grow on any well drained ordinary soil provided it is reasonably firm. Lime may be necessary if the soil is at all acid.

Opposite: Curly-leaved varieties of endive are sown in spring and summer for cutting in summer and autumn. They have a slightly bitter taste which makes them an interesting alternative to lettuce in salads.

Florence Fennel 'Zefo Fino', grown for its swollen bulb-like base which tastes of aniseed, is only worth cultivating in the mildest parts of the country. The soil should be well drained, light and fertile and the site should be sunny.

Kale is an easy vegetable to grow as it is extremely hardy, will tolerate poor soil and is unaffected by the usual brassica problems: cabbage root fly, club root and pigeons.

**Sowing and planting** Sow the seed thinly in April or May, in drills 13 mm ($\frac{1}{2}$ in) deep and in rows 15 cm (6 in) apart. Thin the seedlings to 7·5 cm (3 in) apart and grow them on strongly until they are ready for transplanting at about 15 cm (6 in) high.

Water the rows before lifting and plant out firmly and deeply from late June to early August, 45 cm (18 in) apart between plants and rows. Water in well.

Allow four plants per sq m (sq yd).

**Cultivation** Ensure that the plants are firmly in the soil. Keep down weeds, and water in dry weather. The taller varieties may need staking to prevent wind rock.

**Possible problems** The pests and diseases which afflict other brassicas seldom affect kale. The caterpillars of the cabbage white butterfly may attack young plants. Hand picking the caterpillars is the easiest remedy.

**Growing time** 200–250 days.

**Harvesting** Pick only the youngest leaves, from the centres first, starting in late autumn. Picking stimulates the production of further tender shoots, but do not strip the plants.

**Varieties** 'Dwarf Green Curled': a smaller variety that does not require staking. 'Pentland Brig': less curly and its immature flowers can be used as if they were broccoli.

## KOHL RABI

Kohl rabi is a swollen-stemmed brassica with a taste of mild cabbage – a delicate nutty flavour and a smooth texture when eaten young and small.

**Soil** A firm, fertile, well manured soil with adequate lime, in a sunny position is ideal for kohl rabi.

**Sowing** Sow seed thinly at three-week intervals from April to August, 13 mm ($\frac{1}{2}$ in) deep, in rows 30 cm (12 in) apart. Thin the seedlings gradually until 15 cm (6 in) apart. Do not transplant, and keep well watered.

Allow 18 plants per sq m (sq yd).

**Cultivation** Weed regularly and keep protected from birds.

**Possible problems** The usual brassica troubles are uncommon because kohl rabi grows so quickly.

**Growing time** 56–80 days

**Harvesting** Begin picking when the stems are no bigger than a hen's egg. This should be in July, from April-sown seed, to November or December, from July-sown seed. They do not store: eat them straight from the ground.

**Varieties** 'Green Vienna', 'White Vienna' and 'Purple Vienna': skins of those colours, but all have white flesh and are equally good.

## LEEK

This mild member of the onion family, grown for its white base, is very hardy and thus a welcome winter vegetable. While it has a long growing season, its relatively high yield from a small area makes it an excellent crop.

**Soil** Any good, ordinary soil with reasonable drainage and sufficient humus will grow healthy leeks. Spread manure or compost the previous autumn, or dig in well rotted organic matter before planting.

**Sowing and planting** Rows 15 cm (6 in) apart. Sow seeds 13 mm ($\frac{1}{2}$ in) deep, thinly and evenly along the drill. Under glass (heated or cloches): February or March. Outdoors: March or April, or June for late cropping. Thin seedlings to 4 cm ($1\frac{1}{2}$ in) apart in rows.

Plant maincrop between June and August, earlier in the north, later in the south; May planting will give smaller and earlier leeks. Plant in rows 30 cm (12 in) apart with 15 cm (6 in) between plants. Select the best and largest seedlings, trim the roots and shorten the leaves by half. Make holes 20 cm (8 in) deep with a dibber and drop one plant in each, pour in water to puddle-in the plant and leave it to grow. The deep hole will encourage a longer white stem as the surrounding soil gradually falls in.

Allow 18 plants per sq m (sq yd).

**Cultivation** Leeks do not usually need much water, but keep the soil evenly

Leeks take up relatively little room and have a high yield, so they make excellent winter vegetables for a small plot.

Kohl rabi are not suitable for storing; eat them soon after harvesting. Though the root is usually used, it is possible to boil the young leaves, treating them like spinach.

moist, and mulch and water thoroughly in dry weather.

Allow the planting hole to fill with soil naturally, and gradually earth up to increase the blanched-stem length. Keep soil away from the leaf crown and trim back leaves if they touch the ground. Regular liquid feeding when the plants are growing strongly will increase the girth of the stems. but do not use high-nitrogen fertilizer after August.

**Possible problems** Fortunately, leeks are largely free of pests and diseases. Stem and bulb eelworm can cause distorted stems and leaves, but this is more common in onions. Rust, on the other hand, is more of a problem on leeks. There is no treatment for either bulb eelworm or rust, other than burning the affected plants and not growing this crop on the same soil for as long as possible.

**Growing time** Early and mid season types, 200 days; late types, 300 days.

**Harvesting** Early types: September to November; mid season types: December to January; late types: March to May or even June.

Early varieties tend not to be so hardy and should be used before winter sets in. Mid- and late-season types are perfectly happy left in the soil through the winter and, to release the ground for spring planting, they can be lifted and temporarily heeled-in in a spare corner of the vegetable patch.

**Special points** Their extensive, thick fibrous roots make leeks good soil improvers and thus good starter crops on newly dug land.

**Varieties** Early type – 'Walton Mammoth': an excellent culinary and show variety. Mid-season type – 'Musselburgh': a hardy and reliable favourite. Late type – 'Winter Crop': the flavour of 'Musselburgh' and even hardier.

## LETTUCE

Lettuce will grow in most soils and most gardens. Sown under glass (for transplanting outdoors) or outdoors in succession over spring and summer, it can provide you with a regular supply of fresh leaves.

Loose leaf lettuce varieties such as 'Salad Bowl' and 'Red Salad Bowl' do not have a heart. The leaves are picked a few at a time, with the plant remaining in the ground – and productive – for several weeks.

**Soil** Fertile well-drained soil. Not too acid and kept moist. Dig compost or well-rotted manure into soil in autumn or winter. Before sowing or planting rake to fine tilth and apply general fertilizer.

**Sowing and planting** Indoors: sow in trays or small compost-filled peat pots, two seeds per pot. Thin out leaving the stronger seedlings. Harden off and transplant outdoors, setting 30 cm (12 in) apart in rows. Outdoors: from March to July, sow seed thinly in shallow furrows 10 mm ($\frac{1}{2}$ in) deep and 30 cm (12 in) apart. Alternatively, you can buy strips of young plants and plant them in rows as above.

**Cultivation** Water well, and keep down weeds between rows with a hoe.

**Possible problems** Protect seedlings from birds and slugs. Greenfly and grey mould can affect the crop, and they may bolt if short of water or overcrowded.

**Growing time** For butterhead and cos varieties, 56–100 days; Crisphead varieties, 56–100 days; Loose leaf varieties, 42–56 days.

**Harvesting** Pick when a firm heart has formed. Cut with a knife or pull up the entire plant. Leaves of loose leaf varieties can be picked off when required.

**Special points** Lettuces are suitable for intercropping: grow between rows of

'Webb's Wonderful', with its large, firm heart, is one of the most popular crisphead lettuces.

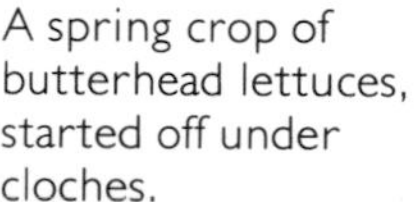

A spring crop of butterhead lettuces, started off under cloches.

slower growing vegetables or with ornamental garden plants.

**Varieties** Butterhead – 'All Year Round' suitable for sowing all year around, unlikely to bolt. 'Buttercrunch': a summer cropper with a compact crunchy heart of creamy leaves. 'May Queen': early summer variety with red-tinged leaves. 'Tom Thumb': early summer variety which matures quickly and has fine flavour, compact and good for small plot. Cos – 'Little Gem': quick maturing and compact early summer cropper with a sweet flavour. 'Lobjoits Green': large deep green very crisp leaves, early summer variety. 'Paris White': large pale green, crisp, variety, for summer cropping. Crisphead – 'Iceberg': crisp, white-hearted lettuce for spring and summer sowing. 'Webbs Wonderful': large-hearted lettuce for summer cropping, succeeds in hot weather. 'Windermere': sow under glass or outdoors for early summer crop, quick maturing and fine head. Loose leaf – 'Salad Bowl': cut and curled leaves which can be regularly picked off plant. 'Red Salad Bowl': reddish-brown leaves for regularly picking off plant, summer cropper.

## MARROW, COURGETTE, PUMPKIN AND SQUASH

These are all frost-tender annuals belonging to the cucumber family. Courgettes are simply young marrows; pumpkins and squashes are the American counterparts. They all take up a lot of room during the heaviest cropping season and, although courgettes can be prolific producers, the low number of fruits cut make them only really worthwhile in a large garden.

**Soil** Any good soil enriched with compost or manure will grow satisfactory marrows, etc, but for large crops the traditional marrow mound or pit is still probably the best way. A 30 cm (12 in) cube is dug out, the soil from it mixed with an equal volume of well rotted manure or compost, and the hole refilled with this, leaving a low mound on which the seedlings or seeds are planted.

**Sowing and planting** Under glass: sow two seeds, not before April, in 7·5 cm (3 in) pots of peat-based compost and keep warm. As soon as true leaves appear between the seed leaves (cotyledons) pull out the weaker ones. Outdoors: sow *in situ* in early June or when all danger of frost is past. Use the same procedure as under glass.

These vegetables are all very cold-sensitive; do not plant out the seedlings until after the last frost. This is usually June, but recent years have been much colder and there are always exceptionally cold areas. Set the plants deeply – they will root from their stems – which will help to prevent wind rock. Leave a shallow saucer-shaped depression around the plant to assist watering.

Allow one to two plants per sq m (sq yd).

**Cultivation** Water copiously throughout the summer. Mulch around plants to conserve water and to keep the fruits clean. Feed continuously with a high-potash soluble fertilizer, such as Phostrogen, or liquid seaweed. Pinch out the tips of trailing varieties.

**Possible problems.** Many of the problems which afflict cucumbers could affect this group, but this is not generally so. Apart from slugs, the only common problem is likely to be cucumber mosaic virus, which causes patterning and stunting of the leaves and fruit. As aphids are carriers of this virus, the plants will have to be destroyed to prevent its spread.

**Growing time** 80–120 days.

**Harvesting** Pick courgettes frequently as soon as they are 7·5–10 cm (3–4 in) long to keep them forming. This will start about mid July. The mature fruits of marrows, squashes and pumpkins will not be ready until a little later but they can be picked and eaten at any size. For winter storage the fruits must thoroughly ripen on the plant before picking.

**Special points** Bees and other insects normally pollinate the flowers outdoors, but in cool or overcast weather they may need assistance. To hand pollinate, take off an open male flower, which is the one with pollen and without a tiny fruit behind it, remove the petals if it helps and then simply rub it into the centre of the female

'Vegetable Spaghetti' so-named because of spaghetti-like strands which form inside the fruit when it is boiled, is a variety of squash.

Marrows, frost-tender vegetables grown in the summer, take up considerable space – they are only worth considering in a large vegetable garden.

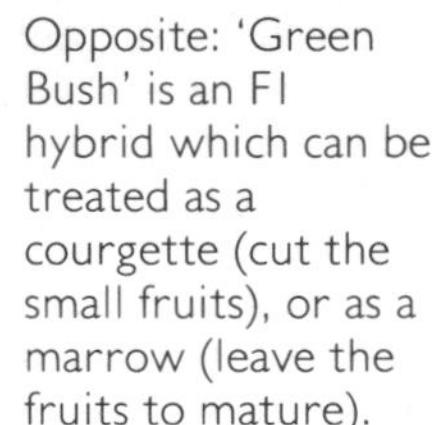

Opposite: 'Green Bush' is an F1 hybrid which can be treated as a courgette (cut the small fruits), or as a marrow (leave the fruits to mature).

Opposite: 'Atlantic Giant', a pumpkin renowned for its record-breaking size and excellent flavour.

flowers, the ones with a tiny swollen fruit behind them.

**Varieties** Marrow – 'Green Bush': the most compact, ideal for small gardens. Courgette – 'Aristocrat': for earliness and high yield. 'Gold Rush': for colour and flavour. Pumpkin – 'Atlantic Giant': not only the biggest, it also has the most flavour. Squash – 'Vegetable Spaghetti' is fun and quite tasty; spaghetti-like flesh. Custard marrows are more attractive than useful except for wine making.

## ONION AND SHALLOT

The leaf-like layers of onions show that they are bulbs and, apart from the leek, they are the only true bulbs grown for eating in this country. Onions are also unique in being grown from both seed and sets (small immature bulbs). Shallots divide to produce a clump of small bulbs from a single full-sized bulb while spring onions are grown from seed. Alternatively use the thinnings from bulb varieties, as spring onions for salads. Whether from seed or sets, they are a good value crop.

**Soil** Onions will grow perfectly well in any good garden soil with sufficient organic content. Sets will tolerate less fertile conditions and less humus in the soil than seed-raised plants.

**Sowing and planting** Rows, 23 cm (9 in) apart. Sow seed 13 mm ($\frac{1}{2}$ in) deep, very thinly, no less than 6 mm ($\frac{1}{4}$ in) apart; Japanese seed, 25 mm (1 in) apart. Remove weakest gradually until they are finally 10 cm (4 in) apart. Under glass: sow in December, traditionally Boxing Day, or into January. Plant out in April. Outdoors: sow in February and March, or August for late sown and Japanese varieties.

Before sowing or planting, fertilize the soil and rake over it when dry. Stamp down the soil and rake the ground again to ensure a fine surface.

Plant sets in rows 23 cm (9 in) apart, with sets 10 cm (4 in) apart. Trim off tips before planting, and plant firmly with tip just showing to help deter birds pulling them up.

Allow 80 bulbs per sq m (sq yd).

**Cultivation** Keep soil moist and mulch

to conserve water. Water only in very dry weather and not at all as the bulbs ripen.

Such a low-growing crop is very susceptible to being swamped by weeds. Hoe carefully, preferably with the traditional short-handled onion hoe. When the leaves fall over naturally to herald the start of ripening, deliberately bend them down away from the direction of the sun. Pulling soil away from the crowns and sides of the bulbs will also assist ripening.

**Possible problems** Birds may pull out sets. The onion fly lays eggs in the soil and the grubs eat into the base of the bulb. Dress seed bed with bromophos or diazinon or use sets which are not affected. Premature running to seed can be caused by planting too early in cold years. The larger sets aggravate this problem, so select small firm ones, no larger than 20 mm ($\frac{3}{4}$ in) across. Pick off any flower heads and use these bulbs as soon as possible. Bullneck, a distinct thickening of the bulb at the point where the leaves start, is the result of too much softening nitrogen fertilizer or too much manure. Feed with a high-potash soluble feed until the bulbs stop swelling.

**Growing time** Spring-sown seed, 150 days; autumn-sown, 300 days. Sets, 150 days. Shallots, 130 days.

**Harvesting** Autumn-sown and Japanese onions are ready for harvesting about June. Spring-sown seed and sets will be ready from about August onwards. Thinnings may be used as salad onions. Use any bolted (those with flowers) or bullneck onions first. About two weeks after the bulbs have had the soil pulled away from them they can be carefully lifted and laid out to dry in the sun.

For storing, onions must be thoroughly ripened and very firm. Japanese onions do not keep well. Store others in plaited ropes or in the legs of old tights, with a knot between each bulb. The next one up will not then fall out when the bottom one is cut off for use.

**Varieties** Seed – 'Ailsa Craig': still the favourite globe-shaped bulb. 'Bedfordshire Champion': a large, round onion, similar to 'Ailsa Craig' but can be stored for longer. Downy mildew is frequently a

As soon as the onion leaves start to fall over, bend them towards the ground and away from the sun to encourage the bulbs to ripen.

Below: For each shallot set planted, 8–12 similar-sized bulbs will be produced in a cluster in the summer. When the leaves turn yellow, usually in July, lift and separate the clusters of bulbs.

'Brunswick', a medium-sized onion with a mild flavour, is grown from seed. It has excellent keeping qualities.

problem. 'Reliance': flat bulbs, stores well, good for autumn sowing in warmer areas. 'Imai Yellow': hardier Japanese variety, medium, flat bulb for autumn sowing. Sets – 'Sturon': globe-shaped, does not easily run to seed and very large. 'Rijnsburger': the best for storage. 'Unwins First Early': for autumn planting. Shallots – 'Hative de Niort': mild. 'The Aristocrat': for quantity. 'Paris Silver Skin' or 'Barletta': for pickling. Spring onions – 'White Lisbon': quick growing with a mild flavour. 'Ishikura': straight sided and does not form bulbs.

## PARSNIP

A biennial root crop used in its first year before flowering. In the same family as the carrot, but a quite different vegetable with a distinct flavour which is not always appreciated.

**Soil** Deep, full-bodied soil, without fresh manure, is best but they will grow perfectly well on any reasonable soil.

**Sowing and planting** Rows 30 cm (12 in). Sow seed 13 mm ($\frac{1}{2}$ in) deep, 15 cm (6 in) apart in threes. For even, long straight roots, sow in deep conical holes made with a dibber or stick and filled with sieved soil or loam-based seed compost, at the same spacings. This is a particularly good method on shallow soils. Sowing seed from late February to April is the normal recommendation, but recent trials have shown that later sowing, until June, still produces a satisfactory, if slightly smaller, crop.

Like most root crops, parsnips are not usually transplanted but sowing in tall sweet pea tubes and transplanting these whole, without disturbing the roots, is successful and allows earlier sowing in warmer conditions and an earlier crop. Fluid drilling is also useful since the main reason for sowing three seeds at each growing position is that parsnips germinate erratically.

Allow 20 plants per sq m (sq yd).

**Cultivation** Overwet conditions encourage canker but this is a deep-rooted crop so you will only need to water in a drought. Weed carefully; damage to the root crown increases the risk of canker.

'White Lisbon' is a quick growing spring onion suitable for sowing in succession.

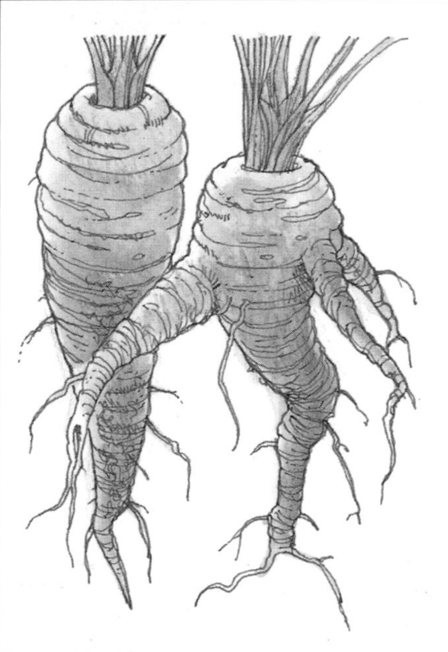

Parsnips grown on over manured soil may develop forked roots.

**Possible problems** Canker is a disease specific to parsnips and is usually worse on acid soil with too much humus. Sowing too early in cold, wet soil aggravates the condition. Liming and choosing a resistant variety helps prevent it.

**Growing time** 250 days.

**Harvesting** Parsnips are ready from a normal sowing by about early November, but as they are perfectly hardy in all but the most severe winters, they may be left in the ground and used as required. There is nothing to stop you digging young, immature roots before the main season, but this crop is the one proven case of frost actually improving its flavour. Lift carefully with a fork. Unless the space is required, there is no point in freezing them although they freeze quite well if cubed and blanched for five minutes.

**Special points** As parsnip seed rapidly deteriorates, always use fresh seed from sealed foil packets.

**Varieties** 'Tender and True': good for flavour, reliability and size. 'White Gem'; shorter, with excellent flavour and resistance to canker.

## PEA

An annual legume, peas are the most popular vegetables for eating whether canned or frozen – but with the home gardener they take second place to their cousins the broad, runner and French beans. In fact, although freshly picked garden peas are superior in flavour, this is the only advantage they have for they are not superior in nutritional value.

**Soil** For a worthwhile crop the soil needs to be very deep and fertile. Deep digging and plenty of organic manure, at least 12 kg per sq m (25 lb per sq yd) are indispensable. Lime should be used to keep the soil neutral to slightly alkaline.

**Sowing** Pea varieties are quite variable in height – from 'Meteor', a round-seeded

Above: To grow long, straight-rooted parsnips, sow the seed in a deep, conical hole filled with fine, sieved soil or a loam-based seed compost.

Right: 'Bikini', a pea bred for easier picking since it has fewer leaves and more tendrils than most peas.

early at about 30 cm (12 in), to 'Alderman', a maincrop at about 1·5 m (5 ft). The distance between the rows should be the same as the variety's ultimate height. It is a good idea to consider growing the taller varieties up leaning wire-covered frames as these will make the best use of the space and deter weeds between rows. Seeds should be sown about 5 cm (2 in) deep, with 7·5 cm (3 in) between them, in three staggered rows in 15 cm (6 in) wide, flat-bottomed drills.

Under glass (cloches): hardier, round-seeded varieties can be sown in October or November, in warmer areas, or February and March in colder ones, for an earlier crop. Outdoors: sow every three weeks from April to June for successional crops.

Allow 30–40 plants per sq m (sq yd).

**Cultivation** Lack of water could prevent pods swelling, but this is not common since peas only suffer in very dry weather. Mulching will probably be sufficient protection.

Nitrogenous fertilizer is not usually beneficial and may be harmful, but one or two extra feeds of liquid potash fertilizer will increase the crop, especially if the weather is at all dry.

All varieties need protection and support. Two or three single strands of black cotton, not nylon thread, above the seed row will hinder birds. Shaking the seed in a little powdered seed dressing before sowing or stretching a renardine-soaked string along the soil surface, will both deter mice.

Late sowings will need the protection of cloches from August onwards if they are to crop reliably.

**Possible problems** Little maggots inside the pods are the tiny caterpillars of the pea moth. The only good prevention is a reasonably persistent spray such as dimethoate or fenitrothion. In cold, dry weather, mildew is quite common and, in addition to conserving water in the soil, an organic sulphur or triforine spray may be necessary.

**Growing time** Autumn-sown, about 200 days; spring-sown, about 100 days.

**Harvesting** The early sowings under cloches will be ready for picking from May or June onwards; later sowings from July to September. Mangetout and petits pois about August.

It is important to harvest peas regularly – if pods are allowed to mature for too long on the plant they will reduce its likely yield.

Peas at their best are soft and sweet – when the pods are well rounded but not completely full. Test harvest one or two to make certain they are at their peak. Mangetout should be 7·5 cm (3 in) long and no more. Pick from the bottom of the plant upwards; do this regularly to keep them coming.

For freezing, shell, blanch for one minute and dry very thoroughly.

Dried peas must be left on the plant to ripen completely. In wet weather cut off the whole plant and hang up to dry in a cool place before shelling. After harvesting, cut off the dried tops and leave the roots in the soil to release their nitrogen.

**Special points** Support is essential; twiggy pea sticks must be pushed in on the rear side of the seedlings when they are no more than 7·5 cm (3 in) high or, for the taller varieties, use the pea frames mentioned earlier. Seedlings easily become damaged or eaten by slugs.

Until the pea plants meet between the rows, the spaces make ideal areas for intercropping salad crops.

**Varieties** First earlies – 'Feltham First': a round-seeded hardier type, 'Kelvedon Wonder': for successional sowing. Second Earlies – 'Onward': the usual choice. 'Bikini': has much reduced leaves and tendrils in their place which makes the pods easier to see and pick. Maincrop – 'Senator': both a heavy cropper and tasty. Mangetout (literally 'eat all') – 'Sugarsnap': the pods and the young peas are eaten without shelling; this variety is also useful for growing on as a maincrop. Petits pois are not simply baby peas but small

Early varieties of seed potato like 'Vanessa' should be sprouted before planting. Stand them, with their eyes uppermost, in shallow trays and keep in a cool, well lit place until 2·5 cm (1 in) long green sprouts appear.

Below: Brown patches on the foliage – the early signs of potato blight.

extra-sweet types, the best variety being 'Waverex'.

## POTATO

A half-hardy perennial in the same family as the tomato, this familiar root crop is always referred to as a tuber, but is strictly an underground stem, as can be seen from its 'eyes' which are the buds that normally appear spaced up the stems of above-ground plants. The early (new) potatoes are worth growing, unless you have plenty of space for a quality maincrop variety.

**Soil** Any reasonable soil, well prepared, dug and manured the previous autumn, will raise a good crop. Never add lime as it encourages common scab disease.

**Planting** Potatoes are supplied as 'Certified Seed' (medium-sized potato 'sets', not real seed), which is raised under special disease-free conditions and certified by the Ministry of Agriculture as being pure and clean.

Plant earlies in rows 60 cm (2 ft) apart, the 'seed' 30 cm (12 in) apart, 10–15 cm (4–6 in) deep. Maincrop in rows 75 cm (30 in) apart, the 'seed' 38 cm (15 in) apart, 10–15 cm (4–6 in) deep.

Sprouting seed potatoes before planting is vital for earlies and advisable for maincrop. Look for the eyes: most are towards the 'top' of the tuber and each has its 'eyebrow' underneath it. Stand the tubers, supported in damp peat if necessary, with their top ends uppermost, in shallow boxes – seed trays will do. Keep the trays in a well lit, cool place until firm, dark green sprouts about 2·5 cm (1 in) long have formed from the upper eyes. This will take a month to six weeks if started in February, and they will then be ready for planting.

For a small supply of new potatoes at special times of the year, allow about twelve weeks before the special occasion and plant some tubers in pots or boxes in a greenhouse.

Allow about two to four plants per sq m (sq yd) of ground.

**Cultivation** The earthing-up and the plant's large leaf canopy conserve water effectively around the roots, but once the tubers begin to form, right through to harvesting, it is vital not to allow the soil to dry out. Up to 20 litres per sq m (4 gallons per sq yd) every week may be necessary.

When the shoots are through the ground by about 23 cm (9 in), draw up the soil from the sides to make ridges around the bases of the plants. An alternative to this is to plant through black polythene sheeting – no earthing-up is then needed, weeds are effectively eliminated and the potatoes can be harvested a few at a time. The tubers form more or less on the surface and earthing-up is intended to keep them covered to prevent them greening (green tubers are mildly poisonous) and to encourage a larger crop. Polythene has both of these effects.

**Possible problems** Potato blight is the most serious disease; there is no cure, only prevention is possible. In warm

Left: By drawing soil into ridges around the base of potato plants when they are about 22 cm (9 in) tall, you help retain moisture around the roots.

Opposite: 'Desiree' is a popular maincrop variety easily distinguished by its pink flesh.

humid weather, soft brown patches appear on the leaves and later spread to the tubers. The only action is to watch the weather and the crop, and if blight is likely, spray with a copper fungicide or dithane. The odd infected plant must be pulled out and burned before the disease spreads to the others.

Flat, warty-like growths on the surface are usually common scab disease, but this is superficial and the crop is perfectly safe to eat provided you peel it first.

All plants that like a high-potash diet may show signs of magnesium deficiency from time to time, in yellowing on the older leaves between dark green veins. Epsom salts, 12·5 g per litre (2 oz per gallon) sprayed on the plants and soil will cure this. Alternatively, avoid the deficiency in the first place by feeding with a high-potash soluble fertilizer to which magnesium has been added.

**Growing time** Earlies, 100 days; maincrop, 150 days.

**Harvesting** Early potatoes are ready for lifting when their flowers open. Check a few plants first to see if they are a reasonable size. Dig them as required.

Maincrop are ready about two weeks after the foliage withers and dies – take it off as soon as this happens and leave the rows exposed until lifting. Use a flat-tined potato fork, keeping well back from the line of the row to avoid spearing the tubers. Always clear the ground completely of even the smallest tuber to prevent problems in the following year.

**Special points** Newly dug ground, especially old turf, will invariably be infested with wireworms which can easily ruin a potato crop. Dressing the soil with

'Wilja' is a reliable early potato with high yields and a reasonable flavour.

'Maris Piper' has high yields and good cooking qualities.

an insecticide at planting time should prevent this.

Potatoes are particularly useful for breaking new ground because their canopy shades-out weeds and the earthing-up exposes a large surface area to weathering, thus improving the soil's structure. Some gardeners maintain that soil becomes more fertile if it is mixed with a potato leaf compost, but this has not been proved.

**Varieties** First earlies – 'Pentland Javelin': not the earliest new potato but a heavy cropper and a good smooth, moist texture for those who do not like dry potatoes. 'Epicure': somewhat hardier. Second earlies – 'Wilja': a solid, good cooker of reasonable flavour and high yield. 'Maris Peer': has useful scab resistance, but objects to dry conditions and thin soils. Maincrop – 'Desirée': a personal favourite with superb flavour; a heavy cropper and resistant to most diseases other than scab. 'King Edward': still a favourite for its reliability and cooking quality, but it is not a heavy cropper.

## RADISH

A quick growing annual root crop belonging to the cabbage family, ideal for salads. In addition to the popular round, red-skinned radishes there are several other summer types: cylindrical (or intermediate) – about the size of a thumb, red- and yellow-skinned; long – white skinned. Although they are not so often grown, there are also large winter varieties of radish, some of which have an unusual black skin.

**Site and soil** Rich and fertile, manured for a previous crop. Add a little fertilizer before sowing and rake the soil finely. The summer crop needs shade.

**Sowing** Summer varieties: in rows 15 cm (6 in) apart in drills 13 mm ($\frac{1}{2}$ in) deep. Under cloches: in January and February. Outdoors: in March. Water the drills before sowing. Sow successionally at two-week intervals until the end of May – results for summer-sown seed are generally unsatisfactory – further sowings can be made from mid August to mid September. It is vital to thin the seedlings to 2·5 cm (1 in) apart. Winter varieties: rows 23 cm (9 in) apart. Sow July to early August and thin to 15 cm (6 in) apart.

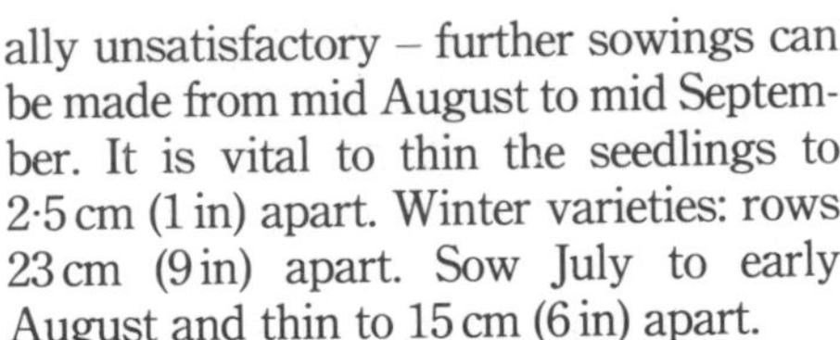

For the winter varieties allow 12 plants per sq m (sq yd).

**Cultivation** Always keep the crop adequately watered to prevent bolting and the formation of woody roots. Keep down weeds.

**Possible problems** Slugs can be a nuisance, particularly with the winter types. Birds may pull out seedlings, so protect with cotton or a net. Holes in the leaves are likely to be caused by larvae of the flea beetle – spray with liquid derris or, better still, use an insecticide when sowing.

**Growing time** Summer varieties, 20–40 days; winter varieties: 70–84 days.

**Harvesting** The round, cylindrical and long types must be pulled while they are still young, before they become woody and hot flavoured. The large winter types are hardy and best left in the soil, protected by a covering of straw or peat until needed; they can be lifted and stored like carrots.

**Special points** Because radishes are so quick growing they are best treated as catch crops or for intercropping when other vegetables will provide some shade.

**Varieties** 'Cherry Belle' (round): red

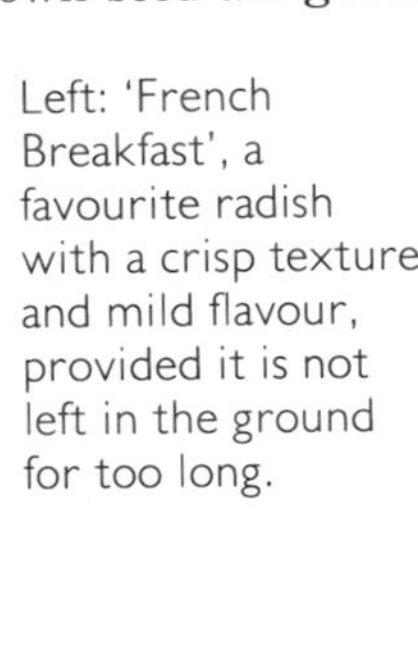

Left: 'French Breakfast', a favourite radish with a crisp texture and mild flavour, provided it is not left in the ground for too long.

Right: Spinach can be sown in succession from March to May to give a steady supply through the summer.

Only pick the younger outer leaves of ruby chard. Carefully pull them off at the base of the plant to include the gorgeous red stems which can be eaten with the leaves.

skin, mild flavoured and crisp. 'French Breakfast' (cylindrical): quick growing with crimson skin and good white flesh. 'Long White Icicle' (long): white outside and nutty in flavour. 'China Rose' (winter): long, oval root, bright rose skin, crisp white flesh. 'Black Spanish Round' (winter): black skin, good flavour.

## SPINACH, SPINACH BEET AND LEAF BEET

Although all the plants used as spinach are members of the fat hen family, they are not all spinach. To the true summer and winter spinach is added the New Zealand spinach, spinach beet, the 'perpetual' spinach, and leaf beet or Swiss chard which is a spinach substitute. Spinach is not to everyone's taste.

**Soil** Good, deeply dug soil with plenty of organic manure is essential. This is not always appreciated and is possibly why spinach often proves so difficult, easily running to seed. Leaf beet is far less demanding, easier to grow and therefore a better choice for the beginner. All spinach likes slightly acid to neutral soil and liming may therefore be necessary.

**Sowing and planting** Ordinary spinach: rows, 30 cm (12 in) apart; sow seed thinly, 2·5 cm (1 in) deep; thin to 15 cm (6 in). Summer spinach: sow successionally every three weeks from March to May. Winter spinach: sow August and September. New Zealand spinach: grow in stations 60 cm (2 ft) apart. Sow three seeds per station, about 20 mm ($\frac{3}{4}$ in) deep, pull out the two weakest as they grow. Sow seed in May. Leaf beet: rows, 38 cm (15 in) apart; sow seeds 10 cm (4 in) apart, 2·5 cm (1 in) deep; thin to 30 cm (12 in) apart; sow seed in April.

Allow 30 plants per sq m (sq yd) for ordinary and New Zealand spinach and three plants to the same area for leaf beet.

**Cultivation** Spinaches are not excessively demanding of water, but mulching will be appreciated and extra watering in dry weather to prevent bolting.

**Possible problems** Downy mildew makes the foliage inedible in cold wet weather. Copper spray is the only answer.

Shading will reduce bolting, so growing on the shady side of, or between, larger crops will provide this condition. Pick off any flowers to keep leaves growing. Protect winter spinach and leaf beet with cloches or by lagging the plants with straw or bracken.

**Growing time** Summer and winter spinach, 75 days; New Zealand spinach, 40 days; leaf beet, 100 days.

**Harvesting** Ordinary summer spinach from successional sowings will crop from May to November and winter spinach from November to May. In theory, this covers the whole year but, in practice, there is likely to be a short gap in May. New Zealand spinach should crop from June to about September, depending on the season. Both types should be picked carefully, nipping off the leaves without tearing. They are quite robust plants and up to half the leaves may be picked at a time.

Leaf beet can be pulled a little in the winter, but mainly in August and September. Take only the young outer leaves while they are tender and pull them off complete with the base, like rhubarb, being extra careful not to pull up the plant. Keep the pickings as clean as possible.

**Special points** Hungry spinach of any kind will be bitter and possibly earthy flavoured. Give extra base dressing and liquid feed well throughout the summer.

**Varieties** Ordinary summer spinach – 'Norvak': a new hybrid, producing large yields and slow to run to seed. Ordinary winter spinach – 'Broadleaf Prickly': a very dark green leaf, slow to run to seed (the seeds prickly, not the plant). New Zealand spinach is sold purely as that; there are no variety names. Leaf beet 'spinach' or Swiss chard, and the red-stemmed ruby chard are grown for their thick leaf stalks as well as their leaves. Spinach beet is the perpetual spinach and is grown like the chards.

Test for the ripeness of sweetcorn by peeling back the outer leaves and squeezing the seed. It is ready if a milky fluid is released.

## SWEDE

A member of the cabbage family and closely related to the turnip, the swede is generally much hardier and milder flavoured. Like the turnip, it is not a great favourite although it was a staple food for most people up until this century. Its reputation undeservedly now rests on the unattractive way it is sometimes served up as mash, particularly by institutions. However, it is worth growing to add variety to the range of crops harvested in the winter months.

**Soil** Like all brassicas, swedes need firm planting in non-acid, free-draining soil which has been amply manured for the previous crop.

**Sowing** Rows 38 cm (15 in) apart. Sow seed thinly 13 mm ($\frac{1}{2}$ in) deep; thin seedlings gradually to leave best and strongest 23 cm (9 in) apart. Sow successionally from April to June.

Allow 10 plants per sq m (sq yd).

Always use a fork to lift swede. Being hardy, it can be left in the soil till needed. Alternatively store in boxes of moist peat.

**Cultivation** Keep soil where the crop is growing evenly moist, to prevent the swedes becoming woody.

**Possible problems** Cabbage root fly can be a pest and is difficult to control culturally with collars. Soil insecticide, such as diazinon, may be the only answer. As with turnips, swedes are susceptible to boron deficiency, but this is more likely to affect swedes in the form of brown heart. Dissolve 36 g of borax in 10 litres (1 oz in 1 gallon) of water and apply evenly over 17 sq m (20 sq yd).

**Growing time** 160 days.

**Harvesting** Lift as required for eating from early autumn. They are completely hardy and can be left in the soil, although they will store equally well in boxes of moist peat if this is more convenient; stored dry, they tend to lose water and become tough. There is no point in freezing swedes.

Always lift with a fork, and do not pull them up.

**Special points** Like brassicas, swedes are very susceptible to club root. Do not grow them on the same soil each year, and dress the seed drill with lime, mercurous chloride or benomyl.

**Varieties** 'Marian': club root resistant and has a good flavour. 'Acme': a quick growing variety.

## SWEET CORN

Sweet corn is a member of the grass family, familiar in the supermarkets but still not widely grown in home gardens. The difference in flavour of the freshly picked and cooked cobs is sufficient reason for growing it.

**Soil** A well drained, humus-rich, water-retentive soil is necessary for success.

**Sowing and planting** Sow two seeds to a peat pot of compost in a greenhouse in April for planting out in early June. Pull out the weaker seedling as soon as possible. In the garden, sow seed in May under cloches or early June in open ground. Sow in blocks rather than rows, perhaps among decorative garden plants, or as a windbreak, again putting two seeds in each position and removing the weaker seedling.

Transplants and seedlings should be planted 45 cm (18 in) apart in both directions to form the planting block which aids wind pollination and thus ensures a good crop.

Allow four plants per sq m (sq yd).

**Cultivation** Sweet corn plants root from their stems and earthing-up helps steady them in windy weather. Keep the plants well watered in dry weather and liquid feed when the cobs are forming.

Tap the plants on a dry, still day to release pollen from the male flowers at the tops. Pollen will drift down on to the 'silks' (the female flowers) below to help ensure a good set of seed.

**Possible problems** The maggots of fruit fly can cause, among other things, poor sized cobs; it is best to play safe by dressing the seed with an insecticide. If any swellings appear on the plants, which is possible in hot summers, cut them off immediately and burn them. After harvesting burn the plants and do not grow sweet corn on the same plot for at least four years.

**Growing time** 100 days.

**Harvesting** When the cobs are swollen and firm peel back the outer leaves to test for ripeness. The seeds should release a milky cream when squeezed if they are ready to eat; a watery fluid means that the cob is still unripe. Another sign that the cobs are nearly ready for picking is that the fine white threads at the top of the cobs start to turn black. Pick just before needed to ensure freshness.

**Special points** This crop is unlikely to be successful unless grown in an open, sunny site.

**Varieties** 'First of All': a reliable early variety and a good choice for cooler areas. 'Northstar': for northern areas. 'Kelvedon Glory': for size and flavour.

'Outdoor Girl', recognized by its slightly ribbed fruits, is one of the earlier outdoor tomatoes to ripen. It is a heavy cropper and has a good flavour.

All cordon varieties of tomato must be supported with bamboo canes and trained (see opposite page).

TRAINING CORDON TOMATOES

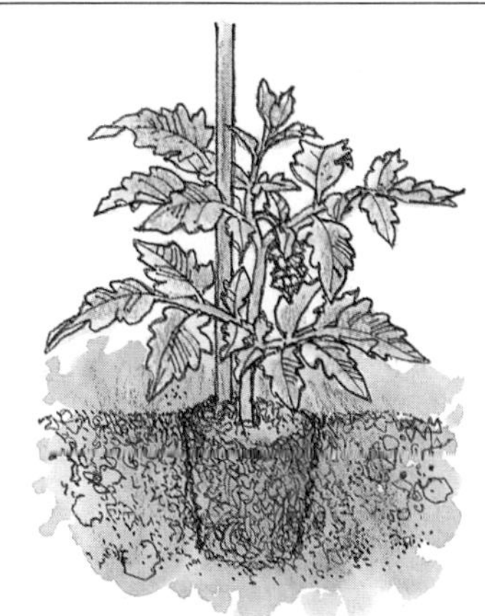

1. Drive in a bamboo cane, before planting seedlings. They are ready when flowers on the first truss are opening.

2. As the tomato plant grows, loosely tie the main stem to the bamboo cane, using string.

3. Where a leaf stalk joins the main stem, side shoots will grow. Pinch these out, before they grow too large, sapping strength from the plant.

## TOMATO

Certain tomato varieties can be grown outdoors in mild parts of the country, given a sunny sheltered spot.

**Soil** During previous winter, dig garden compost and well rotted manure into the soil. Rake in a general fertilizer before planting. They can also be grown in pots or growing bags.

**Sowing and planting** Sow under glass at beginning of April. Set seed 2·5 cm (1 in) apart in trays of seed compost and germinate in propagator or plastic bag. Prick out into pots of potting compost. Plant out six to eight weeks after sowing, when flowers are visible on first truss. Bought, ready-grown seedlings can be planted out in late May to June. Rows 75 cm (30 in) apart for cordon varieties and 60 cm (2 ft) apart for bush varieties. Planting distance 45 cm (18 in) apart. Allow six cordon varieties per sq m (yd) and four bush varieties per sq m (yd).

Tomato seedlings can be planted in growing bags when 15–20 cm (6–8 in) tall.

**Cultivation** Stake cordon varieties. Remove side shoots at leaf joint and pinch out growing tips when four to six trusses have formed. Bush varieties do not need staking or pinching out. Water frequently. Feed weekly with a liquid tomato fertilizer when small tomatoes form on first truss.

'Yellow Perfection' ripens earlier and has a sweeter taste than other yellow varieties.

Bush tomatoes rarely require staking. They will grow in any sunny spot.

**Possible problems** Look out for aphids, grey mould, tomato leaf mould, foot rot and virus diseases.

**Growing time** 140 days.

**Harvesting** Pick in August and September when the fruit is ripe and fully coloured. Hold the fruit in hand and press the stalk with thumb to break it at the 'knuckle'. Before frost arrives, remove unripened tomatoes and ripen in a drawer alongside a ripe apple or tomato.

**Varieties** Cordon – 'Ailsa Craig': gives a heavy early crop of good flavoured medium-sized tomatoes. 'Alicante': resistant to greenback, is an early heavy cropping variety with excellent flavoured fruits. 'Marmande': produces large well flavoured beefsteak tomatoes. 'Sweet 100':

has cherry-sized well flavoured fruit. 'Yellow Perfection': has sweetly flavoured yellow tomatoes. Bush varieties – 'Pixie': a heavy cropper with small well flavoured fruit, ripens quickly. 'Red Alert': early maturing good cropper, small well-flavoured tomatoes. 'The Amateur': early, large crop of medium-sized tomatoes.

## TURNIP

Another member of the brassica family, turnips are grown both for their roots and their tops which are used as spring greens.

**Soil** Like swedes and the other brassicas, turnips require a firm soil with a good residue of humus from the previous crop and sufficient lime to keep the soil neutral (pH 7 or just below).

**Sowing** Sow seed thinly about 13 mm ($\frac{1}{2}$ in) deep. Earlies: rows 23 cm (9 in) apart and thin the seedlings to 13 cm (5 in) apart. Under cloches in February; outdoors in March and April. Maincrop: rows 30 cm (12 in) apart and thin the seedlings to 23 cm (9 in) apart. Sow first batch March or April, then every three weeks or so until July. Spring greens: rows 7·5 cm (3 in) apart in July and August. No thinning is required. Allow 15 plants per sq m (sq yd) for roots; 40 plants for turnip tops.

**Cultivation** As with swedes, too little water causes woody, tough roots. Fluctuation in the soil's water supply can cause roots to split. Extra feeding with liquid seaweed or soluble fertilizer will keep the crop growing strongly.

**Possible problems** Soft rot causes slimy brown rot inside the turnip; outside it appears normal, but leaves droop. Damage by hoeing, too much manure and prolonged wet soil all contribute to this.

**Growing time** 42–82 days.

**Harvesting** Begin to lift early turnips when they are about egg size – at this stage they can be pulled like radishes. Lift maincrop varieties as soon as they are big enough to use, about October. They are not as hardy as swedes but in most areas they can be left in the soil until needed. In cold, wet districts lift with a fork, twist off the tops and store in boxes of peat.

For spring greens, cut the leaves from March or April onwards, depending on the weather; the plants will respond to this by producing several crops of leaves.

**Special points** Early varieties of turnips need more care and better soil conditions than maincrop varieties.

**Varieties** Early – 'Snowball': the best white-fleshed early. Maincrop – 'Golden Ball': tender, yellow-fleshed, mild flavoured. Spring greens – 'Spring Top White'.

Above: 'Sprinter', one of the smallest and earliest of early turnip varieties.

Left: 'Golden Ball', a yellow-fleshed maincrop turnip which keeps well.

# HERBS

A vegetable garden would not be complete without a small selection of culinary herbs. Either grow them in a plot on their own, perhaps in a group of small formal beds edged with clipped box or rosemary (arranged in a geometrical design reminiscent of the Elizabethan knot gardens) or have them alongside your vegetables. The ornamental herbs – thyme, sage, borage and rosemary, for example – can be cultivated in flower and shrub borders, or in pots if space in the beds is at a premium. Herbs also grow well in windowboxes.

If there isn't room in the vegetable garden for herbs, grow them in pots and windowboxes on a sunny part of the patio. Here they will be close at hand for the cook, and their sweet fragrance can be enjoyed by anyone sitting near by.

## GROWING HERBS

### SITE AND SOIL

As most popular herbs come from southern Europe or the Mediterranean region, they need a sunny site sheltered from cold winds – the south or west side of the house, a wall or thick hedge are ideal. With the exception of mint, angelica and parsley, which thrive best in moderately moist soil, all the other herbs listed here need a well-drained medium which is not rich. Too rich a soil produces sappy growth of poor flavour and keeping quality.

### SOWING AND PLANTING

Though most herbs can be raised from seed, it is often simpler, and certainly less trouble, to buy the plants – available in spring. With shrubby herbs like rosemary and bay, you will probably only need one plant of each. Even with the popular perennials like chives and mint, a few specimens are sufficient.

If you decide to raise the herbs from seed (see individual entries for suitable species), sow the seed in February or March in pots of seed compost. Cover the pots with a plastic bag, sheet of glass or place them in a propagator. Keep at a temperature of 18–21°C (65–70°F) out of direct sunlight.

When the seedlings appear, take them out of the propagator, or remove the glass or plastic bag and place them in a lighter spot, perhaps on a windowsill or in the greenhouse. As soon as one or two true leaves appear (after the seed leaves), prick the seedlings out into separate pots. Grow them on, then harden off in a cold frame and plant out in May. Hardy perennial herbs can also be sown directly outdoors in a seed bed in May.

### CARE

Most herbs are easy to grow, given a suitable site and soil. Keep the ground around them well weeded, and pick them regularly, so their shape remains neat and compact. The more invasive plants – mint, for example – should also be trimmed occasionally to prevent them from choking the entire bed. Every three years, the perennial herbs should be replaced, either by taking cuttings or by using division.

### PROPAGATION

Perennial and shrubby herbs can be increased by division or taking cuttings. (See individual herb entries for suitable methods.)

**Division** In late winter and early spring, lift established clumps out of the ground. Divide them into even-sized pieces, using your hands or a fork if the

LIFTING AND DIVIDING CHIVES

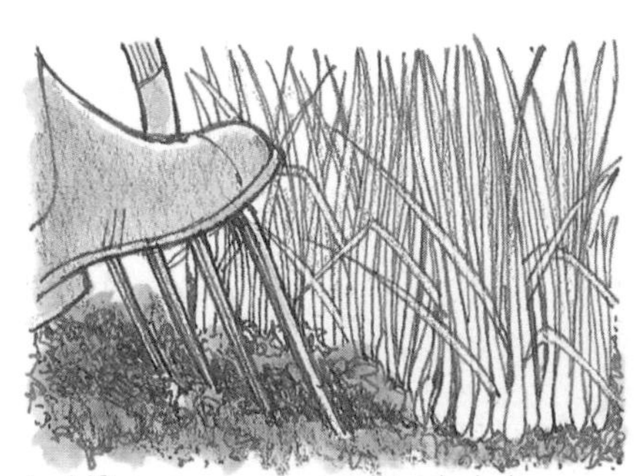

1. Lift mature or overcrowded clumps of chives out of the ground, using a garden fork.

2. Divide into smaller clumps, by prising the roots apart with your hands or a small fork.

3. Plant out the new divisions, without delay, in the desired position. Make sure that the chives are well watered.

roots are entangled, and then replant in the desired position.

**Cuttings** Take cuttings in summer from semi-ripened shoots. Make a diagonal cut into the stem just below the junction with a side shoot; make another cut just above the junction with the side shoot. Dip the cutting in hormone rooting powder and then root it in a pot of seed compost or a half-sand, half-peat mixture. Cover the pot with a plastic bag, sealed with a rubber band and place in a cold frame or on a windowsill.

Both the seeds and young leaves of the caraway plant can be used in cooking.

### HARVESTING AND DRYING

Herbs grown for their young stems and foliage – e.g. angelica, borage, chives, fennel and parsley – must be harvested before flowering. All are best used fresh, but the last three can be dried. A few herbs are grown for their seeds, e.g. dill and fennel. For these, the seed crop must be yellowing and starting to turn brown. Lift or cut the plants at ground level, tie them in small bundles and hang head-downwards in a warm, dry place until the seeds fall easily when you touch them. Strip the seed and store in sealed opaque jars in a cool dry place.

Bulbous herbs such as garlic are lifted when the leaves yellow, dried in the sun or in any dry place, then cleaned and hung up for use. The remaining herbs described below, though best used fresh, can be dried for winter use. Just as the plants come into flower, gather healthy sprays and space them out in trays kept in a warm airy place. An airing cupboard or the warming drawer of a stove are suitable provided there is adequate ventilation. Turn the herbs once a day until they feel brittle to the touch. Crumble them and store in opaque jars. Ideally herbs should be kept somewhere that is both cool and dark so they retain their freshness.

## A–Z OF HERBS

### ANGELICA

A robust, upright biennial or short-lived perennial which, if allowed to flower, reaches 1·8 m (6 ft) or more in height. It has handsome leaves divided into several leaflets and clusters of tiny greenish flowers. Only clusters of the young leaf and flower stalks are used in the kitchen. Raise new angelica plants from seed.

### BASIL

This half-hardy annual, also known as sweet basil, can grow into a bushy, upright plant 60 cm (2 ft) or more in height,

TAKING CUTTINGS OF SHRUBBY HERBS

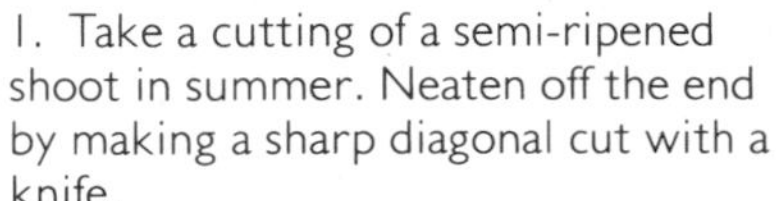

1. Take a cutting of a semi-ripened shoot in summer. Neaten off the end by making a sharp diagonal cut with a knife.

2. Carefully strip the leaves off the lower end of the cutting to leave the stem bare. Do this gently with your hands.

3. Wet the bottom end of the cutting with water and dip in a pot of hormone rooting powder to encourage roots to grow.

4. Fill trays with seed compost or a half-sand, half-peat mixture. Using a matchstick, make holes and insert the cuttings.

5. Firm in the cuttings with your fingertips, and then gently water them, using a fine rose on a watering can.

6. Cover with a clear polythene bag, keeping the polythene off the leaves. Place on a warm windowsill.

Bay, an attractive evergreen shrub or small tree, can be trained into a standard.

with small, oblong leaves in pairs. The tiny tubular flowers are white. Use the clove-scented leaves when they are young. Raise from seed.

**BAY**

Also know as sweet bay, this is the tree whose leaves were used to wreathe famous people in ancient Greece. Although an almost hardy evergreen tree, it stands clipping well and can be easily rooted from cuttings so it is not necessary to provide a lot of room for its growth. The aromatic leaves are best used when newly matured. Propagate by taking cuttings.

**BORAGE**

A decorative hardy annual up to 60 cm (2 ft) tall, but often less. It has large, rough, oval leaves smelling of cucumber and sprays of sky-blue starry flowers used for decorating desserts and summer cocktails. Raise from seed.

**CARAWAY**

This hardy annual forms slim stems 60 cm (2 ft) or more in height, bearing ferny leaves and topped by flat heads of tiny white flowers. Its seeds are used in cooking, but young leaves can be chopped and added to salads. Raise from seed.

**CHERVIL**
Similar in overall appearance to caraway, this biennial reaches about 45 cm (18 in) and is grown for its parsley-flavoured leaves. Raise from seed.

**CHIVES**
This densely tufted perennial has grassy, hollow leaves 25 cm (10 in) long with a delicate onion flavour. If allowed to develop, 2·5 cm (1 in) wide globular heads of small rose-purple flowers top the foliage. Ideally, pinch out the flower spikes when small to promote more leaves, and use young leaves in preference to mature ones. Raise from seed or propagate by division.

**COMFREY**
A tall wide-spreading perennial which has coarse, rough leaves, blue or creamy white flowers and reaches 60–90 cm (2–3 ft) high. It is used as a medicinal herb and can be cooked like spinach or added to a salad. Raise from seed.

**CORIANDER**
An annual grown mainly for its spicy, aromatic seeds, though the leaves are sometimes used as a garnish. Grow in full sun in a light rich soil, sowing the seeds in very early spring. Plants can be thinned to 10–15 cm (4–6 in) apart. When seeds have turned a light greyish-brown, cut down the plant and leave to dry for two or three days. When dry, shake out seeds and store. Raise from seed.

**CUMIN**
A slender annual reaching 30–60 cm (1–2 ft), the plant has long thin leaves and small pink or white flowers. Cumin is grown for its seed alone. Raise from seed.

**DILL**
Much like fennel but with a single stem reaching 90 cm (3 ft) high, this annual is grown for its aniseed-flavoured leaves and seeds. Raise from seed.

**FENNEL**
This is a graceful clump-forming perennial which can be grown for decoration as well as edible values. Its dark, almost blue-green, sweetly aromatic leaves are finely divided. The flowering stems are best removed when young, unless seed is required. Allowed to grow unrestricted,

The graceful, finely divided leaves of fennel make it a suitable herb to grow as a feature, surrounded by a low-clipped hedge.

Left: For a regular supply of chives, remove the flowerheads before they open and cut the leaves when they are still young.

Here, a simple but stunning herb garden has been created by growing the clumps of herbs between paving slabs. Where a large bed was needed, several slabs were lifted and the ground underneath prepared for cultivation.

When the leaves on garlic plants turn yellow in July or August, lift the plants and hang them up to dry in the sun.

fennel will reach 1·5–2·5 m (5–8 ft) high and produce flattened heads of tiny yellowish flowers. Raise from seed or propagate by division.

**GARLIC**
The familiar white bulb of this plant is composed of several narrow bulblets known as cloves. The narrow leaves grow to 45 cm (18 in) tall. Sometimes, rounded heads of tiny, white, purple-tinged flowers are produced on stems above the leaves. Propagate by separating the cloves and replanting them.

**HORSERADISH**
A hardy perennial with large floppy leaves growing from the base of the plant to a height of 60–90 cm (2–3 ft). The flowers are white on a single stem but do not appear every season. The large thick roots are used for cooking. Plant out young shoots, or bury pieces of root.

**HYSSOP**
This hardy perennial grows up to 45 cm (18 in) in height. With its woody growth, technically it is a low shrub but it needs annual pruning to keep it low and compact. The narrow, aromatic leaves are in opposite pairs, and small tubular blue, pink or white flowers form showy upright spikes. Both leaves and flowers can be used to flavour stews and salads. Raise from seed or take cuttings.

**LEMON BALM**
Sometimes simply known as balm, this is a clump-forming hardy perennial with pairs of corrugated lemon-scented oval leaves and clusters of small, tubular, white flowers which form leafy spikes. The leaves can be used fresh or dried. Raise from seed or propagate by division.

**LOVAGE**
In leaf, this clump-forming perennial resembles celery. It will send up stems 2·5 m (8 ft) high which branch and bear clusters of yellowish flowers. Both the seeds and leaves are used. Raise from seed.

**MARJORAM**
Usually listed as sweet marjoram, this is a shrubby-based perennial grown as a half-hardy annual from seed. It has slender stems about 45 cm (18 in) tall with pairs of oval leaves and loose clusters of small, knotted flower spikes bearing minute white or pinkish flowers. Its leaves are mainly used for flavouring meat dishes. Raise from seed.

**MINT**
There are several different kinds of mint. All are hardy perennials 60–90 cm (2–3 ft) high and all can be invasive. They have opposite pairs of simple leaves and spikes of tiny, tubular, mauve flowers. Common spearmint is the form most usually grown, with smooth, bright green lance-shaped leaves. Apple mint has broadly oblong to rounded, white, hairy leaves. Peppermint yields the world's supply of peppermint oil. It is similar to spearmint (one of its parents) but is easily distinguished by its smell. Propagate by division.

**PARSLEY**
This familiar hardy biennial, which can also be grown as an annual, forms a tufted rosette of finely cut leaves which are flat in the original species but in the best known varieties are 'crested' or mossy. If allowed to flower it produces an upright branched stem to 45 cm (18 in) or more with tiny yellowish flowers. Parsley is a good plant for edging the herb garden, and is ideal for growing in a container. Raise from seed.

**PURSLANE**
An attractive tender annual with succulent leaves, small yellow flowers, and upright reddish stems, purslane grows up to 15 cm (6 in) high. It has a sharp clean flavour which is best combined with other herbs. It is essentially a salad herb but the young shoots can be cooked as a vegetable. Purslane must not be sown until

One sage plant will usually provide enough leaves for a household. Every summer after flowering, trim the plant to keep it neat. As it is not long-lived, replace every three years.

Grow purslane, a slightly tender evergreen, in a sunny sheltered site.

Parsley grows best in rich soil in a shaded site. Raise it from seed for picking that year.

May when all danger of frost has passed. It needs sandy soil with a sunny aspect. Raise from seed.

**ROSEMARY**

A bushy evergreen shrub reaching up to 1·5 m (5 ft) or more high, this herb has dark, almost needle-like leaves and lavender, sage-like flowers. The leaves go well with meat dishes. Propagate by taking cuttings.

**RUE**

This 60 cm (2 ft) high evergreen shrub is primarily grown for its dissected blue-grey leaves and open clusters of yellow flowers with cupped petals. The pungent smelling foliage can be used to flavour egg and fish dishes. Propagate by taking cuttings.

**SAGE**

Like mint and parsley, this is a very popular herb. It is an evergreen shrub reaching 60 cm (2 ft) high with finely wrinkled grey-green leaves and spikes of quite large, tubular, two-lipped blue-purple flowers. Raise from seed or propagate by taking cuttings.

**SALAD BURNET**

A clump-forming hardy perennial, reach-

If growing herbs in a large border, set the tallest ones – fennel, for example – at the back and the shorter clump-forming varieties towards the front, so each plant receives maximum sunlight.

ing 60 cm (2 ft) or more when in bloom. The leaves are composed of 9–21 oval leaflets and have an almost fern-like quality. The flowering stems are best removed when young to promote more young leaves, for harvesting and use in salads and sauces. Raise from seed or propagate by division.

**SAVORY**

There are two kinds of savory: summer and winter. Winter savory is a small hardy, wiry shrub 15–30 cm (6–12 in) tall with small narrow leaves and short spikes of small, pale purple flowers. Summer savory is a slender, upright hardy annual with similar but longer leaves and white to pale purple flowers. The leaves of both are used in fish, egg and salad dishes. Raise from seed or propagate by cuttings.

**SORREL**

A low growing herb with acid tasting leaves. It is commonly used in salads and in soups. Raise from seed.

**SWEET CICELY**

A slow growing perennial which may reach a height of 60–150 cm (2–5 ft). It is a fragrant plant with a sweet aniseed flavour and can be used in salads or omelettes. Cut off any small white flowers as they appear; this will help the leaves retain a stronger flavour. Raise from seed.

**TARRAGON**

This not quite fully hardy perennial forms wide clumps of upright stems about 60 cm (2 ft) high. The narrow lance-shaped leaves are a greyish-green and an essential constituent of *fines herbes*. Small, greenish, bobble-like flower-heads may appear in good seasons. Propagate by taking cuttings of rooted shoots.

**THYME**

Several sorts of thyme have herbal uses, but the two most popular are common thyme and lemon thyme. Common thyme produces hardy, wiry, spreading evergreen shrublets to 20 cm (8 in) or more in height with tiny leaves and small pale purple to whitish flowers. Its leaves are grey-green, finely hairy and aromatic.

Lemon thyme has a low-growing neat habit and bears clusters of deep pink flowers. A mild-flavoured herb, it can be used in savoury dishes or in sweet jellies, desserts and drinks. Propagate both common and lemon thyme by division or taking cuttings.

# PESTS AND DISEASES

In extreme cases pests and diseases can cause havoc in the vegetable patch. But if you take simple measures to prevent their arrival in the first place, can recognize the pests and diseases if they do occur, and are well prepared to deal with them, they shouldn't be a problem.

## GENERAL PREVENTION

By following a few basic rules, it is possible to greatly reduce the likelihood of pests and diseases in your plot.

### HEALTHY SOIL

A healthy, well-fed soil with sufficient manure and fertilizer will grow strong disease- and pest-resistant plants. It is worth remembering, however, that lush and over-fed specimens will also be susceptible to attack, so check your plants regularly – at least once a week.

### HYGIENE

Keep your garden clean. Rotting cabbage and rhubarb leaves will harbour diseases and pests. Weeds, likewise, are often 'host plants' carrying pests and diseases to infest your crop. Even dry debris, such as stones, bricks and wood, provides hiding places for slugs, earwigs, millepedes and woodlice, all of which attack plants.

### CROP ROTATION

This method of cultivation helps to prevent a build-up of a particular pest or disease, though in today's smaller gardens it may not be as effective as it was in the larger plots of the past.

### CAREFUL HANDLING

Damaged plants attract pests and encourage disease. Avoid bruising, cutting or crushing them. Thin, pick and hoe between crops with care.

### SOWING THINLY

Sown too thickly, seed rots easily below ground and seedlings are prone to the damping-off disease. Sowing more thickly than recommended is a good way of getting an additional early crop from the same ground, so you need to strike a balance.

### CHOOSING CROPS AND VARIETIES

Some crops are more resilient and many varieties are specially bred for pest and disease resistance of one kind or another. The potato 'Pentland Javelin', for instance, is resistant to scab, and some tomato varieties have virus, eelworm, wilt and 'greenback' resistance. Make sure the variety is suitable for growing in your area. Some varieties only flourish in a particular type of soil or climate, so check carefully before you buy any seeds or

Scarecrows will only deter birds effectively if they are moved occasionally.

seedlings. Always read any accompanying labels or instructions.

**PROTECTION**

Building a high windbreak around the vegetable garden will prevent a great many pests blowing in, but in many cases this is difficult. It's far easier simply to erect a polythene screen around vegetables likely to be affected: carrots and celery, for example, can be hidden from their respective flies which search at or just above ground level looking for food. This, in turn, prevents the flies from laying eggs on the topsoil, so that the roots are then less likely to be eaten by grubs.

Cabbage flies will not be deterred by a polythene screen but you can at least prevent them from laying their eggs in the soil near the base of the brassica stems. Place some carpet underlay, cut in circles with a central hole and a radial split joining this to the circumference, around the young cabbage stems, or buy cabbage collars which serve a similar purpose.

**DISGUISE**

By planting certain crops together (see Intersowing page 24) one crop can be used to disguise the smell of the other from a potential pest. Spring onions, for example, will disguise the smell of carrots and deter carrot fly. This is not considered a very

Leatherjackets tunnel into root crops and eat the stems and lower leaves.

ABOVE-GROUND PESTS

**Greenfly** Small greenfly aphids usually appear outside in the spring, or throughout the year in greenhouses. Spray outside plants with an insecticide such as menazon or diazinon.

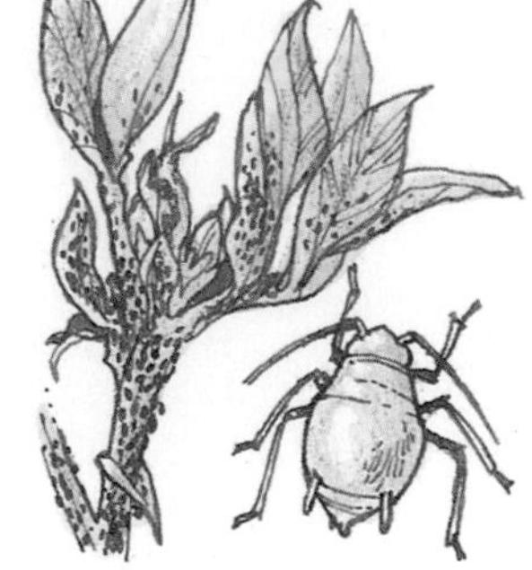

**Black bean aphids** These sap plants of energy. Outside plants are vulnerable between May and July. Before flowering, treat them with an insecticide like pirimphosmethyl.

**Cabbage whitefly** Found on undersides of the leaves of cabbages, Brussels sprouts and other brassicas, and appear from May to September. Spray with dimetheote.

**Caterpillars** Appearing from March onwards, they eat holes in the leaves of most plant varieties. Remove by hand or treat with derris or malathion.

**Celery fly** Maggots appear in April and leave brown blotches on celery and parsnip leaves. They may kill the plant. Treat crops with malathion.

**Earwigs** Eat beetroot, carrot and parsnip leaves, making ragged holes. They appear between May and October. Dust or spray with malathion or HCH.

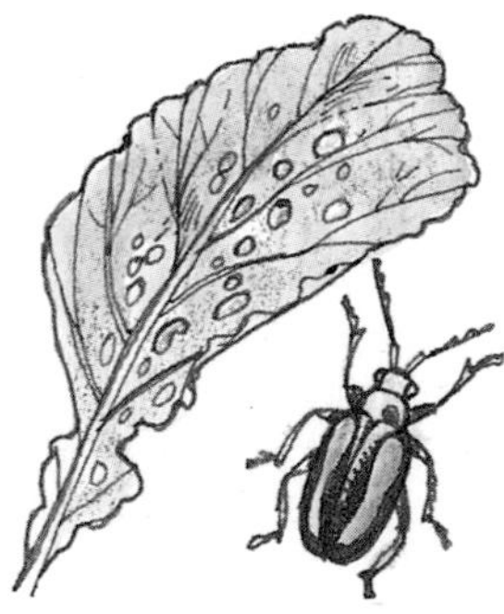

**Flea beetles** Cabbages, turnips and radishes can be affected in May. They make small holes in young leaves. Dust seedlings with derris to prevent damage.

**Pea thrips** Live on pea foliage, and leave a silvery trace behind. They like hot, dry summer weather. Dust or spray plants with malathion or HCH.

**Pea and bean weevils** Eat the edges of pea and bean leaves in a semicircular pattern, between March and June. Dust young plants with HCH immediately.

A colony of aphids on Brussels sprout leaves. Spray them immediately as they will weaken the plant and may be carrying viral diseases.

reliable method of control. Only one out of ten trials seems to work. A better way of dispersing the plant smells which attract pests is, after thinning seedlings, to water the row thoroughly and firm in the seedlings well.

### DETERRING BIRDS

The most practical bird scarers are the quiet ones like scarecrows, flapping polythene strips or tin foil discs and, more recently, imitation birds of prey. Research has shown that even these are only effective if they are moved about from time to time; otherwise the birds soon become accustomed to them.

A variation on the scarecrow theme is a

### BELOW-GROUND PESTS

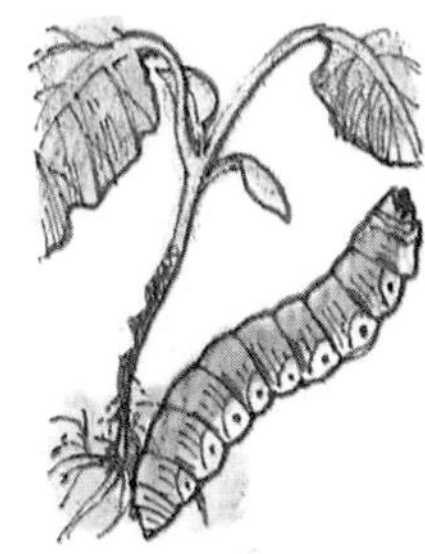
**Cutworm** Eat through lettuce shoots at ground level in early spring and late summer. Weed to reduce the risk of infestation. Alternatively, work bromophos well into the soil.

**Cabbage root fly** Newly transplanted brassicas such as Brussels sprouts will collapse if attacked by the maggots of this fly. Protect between April and September by applying diazinon.

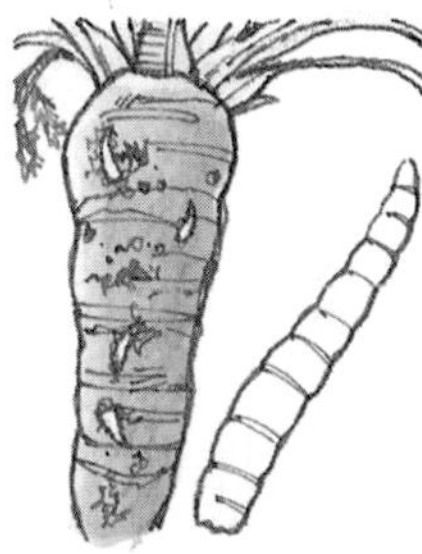
**Carrot fly** Celery, carrots and parsnips are damaged by tunnelling carrot fly maggots. Water plants with diazinon two or three times in August and September to prevent damage.

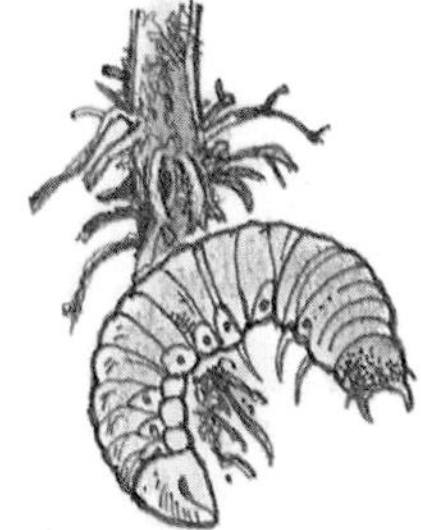
**Chafer grubs** Curved in shape and over an inch long, they feed on a variety of roots. Use a soil fumigant on the larvae and kill beetles by spraying stems with BHC.

**Leatherjackets** The larvae of craneflies, these appear between April and June, usually in wet weather. They attack most vegetables. Protect with diazinon.

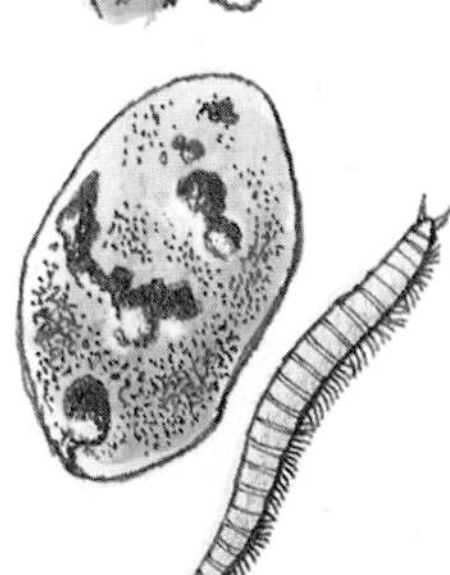
**Millepedes** Tunnel into potatoes and other root crops during late summer and autumn. Deep cultivation in well-manured soil should help to keep them at bay.

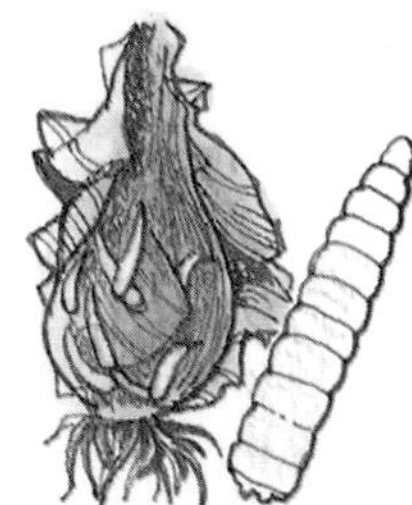
**Onion fly** Between May and August their small, white maggots feed on decaying onion, leek or shallot tissues. Water roots two or three times with trichlorphon.

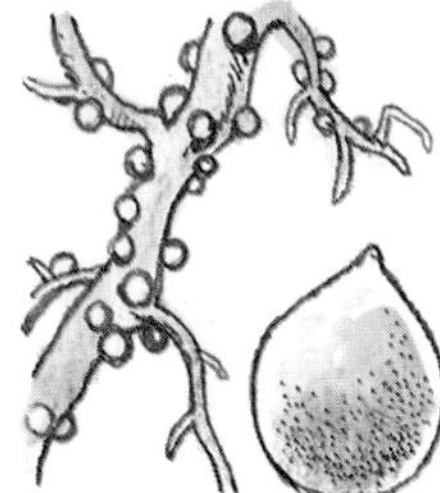
**Potato cyst eelworm** Potatoes and tomatoes are susceptible to these pests between July and September. In severe cases, do not plant on the site for five years.

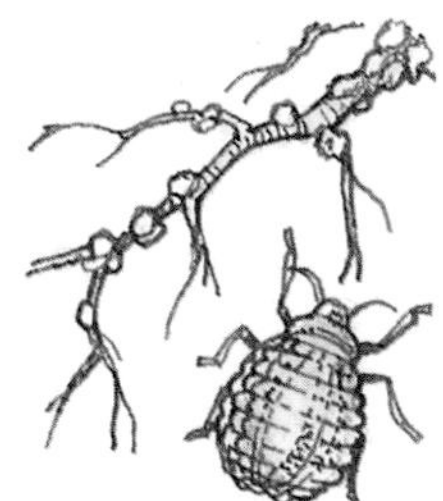
**Root aphids** White colonies affect the young shoots of broad beans from May to July outdoors, causing leaves to yellow and wilt. Water roots with diazinon.

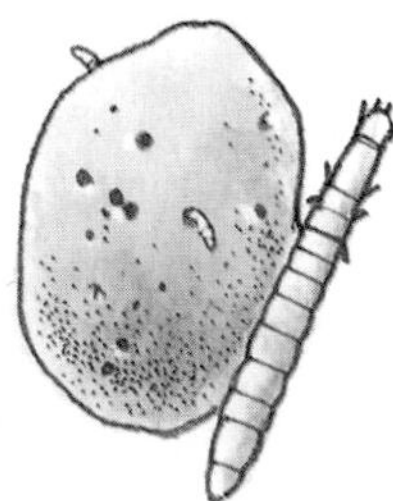
**Wireworms** These feed mostly on tubers, stems and roots of potatoes, tomatoes and lettuces. HCH can be applied to susceptible crops.

**Slugs and snails** Leave a trail of slime and damage the leaves, stems and roots of a variety of vegetables. Water soil with a liquid slug (and snail) killer.

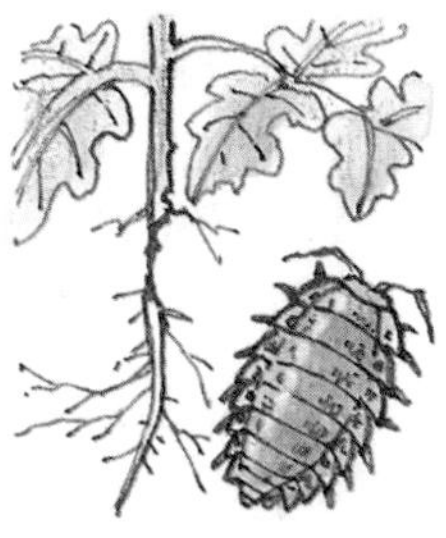
**Woodlice** Generally attack seedlings and young plants in greenhouses at night. Dust or water soil around seed boxes with BHC to deter them.

special wire which, when tightly stretched across the plot, produces a humming sound in the wind that keeps birds away. Black cotton, zig-zagged across the plot – another alternative – is frowned on by conservationists because birds can easily become entangled in it – a particular problem if the thread used is an indestructible synthetic material, which can kill the birds. But a single strand of real black cotton 2·5–5 cm (1–2 in) above a row of seeds or seedlings is most effective, as the birds dislike having to avoid it while they attempt to feed.

If pigeons are a problem the only effective answer is to thoroughly net over the plants. It's worth doing, though, as a couple of pigeons are capable of completely devastating a brassica bed, stripping every leaf to a bare rib.

Look out for cabbage white caterpillars on brassica leaves between April and October. The first indication of their presence will be holes in the leaves.

### DETERRING MAMMAL PESTS

The damage caused by dogs and cats is often difficult to repair. They also represent a health and hygiene hazard so some form of prevention is essential. Pepper sometimes deters them, but it is not always effective. Renardine works reasonably consistently on all larger mammals (rabbits, mice and moles included), but it does have an unpleasant smell when used in large quantities. Small stakes with a renardine-soaked sacking strip wrapped around their tops, pushed into the soil at intervals around the plot, will keep the mammals away most effectively. Alternatively, you can soak a single strand of thick hairy string in the liquid and lay this along the soil of a seed row or seedling bed to deter mice. (Make sure you keep the string off the plants.)

To deter moles mix a tablespoon of renardine into a jam jar full of sharp sand. Tightly seal the jar, and keep it handy so that at the first sign of a mole hill you can put a spoonful of the mixture down the hole beneath the hill. Make sure that the tunnel is completely open and not blocked by earth, so the smell can spread throughout the mole run. You're unlikely to have trouble from moles after that.

Slug damage on radishes. To prevent slugs arriving in the first place, keep garden rubbish well away from the vegetable patch. If you see any slime trails, lay slug pellets around the plants.

## CURATIVE MEASURES

If, in spite of preventive measures, pests still arrive, there are two ways of getting rid of them: cultural and insecticidal.

### CULTURAL CONTROL

These are methods which encourage nature to prevent the pest problems.

**Birds** A vast number of caterpillars and aphids are consumed by birds so it pays to encourage them to feed in your vegetable patch. The problem for the gardener is attracting the beneficial birds without exposing your crop to the ravages of pigeons. Nesting boxes with the right-sized holes and careful feeding of favoured species (leaving out fat for blue tits, for example) can work, but the unwanted bird species are bound to appear from time to time so other cultural practices will also be necessary.

**Exposing pests** Digging and hoeing to expose underground pests will make a bird's job easier. You'll find that just as the

**PHYSIOLOGICAL PROBLEMS**

**General yellowing** of a plant often signals nitrogen shortage in the soil. Treat vegetables with dressings and/or a leaf-feeding fertilizer.

**Wind scorch** causes patchy yellowing of leaves with scorched edges, and can kill plants. Protect with a wind-break or plant under cloches.

**Plants deficient in manganese** may have yellowing on lower leaves between the veins. To avoid, make sure the soil is well manured.

**Wilting foliage,** discoloration and checked growth may be the result of a water shortage. This can be prevented by composting, watering and mulching.

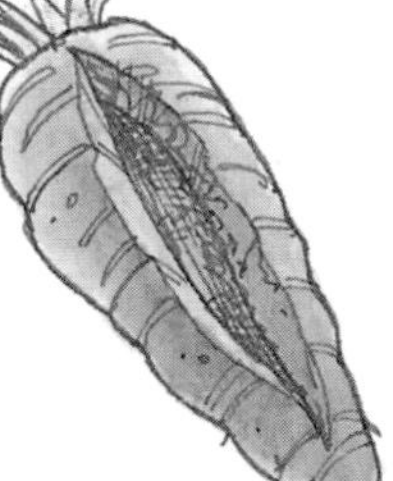

**Split roots** in tomatoes and potatoes are caused by heavy rainfall or overwatering following drought. Avoid by watering before soil dries.

**Forked roots** in carrots and parsnips are caused by over-manuring. To avoid, use land which has been manured for a previous crop; do not add more.

seagulls follow the plough, so will the robin sit close by and pick up cutworms and grubs, as well as fly pupae. After the day's digging, shrews will come out in the evening and lend a hand.

**Hand picking** A daily walk around the plot is useful for spotting pests before they become a problem. Look out for caterpillars and slugs on plants, and pick them off. If you come across a small colony of blackfly on a broad bean shoot, or a clutch of small orange cabbage white butterfly eggs on the underside of a leaf, rub them off between your thumb and forefinger.

In the soil, pick out caterpillars, grubs and slugs while digging and cultivating. With a sharp eye you may also spot slug or snail eggs: little clusters of white pearls.

A minor variation on hand picking is shoot picking: blackfly are often found on the tips of broad bean shoots, for instance. If you pick off the shoots with the blackfly you eradicate the blackfly and remove the succulent shoot which attracted them in the first place.

**Stale seed bed** This technique of weed control, which allows weeds to germinate before burning them to the ground (see page 33) is also a good way of controlling pests as it discourages many pests which would otherwise feed on the weed roots until the vegetables arrive.

**INSECTICIDAL CONTROLS**

Modern insecticides are safe used carefully and wisely, when a pest is multiplying too rapidly to control by other means. Nowadays, there is a choice between synthetic chemical insecticides, plant extracts, and natural organic soaps.

Downy mildew occurs on the undersides of leaves – it often produces a downy outgrowth.

**Synthetic chemical insecticides** A simple selection of four will give good all-round pest control: a soil insecticide, such as bromophos or diazinon; a slug bait, based on methiocarb; a specific aphid (greenfly) spray like pirimicarb, which does not affect any other insects; and a general insecticide for caterpillars and other pests, either containing the systemic insecticide dimethoate, or the contact insecticides permethrin or resmethrin. Systemic insecticides are taken into the plant's sap and kill insects which later suck it. Contact insecticides kill only those pests that are sprayed with it.

**Plant-extract insecticides** are used by gardeners who regard synthetic chemical insecticides as harmful under any circumstances. The common plant extracts are rotenone, sold as derris dust and liquid derris; and pyrethrum, which is sometimes sold under that name, in dust and spray form. The third plant extract insecticide is quassia, but this is not so widely available. All three are most effective as caterpillar, greenfly and fly killers. They are contact insecticides, killing only those pests which are actually sprayed.

## PLANT DISEASES

**Anthracnose** Patchy brown sunken areas may appear at any time on dwarf and runner beans. Destroy diseased plants and sow in a new site. Apply carbendazim, if necessary.

**Black leg** Affects potatoes in June, developing at the base of the stem. The leaves yellow and the stem dies. Plants should be destroyed and healthy tubers replanted.

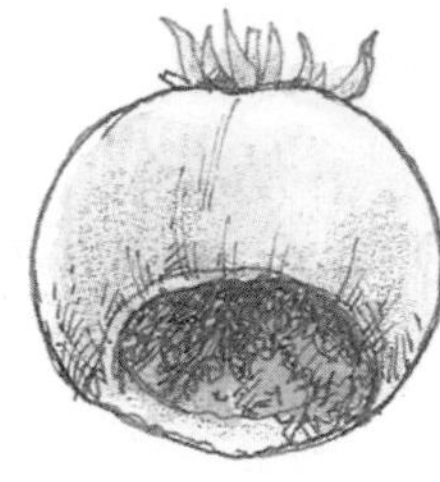

**Blossom end rot** This is a circular brown patch at the blossom end of developing tomatoes and can be prevented by regular watering. If the soil is acid, add garden lime.

**Blotchy ripening** Sometimes parts of developing fruit fail to ripen. Frequent watering and shading the fruit in hot weather will help prevent this, or try growing another variety.

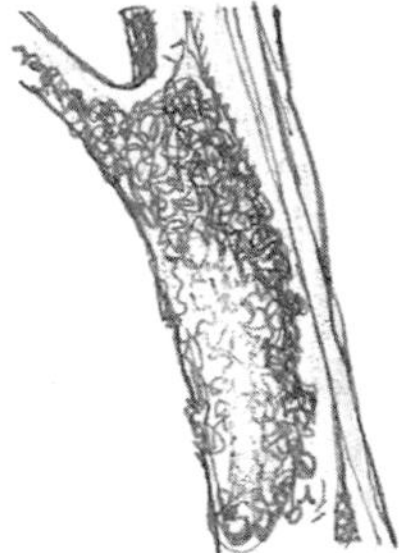

**Botrytis** This grey mould affects tomatoes and, in wet weather, pea and bean pods. Prevent by having good ventilation and avoid overcrowding. Burn any diseased vegetables.

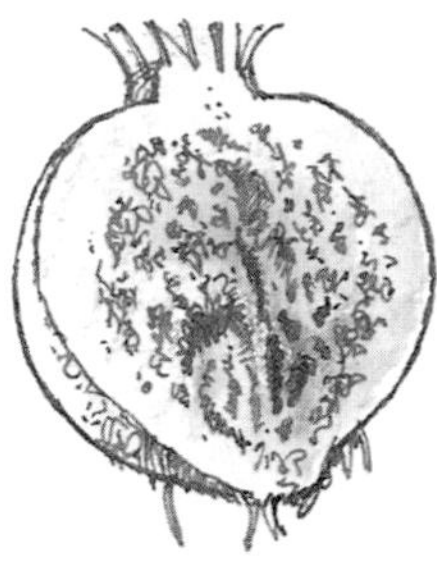

**Brown heart** This internal root decay affects turnips, swedes and beetroots. Regular watering prevents it; or sprinkle topsoil with powdered borax before sowing.

**Chocolate spot** In spring, beans may become covered with chocolate brown blotches – signalling potash deficiency. Prevent it by sowing early under shelter.

**Club root** Roots swell and decay, and leaves yellow. Lift and burn diseased plants. Dress soil with lime and/or put four per cent calomel dust in the new planting holes.

**Crown gall** These large, harmless galls sometimes develop on roots of fruit and vegetables in the growing season. Cut off and burn, provided doing so will not damage the fruit.

**Cucumber mosaic virus** This virus also affects raspberries and causes yellow mottling on fruit and leaves. Control insects which carry the disease by spraying.

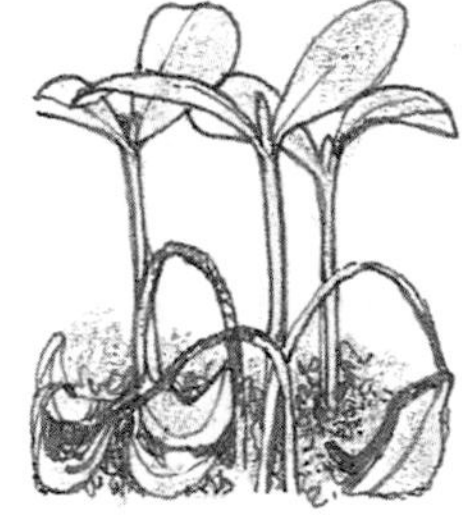

**Damping-off** Young lettuces are particularly susceptible: stems decay and seedlings collapse. To avoid, sterilize compost and do not overcrowd or overwater.

**Downy mildew** This furry coating appears on onions and the underside of brassica, lettuce and spinach leaves. Treat spinach and onions with zineb, and lettuces with thiram.

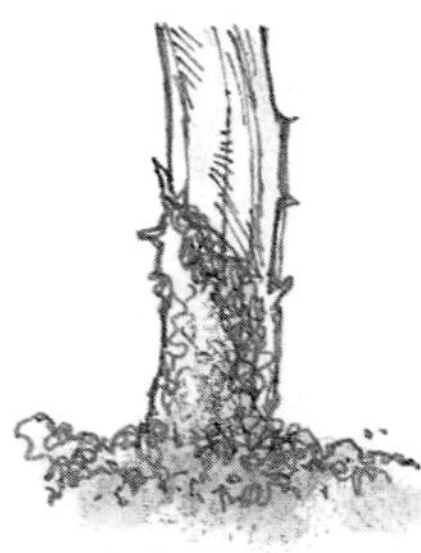

**Foot rot** This discoloration and rotting at the base of the stem can kill tomato, pea and bean plants. Treat plants by watering with cheshunt compound.

**Halo blight** French and runner beans are susceptible to these dark, circled spots. Blistered seeds should not be planted. Spray diseased plants with copper fungicide.

**Leaf spot** This is revealed by dark, irregular spotting. Diseased leaves should be removed and burnt, and the affected plants sprayed with a fungicide.

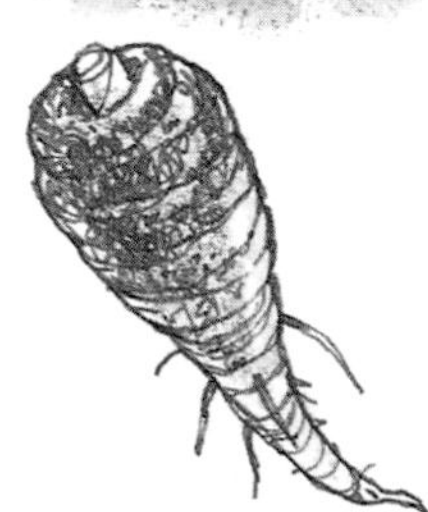

**Parsnip canker** These orange-brown or black cankers rot parsnip roots. Prevent by them by dressing the soil with lime and sulphate of potash.

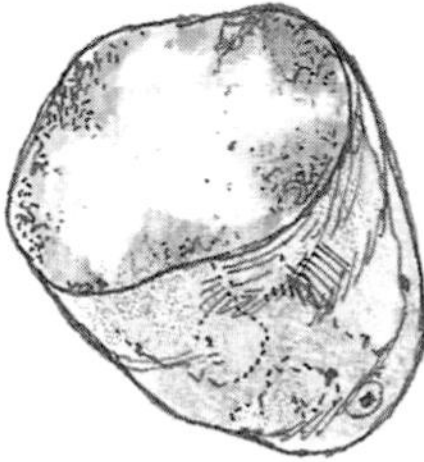

**Potato blight** Black spotting of leaves, withering of the stem and rotting of tubers or fruit are signs from May to August. Spray stems with copper compound.

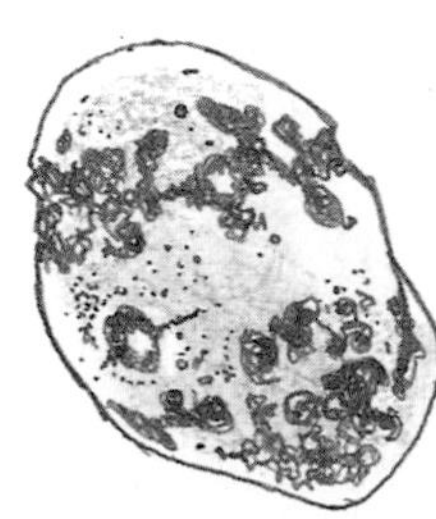

**Potato scab** These rust-coloured fungal scabs appear on potatoes – which can still be used, if peeled. Grow potatoes in slightly acid soil. Peat helps prevent infection.

PLANT DISEASES

**Sclerotinia disease** In spring and summer, tomato plants may develop stem rot. White fluffy fungus appears on the rotting stem. Affected matter should be destroyed.

**Tomato blight** Outdoor tomatoes with blight gradually turn brown and rot. Spray with copper compound once a fortnight in damp weather.

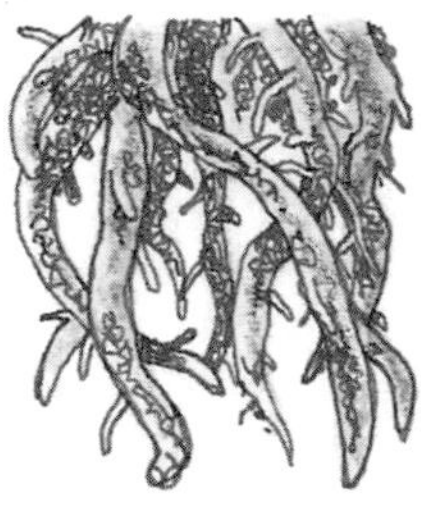

**Violet root rot** Asparagus is prone to develop this. Purple threads cover the roots and kill the plant. Infected plants must be destroyed and the bed not re-used.

**Whiptail** This deficiency is likely to develop in cauliflowers and broccoli. Leaves become thin and curl. Water infected vegetables with sodium molybate.

**White rot** This white fungus rots onions, leeks, shallots and garlic, and contaminates the bed for eight years. Burn the crop and dust new seed drills with benomyl.

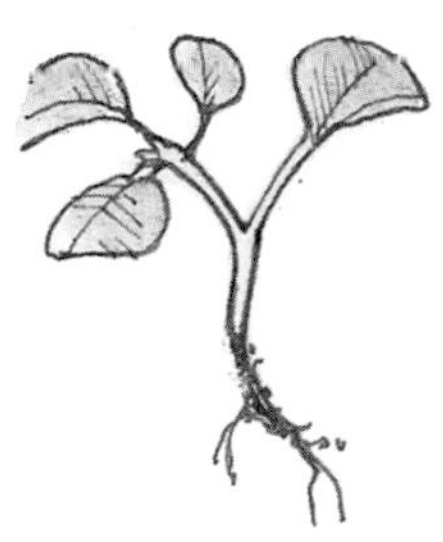

**Wire stem** This causes brassica seedlings to brown and wither at the base of stems. To prevent disease, plant outdoors in soil raked over with quintozene.

**Natural organic soaps** are an old method of controlling pests, now seeing a return in popularity. Their insecticidal properties have been known since pre-Victorian days. The soaps available now are contact insecticides only. They will not affect insects beneficial to your vegetables to any degree because such insects are generally larger, have a more resistant body structure and are faster moving.

Fatty acids attack the cell structure of the pest rather than its nervous system or body chemistry so, unlike chemical pesticides, the pests cannot become immune to them. When applied, the soaps also decay rapidly to form simple carbon dioxide.

## PLANT DISEASES

### FUNGUS DISEASES

Fungi are responsible for many of the plant diseases which occur in the vegetable plot: mildew, chocolate spot and grey mould for example. The part of the fungus which you usually see on your crop is only the fruit, not the entire fungus plant. The growing part (equivalent of a normal plant's stem and leaves) is inside the leaf or whichever part of your plant is affected. Unlike pests, therefore, which can only be sprayed after the insects are seen, it is imperative that fungus diseases are prevented from becoming established by cultural means and by preventative spraying.

The weather, temperature, soil condition, planting distance, season and variety of crop all determine the likelihood of fungus diseases occurring. Powdery mildew for example thrives on warm days and cool nights and is not dependent on damp conditions. Downy mildew, the bane of lettuce, however, is a warm, moist-weather disease, as is potato blight, which can also attack tomatoes. Knowing the conditions that encourage fungus diseases will help you identify them if they arrive and point you towards the best treatment.

Choosing resistant vegetable varieties; planting or thinning sufficiently to obtain good air circulation through the crop; ventilating young plants when they are in the greenhouse; keeping soils and composts evenly watered; protecting from cold with cloches or covers, using the greenhouse, and taking care in handling and cultivating seedlings and plants all help to keep potential fungus diseases at bay. Sooner or later, however, a fungicide spray will probably be needed.

**Fungicides** Four fungicides should take care of all the common fungus diseases: fungicides which contain benomyl, thiophanate-methyl, bupirimate and triforine as their active ingredients are still reasonable mildew preventers despite their age. Mancozeb is also a reasonable rust control.

Copper oxychloride is used for preventing damping-off disease developing in seeds and seedlings.

Sulphur is a more natural fungicide and, since the death of the smelly lime sulphur, which was also a little dangerous to plants, it is only available as the unmodified element. Today there are micronized or colloidal sulphurs which, mixed with natural soaps and sticking agents, give much better leaf cover and persistence as well as penetrating the leaf pores to give some curative effect as well as protection.

### VIRUS DISEASES

Once a plant has a virus disease there is nothing the gardener or even the professional grower can do about it. For the amateur gardener the only two courses of action are prevention and destruction.

Viruses are spread mainly by aphids and some by eelworms. Spraying and cultural controls (see page 90) will prevent serious aphid infestations. Rotation and avoiding susceptible crops are the only precautions against eelworms.

Burn infected plants if possible or at least put them in the dustbin for removal.

### BACTERIAL DISEASES

While fungi and viruses are by far the most important causes of diseases in vegetables, bacteria (notably cucumber canker) can sometimes be a problem. In common with other bacterial diseases there is no satisfactory cure. It is best prevented by using sterile compost and watering accurately, especially around the plant's stem collar, where it touches the soil.

# INDEX

*Page numbers in italics indicate captions*

# ACKNOWLEDGEMENTS

The Publishers wish to thank the following photographers and organizations for their kind permission to reproduce the following pictures in this book:
Eric Crichton 15, 21, 22, 23t, 25, 27, 28, 38, 38, 39, 44, 47b, 49l, 50, 53, 56, 58, 67b, 70c, 76, 78t, 84; Photos Horticultural 6, 9, 14b, 33, 36b, 41, 46, 48, 52b, 57, 65b, 68b, 71tr, 72r, 88, 90b, 91; The Harry Smith Collection 32, 34, 59, 64t, 66b, 71r, 74b, 75, 77r, 81, 82b, 85tl & b, 87, 89, 90t; Suttons Seeds Ltd 61b, 65t, 78b; Sue Stickland 13.

The following photographs were specially taken for the Octopus Publishing Group Picture Library: Michael Boys 18, 19, 24, 29, 40, 43, 47t, 49r, 61t, 63b, 66t, 70t, 74t, 79, 80, 82t, 83, 86; Jerry Harpur 17, 20, 36t, 42, 63t; Neil Holmes 31, 37, 45, 51, 52t, 62, 68t, 69, 70b, 72l, 85tr; John Rigby 8; George Wright 10, 14t & c, 23b, 30, 60, 64b, 67t, 71l, 73, 77l.

# GREENHOUSE GARDENING

# GREENHOUSE GARDENING

Sue Phillips

# CONTENTS

# INTRODUCTION

Greenhouse gardening is gardening with a difference – you can grow a fascinating range of unusual and out of season vegetables, and even flowers for cutting. Furthermore, you can cultivate subtropical plants that don't flower or ripen properly outside in our climate.

The greenhouse is also a handy place to keep houseplants while they are recuperating, and you can have a lot of fun by raising all your own plants. It'll save you a fortune! If you get really hooked, it's easy to pursue an interest in a particular group of plants and end up with a specialist collection of perhaps cacti, fuchsias or geraniums.

The greenhouse gardening year starts in spring, with propagation playing a major part in your activities. There are seeds to sow, cuttings to take, and pricking out and potting up to follow on soon. It is also the time when greenhouse pot plants begin growing again after their winter rest, so you'll need to begin watering and feeding.

By early summer, edible crops like tomatoes and peppers can be planted, and everything will be growing away strongly. Keeping up with the watering will be your biggest job. This is when it is useful to shade the greenhouse and make use of semi-automatic watering.

In mid summer, keeping the greenhouse cool and humid is a problem. It helps to damp down the greenhouse with a cool spray of water over the floor, border soil and under the staging. Ideally do this early each morning and again at midday. Meanwhile plants are growing at their very fastest now, so keep well up to date with watering and feeding. It's also the most colourful time under glass if you grow pot plants.

Towards the end of summer, everything starts to slow down as the weather cools down. Gradually reduce watering and feeding as plants start to prepare for their winter rest. Take late cuttings of perennials like geraniums and fuchsias.

In autumn, tomatoes etc will be just about finished and need pulling out – any remaining fruit can be ripened indoors. This is the perfect time to clean the greenhouse and everything in it. By doing this, you'll cut down enormously on common winter greenhouse problems like fungal disease and slug damage. Watering should be reduced to a bare minimum when the weather is cold or foggy and dull.

In winter, there is very little to do in the way of chores, apart from removing dead leaves and making sure slugs, mice and other pests are kept at bay. Watering is rarely necessary as most plants are best kept very dry and feeding is not required.

Opposite: For the keen gardener, a greenhouse provides endless hours pleasure, greatly extending the range of plants which can be grown.

In summer, the greenhouse becomes a riot of colour with potted geraniums in shades of pink and red.

# CHOOSING AND ERECTING A GREENHOUSE

The first consideration is to decide what kind of greenhouse you want, which can be difficult given the huge number of different makes, shapes and sizes on the market. Your decision must be based on how much space you have and the range of plants you plan to grow.

**LEAN-TO OR FREE-STANDING?**
A free-standing greenhouse is the sort most people choose, but a lean-to can be much more practical if you only have a small garden. This is because it takes up space that might otherwise be left empty, perhaps next to a wall or over the back door. A lean-to can also be warmer than a free-standing greenhouse since one glass wall is replaced by brick, which retains the heat over a longer period. If the lean-to is built over a back door, you'll be surprised how much heat it traps escaping from the house. This not only helps save on your indoor central heating bill, but in a mild area can be sufficient to keep the lean-to free of frost in winter.

But while lean-to greenhouses are naturally warmer, a free-standing house receives more light. Provided it is correctly sited, there can be continuous sunlight, whereas a lean-to will be in the shade for at least part of the time, even if it has been built on the south side of the house. This makes a lean-to much more suitable for growing ornamental plants than for tomatoes or propagation, for which good light at all times is essential. In any case, being so close to the house ornamental plants in a lean-to can be admired.

**WOODEN OR METAL FRAMES?**
Cost is probably the most important consideration, with appearance and cheap maintenance being extra factors to consider. Aluminium greenhouses are undoubtedly cheaper to buy, but cedarwood, or other similar woods, do look very much nicer in the garden. On the practical side, metal greenhouses need no maintenance at all, whereas wooden

The glass-to-ground aluminium greenhouse is a popular choice, being suitable for growing plants in borders or pots on staging.

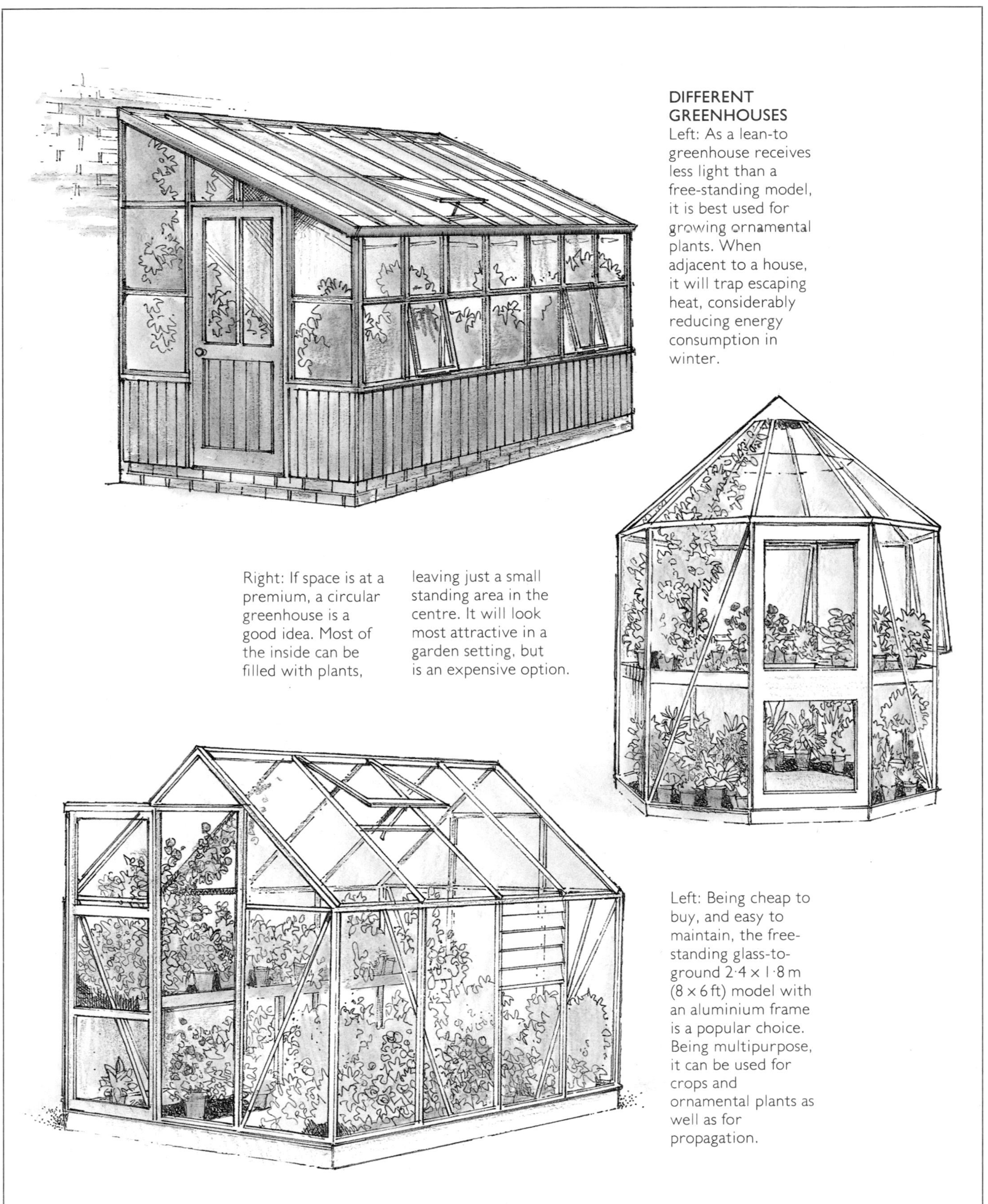

**DIFFERENT GREENHOUSES**
Left: As a lean-to greenhouse receives less light than a free-standing model, it is best used for growing ornamental plants. When adjacent to a house, it will trap escaping heat, considerably reducing energy consumption in winter.

Right: If space is at a premium, a circular greenhouse is a good idea. Most of the inside can be filled with plants, leaving just a small standing area in the centre. It will look most attractive in a garden setting, but is an expensive option.

Left: Being cheap to buy, and easy to maintain, the free-standing glass-to-ground 2·4 x 1·8 m (8 x 6 ft) model with an aluminium frame is a popular choice. Being multipurpose, it can be used for crops and ornamental plants as well as for propagation.

Careful use of space, with plants growing in borders, in pots on shelves and in hanging baskets, makes it possible to put together an impressive collection in the greenhouse.

structures will occasionally need painting with wood preservative to retain their colour and prevent rotting. Also note that wooden framed greenhouses are likely to retain heat slightly better than metal versions, which conduct heat away faster. On the other hand metal greenhouses will usually let in more light, because the glazing bars are much narrower than wooden ones.

**RECTANGULAR OR ROUND?**

Selecting the shape is a matter of comparing looks and space-saving against price. Most greenhouses are rectangular, but in very small gardens, or those where appearance is particularly important, a round greenhouse can be a much better idea. Since they are usually made of cedarwood, they look very attractive – like a small gazebo. What's more, there is no wasted space inside. The staging runs right the way round, leaving just a doorway and a small space in the middle where you stand. But attractive though they are, they have one disadvantage – the price!

**WHAT SIZE?**

There's an old saying about greenhouses – whichever size you buy, one year later you'll wish that you had bought one twice as big!

If money is no object, you can buy greenhouses as big as you like, right up to the size used by small commercial growers. But for many of us, the most sensible buy is the standard 2·4 × 1·8 m (8 × 6 ft) greenhouse, though in many cases that's been reduced to 2·1 × 1·5 m (7 × 5 ft). The reason – manufacturers can produce the most popular size more cheaply than any other! If you buy a standard size but later find you need more room, it is often possible to extend by building an identical greenhouse at one end. So if you think there is any chance this may happen, do check before siting your first greenhouse that there will be sufficient space for a second one. Also, make sure the design allows you to do this without keeping them separate, although this isn't a handicap. In fact, having two greenhouses can be an advantage, because you can heat one and use the other cold, or provide two completely different sets of growing conditions for different types of plants. Or, you can use one greenhouse for a general collection, and the other one for specialist use, such as growing exhibition chrysanthemums.

**HEATED OR COLD?**

Most people start with an unheated greenhouse, and add heating later if they need it. Although it is generally assumed a cold greenhouse is a bit limited in scope, it is surprising just how much you can grow without heat. In summer, for instance, the greenhouse can be used for the same sort of crops as a heated greenhouse – tomatoes, melons, cucumbers, etc – plus a very good range of summer-flowering annual pot plants. The only difference is you can't start quite so early as in a heated greenhouse. You can also propagate winter-flowering pot plants, herbaceous garden flowers and shrub cuttings, since these don't need heat in the winter months.

Another use for a cold greenhouse is to grow a lot of interesting, out of season or exotic edibles – figs and grapes, early baby beetroot, new potatoes and finger carrots – as well as extra early strawberries, and you can grow lots of fascinating bulbs and alpines for winter flowers. It is even possible to grow frost-tender plants such as fuchsias, geraniums and tuberous begonias, provided you only keep them in the greenhouse between mid May and mid September, and then move them indoors to a warm windowsill for the winter.

Below: Begonias, geraniums and fuchsias can all be grown in a cold greenhouse in summer.

Right: Grown in a cold greenhouse, spring bulbs such as *Narcissus triandrus* will bloom in winter.

The advantage of a heated greenhouse is that you can get everything off to an earlier start, and also have a later finish, while growing a much bigger range of plants. Tomatoes, for example, can be kept cropping almost until Christmas, while in an unheated greenhouse the cold would kill them off. You can also grow lots of winter-flowering pot plants and exotic greenhouse perennials, including collectables such as cacti and carnivorous plants.

The heat will also enable you to keep tender potted patio shrubs for the winter. You can begin your normal year's propagating earlier, and produce all your own bedding and tomato plants (which need an early start with plenty of heat). Of course, you no longer need to move all your geraniums, fuchsias and begonias indoors for the winter – you can just leave them in the greenhouse.

Finally, a heated greenhouse makes a very cosy winter retreat. It's a good place to take a cup of tea and the radio, while spending an hour or two pricking out seedlings. Or you could quite simply admire your plant collection! Winter-flowering pot plants should now be at their best, and early flowering bulbs and alpines will soon be flourishing.

## PREPARING THE SITE AND ERECTING THE GREENHOUSE

### THE RIGHT POSITION

In a very small garden, you probably won't have much choice where you site your greenhouse – it will have to go wherever there is room. But if you do have plenty of space, choose a site that gets plenty of sun all day long, well away from overhanging trees or nearby buildings that may shade it. Pick a well-sheltered spot where there is little risk of glass being broken by strong winds, and within hose-pipe distance of a tap for watering. If possible, also keep it close to the electricity supply in case you later decide to provide heat, light, and an electric propagator.

### THE SITE

Regardless of whether you are building the greenhouse yourself or getting someone to do it for you, prepare the site well in advance. (Note: if you are paying a firm to construct the greenhouse, you'll usually find there is likely to be an extra charge for additional work such as levelling the ground and constructing the base for it.)

Preparing the site is not difficult, and merely involves making it level and uniformly firm so that it is ready for the foundations to be laid. However, many greenhouses, especially the metal kinds, now have pre-formed bases available as an optional extra. These are often made of metal and are easily assembled on the lines of a meccano set. The bases are lain on top of the prepared soil, with the greenhouse neatly being bolted into place.

If you don't buy the manufacturer's base, you will need to build a dwarf wall, about two or three bricks high for the greenhouse to be built on to. Needless to say, if you opt for this method it is vitally important to get your measurements exactly right.

Whether choosing a brick or metal base, it is essential to make sure that the base is perfectly level not only from side to side and front to back, but across the diagonals as well. Use a spirit level. If the base is at all skewed, you can be certain the greenhouse will be extremely difficult, if not completely impossible, to put up.

### CONSTRUCTION

If you decide to build the greenhouse yourself, do read the manufacturer's instructions thoroughly before you start, and make quite sure you understand them. You should find they tell you everything you need to know.

It's always a good idea to begin by laying out all the parts. Use a felt tipped pen to label each piece so you can easily see what it is and where it goes according to the manufacturer's plan. Not only will this let you envisage how you must tackle the project, but it also enables you to check that all the pieces are there.

The structure is usually assembled flat on the ground, each side being constructed in turn before they are bolted to the base. The glazing bars in the roof are normally put in last. Allow a complete day for assembling the structure; don't start putting the glass in now, but leave this task for another day when you can complete the job all at once.

To glaze the greenhouse, you need a very still, dry day. Again, you can expect it to take virtually the whole day to finish. Don't worry about the shelving and staging while you are building the house. These items can easily be put up later, being constructed inside the greenhouse. It is essential you complete the glazing in one day. A half-glazed greenhouse could be damaged by overnight winds.

A greenhouse should be sited away from overhanging trees and tall buildings so it receives plenty of light.

Opposite: The standard aluminium frame free-standing greenhouse comes in a kit form that can be readily assembled.

# RUNNING A GREENHOUSE

## BASIC EQUIPMENT

There is no reason why you should not start using the greenhouse just as it is, without inserting any extra equipment. If you are planning to grow crops, such as tomatoes, in a bed within the greenhouse, you don't need any accessories. However, if you plan to do any propagating, or grow potted plants, then it is a good idea to put staging along one or both sides of the greenhouse.

Staging can be either slatted or solid, and made of aluminium or wood. Aluminium staging does not rust or rot, and is probably the most practical. Wooden staging may need attention in later life, though like wooden greenhouses it looks much more attractive. If you envisage using any kind of semi-automatic watering system, then choose solid staging. With slatted staging the plants tend to dry out faster as the air passes up through the gaps.

However, there is a third kind of staging available. This is very lightweight, often made of metal wire coated with plastic, and is secured at one end by hinges attached to the side of the greenhouse, while the front is supported on legs. The advantage of this form of staging is that it can easily be folded down, and stored flat against the side of the greenhouse taking up minimal space. This will be particularly useful if, for instance, you want to grow tomatoes in the border underneath.

Shelves are not essential, but some people find them a very useful way of making extra room for growing potted plants when all the staging has been filled. They can also look most effective when supporting trailing plants.

Another useful extra is a second roof ventilator. Most small greenhouses only have one vent fitted as standard, which really is not enough on a hot summer's day, unless you are able to prop the door open as well. Better still, put a louvered ventilator in a side wall. This will be particularly useful as it can be left open even on windy days without risk of damage, and, since it will be placed about halfway up the side of the greenhouse, it will create 'forced ventilation'. This term describes the process by which hot air rises, escaping through the open roof vent, while at the same time new cool air is drawn in through the louver in the side of the house. This gets the air moving through the greenhouse much faster than with a roof ventilator.

The other piece of equipment you'll find almost indispensable is an automatic ventilator opener. This saves you the bother of going down to the greenhouse every time the sun comes out, or whenever it turns dull, to open or close the ventilator. An auto-vent, as it is called, is very cheap and

Traditional tiered staging made from wooden slats will show off a collection of decorative potted plants in an attractively banked display, yet still make good use of the space available in the greenhouse.

Two storey aluminium staging is only suitable in a greenhouse which has glass down to ground level. Without this, the plants on the lower level – even shade-lovers – will receive insufficient light. The staging must be solid for watering if you plan to use capillary matting.

Temporary staging, secured to the side of the greenhouse by hinges, can be folded away when it is not required. Use it to raise bedding plants in spring, then put it away in summer, to free the ground below for cultivation.

Stand ferns on wooden staging to show them off to best effect. As the compost must always remain moist, it's worth having solid staging which will take an automatic watering device. Always keep them shaded.

easy to fit, and does not need to run off electricity, being powered by the sun's heat. The gadget is very simple, and consists of a sealed tube of paraffin wax, the contents of which expand and contract according to the temperature. When the paraffin wax expands, it acts like a piston and operates a 'plunger' device that is linked via a crank to the greenhouse ventilator, which is automatically raised or lowered. The typical auto-vent operates roof ventilators, but you can also get a specially designed version for opening the louvered ventilators.

## THE BARE ESSENTIALS

Now that you've tackled the greenhouse, it's time to equip yourself for raising seeds and plants. First of all you need pots, seed trays, and composts.

**Pots** They come in a variety of sizes, such as 9 cm ($3\frac{1}{2}$ in) or 13 cm (5 in), the measurements denoting the distance across the top. The 9 cm ($3\frac{1}{2}$ in) pots are the most useful size for general purposes, but it's also handy to have a few larger ones – 13 cm (5 in) and 18 cm (7 in) for instance – plus a few half pots (the same distance across the top, but only half as deep).

Plastic pots are more commonly used, since they are cheaper to buy and much lighter in weight than the old clay pots. However, clay pots are useful for large, top-heavy plants, especially if they are likely to be stood outdoors for the summer – their weight makes them less likely to be blown over. If you are using clay pots in a glasshouse, you'll soon discover that modern greenhouse staging is not always sturdy enough to take the weight. The staging is designed mostly to support plastic pots. So if you do use clay ones, it is best either to stand them on the floor or make your own staging. This can be done using a series of planks supported on bricks.

**Seed trays** They come in two sizes, full size and half size. The best sort to buy are made from polypropylene which can be washed in very hot water, and is almost impossible to break. Cheap plastic trays eventually become brittle and break, but since they are very cheap to replace, this barely matters.

The old wooden seed trays are rarely seen now, and though they look picturesque, are terribly difficult to clean and always seem to need repairing. If you don't want to buy seed trays, you can always adapt household objects instead. Old margarine tubs, vending cups, yoghurt pots, or strawberry punnets all make excellent alternatives.

**Composts** These are special mixtures for growing plants in, not the compost you make at the bottom of the garden! Proprietary composts are much better for plants growing in pots. Do not use garden soil – it is not as nutritious and will not produce such good results. Some gardeners mix their own composts, but this is not really a job for the beginner as it is very difficult to ensure the ingredients are evenly mixed.

Ready mixed composts come in two basic sorts, those made from peat (such as Levington), and those made from soil (John Innes). Some people prefer one kind

Trays are used for raising large numbers of plants from seed. Though trays this size will take up to 250 seedlings, try not to sow the seed too thickly.

and some another, so it's really a case of trying both and sticking to what you find works best for you. In practice, the main differences are in weight – soil is heavier than peat – and the fact that plants grown in peat composts need more feeding but less watering than those grown in the soil composts.

Both soil and peat-based composts come in several different types, according to what you intend growing. Seed composts are for sowing seeds or raising cuttings. Potting composts are suitable for most young plants from the time they are ready to be potted. You will also find ericaceous compost for growing lime-hating plants such as camellia and heathers; cactus compost for cacti and succulents; and occasionally special composts for growing orchids, or other plants with particular needs.

If you are a beginner, one bag of seed, and one of potting compost is all you need to get started. Or if you want to buy just one bag, choose a universal compost (sometimes called sowing and potting compost) which can be used for both jobs. Either way, always use bought composts straight from the bag – there is no need to mix them with anything – and keep the top rolled firmly down and secured after use so no weed seeds, or diseases can get inside.

## PROPAGATING

This is one of the most exciting parts of greenhouse gardening. If you want to take up plant propagation seriously, then an efficient, electrically heated and thermostatically controlled propagator will enable you to have a high success rate all the year round. But if you only want to do a little propagating, perhaps in spring or summer when cuttings and seeds are easiest to grow, you can get by with nothing more than a few seed trays. Buy or make transparent plastic seed tray covers, which will create a beneficial humid atmosphere when water is sprayed within.

### PROPAGATING FROM SEED

This is normally a spring job, though there are some plants (such as annual winter-flowering pot plants, and garden perennials and biennials) that are sown in mid summer. Some plants, such as shrubs and hardy annuals for early flowering the next spring, may be sown in early autumn.

The key to successful seed raising is cleanliness. Everything you use – pots, trays, plastic covers and the propagator itself – must be perfectly clean. You must

Space sow large seeds, setting them approximately 2·5 cm (1 in) apart in rows on the surface of the seed compost. Press them gently into the compost to cover.

Wax begonias (*Begonia semperflorens*) are grown as half-hardy annuals. They can be raised from seed in the greenhouse in February and March and then planted out as soon as danger of frost is over in flowerbeds, windowboxes, hanging baskets and tubs.

therefore begin by washing out everything you intend to use in warm water and washing-up liquid, followed by a rinse in a solution of garden disinfectant and then a good final rinse in some clean water. You must also use fresh seed sowing compost. (Don't buy more at one time than you can use within a few weeks, and keep the top of the bag rolled down after it has been opened to prevent disease organisms getting into it.)

To sow seed, fill a tray or small pot loosely with compost, level it across the top, and then firm it very gently down with a flattener – a small piece of wood you have cut to fit the inside of the pot or tray. Sow small seeds by scattering them evenly over the surface of the compost. Cover them to their own depth with a fine sprinkling of compost. Very tiny seeds are best not covered at all, but left on the surface of the compost. Large seeds, such as sweet peas, are best 'space sown' – laid out about 2·5 cm (1 in) apart in rows all over the surface of the compost, and then gently pressed in until they are just covered (this makes them easier to separate when they come up).

Water the seeds by standing the seed container in several centimetres of water until the compost turns a dark colour – this indicates that the water has soaked right through to the top. Then place the pot or tray inside the propagator or under a plastic cover. If you don't have either, stand the container of seeds inside a large plastic bag, for humidity, keeping the bag well away from the soil using a twig or stick. Then place the container in a well-shaded spot but not in the dark, because many seeds need light to germinate.

Seeds sown in late spring will not need extra heat, but if you sow early in the season a heated propagator is advisable, as is a heated greenhouse to grow the seedlings on. The temperature should be set according to that recommended on the seed packet, 16°–21°C (60°–70°F) being normal. Take a look at the seeds occasionally and water as often as is necessary to keep the compost just moist.

Remove the containers from their plastic bags when the first shoots begin to emerge. However, the seeds being raised in a propagator or under cover can stay put for a while, but do open the ventilator slots in the tops to provide them with fresh air, or they may start 'damping off' (being attacked by a fungal disease, marked by wilting and rotting). When the seedlings have grown their first pair of leaves (seed leaves), they are ready for 'pricking out', though if they are well spaced apart you can leave them in their seed trays a bit longer before moving them.

To prick out seedlings, prepare a tray or pot of fresh seed compost in the same way as described for seed sowing. Lift each seedling out by a leaf, after loosening the roots with a pointed stick or dibber. (Don't handle seedlings by their stems – if you bruise them they can die.) Now make a hole with your pointed stick, big enough to take the roots, and plant the seedling up to its neck, with the seed leaves just resting above the compost level. This is important, or you will get tall leggy seedlings that easily die. Space the seedlings about 2·5–5 cm (1–2 in) apart, depending on their size, and when you have filled the tray or pot, water the seedlings in with a fine rose on the end of a watering can spout, or by standing the tray in several centimetres of water. Keep the newly pricked out seedlings well shaded for a few weeks while they acclimatize.

Seedlings that were germinated in a propagator should ideally be returned to the propagator for a week or so after pricking out. Over this period you should gradually lower the temperature and increase the ventilation to get the seedlings acclimatized to life in the open.

## PROPAGATING FROM CUTTINGS

Many plants can be propagated from cuttings taken at any time between early spring and late summer. Late summer is a good time to strike cuttings of plants such as geraniums and fuchsias because they will root before winter, and can be left in their trays or small pots ready for final potting the following spring.

Cuttings rooted the previous autumn will start flowering much earlier than spring-struck cuttings. However, some garden plants – such as chrysanthemum, dahlia, delphinium, etc – are usually grown from cuttings taken very early in the spring. This is deliberately done to allow the young plants enough time to develop adequately and flower during the season. Any plants with corms, such as tuberous begonias, are also best propagated from cuttings in spring. This gives them enough time to grow a new corm, which is essential if they are going to survive the winter. There are several different types of cuttings.

**Tip cuttings** They are the commonest means of taking a cutting, and are obtained from any plant that has normal stems such as geraniums, fuchsias, etc.

To take tip cuttings, prepare and fill pots or seed trays as when sowing seeds. Use a sharp knife or secateurs to snip off 7·5–10 cm (3–4 in) from the ends of young shoots. Then trim the cutting by making a clean cut with a very sharp knife just below the lowest leaf joint. Next, remove the leaves from the bottom half of the cutting, and any flowers or buds. Then dip the cut end of the shoot into rooting powder. Push the cutting into the compost to about half its length, spacing each one about 5 cm (2 in) apart. (It is usual to put four or five cuttings into a 9 cm [$3\frac{1}{2}$ in] pot; a tray is only used if you have two dozen or so cuttings.) Water the cuttings in by either standing them in water, as for seed, or by using a fine rose on a watering can.

If you take cuttings before the middle of May, it helps them to root if you place the pot in a plastic bag, under a cover, or in a heated propagator. But if you take them later in the spring, or in summer, when they are easier to root, most cuttings will grow perfectly well in a shady spot

Above: Geranium cuttings usually take four to six weeks to root. When they start producing new leaves at the top, check to see if they have rooted and pot on.

Left: Ivy-leaved geraniums can be enjoyed year after year, if you take cuttings from them in late summer.

provided they are kept just moist and humid. Hairy leaved cuttings should never be put in a polythene bag to root as too much humidity tends to make them rot.

Regularly look at your cuttings. Water them whenever they need it, pick off any dead leaves, and check to see if they have rooted. Stem cuttings normally take from four to six weeks to root. You can tell when they are ready for potting on as the cutting starts to grow and produce new leaves from the top. You may also see roots growing out through the holes in the bottom of the pots or trays, a sure sign that they need a larger pot.

**Leaf cuttings** Plants that do not have shoots, where the leaves grow from a central rosette or rootstock, as with tuberous begonias and streptocarpus, are grown from leaf cuttings. This method requires a whole leaf, complete with its stalk. (It must be a fairly young leaf from near the centre of a plant but which has entirely opened out.) It can be treated just like a tip cutting, with its stalk being pushed into a pot of compost. Or, if you want lots of cuttings, you can slice up the leaf into squares about the same size as a postage stamp, and push them edgeways into a tray of compost, leaving half of each cutting sticking out.

Cuttings made from a whole leaf root easily, but the cut-up squares must be treated with care – if they dry out they will shrivel up and fail to root. It is therefore best to lay a sheet of cling-film polythene loosely over them after watering. This can be left on for four to five weeks. Leaf cuttings should be left in their trays until you can see new shoots growing up from the compost, which indicates that they have rooted and begun to make new plants. This is the time to pot them. Keep newly potted cuttings well-shaded for a few weeks, while they acclimatize.

**PROPAGATING BY DIVISION**

Plants that naturally form clumps instead of growing from one main stem can be propagated by division. This will immediately provide you with a supply of new plants. There's no waiting while roots grow, and little likelihood of failure. Suitable plants for dividing include aspidistra, and asparagus and maidenhair ferns.

Some plants such as mother-in-law's tongue don't clump, but produce offsets instead; these are like little plants that grow a short distance away from the parent. To take an offset split up a large potful of plants to make several new ones. The best time to split up plants in this way is in the spring when they start growing, or in autumn when they stop.

Knock the plant carefully out of its pot, and carefully prise the ball of roots apart with your fingers. Divide it into two or three pieces, each of which contains a roughly equal portion of plant. Try to avoid breaking off any roots, or removing more compost from the root ball than you have to. If the roots are too solidly packed for you to divide with your hands, use a long knife instead and cut through the root ball to separate each new clump. Trim off the damaged bits of root afterwards, and dust the cut ends with rooting powder. Then pot up each section of plant individually. Water, and keep them shaded for a week or so while they get established.

Plants cut apart with a knife should be kept slightly drier to start with, to prevent damaged roots from rotting.

## POTTING AND REPOTTING

When cuttings have rooted, and seedlings which previously have been pricked out have filled their tray, they are ready for potting. Since the young plants will have a reasonably good root system, they can be grown in potting compost from now on. If using John Innes compost, choose No. 1 which is the weakest and most suitable mix for potting young plants. Otherwise, use a peat-based potting compost or a multi-purpose seed and potting compost.

For the first potting, 9 cm ($3\frac{1}{2}$ in) pots are normally the best size to use. You should begin with a pot only a little larger than the young plant's root system, and repot into a larger size each time the pot fills with root, moving the plant to a pot one size bigger each time. Plants don't grow so well if you put them in too big a pot to start with.

To pot up a young plant, remove it carefully from its previous tray or pot, disturbing the root ball as little as possible. Place just a little fresh compost in

REPOTTING
1. Repot a plant when its roots have filled the pot. Remove it carefully, trying not to disturb the root ball.
2. Place a little fresh compost in a new, larger pot, and then stand the plant in it. Fill in around the roots with more compost.
3. Fill almost to the top of the pot with compost, and then firm down well.

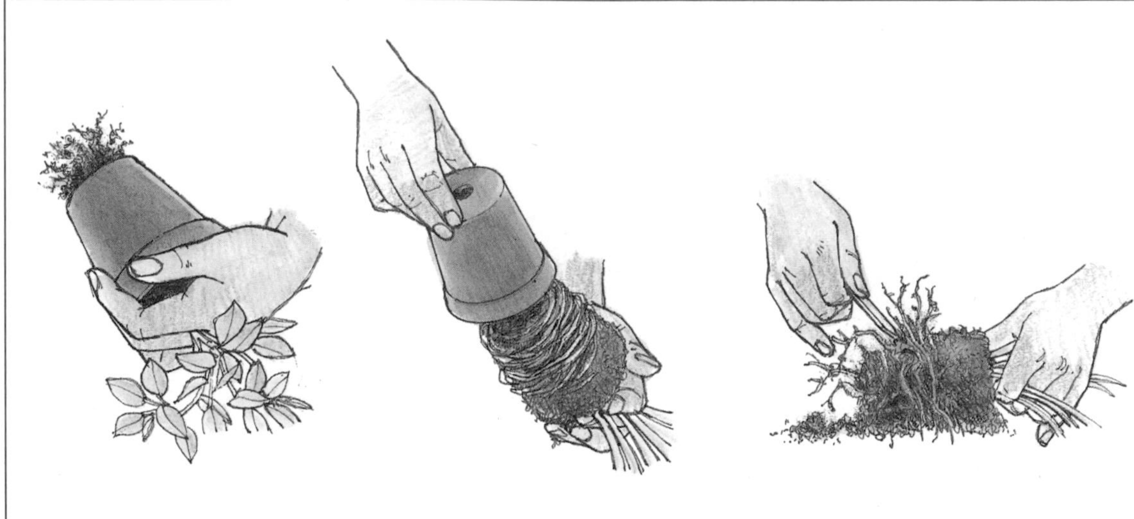

**POT BOUND**
1. A plant is pot bound when its roots start growing out of the drainage hole.
2. When you knock it out of its pot, you will see that the roots coil around the outside of the root ball.
3. Tease a few of the large roots out from the tangle, so that when you repot they can start growing out in the new compost.

the bottom of the new pot, and stand the plant in it. Hold it loosely in place, well centred, while you fill in around the roots with more compost. Fill almost to the top of the pot, and then firm the compost very lightly down with your fingers. Check the plant is still at the same depth it was originally growing, and water it well. Always grow newly potted plants in slightly shaded conditions for a few weeks before moving them into full sun. This will help them get their new roots properly established.

It's impossible to give one absolute period after which plants will require a larger pot and more space for their root system, because they grow at different rates. So the best way to check if this is necessary is by looking underneath the pot. If roots are growing out through the drainage holes, it is time to repot. Choose a pot one size larger than the old one and repeat the same process as before. Avoid breaking up the ball of roots, unless the plant is badly pot bound, with the roots tightly coiled around the edge of the old pot forming a solid mass which is difficult to tease apart. In this case, it is a good idea to loosen gently a few of the thick coiled roots from the bottom of the root ball, helping them start spreading out into the fresh compost in the new pot.

Annual plants will probably never need

If a greenhouse is built on good soil, dig the border for growing tomatoes, chrysanthemums and other tall plants.

potting into anything larger than a 13 cm (5 in) pot or half pot. But long-lived greenhouse plants, such as lemon trees, aspidistra, figs or grape vines, grown in pots will probably end up in very large containers indeed – perhaps 30–38 cm (12–15 in). By the time they reach pots this size you clearly cannot keep transferring plants into a larger pot each time they need it. The solution is to top dress the pots once a year, in the spring, just as new growth begins. Scrape away the top layer of old soil and replace it with new potting compost. If you use John Innes compost, then No. 3 is ideal for potting large plants or top dressing them. Otherwise you can just as easily use your usual potting or multi-purpose compost.

## PLANTING INTO THE BORDER

Not all of the plants you raise in the greenhouse will be grown in pots throughout their lives. Some, such as tomato, pepper, lettuce and cucumber plants, will be planted out in the greenhouse border.

In the early stages these plants are grown in the same way as pot plants, with individual seedlings being pricked out into trays or small pots. But instead of potting them on as you would pot plants, they are planted out into the border. With edible crops particularly, it is very important to plant them out as soon as the pot or tray they are growing in is filled with roots. You can tell when this is happening just by looking at the bottom of the pots – in the case of plastic containers and trays you can see the roots just starting to grow out of the holes in the bottom, and if you use peat pots, you'll see roots starting to appear through the sides.

Don't let the plants get pot bound, or they will suffer a bad check in growth and take a long time to recover – which means your crop will be late starting. If by chance plants do become pot bound, give them a good soaking in diluted liquid feed, at its normal strength, before planting, and tease out the largest roots from the coiled mass when you plant. Make sure the ground is well prepared before planting, so it has a light consistency.

To plant, make a hole slightly bigger than the root ball of each plant, knock the plants gently out of their pots or trays (if grown in peat pots, plant the pot too) and sit the root ball in place. Do not damage the root ball. Fill in around it with soil, leaving it at the same depth it was growing in its pot. Then water it well.

Trained as standards, fuchsias make a good display in a greenhouse for decorative plants.

## STOPPING, PRUNING, TRAINING AND TIDYING

Many greenhouse pot plants, such as geraniums and fuchsias, tend to become tall and leggy. If left to their own devices they can look rather flimsy and insubstantial, instead of being bushy shaped, more interesting, and decked with greater numbers of flowers.

To encourage plants to become bushy, it is usual to stop them once or twice soon after they are potted. This means pinching out the growing point of the plant between your thumb and forefinger, just above a leaf. You can do this either when you pot the plant up, or wait until it has been growing for one to two weeks. Soon after, three or four new shoots will sprout from lower down on the stem.

If you want to grow an especially bushy

STANDARD FUCHSIAS

1. To grow a standard fuchsia, pot up an upright plant, and tie it, at intervals, to a 90 cm (3 ft) long split cane, to encourage it to remain straight.

2. Pinch out the side shoots as they appear, leaving only the main stem intact. Continue to tie the stem to the cane as it grows.

3. When the main stem reaches 15 cm (6 in) above the cane, pinch out the growing tip. Leave the side shoots to form the standard's head.

4. Allow the side shoots to grow 5 cm (2 in) long, then pinch out their growing tips. Repeat with new side shoots until a good ball-shaped head has formed.

plant that you intend potting on into a bigger pot at a later stage, you could even stop the plant a second time, a few weeks later. This time you should pinch out the growing tips of each of the new shoots when they are 5–7·5 cm (2–3 in) long. Older plants that have lost their shape, or are getting too big, can be pruned back to improve their appearance and keep them to a manageable size. This is normally only necessary for perennial plants, such as the eucalyptus or other greenhouse shrubs, which you will be keeping for several years.

Pruning is a useful way of rejuvenating old geraniums and fuchsias when you want to keep them instead of propagating new ones. The best time to prune is in the autumn, when plants have finished their growth, or in early spring just as growth starts. But if necessary it can be done during the growing season. Plants can either be cut back hard, to within several centimetres of the top of the pot, or pruned lightly to remove straggly branches, so reshaping the plant. Either way, use sharp secateurs and cut just above a leaf joint, or just above the junction of a new shoot with an old stem.

Some kinds of plants are occasionally trained as standards – tall stems with a ball-shaped head of flowers and foliage at the top. Fuchsias are often grown this way, though you can also train geraniums and many other perennial plants – even grape vines – as standards.

To grow your own standard plant, select a strong cutting with a straight stem and root it. When you pot it, do not pinch out the growing point. Instead, place a 90 cm (3 ft) cane in the pot by its side (you can grow a taller standard if you like, simply by using a taller cane) and, as the stem grows, tie it loosely to the cane with raffia or string. Pinch out any side shoots that grow, leaving only the single main stem. When it reaches the top of the cane, allow the shoot to produce an extra 15 cm (6 in) of growth and then pinch out the top. This time, do not remove the side shoots that grow. They will form the head of your standard.

When these shoots are 5 cm (2 in) long, pinch out the tips of their growing points. And when they produce side shoots once again pinch out the growing points after 5 cm (2 in). Keep doing this until you have an attractive, densely packed, rounded head. Don't expect results immediately though – it will probably take two years to grow a good specimen – and remember, always keep the head of the standard securely tied to the supporting cane, or it may be broken off.

As a change from normal standards, you can can also train plants such as box or bay into pyramids or fancy topiary shapes. These make fascinating specimens for patios or tubs outside a front door, though if growing dubiously hardy specimens, it is advisable to keep them in the greenhouse for winter.

In addition to stopping, pruning and training, which are only done occasionally, most ornamental greenhouse plants also need a little regular tidying to keep them looking their best. So check them over frequently and remove any dead leaves and flowers, nipping dead stems right back to where they join a healthy stem. This not only keeps plants looking tidy, but encourages them to produce new flowers, and helps prevent the occurrences of plant diseases.

## WATERING

Watering will probably take up more of your time in the greenhouse than any other task. But watering isn't as easy as it sounds. Unfortunately, there are no hard and fast rules – you can't say you should water once a day or once a week – what matters is that you water when the plants need it, and the only way to check if they do is by regularly examining them.

With plants growing in the greenhouse border, it's easy to tell when they need watering because the soil surface looks and feels dry. Provided the soil is given an occasional thorough soaking, plants growing there can last quite a long time between waterings without ill effect, for their roots have access to a great deal of moisture. In summer, the border may only need damping over daily, with a thorough soaking once a week. In winter, even if you are growing vegetable or salad crops, the border will hardly need watering at all provided it was soaked well before the crops were planted.

Pots, on the other hand – especially small ones – dry out very quickly in summer, when you will probably need to water them at least once a day, particularly during a hot spell. In winter, they won't need watering nearly so often – once a week at the most. If in doubt about when to water, it is best to check by testing the compost with your finger or a special watering meter. Push the tip of your finger, or the point of the water meter, about 2·5 cm (1 in) into the pot. The meter will indicate how wet or dry the compost is; but with the finger method you have to judge for yourself whether the compost is bone dry, just right or too wet, and decide whether to water or not.

**AUTOMATIC HELP**

If you are out at work during the day, you may find it is difficult to find enough time to water the greenhouse regularly. However, the problem is solved by using one of the automatic watering devices now on the market. They usually work by having a tank or large plastic bag full of water hanging from the roof of the greenhouse, from which plastic tubes slowly leak water directly into pots or border soil, which are kept permanently just moist. All you have to do is top up the tank.

Another system uses special water matting (known as capillary matting) which is laid across the staging, beneath the pot plants. The tubes from the overhead tanks or bag of water then leak into the matting, which is kept permanently moist, allowing the plants standing on it to draw up as much water as they require. The advantage of this system is that it is much cheaper than those which require a tube to be inserted into each pot.

If you are good at DIY, you can easily make your own automatic watering system, using sheets of capillary matting that you can buy individually. The very simplest home-made scheme involves nothing more than standing plants on staging which has been covered with capillary matting, and wetting the matting thoroughly with a hose pipe each morning. You can also use strips of the matting to water large pots standing on the floor. Fill a bucket with water, and drape strips of the matting so that one end hangs in the bucket, with the other being tucked into the compost of a nearby pot. Provided you don't use one bucket of water to supply too many plants, you should find this is adequate for a day, or possibly even a weekend.

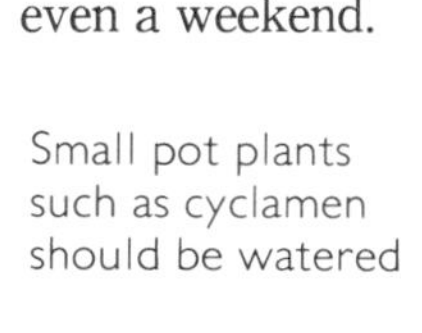

Small pot plants such as cyclamen should be watered only when the compost feels dry in winter.

For longer periods of time, perhaps while you are on a two-week holiday, it is best to take an alternative approach. Remove the pot plants from the greenhouse and plunge them up to their rims in soil in a damp shady part of the garden. Give them a good soak just before you go away, and they should still be fine when you get back.

During the colder season (mid September to mid March or early April), the golden rule for watering is, 'If in doubt, don't'. This is because when the weather is dull, plants do not grow so fast, and they don't need nearly so much water. If you have been using semi-automatic watering in summer, stop and return to hand watering instead. Plants will no longer require a continuous supply of water, only a feed once (or even less) per week.

Some plants become dormant during the winter months and need no water whatsoever, the corms of tuberous begonias being a good example. Others, like geraniums and fuchsias, are semi-dormant and can safely be left dry for long periods of time with only very occasional and modest watering.

## FEEDING

In addition to watering, you will also need to feed greenhouse plants fairly frequently during the growing season. Although seed and potting composts contain plant food, it only lasts a short time. Once it has been used up, it has to be replaced by regular feeding of some kind.

The best products to use, for both potted plants and those in the border, are either liquid or soluble feeds, or the new slow-release feeds (which mostly come as sticks or granules).

Liquid and soluble feeds are mixed with water and applied with a watering can. They should be used regularly throughout the growing season. Slow-release feeds are more convenient if you don't have time for regular feeding. They are applied only occasionally, about every three months. To apply this sort of slow-release feed, you just scatter it over the compost or press it in, and it dissolves bit by bit, releasing a little plant food every time you water the pots or it rains.

The plant foods to avoid using in pots are solid fertilizers which are for outdoors. They are risky to use where roots are in a restricted space as the strong chemical concentration can easily scorch or kill the roots and harm the plant.

There are countless brands of plant food available. Any good general-purpose feed is fine for most greenhouse plants. But if you grow tomatoes, they will require a feed high in potash to encourage heavy fruiting, so in this instance use special liquid tomato feed.

Another method of feeding plants involves a foliar treatment. Instead of watering the feed into the soil, you spray it on to the leaves. Foliar feeding is therefore a very useful way of feeding plants that don't have much root, such as young seedlings or cuttings, or plants whose roots have been damaged perhaps by rotting or insect attack. It is also a good way of giving plants a quick boost, in spring, or when they are recovering from ill-health. You can apply a foliar feed and root feed at the same time to plants that are growing fast.

Special foliar feed products are available, though many normal liquid or soluble feeds can also be used as foliar feeds, provided they are diluted more than usual. When using foliar feeds, follow the normal precautions for spraying – take care not to use a sprayer that has previously been used for weedkiller, and avoid spraying on hot days or when the sun is on the plants.

Whichever method of feeding you choose, the golden rule is always follow the manufacturer's instructions as to the dilution rate and the frequency of feeding. As a rough guide, plants will need feeding regularly when they are growing fast in summer, and hardly at all, if ever, in winter. The need for feeding varies, too, according to a plant's stage of growth. Seedlings or cuttings are unlikely to need feeding until after they have been potted – the seed compost provides enough feed until this time.

Plants that have just been potted or repotted into new compost will not need feeding until they too have used up the available nutrition. This will take from six to eight weeks in a peat compost, and a few weeks longer in a soil-based compost. Bear in mind that plants grown in soil-based composts will need feeding less often than those which are grown in peat-based composts.

AUTOMATIC WATERING

Left: Water from a header tank, secured to the side of the greenhouse, passes slowly but continuously through layflat tubing which lies across the capillary matting. This layflat tubing is stitched along one side, allowing water to seep out on to the matting.

Right: The individual pot system, in which water passes from a header tank down a main tube and then into smaller tubes which lead to specific pots, is generally used for watering large pot plants – using this system for an extensive selection of small pot plants would involve too many tubes.

A traditional sprayer is ideal for applying a foliar feed to the leaves of plants, though you should be careful not to use equipment which has previously held weedkillers. When applying liquid or soluble feeds to the plant compost, use an ordinary watering can.

If all this sounds a bit vague, that's because plants are individuals growing at different rates, according to their size, health, age, the weather, and many other factors. But with practice, you'll find you can soon start to tell when a plant needs more feeding – its rate of growth will slow down, its foliage will tend to be yellowish green instead of deep green, and there may be fewer flowers or new buds produced. Shorter flower stems are another sign of food shortage.

## VENTILATION

Whenever the sun comes out, the temperature inside a greenhouse rises sharply. But while plants like warmth, too much heat will make them dry out fast and wilt, and can even kill them. Ventilation is therefore essential for keeping the temperature down to a level at which plants will thrive. Ideally you should keep the greenhouse below 27°C (80°F), though provided plants are well watered they should be able to survive slightly higher temperatures for short spells.

Ventilation is also vital for letting fresh air into the greenhouse. Plants require carbon dioxide, as well as water, nutrients and sunlight, and if any one of these ingredients is in short supply, they won't grow properly. So constant ventilation is essential for topping up the carbon dioxide in the greenhouse, replacing that used by the plants.

Most greenhouses come equipped with a single ventilator in the roof. This is usually adequate, provided you are around during the day to open and close the door of the house for extra ventilation. If not, it is a good idea to put in an extra ventilator, either in the roof or in the side of the house, as described under Basic Equipment (see page 14).

Another useful extra is an automatic ventilator opener (see pages 14 to 15). This varies the amount of ventilation according to the temperature. An auto-vent is essential if you are away from home during the day, but even if you are about you will still find one very useful. Don't worry if you discover the ventilator open in the evening or in winter – provided it has been correctly installed it will only open when the temperature inside the greenhouse needs it open – and it's surprising how the heat can build up. If you don't have automatic openers, it is a good idea to open the vents in the winter for an hour or two in the middle of the day, if the weather is fine, just to let in some fresh air. Don't forget to close them again before night fall.

## SHADING

During the height of summer even good ventilation is not sufficient to keep the temperature down. Not only will plants suffer badly from the heat; many delicate plants, including young seedlings and shade-loving varieties, can be scorched and killed by exposure to the strong, direct sunlight.

To prevent both problems you must shade the greenhouse. Most people do it by painting the outside of the glass with a special greenhouse shading liquid. It resembles a weak white emulsion paint, which washes off easily at the end of the summer, allowing maximum light into the greenhouse for the rest of the year. For more temporary shading, old net curtains or sheets can be draped over a framework of canes or strings inside the greenhouse. This is a very useful way of shading young seedlings at the beginning of the season, when you may not want to paint the more long-lasting shading over the glass panes.

## HEATING

By the time you have too many plants to bring indoors for the winter, you'll have to start thinking about heating the greenhouse. To be certain of keeping tender plants, such as geraniums, fuchsias, etc, safely through the winter, you will need to heat the greenhouse from the first frost in autumn until there is no more risk of serious frost the following spring. In practice, this means from around mid to late September, until late April or mid May, depending on where you live.

### CUTTING YOUR COSTS

Heating can, of course, be expensive. To cut costs, try to keep the heat down as low as possible, without putting the plants at risk. Most commonly grown greenhouse plants can be kept through the winter at a temperature of 3·5°–4·5°C (38°–40°F), which is just enough to prevent a frost.

If you are only providing such background heat, it is essential to keep the plants as dry as possible, otherwise there is a big risk of them rotting or going mouldy. It is also advisable to spray them every few weeks (on fine days) with a fungicide as a precaution. If you want to keep more exotic plants, you will need to provide a little extra heat, from 7·5–10°C (45°–50°F). But provided there are only a few plants requiring this much warmth there is no need to heat the whole greenhouse to 10°C (50°F). You could either section off part of the greenhouse with polythene to keep it warmer, or move the exotic plants indoors to spend the winter on a windowsill.

### TYPES OF HEATER

There are three basic kinds of heater – paraffin, gas or electric.

**Paraffin** heaters were popular a few years ago, being cheap to buy and run. But sadly this is no longer true, for the price of paraffin has since risen considerably. Another disadvantage is that as paraffin heaters do not have thermostatic controls, you will always have to light them in the evening, fill them, and turn them off in the morning, which may not be convenient. Nor can you adjust the temperature – such heaters are either on or off. If you go to work on a cold winter's morning you may have to leave the heater running, despite the fact that the weather can greatly improve later in the day.

**Gas heaters** are much more convenient. They are available with thermostatic controls and will run for some time before you need to fit a new gas cylinder. Some gas heaters will run off the mains, but they are even more expensive to purchase than those needing gas cylinders. The big advantage of both paraffin and gas heaters is that they can be used in a greenhouse which does not have electricity.

**Electricity** If available, it is the most reliable form of heating and the most economical. By using an accurate thermostat, the heat is only on when you need it, and cuts out the minute the required temperature is reached, so you don't waste any fuel. As electric heaters can be left to switch themselves on and off, you can go away for a few days without needing to worry. Another advantage is that they give out dry heat which discourages moisture-loving fungal diseases in winter. The only possible problem can be a power cut. So if you have a valuable plant collection, it pays to keep a small paraffin heater as well, as a stand by.

## CLEANING

Once a year it is a good idea to give the greenhouse a thorough clean out. The best time for this may not in fact be the spring, since this can be a very busy time of year. Autumn is usually more convenient for most gardeners.

Choose a fine day, when the weather is warm and sunny, and empty the greenhouse entirely. Take out all the plants, together with any pots, canes, etc, that have accumulated under the staging, and pull up any weeds from the path and border. Then scrub down the inside of the glass, frame, staging, shelves, paving slabs or concrete floor, and anything else that is left permanently in place, with warm water and detergent, and a soft brush. Scrape off any moss or algae growing on the glass, paying special attention to the cracks where adjacent glass panes overlap.

Next, wash everything inside the house, including the glass, with clean water and garden disinfectant, and drench the borders thoroughly with more of the same solution. Finally, rinse everything down with a strong jet of water from the hose, and leave the door and ventilators open so that the house can dry out before returning all the plants.

In the meantime, take this opportunity to tidy up plants that will be going back inside, removing all the dead leaves or flower heads, and cleaning up any dirty pots. Empty pots are best stored away from the greenhouse in winter as they often provide homes for mice, woodlice, etc, but if they have to be stored under the staging wash them well with a solution of greenhouse disinfectant before putting them back. If you clean the greenhouse in autumn, wash off any remaining shading from the outside of the glass at the same time, to improve winter light.

Your last task is to prepare the borders for planting. Fork them over, and dig in plenty of peat, well-rotted manure or garden compost to improve the soil. Rake the soil level, and remove any large stones, dead leaves and other debris. There is no need to add fertilizer before planting or sowing in the autumn. But before planting or sowing spring crops, sprinkle 96–128 g (3–4 oz) of solid fertilizer to every $\frac{1}{2}$ sq m (1 sq yd) of border, and rake it in lightly.

Opposite: Paraffin heaters are one way of keeping a greenhouse frost-free in winter.

Right: Clean the greenhouse once a year. Scrub all the glass panes with clean water and a garden disinfectant, and then rinse well with a strong jet of water.

# PLANTS FOR THE COLD GREENHOUSE

## ORNAMENTAL PLANTS

### ALPINES

Alpines and other small rock plants make very attractive pot plants to grow in an unheated greenhouse in winter. The best kind to choose are those that flower in early spring and those with interestingly shaped forms or colours. Many such species grow better under glass than out in the garden, as they are protected from damp, which does them more harm than the cold.

**Interesting kinds** Look for pasque flowers, saxifrages (some of which are grown for early flowers, and some for their fascinating silvery rosette-like form); sempervivums (available as the familiar cobwebbed houseleek [*Sempervivum arachnoideum*], and varieties with red or red-tipped leaves); and many kinds of small, winter and early spring flowering

The rich blue and yellow flowers of *Iris reticulata* 'Harmony' make a stunning display in late winter. Their delicate scent is an added attraction.

Opposite: Pasque flowers (*Anemone pulsatilla*), which come in white or crimson forms as well as the stunning shade of purple seen here, bloom in spring. Try to avoid repotting these alpines as they resent root disturbance.

Alpine plants in the greenhouse are best grown on solid staging covered with shingle. This ensures free drainage of moisture from the pots – an essential requirement for these plants.

bulbs such as hardy cyclamen, *Iris reticulata*, and miniature narcissi, including *N. bulbocodium* and *N. cyclamineus*.

**Cultivation** Grow alpines in a gritty compost, similar to that used for cacti. Or make your own alpine compost by mixing half and half John Innes potting compost No. 1 and horticultural grit. Stand the plants outside in the garden over summer, and avoid overwatering at all times. Most kinds need a sunny position, but a few, such as alpine primulas, prefer some shade. Protect plants from slugs and mice, especially in the winter months.

## ANNUAL BEDDING PLANTS

Many annual bedding plants that are normally planted outside in the garden, make very pretty pot plants for growing under glass in summer. The advantage of growing them this way is that if you live in a cold or windy area the plants will grow and flower much better under cover than out in the garden. This is particularly true of varieties, such as petunias, whose blooms can get badly battered by adverse weather conditions.

**Making a choice** Select dwarf varieties for use as pot plants because of their compact growth, though trailing and climbing annuals can be good too. Try petunias, black-eyed Susan (*Thunbergia*), busy Lizzie (*Impatiens*), salvia, ageratum, French marigold (*Tagetes*), and morning glory (*Ipomoea*). Plants are available from early to mid May. Plant them in 9 cm ($3\frac{1}{2}$ in) pots. Trailing kinds, such as petunias, can be planted in hanging baskets and hung from the greenhouse roof where they make a spectacular display. Climbers, such as morning glory, can either be planted in hanging baskets, where they climb up the chains as well as dangling over the sides, or they can be planted in large pots with twiggy sticks for support.

**Winter display** Although annuals are normally planted in May to flower over the rest of the summer, you can also grow some types under glass in winter for an early show of flowers in the greenhouse in spring. You must choose hardy annuals – suitable kinds include dwarf pot marigolds (*Calendula*), nasturtium, clarkia, and Beauty of Nice stocks. They can be sown under cold glass in late summer or autumn, and potted when big enough to handle. They will flower in the greenhouse early the following spring. Throw the old plants away when they have finished flowering or, if you want room for other plants before then, put the annuals out in the garden.

## BULBS

Spring-flowering bulbs are useful for providing early spring colour in a cold greenhouse, where they will flower several weeks earlier than out of doors. The most successful kinds for growing in pots are small species, and dwarf growing varieties such as *Narcissus triandrus albus*, 'February Gold', 'Jenny', and 'Tête à Tête' for example.

**Cultivation** Plant the bulbs in half pots of normal potting compost in autumn, with their tips just showing above the compost. Space them close together, so that the bulbs are almost touching. Keep them in a cool dark place, such as the foot of a north-facing wall, or in the back of the garage, until shoots appear, and then place under the greenhouse staging for a week or two while they acclimatize to the light. Move them to the top of the staging when their buds are well developed.

PLANTING SPRING BULBS IN POTS

Cover the drainage hole with crocks and then half fill the pot with compost. Press the bulbs firmly into position, so they are close together but not touching. Fill the pot to within 15 mm ($\frac{1}{2}$ in) of the rim.

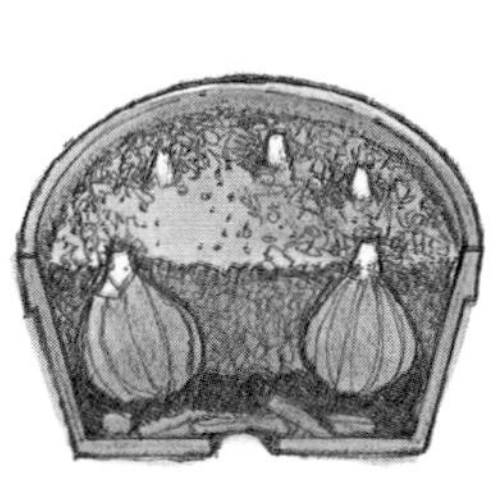

The flamboyant red and orange blooms of tuberous begonias can be relied upon to introduce a splash of colour to the greenhouse in summer. Store the tubers in a dry, frost-free place over winter, and start them into growth again in the warmth the following spring.

GROWING BEGONIAS FROM TUBERS

1. Lay the tubers concave-side-up and 5 cm (2 in) apart on dampened potting compost in a seed tray. Press them in lightly, to no more than half their depth.

2. When the shoots appear and two or three leaves have opened out, pot up into 13 cm (5 in) pots so that the top of the tuber is just visible above the compost.

After flowering, plant the bulbs out in the garden, or leave them in their pots for next year. If you do keep them in pots, continue watering and feeding the plants regularly until the foliage starts to die away naturally, and then allow the compost to dry out gradually. The bulbs should be kept perfectly dry in summer while they are dormant.

### BEGONIA

Tuberous begonias are large, colourful, summer-flowering pot plants, grown from tubers, which are frost tender and need to be dried off and stored indoors overwinter. Buy plants in mid May, or from March onwards. Start tubers into growth on a warm indoor windowsill by laying them hollow side up on a tray of moist potting compost. When shoots start appearing, pot each tuber into a 13 cm (5 in) half pot, with the top of the tuber just visible above the compost.

Move the plants out to the greenhouse after the risk of frost is past, and grow them in slight shade. Pot large specimens on into 18 cm (7 in) pots, and keep them well fed and watered during the summer. Remove dead flowers to encourage new buds to form. Support the plants by tying their stems to split canes if necessary. They will grow to a height of about 30–45 cm (12–18 in). Towards the end of September, when the leaves start turning yellow, gradually reduce the amount of water until the old stems fall off, leaving just the dormant tuber in the pot. Keep this completely dry and in a frost-free place overwinter, away from ice and damp.

### BUSY LIZZIE

An easy flowering pot plant that is technically a half-hardy perennial, although it is most conveniently treated as an annual. Busy Lizzies bloom throughout summer; the plants are about 15–20 cm (6–8 in) high, and come in a good range of colours, with single or double flowers. Feed and water the plants well during the summer, and keep them slightly shaded from direct sun. To keep the plants flowering well, regularly remove dead flower heads. Propagate new plants from cuttings taken any time during the summer.

### CAMELLIA

Choice, hardy outdoor shrubs which

Grow camellias in tubs which can be carried into a greenhouse, away from frost, for flowering.

flower very early in the spring, and make spectacular pot plants for growing in large tubs in a cold greenhouse during winter and early spring. Such protection produces a much better display of flowers than you would get outdoors.

Feed and water plants well while they are in bud, and later remove the flower heads when they have died. Place plants back outdoors after flowering, and keep them on the patio in slight shade for the summer. Bring them back under glass in November, ready for flowering. When repotting is required, use some ericaceous compost, and try to water with rainwater or water that has been first boiled in the kettle and then cooled, as camellias are lime-hating plants.

### CELOSIA

Half-hardy annual greenhouse pot plants, grown for their striking flowers. There are two different types: cockscomb (*Celosia argentea* 'Cristata') which produces a large, wavy crest of flowers, and Prince of Wales feather (*C. argentea* 'Plumosa'), which has an upright spire of feathery flowers. Both types come in very bright, eye-catching colours, and always attract a lot of attention.

Plants are grown from seed, which should be sown in late spring. If you want early-flowering plants, sow the seeds indoors on a warm windowsill in March. Prick the seedlings out when they are big enough to handle, and later pot the young plants into 9 cm (3½ in) pots. Young plants and seedlings need shade and moisture, but full-grown plants need more light – shade them from very strong sun though. The plants will continue flowering for about two months. When they are past their best throw the old plants away.

### COLEUS

These are half-hardy plants grown for their brilliantly coloured foliage, which makes a superb show all summer long, and acts as a good background to flowering plants. The colour range includes purples, reds and yellows, but coleus leaves are usually strongly patterned with different coloured mottles, stripes or spots, and some varieties even have attractively fringed foliage.

**Propagation** Coleus are grown from seeds sown on a warm indoor windowsill in spring. Seeds are available in a good range of mixtures, but also as individual named varieties. In addition, they can be grown from cuttings, which root easily at any time during the late spring and summer. Pot the seedlings or rooted cuttings into 9 cm (3½ in) pots; for larger specimens, pot on into 13 cm (5 in) pots.

Keep young plants slightly shaded at first, but older plants tolerate quite bright

direct sun, provided they are kept well watered. Coleus plants should be constantly kept just moist, or they soon start to wilt. Feed regularly to maintain good leaf colour. Also, remove any flowers as soon as they start to appear (usually later in the summer) or the leaf colour will fade (you are not missing anything for coleus flowers are not very attractive anyway). At the end of the summer throw the old plants away, unless you have a very warm place indoors where you can keep them during the winter months.

**EUCALYPTUS**

A very large group of Australian trees, not all of which are hardy, some making good pot plants for the greenhouse. Eucalyptus are grown for their foliage, which in many varieties is an attractive silver-grey colour, and makes a good background for flowering plants. The juvenile foliage of some types is round, and looks like rows of silvery discs threaded together. All the species have scented leaves.

Hardy species such as *E. perriniana*, *E. gunni* and snow gum (*E. niphophila*) may be grown in a cold greenhouse for a few years until they get too big, and then planted out in the garden. Tender species, such as *E. cordatus* and lemon scented gum (*E. citriodora*), can be grown in large pots and cut back every spring to keep

Above: Coleus are half-hardy plants grown for their brightly coloured and patterned foliage. Raise them either from cuttings, or from seed – packets including a mixture with a good range of leaf colours are readily available.

Left: Fuchsias with large blooms are not hardy and must be kept in a frost-free greenhouse over winter. In summer they can be moved outdoors, but if you keep them under glass, make sure ventilation is good and they are shaded from the sun.

them small and bushy. These tender species, however, should be kept indoors as they need frost protection during the winter. Propagation is by seed sown in spring or summer.

**FUCHSIA**
Showy, frost-tender, flowering shrubs, with characteristic 'skirts' to their flowers. Plants bloom profusely from spring until autumn. A wide range of cultivars are available in a good choice of colours – some also have gold or bronze-orange coloured leaves.

Fuchsias should be moved into the greenhouse in May when the risk of frost is past. Repot old plants, or pot up rooted cuttings taken the previous year into 9 cm ($3\frac{1}{2}$ in) pots. Stop the young plants once or twice to make them bushy. Grow the plants on in lightly shaded, humid conditions, and ventilate the greenhouse well to prevent it from becoming too hot. Keep them regularly fed and well-watered – the compost should be kept just moist throughout the summer.

Towards late September, when the leaves start turning yellow, gradually reduce the amount of watering and stop feeding as plants are preparing for their winter rest. When all the leaves have fallen, give a little water about once a month to lightly moisten the compost and cut the plants back to within 5 cm (2 in) of the top of the pots. Keep them in a frost-free place for winter, hardly ever watering until new growth starts the next spring.

Fuchsias are easily propagated from cuttings taken at any time during the spring and summer. The best flowers are produced by young plants, so if possible propagate new fuchsia plants every year.

**GERANIUM**
Correctly speaking, these should be called zonal pelargoniums to distinguish them from the true geranium which is a hardy perennial border plant, otherwise known as cranesbill.

Greenhouse geraniums are frost-tender plants that flower from early spring well into the autumn, and are available in all colours except yellow and blue. Plants are available usually from spring onwards – do not put them into an unheated greenhouse until after the risk of serious frost is over, in May. Geraniums like plenty of

Above: The beautiful scarlet blooms of *Fuchsia* 'Thalia' contrast well with its deep bronze-green foliage.

Left: Gloxinias come in varying shades of red, pink, violet and purple, often with a contrasting light or dark centre. They are particularly attractive pot plants for display indoors.

sun, and flower best if not over generously fed or watered.

Towards late September the plants will start shedding many of their leaves, which indicates that they are getting ready for their winter rest. When this happens, gradually cut down on watering and stop feeding. Finally cut down the old plants to within 5 cm (2 in) of the top of the pots. During the winter, plants must be kept dry and in a frost-free place, such as an indoor windowsill.

Geraniums are easily propagated from cuttings taken any time from spring to late summer. Bedding geraniums can also be propagated from seeds sown either very early in the spring, or better still in early autumn, to flower the following year. Either way, they must be grown in heat until May – on a warm indoor windowsill, or in a heated propagator. Young plants have a tendency to be leggy, and are best stopped when only several centimetres high to encourage them to produce lots of side shoots and become bushy.

### GLOXINIA

Also known as *Sinningia*, these tender perennial plants are grown from corms in much the same way as tuberous begonias. Plants can normally be bought throughout the spring and summer. However, if growing your own, start the corms into growth in a warm place (such as an indoor windowsill) in spring, laying them on top of moist compost until they start to sprout. Be sure to lay them the right way up – the

Geraniums are attractive plants, available in colours ranging from white to many shades of pink and red.

**TAKING GERANIUM CUTTINGS**
Choose shoots 7·5–10 cm (3–4 in) long, cutting off neatly just below a leaf joint. Remove the leaves from the lower 5 cm (2 in). Plant four or five cuttings in a pot, with the lowest leaves just above the surface.

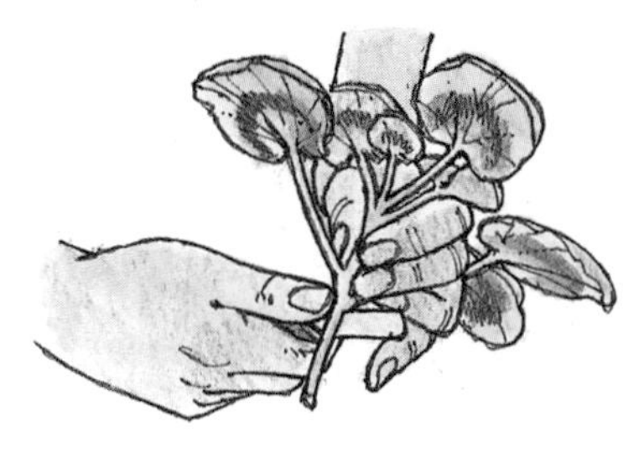

Although hydrangeas are usually thought of as garden shrubs, they also make excellent subjects for a cold greenhouse and are easy to care for, producing masses of showy blooms.

side which has a slight hollow in the middle is the top.

When shoots start to appear, pot each one individually in a 13 cm (5 in) half pot, with the corms just showing above the top of the compost. Water sparingly to start with, but when the plants are growing well they will need feeding and watering frequently. Move them out to the greenhouse in May after the risk of frost is over, and grow them in a slightly shaded spot. In the autumn, when gloxinia leaves start to turn yellow, gradually reduce the amount of water given until the corms eventually dry out. Store in a frost-free place over winter.

**HOUSEPLANTS**

During the summer the greenhouse is a useful place to keep indoor houseplants temporarily, after they have finished flowering, or when they are in need of rest and rejuvenation. This treatment is suitable for most perennial houseplants, other than tropical kinds. Good candidates include flaming Katy, Christmas cactus, fuchsias, geraniums, poinsettia, hydrangea, azalea, winter-flowering begonias, cyclamen and aspidistra. Hardy houseplants, such as fatsia, ivies, and fatshedera, can be kept in the greenhouse in summer, and if necessary in winter too.

**Cultivation** As a general rule, keep houseplants moist, humid and well shaded while they are in the greenhouse, and don't forget to feed them regularly. In warm weather spray them with water daily to maintain high humidity.

To rejuvenate old houseplants that have become tall and leggy, or which have lost a lot of their leaves, start by pruning them back quite hard. In most cases, they can be cut back to several centimetres above the top of the pot. If less drastic action is called for, cut out untidy or dead shoots and generally reshape the plant.

If the roots are beginning to grow out through the holes in the bottom of the pot, repot into the next size pot using fresh potting compost. While they are recovering from repotting, only water to keep the compost just moist; plants that have been pruned hard will not need much water until new shoots are growing strongly. Feed the plants regularly from then on. Do not forget to move all houseplants (apart from hardy kinds, such as ivy) back into the house by the middle of September when the weather will start getting too cold for them at night.

**Special requirements** Some kinds of houseplants are extremely fussy. Cyclamen corms, for instance, must be allowed to dry off and have a dormant summer. Azaleas and the Christmas cactus are best put out in a shady spot in the garden during the height of summer, though they can be kept under glass in spring and autumn. Poinsettias are notoriously difficult to keep – cut the old plants back hard when the flowers are over, repot if necessary and keep shaded and on the dry side. They probably won't flower until Easter the following year. (Note: see individual entries for full details of each plant's needs.)

**Tropical plants** These include foliage plants, such as prayer plant (*Maranta*), figs and rubber plants (*Ficus*), *Dieffenbachia*, etc, which are not suitable for moving out to the greenhouse during the summer because they find it difficult to adjust to the change in conditions. Their leaves will frequently turn yellow or brown, ruining their general appearance.

**Annual flowering pot plants** Plants such as Persian violet (*Exacum*), cineraria and calceolaria, are not worth moving to the greenhouse after flowering. They will die when they have finished flowering, and should then be thrown away. You can, however, use the greenhouse to raise a new crop of these plants from seeds, which will give you enough to keep both the house and greenhouse well supplied.

### HYDRANGEA

These garden shrubs are often grown as flowering houseplants, either indoors or out in the greenhouse. Being hardy, hydrangeas can be grown in an unheated greenhouse all the year round, or you can use the greenhouse to keep hydrangeas normally grown indoors, when they are not in flower. The plants flower in late spring and summer, with large mophead-shaped blooms in pink, blue or mauvish purple.

Hydrangeas are very easy to look after. They need plenty of feeding and watering while they are growing and flowering, between April and September. It is particularly important that they do not dry out when in flower or bud. After flowering, remove the dead blooms, cutting their stems back to within several centimetres of the pot, or to a natural junction with another shoot. Do not cut back new shoots which have not yet flowered, for they will bear next year's blooms. Repot old plants that are pot bound in late autumn or early spring. New plants are easily propagated by cuttings which root any time during the spring and summer.

### IVY

Ivies are popular hardy pot plants available in a range of leaf shapes and sizes, including several variegated types. As well as the commoner kinds, a fascinating selection of very unusual varieties is available. You can get ivies with spotted, speckled, curled, crimped, bird's foot or heart-shaped leaves.

Ivies grow very well in the greenhouse, provided you keep them shaded from direct sunlight and spray them with water in warm weather to keep the surrounding air moist. They dislike being too hot, so unless the greenhouse is very well ventilated and shaded in summer, it is a good idea to put ivies outdoors during the hottest months.

Propagate new plants by cuttings, which root easily during the spring and summer, and even early autumn. Pot the rooted cuttings into 9 cm ($3\frac{1}{2}$ in) pots, and repot into 13 cm (5 in) half pots when necessary. Trailing ivies can be trained upwards to save space; insert a split cane into the pot and use plant ties to hold the stems in place.

Ivy makes an excellent decorative climber for the cold greenhouse, provided you can keep it shaded from direct sunlight.

**LILIES**

Some kinds of lilies are sold in summer as flowering houseplants. They can be planted out in the garden after the flowers are over, or repotted into bigger pots and grown in the greenhouse to flower again the following year. You can also buy lily bulbs in spring; plant them in pots for an excellent greenhouse flower display possibly with a gorgeous scent.

**Choice and cultivation** The most suitable varieties for growing in pots are those that are not too tall – *Lilium speciosum* cultivars are ideal (they mainly have white flowers with red or pink spots); also consider Mid Century hybrids, such as 'Paprika' and 'Enchantment' (which have respectively crimson and orange flowers), and the old favourite *Lilium regale* (fragrant white flowers with a brownish maroon reverse).

Plant the bulbs immediately into any good potting compost. One bulb in a 15 cm (6 in) pot makes an attractive plant on its own, but for an even better display plant a group of three in a 25 cm (10 in) pot. Plant them fairly deep, so there is 5 cm (2 in) of compost over the top of each bulb. Water just enough to slightly moisten the compost, but no more. Keep the newly planted bulbs somewhere cool and shady – you can even stand them outside to start with. When the shoots are 7·5–10 cm (3–4 in) tall, move the pots into the greenhouse but continue to water very sparingly, and keep the plants well ventilated and shaded from strong sun. Plants can be taken indoors when they are in flower, or kept in the greenhouse for summer decoration.

The lily variety 'Enchantment' is a good choice if you have never grown lilies before, as it is easy to cultivate and will do well in a garden border after flowering in the greenhouse.

Polyanthus, and other very small seeds, should be sown on the surface of the compost. Stand the pot in water until the compost is thoroughly dampened, then place inside a polythene bag to retain the moisture until the seeds have germinated. Secure the bag with an elastic band.

**PELARGONIUMS** (See Geraniums pages 33 to 34)

**POLYANTHUS**

Small hardy plants, 20–25 cm (8–10 in) high, that are invaluable for providing a good show of colourful flowers under glass during March and April. The individual flowers are much the same shape as those of primroses, but are produced in large clusters at the top of tall stems.

Polyanthus are available in a very good range of colours including red, blue, maroon, pink, orange and yellow; old fashioned gold-laced polyanthus (with a gold rim around the edge of the petals) are also occasionally sold.

Plants are on sale from early to late spring. They should be kept moist and well shaded from bright sun. They dislike too much heat, and are therefore best placed outdoors over summer. Better still, plant old polyanthus out in the garden after flowering, and grow or buy new plants for the greenhouse the following year – young plants produce much better flowers than old ones.

New plants can be propagated by dividing old clumps, or by sowing seeds in the greenhouse in spring. Sow the seeds on the surface of the compost and do not cover them. Instead, put the pot or tray inside a polythene bag after watering – this will maintain the necessary humidity. After the seeds have germinated take the container out of the bag, but continue to keep

Polyanthus hybrids are availabe in a wide range of colours, including many varieties with contrasting centres or rims to the flowers.

the compost moist all the time – this is important, for seedlings will not recover if they dry out. Keep them very well shaded, even after they are potted, and stand young plants outside for the summer.

### PRIMROSES

Primroses are now bred in a large range of colours similar to those of polyanthus, and make very useful and colourful early spring flowering plants, normally about 7·5 cm (3 in) high. They belong to the same family of plants as polyanthus, and need similar conditions – shade, moisture, and not too high temperatures, so again stand them outside in the summer or plant them in the garden after flowering. Propagate by dividing the old clumps, or by sowing seeds in the greenhouse in spring, following the same method as for polyanthus.

## VEGETABLES

### AUBERGINE

The growth of holidays abroad and our exposure to foreign foods has increased our taste for aubergines. But you don't have to rely on a good greengrocer for a supply, since they can be grown easily in an unheated greenhouse in summer.

Plants are often available in spring. Alternatively, grow your own in a heated propagator – since the plants are slow growing the seeds must be sown in February or March.

Aubergine plants are short and bushy. The backs of the large grey-green leaves are covered in vicious spines as are the stems of the plants, so take care when handling them.

**Cultivation** Aubergines are grown in much the same way as tomatoes, except that they do not need to have their side shoots removed, nor do they need training up canes or strings.

Plant from mid to late May, but if the weather is cold delay buying plants until the end of the month, or keep them on an indoor windowsill until the weather improves. Grow the aubergines in a well-prepared greenhouse border, spacing the plants about 75 cm (30 in) apart. They can also be grown in large 30–38 cm (12–15 in) pots, although they will not produce such large crops as they would in a border. Feed the plants immediately after planting with liquid tomato feed (at the manufacturer's recommended rate for tomatoes). Keep the plants well watered throughout the summer.

Plants do not have to be supported, but if required push three 90–120 cm (3–4 ft) canes in a circle around each plant and tie the branches to them in case they flop. Check the plants regularly for whitefly, red spider mite and greenfly, and spray them if necessary. Grey mould may be troublesome in very damp weather in the autumn, but normally the plants are relatively disease-free.

**Cropping** Aubergine plants start flowering soon after planting, and their strange purplish flowers are quickly followed by fruits which can be picked as soon as they are big enough to use. They do not need to ripen. The more often you pick, the more aubergines you will get. If you leave fruit on the plants too long they become full of hard seeds and prevent the plants from producing more fruit in the meantime. Plants will continue cropping until the weather gets too cold for them, probably around late September.

### CARROTS (EARLY)

You can get a useful crop of early carrots from a sowing made in the border in late February or early March. Sow an early variety such as 'Amsterdam Forcing', 'Chantenay Red Cored', 'Early Scarlet Horn' or 'Nantes' in the border, in rows 22 cm (9 in) apart. Thin the seedlings to 5 cm (2 in) apart when they are big enough,

Aubergines are an unusual yet easily cultivated vegetable for the greenhouse. They require much the same treatment as tomatoes, although it is unnecessary to provide any support unless the branches are in danger of collapsing under the weight of their crop.

and keep the border soil just moist.

The carrots will be ready to pull in late May, in time to plant cucumbers, peppers or aubergines afterwards. Early varieties of carrot can also be sown in the greenhouse border in late August or early September for a late autumn crop of 'early' carrots. Do not allow the soil to dry out or the greenhouse temperature to get too high if growing late crops.

## CUCUMBERS

Cucumbers are one of the most productive greenhouse crops you can grow. One plant should be enough to keep a small family supplied with all the cucumbers they can use; grow two to be on the safe side or if you eat lots of cucumber sandwiches!

**Cultivation** The fruit grow on a long rambling vine-like plant that is normally trained up a cane or string, so that it does not take up too much room. The plants are usually grown in the border or in growing bags, though large 30–38 cm (12–15 in) pots are also suitable.

Plants in the border are easiest to look after, but if you have previously grown cucumbers in the same soil for several years or had plants die from root rot, it is advisable to grow in pots or bags instead. This is because cucumber plants are very susceptible to their own set of root diseases which persist in the soil from one crop to the next. Young plants are available in the spring, but as they are fast growing you can raise your own from seed on a warm indoor windowsill.

**Varieties** The new F1 hybrid varieties such as 'Diana', 'Monique' and 'Pepinex 69' (which only produce female flowers) are the least trouble to grow, and the above are all especially suitable for cold greenhouses. Alternatively you could grow a good outdoor variety, which does very well under glass especially in a poor summer.

Modern outdoor cucumbers are a great improvement on the old ridge cucumbers which were rather coarse, did not taste good, had a thick skin covered in prickles and lurid yellow stripes and spots! The Japanese outdoor varieties, such as 'Tokyo Slicer' and 'Kyoto' produce normal looking cucumbers, and give excellent crops under glass.

**Propagation** Cucumber plants can be slightly temperamental to grow in the early stages, so it pays to take special care. If you are growing your own, sow the seeds remembering that they take four weeks to develop into plants.

Sow each seed individually into a 9 cm ($3\frac{1}{2}$ in) pot of seed compost (see Cucumber and Melon Plants, page 72, for details of plant raising). Whether you buy plants or grow your own, it is important to time them just right. They should be ready to plant in late May or early June, just as the plants fill their pots with roots, so sow the seed about 4 weeks earlier. Cucumber plants should not be allowed to get pot bound – if you have to delay planting for any reason, it is better to pot them on into a larger pot. However, if the weather is cold at planting time, wait until it becomes warmer because the cold can check cucumber growth badly – and they take a long time to recover.

The new all-female cucumber varieties are the most straightforward for growing under glass. These healthy young plants are ready for planting out into the greenhouse border, growing bags or large pots. You are unlikely to need as many plants as this, but it is a good idea to grow a few spare plants in case of disasters in the early stages.

When planting in the border, space cucumbers about 75 cm ($2\frac{1}{2}$ ft) apart. In bags, insert two or three plants in each row, or if using pots, plant in 30–38 cm (12–15 in) size containers filled with good potting compost. Water in lightly after planting, but be very careful not to water any more than you need for the first two or three weeks while the plants are developing a good root system.

During this time they are liable to rot off if the soil is too damp. Instead, spray the leaves once or twice on a fine day, which helps to keep the air around the plants humid (put your thumb over the end of the hose to produce a fine spray). It is also a good idea to damp down the whole greenhouse daily by spraying the floor as an additional means of creating humidity.

These cucumbers are ready for harvesting, as they have reached the right thickness – do not leave them on the plant to grow larger, as the flavour deteriorates and the plant will stop producing new fruits.

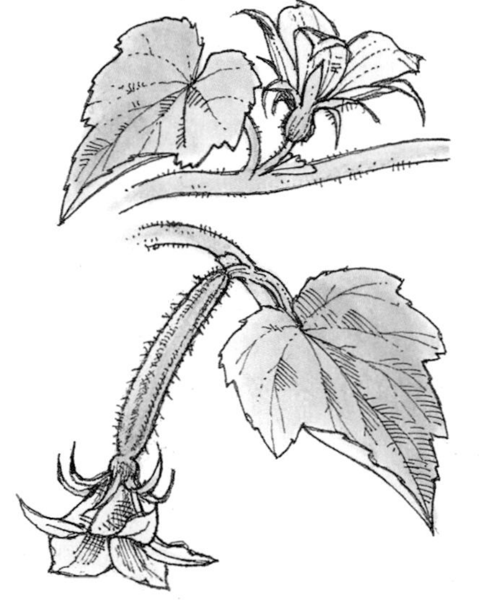

**MALE AND FEMALE CUCUMBER FLOWERS**
Male flowers (above right) are attached to the plant with a short stalk, while female flowers (below right) are produced at the end of a miniature cucumber. The male flowers should be removed as soon as possible to prevent them pollinating the female flowers, resulting in bitter, inedible fruits.

**Providing support** As the plants start to grow they will need support. You can either grow them up canes or strings. If using canes, place a 1·5–1·8 m (5–6 ft) cane alongside each plant, and tie the stem to it with twist ties or thick string (thin string can cut into the stems, causing damage).

If you prefer to grow the plants up strings, they should be put in place before planting the cucumbers. Again, use very thick string reaching from the roof to the floor of the greenhouse, with about 30 cm (12 in) over. Make planting holes for the cucumbers, and fix one string to a hook in the roof of the greenhouse above each planting hole. Then when you plant, bury the bottom of the string underneath the root ball of each cucumber. To hold the stem upright, you just twist it round the string every few days as the plant grows.

**Troubleshooting** Besides keeping the main stem of the plants upright, there are also side shoots to be dealt with. (These are small shoots growing out from the main stem of the plant in the junction where a leaf stalk joins the main stem.) The way to handle these side shoots depends on whether you are growing all-female cucumber varieties.

With all-female varieties, the cucumber fruits are produced in the leaf joints, along with the side shoots. So with these varieties you should remove all the side shoots every few days, nipping them off between thumb and forefinger while they are still small. Take great care, when side shooting, not to remove the tiny baby cucumbers by mistake – it's easily done.

If growing varieties other than all-female, the technique has to be slightly different because here, cucumbers are not grown in the leaf joints, but only on side shoots. Therefore, leave the side shoots to grow until they produce cucumbers.

Normally, each side shoot will produce one cucumber by the time it has grown about four to six leaves. As soon as a cucumber has formed, stop the shoot by pinching out its growing tip one leaf beyond the developing fruit. To complicate matters slightly, this group of cucumbers does not just produce female flowers (the ones that become cucumbers) but male flowers too. It is important to remove all the male flowers as soon as they appear, otherwise the cucumber fruits will be pollinated. This makes them virtually inedible, as they become bitter and eventually fill up with hard seeds.

You can always tell when a cucumber has been pollinated because it swells up at one end – growers call them 'bee stung' cucumbers. Incidentally, it isn't difficult to tell male and female flowers apart. Male flowers have only a short stalk behind them, whereas female flowers have a quite distinct small baby cucumber at the back of them.

**Harvesting** Once the plants are growing strongly, increase the amount of water and start feeding regularly with a general-purpose liquid or soluble plant food, following the manufacturer's instructions. Continue spraying the plants and damping down the greenhouse daily whenever it is warm, and start picking cucumbers as soon as they fill out all the way along their length.

Pick regularly and cut off the cucumbers at the stalk with secateurs or a sharp knife. If you leave fruit on the plants to get bigger, the flavour deteriorates and the plants stop producing new cucumbers until the mature fruit have been cut.

**Pests and diseases** Watch for greenfly and whitefly, and spray when necessary, checking with the instructions that the chemical is suitable for cucumbers, because many products are not. Where possible, use one that allows treated crops to be eaten within a day or two of spraying.

Towards the end of the summer, around early September, cucumber plants are often affected by powdery mildew which looks like talcum powder on the tops of the leaves, so spray with benomyl. Then, as the weather begins to get cold at night, the plants will be more severely affected by mildew and will also stop producing more cucumbers. When this happens, cut the last of the crop and pull out the plants.

## FIGS

When they are grown outside in the garden, figs take up a great deal of room and rarely produce much ripe fruit. If you live in the north of the country, you are unlikely to get any at all. By growing a potted fig in the greenhouse, however, you can get a good crop of ripe fruit from a plant only about 90 cm (3 ft) tall.

The ordinary outdoor varieties such as 'Brunswick' and 'Brown Turkey' can be grown under glass, but you can buy varieties especially for growing in greenhouses, such as 'White Marseilles', 'Negro Largo', etc, which bear better flavoured fruit than outdoor figs.

**Cultivation** Fig plants are easy to grow. In spring select a bushy young plant. Put it into a larger pot if the roots are starting to grow out through the holes in the bottom of the old container, and use John Innes potting compost No. 3.

As new growth begins, do not water much to start with until the plant has produced several new leaves. As the summer progresses, you will gradually need to increase the amount of water. By the time small figs start to appear at the tips of the shoots, the plant will need quite heavy watering.

It is vital to keep the compost evenly moist from this stage onwards, as the developing fruit will drop off if the plant is allowed to get dry. On hot sunny days, up to $4\frac{1}{2}$ litres (1 gallon) of water a day may be needed. Figs also need extensive feeding during this time.

**Harvesting** The fruit will start ripening towards late summer. You can tell if it is ripe by gently squeezing the figs. If they are very soft, and the skin splits open easily, or the fruit falls off into your hand, they are ready to eat. This is also the time when purple-skinned figs develop their distinctive colour. Not all the figs will ripen at once, for the crop comes to fruition over about four to six weeks. Pick them regularly.

Not long after the last fig has ripened, the leaves start to turn yellow and fall off. This is a sign that the plant is preparing for its winter rest, and you should therefore gradually reduce the amount of water given. By the time all the leaves have dropped off, stop watering altogether. The plant can be kept completely dry throughout the winter months.

**Pruning** The plants need to be pruned to stop them from growing too big. This should be done in winter when they are dormant. Cut the main branches back by about half or a third, and cut out any that are crossing, badly placed or which have grown too close together.

Growing figs in pots under glass is a reliable way of producing a good harvest of ripe fruit. Gently squeeze the figs to see if they are ripe – they should feel very soft and should easily come off in your hand. Purple-skinned figs develop their distinctive colour as they ripen.

Aim for a pleasing overall shape within which branches are well spaced out round the trunk, and not crossing or touching each other.

However, if you prefer, you can summer prune instead. This is the best method, since it makes the plant grow very slowly keeping it compact and bushy, which means it can produce more fruit. It is a bit more trouble than winter pruning though. First, establish the basic shape of the plant in winter, either as a low bush, or short standard, by cutting out surplus shoots with sharp secateurs. Then, in spring when the plant starts to grow, allow each shoot to produce four full-sized leaves, and then nip out the very tip of the growing point. Side shoots will grow which in turn must be stopped after they have produced four full-sized leaves. Keep doing this every time new shoots are produced, and you will have a very neat, compact and fruitful miniature fig tree. If you want more plants, they can easily be propagated from cuttings taken any time during the summer.

Each year as fig plants start growing in the spring, repot them into larger pots, using John Innes potting compost No. 3. However, when they end up in 33–45 cm (15–18 in) pots eventually, it is clearly not practical to keep moving them into bigger containers. Instead top dress by scraping away the top layer of compost, replacing it with fresh matter.

Training a vine so that it produces heavy bunches of ripe grapes is a long and careful process, but after about three years you can expect a delicious crop like this every summer. A well-pruned pot-grown plant is the most fruitful and convenient for a small greenhouse – left to itself a vine will soon take over the entire greenhouse.

## GRAPES

Grapes are another crop that traditionally take up a lot of room, and one vine can easily dominate the entire greenhouse. The best means of keeping a vine compact is by growing it in a pot, although this will produce a smaller crop.

**Cultivation** A pyramid is probably the most suitable shape for training a pot-grown vine. It takes up least space and produces most fruit.

Start with a pot-grown vine in spring. Make sure you buy a greenhouse variety rather than the sort sold for growing out of doors, whose fruit will normally only be suitable for making into wine. Garden centres often sell vines such as 'Black Hamburgh', for growing under glass. Repot the young plant into a larger pot using John Innes potting compost No. 3, and begin training it straight away. Each spring, repot it into a larger pot. Eventually it will need a 38–45 cm (15–18 in) pot, after which you should only provide a new top dressing each year, as with figs. As growth commences, gradually increase the watering and also begin feeding the plant again.

**Forming the shape** The first year will be spent getting the vine properly established and growing it into the right shape, so unfortunately there won't be any fruit at this stage. Using secateurs, cut back the vine to within about 15 cm (6 in) of the top of the pot, cutting just above a leaf joint.

When the shoots start to grow out from the base of the plant, select the strongest three, ensuring they are well spaced out round the plant. Rub the rest out by gently picking them off with your fingers, and removing them flush with the main stem of the plant.

Push three 1·5–1·8 m (5–6 ft) canes in around the edge of the pot (next to each shoot) and tie them together at the top to form a tripod. As the three main shoots grow, train each one up its own cane, tying it in place at regular intervals with soft string or raffia. When the stems are 1·5 m (5 ft) high, stop them by pinching out the growing point. If any side shoots develop, allow them to grow two or three leaves and then pinch out their growing points too. This will build up a strong framework which forms the basis of your plant for future years.

**Feeding** Keep the young vine well fed and watered while it is growing strongly, using general-purpose liquid or soluble feed. In the autumn, when the leaves start to turn yellow, gradually cut down the amount of water until the leaves have all fallen off and the compost feels almost completely dry when you touch it.

The vine will remain dormant over winter, during which time it should not be watered at all.

**Pruning** Each winter cut down each stem to about 20 cm (8 in) from the point where it branches out from the main trunk.

**Training** As before, select the strongest three shoots (one from each of the three stumps you have left from last year), and train them up the three canes. They will produce a few flowers and some fruit in the second year, but you should get better crops after that. It is specially important the vine does not dry out or go short of feed when flowers or fruit are present. At the end of the year, after the leaves have fallen from the vine, prune it back as before, leaving just three short stubs at the base.

If you cannot be bothered to train and prune a vine properly you could just let it scramble up wire netting or a trellis. However, this method will produce a lot of tangled shoots and foliage, and not much fruit. It is also something of a health hazard, for it spreads over all the greenhouse, preventing you keeping it clean.

## HERBS

In summer, herbs grow so well outside that there is little point in having them in the greenhouse. But towards late summer they stop growing and by autumn even the perennial kinds, such as chives and mint, start to die down for the winter. This is when it is valuable to have a supply of fresh herbs growing under glass. Even in a cold house you can keep herbs going for several months after they would have died down outdoors.

**Transfer under glass** Dig up clumps of chives, parsley, and marjoram in September, choose pots that comfortably hold all their roots with a bit of room to spare, and pot them up. If you have evergreen herbs, such as sage, rosemary or thyme growing in pots on the patio, move them into the greenhouse too. This saves their leaves from being browned by the frost.

Mint roots can also be dug up from the garden in winter, any time between November and February, and forced into growth early in the cold greenhouse. Half fill a seed tray with compost, and spread the roots out on it. Cover them with several centimetres of compost, and water lightly. If you have a heated propagator, a week or two inside with the temperature set at 16°–21°C (60–70°F) will provide an excellent start. Avoid overwatering herbs in the greenhouse during winter, and remove dead leaves regularly.

With care lettuces can be grown in the greenhouse border to provide a welcome supply of salad leaves in the winter months. They should be planted about 20 cm (8 in) apart and it is a good idea to grow rows of different varieties to obtain the longest possible cropping period.

## LETTUCE

It is not worth trying to grow lettuces in the greenhouse in summer as it is much easier to have them outside in the garden. But if you want lettuce for Christmas or early spring, before the garden crops are ready, then the only way is by growing them under glass, in the greenhouse border.

**Problems** Winter lettuce is not very easy to grow. The naturally poor growing conditions at that time of year make the plants terribly susceptible to grey mould and other fungal diseases, so it is very important to take great care with the crop.

It is also important to choose the right varieties for growing under glass in winter – you can't use the same sort you sow outside in summer. Unlike summer lettuce, which can be sown over a long period of time, winter lettuce must be sown at precisely the right time, which will differ with each variety. The seed packets always specify these sowing times, so follow the instructions.

**Varieties** Good choices for unheated greenhouses include: 'Kwiek', a traditional round lettuce sown in August to cut in time for Christmas; 'Marmer', a compact iceberg type lettuce sown in late August or early September for cutting early in the New Year; 'Plus', another round lettuce, sown in October or November for cutting in April and 'Kelly's', an iceberg type sown from November to January, for cutting from the end of April and early May. In February and March you can sow the outdoor variety 'Little Gem', a miniature cos lettuce with a superb taste, to grow in the greenhouse for cutting in May. For continuity of cropping, try growing a row each of several different varieties.

**Sowing and growing** Sow the seeds very thinly in a pot. Later, when the seedlings are big enough to handle, prick them out into small individual peat pots filled with seed compost. Plant as soon as the first roots start to appear through the sides of the pot (remember that when using peat pots the roots grow straight through the sides so you must plant 'pot and all').

Space the lettuces about 20 cm (8 in) apart. Do not plant them too deeply; ideally the edges of the peat pots should stand about 13 mm ($\frac{1}{2}$ in) above soil level when they are planted. Water the plants well in, but from then on try to avoid watering any more than is absolutely essential. Test by pushing a finger down into the soil and if it feels really dry then water again. Water in the morning so the foliage is dry by night time. Water again when the plants have grown so big that they are just touching each other. Then, unless they start wilting, try not to water again. This is the point when mildew and rotting is most likely to occur. Spray with a fungicide the minute you see any disease, or it spreads like wildfire.

Lettuce is ready to cut once a small heart has formed. The winter types do not form such big hearts as summer outdoor types, and are generally much smaller lettuces anyway, so don't wait too long. Since winter lettuce is such a tricky crop to grow, and the lettuces are not as good as the summer types, lots of people avoid the problem by growing an easier winter crop as the basis for winter salads. Raw spinach leaves or corn salad, for instance, are both far tastier and easier to grow.

## MELONS

Melons are close relatives of cucumbers. The plants look almost identical until they start bearing fruit, and they are similar to grow although there are one or two important differences.

**Varieties** The plants are grown from seed sown in spring, in exactly the same way as described for cucumbers. Plants can usually be bought around May. There are three different basic families of melons: musk melons (which are the old hot-house kind); watermelons (which also need a heated greenhouse to grow well); and canteloupe melons. Canteloupes are the kind to choose for growing in an unheated greenhouse. Of these, the best variety by far is 'Sweetheart', which will give you lots of ripe melons even in a poor summer. 'Sweetheart' melons are small, with a green rind and beautifully scented salmon-pink flesh inside. The flavour is superb. Other good varieties include 'Gaylia' (yellow netted rind with green flesh), 'Blenheim Orange' (cream netted rind with red flesh) and 'Ogen' (orange and beige striped rind with greenish-yellow flesh).

**Cultivation** Plant melons under glass in late May, either in the border, in growing bags, or in large pots as for cucumbers (see page 39). If planting in the border, it is a good idea to pile some soil up into a mound about 15 cm (6 in) high and plant into the top of that. This makes excess water drain away quickly from around the roots, and helps prevent them from rotting.

Water sparingly at first and damp over

Melons are grown in much the same way as cucumbers, and canteloupe varieties are ideal for a cold greenhouse. Unlike cucumbers, the flowers must be pollinated or fruit will fail to develop. Restrict the fruit to three or four per plant and if you are training the plants upwards remember to support the fruit with netting unless you are growing a small fruited variety such as 'Sweetheart'.

frequently as suggested for cucumbers. But when plants start growing strongly they will need more water and regular feeding. It is better to feed little and often rather than risk scorching the roots by giving the plants a solution of feed which is far too strong.

**Training** Cantaloupe plants can either be allowed to ramble over the ground, without any training or pruning, or you can train them up canes just like cucumbers. Although you will get a good crop by just letting them ramble, they take up a lot of room. Also because they are laying on the ground, you will need to protect them from slugs and from rotting. Do this by lifting developing fruit up off the ground, resting them on tiles to prevent them from rotting. Remember to scatter slug pellets regularly around the plants.

Growing melons up canes takes up less room than if they are left to ramble over the ground, and makes it easier to control pests such as greenfly and whitefly. To grow cantaloupe melons up canes, train them in exactly the same way as the cucumbers that are not 'all-female' flowering. Train the main stem of the plant up the cane, tying it in place at 2·5 cm (1 in) intervals with soft string or raffia.

Remove all side shoots from the lower 45 cm (18 in) of stem, and allow them to grow out above this height until they have produced a female flower (which is recognizable by the tiny baby melon just behind it). Stop the side shoot one leaf beyond the developing fruit, to encourage the fruit to swell to a good size.

**Pollination** Unlike cucumbers, melons must be pollinated or they do not set any fruit. If you leave the door open during the day, bees may find their way into the greenhouse and do the job of pollination for you.

But if you want to guarantee pollination occurs every time, you will need to hand pollinate to do this. Find a female flower that has just opened and pick a male flower (which has a short stem behind it, and no small melon). Then remove its petals, and gently dab the centre of the male flower into the middle of the female flower. Do this every day or two, and it should ensure a good crop. As the fruits swell, remove any that are unusually large, or they will continue to grow at the expense of the rest.

Although in the right conditions bees will pollinate your melon flowers, it is safer to hand pollinate them. Pick a fully-opened male flower, remove the petals and dab into the centre of a female flower. For the best results, treat all the female flowers that are open every day in this way.

If you want to grow melons and cucumbers together in the same greenhouse, it is important to keep bees out of the greenhouse as they will pollinate all-female cucumbers with pollen from melons. To prevent this from happening, attach fine netting over the ventilators and drape it over the doorway, and pollinate the melons by hand.

**Harvesting** Once the melons have been pollinated, they swell up fast and need much more feeding and watering than before. The first melons will normally start ripening around July or early August in a warm summer.

You can tell when one is ripe the moment you walk into the greenhouse, because of the sweet musky scent. Also, the ripe melon will have changed colour slightly, and if you gently press the end of the fruit furthest from the stalk, you'll find it slightly 'gives'. A melon should come away easily from the plant when you lift it.

Canteloupes will keep ripening in succession until the weather gets too cold for them in early autumn. Any fully grown fruit still on the plants by then may ripen in a warm shady place indoors. Pull the old plants out when all the fruit has been picked, and no more new fruit are setting.

## PEPPERS

Sweet peppers are now available in supermarkets in a wide range of colours; orange, purple and yellow, as well as the familiar green and red. In addition to the more usual squarish shaped peppers you can also get long pointed kinds, sometimes called 'banana' peppers, and the fiery hot chilli peppers.

You can usually buy plants of ordinary green and red peppers in the spring. If you want the unusual kinds you will have to grow your own from seed.

**Sowing and growing** To raise your own plants you need a heated greenhouse and ideally a propagator, though you can often get by with a warm indoor windowsill. Sow the seeds in March, three or four to a 9 cm ($3\frac{1}{2}$ in) pot, and pull out all but the strongest seedling when they develop, leaving just one plant to grow in each pot.

Peppers are ready to plant when the pot is full of roots. In a cold greenhouse, plant the peppers from mid May to mid June when the weather turns warm. They are not difficult to grow, being cultivated in exactly the same way as aubergines. The plants are similar in habit to aubergines – low growing and bushy – but unlike aubergines they do not have any spines.

**Harvesting** If you want green peppers, they are ready to pick as soon as they are large enough to use – you don't have to wait for them to ripen. If you want red, purple, orange or yellow peppers, you will have to leave them on the plants until they ripen – they are green or creamy green to start with, and their colour only develops when they ripen. However, this takes quite a long time and while they are ripening the plants don't produce any more peppers. This means that your total crop will be very much smaller if you want ripe fruits. So just grow a few extra plants to keep up your supply.

## POTATOES (EARLY)

Very early new potatoes are not only delicious, they are very easy to grow in a cold greenhouse. What's more, they also produce a good crop. Choose an early variety such as 'Duke of York', 'Epicure',

'Chit' seed potatoes for forcing by standing them in a seed tray, eye end uppermost, in a cool dark place indoors. They are ready for planting when the shoots are 3–5 cm ($1\frac{1}{4}$–2 in) long. Don't wait too long, or the shoots will become weak and spindly, and will not grow so quickly once planted out.

'Maris Bard', 'Pentland Javelin', 'Sharpe's Express' or 'Sutton's Foremost'.

**Starting from seed** Buy seed potatoes for forcing under glass as early as you can get them, if possible, in early February. Set the seed potatoes to sprout in a cool dark place indoors. Then stand them in a seed tray with all the 'eyes' uppermost. When the potatoes have sprouts about 2·5–5 cm (1–2 in) long, they are ready for planting.

**Cultivation** Plant in the border soil spacing them about 2·5 cm (1 in) apart. Alternatively, you can grow them in pots or growing bags. If so, you can move the plants outside if you later need space in the greenhouse, but you won't get such a big crop as you would from the border.

Water sparingly until the foliage is growing vigorously. Feeding is not necessary if you applied Growmore when preparing the soil before planting. When the foliage is about 45 cm (18 in) high, the first potatoes should be ready.

**Harvesting** There is no need to dig up the plants; feel around in the top layers of soil surrounding each plant and you will be able to pick the first harvest of baby new potatoes.

After you have picked over all the plants in this way, two or three times, dig up the plants a few at a time and gather the rest of the crop as you need them. Early potatoes grown in the border will have been harvested in time to plant summer crops such as cucumbers, peppers and aubergines.

Potatoes are an excellent vegetable for forcing under glass, as they are easy to grow and produce a good crop. Buy the seed potatoes as early as possible – preferably in early February – and be sure to choose an early variety like these well-grown Pentland Javelin potatoes.

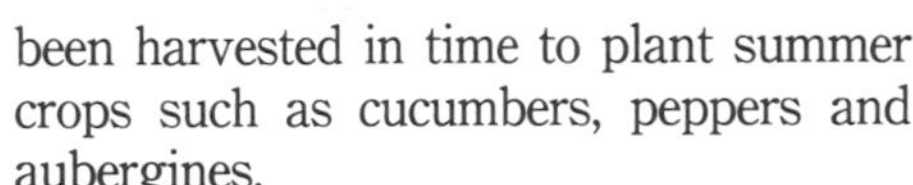

Potatoes grown in pots and growing bags can be moved outside to make room for, perhaps, earlier planted tomatoes from the end of April.

**RADISH**

Radishes are a fast growing crop and they take up little room. This makes them a very productive way of filling any odd gaps between rows of other slower growing crops. They can be sown, for instance, between newly planted rows of tomatoes, cucumbers, peppers or aubergines, early spring-sown carrots or turnips.

For the best results, choose a variety of radish specially intended for growing early under glass, such as 'Ribella', 'Cherry Belle' or 'Saxa Short Top'. These can be sown in a cold greenhouse in spring from February until late April, and again in early autumn for a late crop.

Sow thickly in rows allowing at least 10–13 cm (4–5 in) between surrounding crops, and thin to 5 cm (2 in) apart when the seedlings are large enough. Pull individual radishes as soon they are big enough to eat, leaving the rest to grow on. Don't leave in the ground too long.

**SPINACH**

A very fast maturing crop, handy for making good use of any empty rows in the greenhouse border in early spring or autumn. The leaves can be cooked or used raw in salads.

Choose a summer-cropping variety of spinach such as 'Symphony' or 'Monarch' for spring sowing, and later in the year use a variety specially recommended for autumn sowing such as 'Norvak'. Sow thickly in rows 15–20 cm (6–8 in) apart, and thin in several stages. The thinnings can be used in salads. If large leaves are required, thin seedlings to 15 cm (6 in) apart: if they are left 2·5–5 cm (1–2 in) apart, you will get much smaller leaves.

Protect the plants from slugs as they grow. When the leaves are large enough, begin regular pickings. Finally, pull the plants out when space is needed for other crops, or when the spinach plants start going to seed.

**SPRING ONIONS**

Spring onions are slow growing, but you can get a worthwhile crop from a small space. Sow seeds of the variety 'White Lisbon' in rows 20 cm (8 in) apart in the border. Seeds sown in early February will give spring onions ready to pull in early June; sow in autumn for an earlier spring crop. Sow thickly, and thin the seedlings out using them for salads.

**STRAWBERRIES (EARLY)**

Early strawberries are a very productive crop for a cold greenhouse. The plants only occupy the greenhouse for a few months in late winter and early spring, leaving space for summer crops the rest of the time. Early varieties such as 'Cambridge Vigour', 'Grandee', or 'Red Gauntlet' are the best for forcing, though you will get earlier fruit than usual from any variety of strawberry grown under glass.

**Cultivation** Start to grow strawberries in late summer or early autumn with new plants – which should be potted into 13 cm (5 in) pots on delivery, or use runners from your own fruit garden. These should be pegged down into 9 cm ($3\frac{1}{2}$ in) pots of good compost while still attached to the parent plant, and encouraged to root. When well rooted, cut the runner and move the pots outdoors where you can look after them. Pot them on into 13 cm (5 in) pots when necessary.

To obtain strawberry plants for forcing in the greenhouse propagate from runners on plants outside. Peg the runners into 9 cm ($3\frac{1}{2}$ in) pots of compost in mid to late summer, and cut the connecting stems when the young plants are well rooted.

Radishes are a useful crop for making your greenhouse as productive as possible, as they grow quickly and can be planted in between other, slower growing crops. Sown in early spring or the autumn, they will provide fresh salad vegetables when little else is available in the vegetable garden.

To obtain a good crop of forced strawberries you must start with new plants every year. Allow the fruit to become completely ripe before picking, so that the full flavour develops. Do not force the same plants twice – your second crop will be disappointing.

Leave the young plants out of doors for the first part of winter, choosing a north facing spot where the roots will get a good chilling. In January, move them into the greenhouse. Stand them on the staging, and protect from slugs and mice. When they start growing, gradually begin watering and feeding with a general-purpose liquid or soluble feed, but be very careful not to overwater or the plants may rot.

**Fruiting** When the first flowers appear, pollinate them with a soft artist's brush. This is necessary because it is too early in the season for large numbers of pollinating insects to do the job for you.

To hand pollinate, dab the brush gently into the centre of all the open flowers. Later, when the fruit starts setting, keep the compost in the pots just moist and shade the plants from strong sun on very bright days. Ventilate the greenhouse well when the weather is warm so the temperature does not get too high, otherwise the plants may be scorched.

Leave the fruit to ripen fully on the plants so they develop their full flavour, and continue feeding regularly while you are picking to encourage further flowering and fruiting. When all the fruit have been picked, the plants can be put out in the garden to fruit again next year. Do not force the same plants twice, as they won't give such a good crop second time round – instead, raise new plants from runners each year.

## TOMATOES

They are the number one cold greenhouse crop. Many different varieties of tomatoes are available and it is largely a matter of personal choice which you grow.

**Varieties** Old favourites such as 'Ailsa Craig' and 'Alicante' are still considered among the best for flavour, while many people prefer the heavy cropping 'Moneymaker'. 'Beefsteak' tomatoes, large often ugly shaped fruit of the sort found in Spain, are available in this county now; 'Marmande' is very much like the Spanish tomatoes, while 'Dombo' and 'Dombello' are the same shape as normal tomatoes but very much bigger.

These two varieties are particularly interesting because they lack the unpleasant hard core often found in many beefsteak tomatoes. Also very popular now are 'cherry' tomatoes – varieties such as 'Gardener's Delight' and 'Sweet 100' – which have very tiny, bite-sized fruit with a particularly superb flavour.

Yellow tomatoes, though less well known, also have a very good flavour – try 'Yellow Perfection', or the orange and yellow striped 'Tigerella'. Also worth considering are modern tomatoes, specially bred for disease resistance. If you have experienced problems with root disease in tomatoes and do not want the bother of changing the border soil or growing in bags, try the variety 'Piranto'. There is also a trend towards low bush tomatoes that do not need all the staking, training and side shooting required by normal tomatoes. Of these, 'Tornado' is exceptionally well flavoured. Many of these varieties are available as young plants in spring. Don't be put off if some are described as outdoor tomatoes – they will grow even better in a cold greenhouse.

**Growing from seed** You need a lot of heat and an early start to grow your own tomato plants. Sow three to four seeds to each 9 cm ($3\frac{1}{2}$ in) pot in February or early March, and thin out to leave only the strongest seedling. Keep the plants growing in pots until the first flower has opened (this method avoids plants with abundant leaves but few tomatoes).

**Cultivation** Plant tomatoes in a cold greenhouse from the third week in April in

**CULTIVATING TOMATOES**
1. Plant tomatoes in tubs, growing bags or the greenhouse border when the first truss of flowers is just starting to open. This prevents the plants growing leafy and unproductive.

2. Tie the top of each plant to its cane regularly, to keep up with the rate at which it is growing. Don't tie too tightly, as the stem will swell as the plant grows.

3. Pinch out the side shoots (unless you are growing a bush variety) before they grow too large, taking care not to remove any flower trusses by mistake. When the plant reaches the roof of the greenhouse, pinch out the growing tip.

Yellow tomatoes, like 'Yellow Perfection' shown here, are unusual and attractive, and their fruit is of excellent flavour.

a mild season and in the south of the country. If the weather is cold or you live in the north, wait for mid or late May. After planting, water the plants in with a solution of liquid tomato feed diluted to the normal strength, and then keep them distinctly dryish. For the first two weeks, water them sparingly – just enough to prevent them from wilting.

Meanwhile, push a tall cane in alongside each plant for support and, as it grows, tie the main stem to the cane every 20–30 cm (8–12 in) with soft string. Remove all the side shoots as soon as you see them, taking care not to snap off the top of the plant by mistake.

If you are growing bush varieties, don't tie plants up or remove the side shoots. Instead, just use two or three short canes and some string to keep the plants off the ground, as for peppers and aubergines. As the plants grow, water them sparingly until the bottom truss (bunch) of tomatoes has set and you can see the small fruit just starting to swell.

**Feeding and watering** It is important to both feed and water the plants regularly. From the time the first fruit start swelling, increase both feeding and watering in order to keep pace with both the larger number of leaves and the developing tomatoes.

Try to keep the compost or soil moist all the time to prevent problems such as blossom end rot, or split fruit, from occurring later. This is particularly important with plants growing in pots or growing bags, which dry out much faster than those growing in the border. Spray the plants over with water from a hosepipe on warm days to help the fruit to set (putting your finger over the end will produce a fine, gentle spray).

**Harvesting** The first tomatoes should start ripening when the plants are around 1·2–1·5 m (4–5 ft) tall. By then they will be carrying a large crop of unripe fruit. At this stage they will need watering every day and feeding frequently, otherwise you will not achieve maximum cropping from your plants.

When the first tomatoes start changing colour, leave them to ripen fully on the plants for maximum flavour. To pick them, snap them off at the knuckle, a natural kink in the short stem attaching the fruit to the plants. Bend up against the direction of the knuckle and the tomatoes will come away complete with their green calyx (sepals) round the top – picked this way they will keep longer than if just pulled from the plant.

Do not be tempted to remove any leaves from the bottom of the plant to speed up ripening because this can spoil the flavour of the tomatoes and lead to them being scorched by the sun. Only remove lower leaves when they have turned yellow, which happens naturally as they age – it does not mean there is anything wrong with the plants.

**Problems** If all the leaves turn yellowish, it may be a sign that the plants are not being fed enough. In this case, feed them

'Sweet 100', like all cherry tomatoes, has a particularly intense flavour. The heavily-cropping trusses of fruit must be harvested regularly to keep the plant producing tomatoes for as long as possible. The plants must also be fed and watered regularly so that the trusses forming at the top of the plant have a chance to develop fully.

more often while using the same strength solution as usual.

Also watch out for whitefly and greenfly, the commonest pests of tomatoes, and spray when necessary. Use a product which allows you to eat treated crops within a day or two of them being sprayed, since once tomatoes start ripening you will have some ready to pick almost every day.

**Early autumn** Around mid August to early September, encourage the remaining green tomatoes to ripen before the plants are killed off by cold autumn weather. To do this, first stop the plants. Remove the growing tips of the main stems one leaf beyond the last truss of small green fruit that is just starting to swell.

Also start reducing the amount of water you give the plants (they won't need so much now anyway since much of the crop will have been picked, and the weather is cooler). In addition, you can stop feeding altogether because the plants will soon be pulled out. Remove some of the leaves, particularly on bush tomatoes, to let the weaker sun into the plants to help ripen the remaining fruit.

Six to eight weeks later, stop watering altogether, and after a few more days cut through the base of the stems just above ground level. Leave the plants hanging from their canes. This works wonders, and will ripen up most of the remaining full-sized green fruit.

Just before pulling out the plants, strip all the remaining large green tomatoes from the plants and put them in a cool, darkish place indoors, where they should ripen within two weeks. You can speed up the process by shutting them in a box or drawer with some ripening apples; the ethylene gas given off by the apples helps to ripen the tomatoes. (The traditional way of ripening green tomatoes, on a warm sunny windowsill, makes them shrivel very quickly.) Any tomatoes that do not ripen within two weeks should be thrown away.

If the old tomato crop can be pulled out and the greenhouse given its thorough annual clean before the middle of September, there will be time and space to sow a crop of autumn salads or other fast maturing vegetables. This will probably be more productive than leaving the tomatoes until they are killed by the frost, because as the temperature begins to drop very few new tomatoes will develop – and even if there are any, they will take a long time to ripen.

## TURNIPS

Another very useful quick crop that makes profitable use of a spare row or two in the border in early spring. Turnips can also be sown between newly planted rows of tomatoes, peppers or aubergines, which take time to fill all their allotted space.

Choose a fast maturing variety suitable for use when very small, such as 'Tokyo Cross', 'Snowball', or 'Milan White Forcing'. Sow thinly in rows 15–20 cm (6–8 in) apart, and thin when the seedlings are big enough, leaving them 10 cm (4 in) apart.

Apply a soil insecticide to prevent larvae from spoiling the roots. Keep the soil just moist – there is no need to feed this crop. Start pulling turnips as soon as they are the size of golf balls; they will be tender and more flavoursome when small.

Left: If you grow tomatoes in the greenhouse border dig plenty of garden compost or manure into the soil each year, to provide the plants with a rich growing medium.

Above: 'Snowball' is a good variety of turnip for the cold greenhouse, and its tender white roots are best harvested when they are still quite small – the size of golf balls.

# PLANTS FOR THE HEATED GREENHOUSE

If you have a greenhouse that can be kept free of frost in winter, or better still at around 4·5°C (40°F), the scope of your growing activities increases enormously. For a start you can try all the plants you could grow in a cold house, but earlier and more easily. You can also grow frost-tender plants such as geraniums and fuchsias in quantity, as you no longer need to restrict yourself to numbers that can be housed on an indoor windowsill in winter. But best of all, a slightly heated greenhouse makes it possible to grow many fascinating plants which it is only really feasible to keep there, including some delightful collector's plants.

Many greenhouse plants, including azaleas, require plenty of humidity in the summer. During particularly dry, sunny weather it is a good idea to damp down the greenhouse path with a hose or watering can. As the water evaporates from the surface of the path, it will keep the atmosphere in the greenhouse humid. This also helps tomatoes, peppers and aubergines to set, and is a deterrent to red spider mite.

## ORNAMENTAL PLANTS

### AZALEA

Indoor azaleas (*Azalea indica*) are not ideal plants for greenhouse cultivation because they like a steady temperature of 10°–16°C (50–60°F) and moist, shady growing conditions. Also note that when the flowers are over, the plants can be kept for another year if they are temporarily placed in the greenhouse.

Azaleas aren't the easiest of plants to keep, let alone to get to flower again the following year. If you decide to have a go, they need special care. After flowering, remove the dead flower heads, and spray the plants with a systemic fungicide as protection against grey mould. Keep the plants just moist but not saturated, and shade them from direct sun.

In April, pot them carefully into new pots only slightly larger than the previous ones (this is important), using lime-free or ericaceous compost. From time to time give a weak liquid feed, and it also pays to use an occasional foliar feed, such as one based on seaweed. In addition, use a spray containing sequestered iron once or twice to keep the leaves a healthy green colour, and repeat when necessary if the leaves start to look pale.

Make sure the greenhouse is well ven-

Azaleas (*Azalea indica*) are not the easiest plants to grow under glass, but if you are successful you will be rewarded with a glorious show of brightly coloured blooms.

tilated as spring progresses, so the plants do not get too hot. From June until September put the pots outside in the garden. Choose a sheltered and lightly shaded spot where the soil is moist, ideally under trees, and plunge the pots up to their rims into the soil. Keep them lightly watered, occasionally spray with water, and continue feeding as usual. In mid September put them back in the greenhouse, and keep them moist and shaded from direct sun. Spray as before with benomyl if any grey mould appears.

Azaleas prefer a minimum temperature of 10°C (50°F), though they will tolerate 7·5°C (45°F) so long as they are kept slightly drier than usual. If you cannot maintain the latter temperature, it is probably safer to move plants back indoors when the nights start getting cold, around late October. Otherwise, keep them in the greenhouse until most of the buds are showing colour, then move them indoors to flower.

While they are in bud or in flower, keep azaleas moist but not waterlogged, and regularly fed. It is not practical to propagate new plants at home; if you find you can keep them succesfully however, a very cheap way of increasing your stock is to buy plants that have finished flowering after Christmas (often half price or less) and grow them on.

### CACTI AND SUCCULENTS

These are fascinating little plants. They are very collectable, and as a result of their popularity there are now countless varieties to choose from. Contrary to popular belief, cacti do not just flower in deserts; nor do they just flower every seven years or only when they are 100 years old – many kinds flower every year, even from an early age.

**Display** Species of Mammillaria and Rebutia can be relied upon to produce a particularly good show of spring flowers.

Cacti and other succulents can make a fascinating collection for the greenhouse. There are hundreds of varieties to choose from, many of which produce beautiful flowers.

*Mammillaria zeilmanniana*, one of many members of the Mammillaria family that are relatively easy to bring into flower every year.

Orchid cacti (*Epiphyllums*) also flower freely each year and have large, spectacular flowers. Some cacti are grown for their weird shapes, such as the prickly pears (*Opuntia),* or for their ferocious spines, such as *Ferocactus*.

Succulents, too, normally flower quite well from early in life; some kinds, like the living stones (*Lithops*), are very small and actually resemble stones. Many, like *Euphorbia*, have strange shapes, or spiky leaves, like *Aloe* and *Agave*.

**Cultivation** As a general rule, cacti and succulents are desert plants that like plenty of sun, a good gritty compost, and not too much water, especially in winter when most kinds are best kept entirely dry and at a temperature only just above freezing 4°–5°C (38–40°F).

In spring, when plants begin growing naturally, water by spraying once or twice a week. Do not begin watering the soil until plants have quite clearly made some new growth – start watering too early and they may rot.

Repot plants that need it in the spring, again just as they start to grow. Use a proper cactus compost, or mix half grit with John Innes seed compost. Water sparingly for several weeks.

**Feeding and watering** Compared to most greenhouse plants, cacti and succulents need very little watering at the best of times – they should be allowed to dry out between waterings, even in summer. If they are overwatered, there is a strong risk that they may rot.

Being slow growing, the plants need little feeding, perhaps just once or twice a year – in the spring when they start into growth, and again when they are in bud or flower. Special cactus fertilizers are available, and are ideal.

**Forest cacti** Many kinds of cacti do not grow in deserts, but in trees in the tropical rain forests. These plants, which include orchid cacti, Easter and Christmas cacti, have different cultivation requirements from desert cacti.

During the growing season, feed and water them rather more than normal cacti, and shade them from strong direct sun. They tend to flower better if placed out in the garden for the summer, with their pots plunged up to their rims in moist soil in a sheltered, slightly shaded spot.

Bring them back into the greenhouse in September. Keep the plants much drier in winter, but not completely dry (like normal cacti), watering them just enough to stop the leaves from shrivelling. Rain forest cacti and most succulents need a slightly higher minimum winter temperature than desert cacti – about 4·5°–7·5°C (40°–45°F) is best.

**Living stones** These plants also require slightly different treatment from other kinds of cacti or succulents. They originate from particularly inhospitable

This Mammillaria produces gorgeous bright red flowers in the spring.

Lithops, or living stones, are among the most unusual plants that can be grown in the greenhouse, with their strange, pebble-like appearance and daisy-like flowers.

deserts where they are only able to grow for a limited part of the year. You must therefore duplicate this short growing season, or the plants will soon die. You must also keep them completely dry until they show signs of starting to grow naturally (which is not normally until quite well into summer), when they may be watered.

The new plant bodies will emerge from the dried up remains of the old ones, flower (if large enough to do so), and within a few weeks start to shrivel again. When this happens, reduce the watering gradually and allow them to dry out when they are ready. Don't try and make the plants keep growing by giving them water when they want to be dry – it doesn't work!

**Propagation** Cacti and succulents are surprisingly easy to propagate. Those that produce stems, including the Christmas cacti and orchard cacti, can be propagated by cuttings placed in sharp sand; opuntias are propagated by detaching a fully grown young pad and pushing it half way into a pot of sharp sand.

Globular cacti that have rotted off at the base due to overwatering can often be rerooted by slicing the rotten part away, dipping the cut section in hormone rooting powder, and treating it as a cutting. Some plants, such as small clump-forming Mammillarias and Rebutias naturally produce lots of small bodies. With these, individual bodies can be detached from the group and rooted like cuttings.

Many kinds of cacti and succulents, including living stones and mother-in-law's tongue (*Sanseveria*), can be propagated by dividing large old plants or removing well established offsets and potting them separately – the best time to do this is just when growth starts. Many cacti and succulents can also be propagated from seed, though this is a slow and specialist job.

If you get really interested in this group of plants, it pays to join one of the specialist societies; many large towns have a branch holding regular meetings. They will give you the chance to learn more about them – many individual varieties have special demands and you can also swap plants and obtain unusual seeds.

Calceolaria, or slipper flowers, are colourful pot plants that can be raised from seed each year as annuals. They are available in a range of yellows, reds and oranges.

Below: Carnivorous plants require humidity and should be protected from bright sunlight. They are fascinating plants to grow, although their unusual requirements make them a little more difficult to accommodate than most other greenhouse plants.

**CALCEOLARIA**
Pretty annual pot plants which flower in winter and early spring, producing large groups of brightly coloured flowers shaped like segments of an orange. Plants just starting to flower are available in autumn and winter, and will keep flowering for about six weeks in the greenhouse. But it can be fun to raise your own plants from seed.

**Sowing and growing** Calceolaria are slightly tricky to grow, and need a little care to be successful. The seeds must be sown in mid summer, sprinkled thinly on the surface of the compost, and not covered over; just put a piece of cling film plastic over the top of the pot.

When the seedlings are big enough to handle, prick them out into 9 cm ($3\frac{1}{2}$ in pots). The largest, fastest growing plants can be potted on again, into 13 cm (5 in) pots if you want a few big specimens. Both seedlings and young plants must be kept as cool and shady as possible, and never allowed to dry out. They also need humid air around them all the time. The best way of providing the right conditions is to grow them under the staging in a greenhouse with glass down to the ground, standing them on capillary matting which is kept permanently damp.

Feed and water regularly, and gradually get the plants accustomed to more light as they grow bigger, though they will always need to be shaded from very bright sun. Spray over with water and damp the house down on hot days to maintain high humidity. In the autumn it may be advisable to spray against grey mould, to which the plants are rather prone.

When flower buds are well formed and colourful, plants can be moved into the house if you wish, or left to make a winter display out in the greenhouse. When the flowers are past their best, throw the old plants away because they are annuals and die after flowering.

**CAPSICUM**
Another popular winter pot plant, grown for its brightly coloured fruit, which resemble miniature peppers in shades of red, purple, orange, green and gold. Plants are available from early autumn onwards and last for two to three months after they start

Cineraria is a pretty annual that provides attractive flowering pot plants during the winter months. Like calceolaria, they demand extra care if they are to be successfully raised from seed.

producing peppers. But you can grow your own from seeds which are sown any time during spring and summer.

**Sowing and growing** Keep the pots of seed moist and shaded from the sun, and grow the young seedlings on in the same conditions. When they are big enough, pot them individually into 9 cm ($3\frac{1}{2}$ in) pots, and gradually accustom them to more light. They will still need to be kept permanently moist, but not saturated, and shaded from the strongest sun.

Peppers will start forming from autumn onwards, depending on when you sowed the seed. It is best to sow several batches at different dates to give you a succession of plants lasting all winter. Plants may be taken indoors when they are in fruit, or left to make a display in the greenhouse. After fruiting has finished, the plants should be thrown away.

### CINERARIA

Most attractive winter and early spring flowering pot plants, with large single daisy-like flowers in a wide range of bright colours. Plants in flower are available from autumn onwards. They last about four weeks indoors but up to six or seven weeks in the greenhouse where conditions are cooler.

You can also grow your own plants from seed, but like calceolaria they are slightly tricky to grow as the seeds must be sown in the greenhouse in summer, and kept cool, moist and shaded. Sow the seeds and grow the young plants on in the same way as described for calceolaria (see page 56). A June sowing will give you flowering plants at Christmas. You could also make two or three other sowings in May and July for plants to provide a succession of flowers from late autumn through into early spring. Throw the old plants away when they finish flowering, and raise new plants each year.

### CARNIVOROUS PLANTS

Carnivorous plants include the well-known sundews, pitcher plants, and Venus fly traps that are popular despite their unusual feeding habits.

They have rather different requirements from most greenhouse plants, and in fact many people set up their greenhouses specially to grow nothing but carnivorous plants, thus making it easier to provide the conditions they need. However, with care, you can grow them successfully alongside other plants in a mixed collection. It is worth trying one or two plants, as they are fascinating to grow.

**Cultivation** In general, carnivorous plants need humid conditions and slight shade – enough to protect them from bright sunlight. They need constant moisture in summer, when their pots should be stood in a trough containing 2·5–5 cm (1–2 in) of soft water (either rain water, or water that has been boiled in the kettle and cooled). Just as important, they should never be fed with normal plant food – instead they must always be allowed to catch insects, which they digest and use as their source of nutrients.

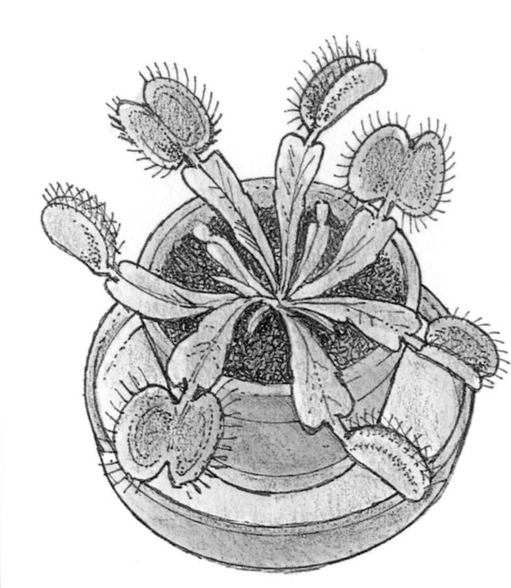

**GROWING CARNIVOROUS PLANTS**

To help carnivorous plants thrive in summer, stand them in a trough or saucer containing 3–5 cm ($1\frac{1}{4}$–2 in) of soft water – either rain water or water that has been boiled and allowed to cool. Keep the plants humid and shaded, but never feed them with plant fertilizers of any kind. If their natural food (flies) is in short supply, you can attract more by hanging a small piece of meat nearby.

*Dionaea muscipula*, the Venus fly trap, is the most popular of all the carnivorous plants. It does not require very deep compost and is quite happy grouped with others in a shallow pan.

From October to early April the plants should be kept rather drier; take them out of the watering trough and just hand water occasionally when the compost becomes very dry. During this time it is important that a minimum temperature of 4·5°C (40°F) be maintained.

**Growth and propagation** Carnivorous plants are not the easiest of species to cultivate; nor do they grow very fast – in fact they will be perfectly happy in their original pots for one or two years.

When repotting is necessary it is best to buy the special compost for carnivorous plants; normal potting compost will not do.

These plants are not the easiest to propagate; they do not make the sort of growth that allows cuttings to be taken, and all except the sundews are slow and difficult to raise from seed.

Established plants can be divided up when they have grown into large clumps. Sundews may occasionally seed themselves into other pots, and these seedlings can be potted individually. Again, if you take a real fancy to this group of plants, it is a good idea to join the Carnivorous Plant Society for both information and supplies of seeds.

**CHRYSANTHEMUMS**

Chrysanthemums are a large group of plants which are categorized primarily according to when they flower. Early varieties flower in late summer or early autumn, and are planted outdoors in the garden. Later flowering chrysanthemums bloom after the frosts have started, so they are grown in pots which are stood outdoors in summer and brought into the greenhouse in September to protect the flowers from frost. They generally flower in November or December. New chrysanthemum plants are grown each year from cuttings and it is possible to buy them already rooted.

**Propagation** If you have grown chrysanthemums before, the old plants can be kept and used to take cuttings. To do this, cut the old plants back to several centimetres above the ground after flowering, and store them in a frost-free place overwinter. They should be potted up in peat in January or February, and kept in a warm place – such as a propagator – to force them into growth.

When shoots start to appear, take them as cuttings when they are 10 cm (4 in) long. Chrysanthemum cuttings root easily in pots of seed compost or sharp sand in the propagator, in temperatures of 16–18·5°C (60–65°F).

**Cultivation** Whether you root your own cuttings or buy them, pot them up into 9 cm ($3\frac{1}{2}$ in) pots and grow on in a frost-free greenhouse. Water them sparingly to start with, giving the young plants just enough water to prevent them from wilting until they are established.

It is also usual to stop chrysanthemum cuttings once or twice before they are more than several centimetres high, making them produce more shoots and an abundance of flowers.

When they begin growing strongly, increase the watering and start feeding

Above right: Chrysanthemums can provide a plentiful supply of long-lasting cut flowers for the home.

Below right: 'Autumn Days' is an intermediate type: the petals are partly 'incurved' and partly 'reflexed'.

regularly with a general-purpose liquid feed. Pot the greenhouse flowering varieties into 13 cm (5 in) pots once the roots start growing out through the drainage hole in the bottom of the original containers.

**Hardening off** Two weeks before chrysanthemums for the garden are planted out, they should be hardened off – stand their pots outdoors during the day, but bring them in at night. This should be done during a warm spell in April or May.

Winter flowering greenhouse chrysanthemums should be similarly hardened off and moved outside at the same time. Pot them on into 20–25 cm (8–10 in) sized pots when they outgrow the 13 cm (5 in) sized ones.

**Support and training** Both types of chrysanthemums will need to be supported to keep their stems straight – push one or more 13 cm (5 in) canes in beside each plant and tie the stems loosely to it with soft string or raffia. When the first tiny flower buds appear at the tops of the stems, decide whether you want 'spray' chrysanthemums (which have several small flowers on each stem) or 'bloom' (which have one very large flower per stem).

To grow sprays, nip out the crown bud (the large one at the very tip of the shoot), leaving the cluster of smaller buds behind. If you want large single blooms, remove all the small buds from the stem and leave only the large crown bud. Do this disbudding while the buds are still very small.

**Autumn** Towards the end of September move the pots of winter flowering chrysanthemums back into the greenhouse. The house should be heated just enough to keep it frost-free, and ventilated well at every opportunity to avoid grey mould, which can spoil the developing flowers. If it does become troublesome, rather than spray, use smoke cones to control grey mould. These are similar to fireworks – you just light the touchpaper,

SPRAY AND BLOOM CHRYSANTHEMUMS

1. To produce spray chrysanthemums, with lots of small blooms on each stem, pinch out the larger 'crown' bud when the buds are still very small.

2. To produce bloom chrysanthemums, with a single, large flower on each stem, pinch out all the side buds, leaving just the crown bud to develop.

The spray chrysanthemums make beautiful pot plants for the home, with masses of long-lasting blooms on each plant.

Another popular subject for flowering pot plants, cyclamen can be raised in a shady part of a heated greenhouse and will last longer there than plants grown indoors. A few named varieties are obtainable and there is a range of white, pink and red shades from which to choose.

and then shut the greenhouse door, and watch it fill with fungicide smoke.

**Cut flowers** Cut both indoor and outdoor chrysanthemums when the flowers are just fully open. Provided they are put straight into clean water, the cut flowers can last from four to six weeks indoors. When all the flowers have been cut, prune back the old stems and either dig up the roots or allow the pots to dry out, keeping them for cuttings the following spring.

**CYCLAMEN**

Popular flowering pot plants for winter and early spring decoration. Cyclamen plants are sold in flower throughout the autumn and winter. Although they are usually grown indoors, they also make ideal plants for a heated greenhouse as the flowers will last longer there. Do not raise them indoors – it can be too warm.

**Cultivation** Under glass, cyclamen like a minimum winter temperature of 4·5°C (40°F). While they are growing and flowering, they need to be kept just moist, and occasionally fed with a well-diluted liquid feed. They must also be shaded from direct sun.

By late March the plants will be starting to decline – no new flowers will be produced and the leaves turn yellow. This is quite natural, and indicates that the plants are preparing to become dormant. When this happens, gradually reduce the watering and stop feeding the plants. The leaves will soon dry out and fall off, leaving just the dormant corm. The pots can be tipped on their sides and stored under the greenhouse staging for the summer. During this time they should be kept perfectly dry. (Putting them on their sides prevents water dripping into the pots which make the corms rot.)

**New growth** Around the beginning of August cyclamen will start growing again. When the first new leaves appear, stand the pots upright and put them back on the staging, keeping them heavily shaded. (In a glass-to-ground greenhouse, grow them in the shade under the staging.) Begin watering, a little at first, and delay feeding till the first flower buds appear. Feed occasionally from then on. Plants can be taken indoors temporarily while they are looking their best, or left in the greenhouse to make a winter display. The same corms can be re-used for several years, though the best flowers are generally produced on younger plants.

**Seedlings** New plants are grown from seed which can be sown any time in spring or summer. Keep the young seedlings permanently just moist, and well shaded from the sun. Pot them individually into 9 cm ($3\frac{1}{2}$ in) pots when they are big enough, leaving the top half of the corm above the level of the compost. Repot them into 13 cm (5 in) pots when they outgrow the original containers, after which the plants will not need further repotting. From the time you sow seeds, it takes about 18 months to have young cyclamen ready to start flowering.

**FREESIAS**

Freesias make interesting, if slightly untidy, plants to grow in a greenhouse, which must be heated to 4·5°C (40°F) in winter. The flowers, which are brightly coloured and highly scented, are produced in spring. They make a good display under glass if left on the plants, but are normally used as cut flowers indoors.

**Cultivation** Freesia corms are available in the autumn. Make sure you buy

Cyclamen add a beautiful splash of winter colour in the heated greenhouse among other tender subjects – here they are displayed with some Agave and Smithiantha.

those for greenhouse cultivation and not the kind intended for growing out in the garden. Plant the corms as soon as they arrive. Put six in around the sides of a 13 cm (5 in) pot filled with potting compost, so the tips are just below the surface of the compost. Water them in lightly, and do not water again until the foliage starts to grow. From then on, water freesias sparingly at all times.

Meanwhile push a few split canes in round the sides of the pot, and crisscross between them with soft string. This supports both foliage and flower stems, keeps the plants from sprawling too badly, and is also essential for keeping the flower stalks straight. If you want particularly straight stems, tie each flower spike individually to its own split cane.

**Flowering and dormancy** From the time the flower spikes start to appear, reduce watering to the bare minimum. Flowers may be cut when each stem has one flower fully open, and most of the remaining buds showing their true colour. They last well in water when cut fresh. After the flowers have either been cut or there are no more on the plant, resume watering normally and give regular liquid feeds, building up the corms for next year's display.

When the foliage starts to yellow, the bulbs are preparing to become dormant for the summer and watering should gradually be reduced until the old leaves die and fall off. When the corms are completely dormant and dry, knock them out of their pots and keep them in a cool, dark place before replanting again in the early autumn.

**Propagation** Freesia plants propagate themselves – your original six corms will most likely have increased themselves to twelve, or more, by the end of their first season's growth. When you replant them, it is a good idea to put the largest corms together in the same pot, since this is the way in which they will flower best. Small corms may not flower in their first year, needing to reach a good size first.

Freesias can also be grown from seeds, which are sown in the greenhouse in spring. Keep the seedlings well shaded from the sun, and constantly just moist – but not too wet. Feed them regularly throughout the summer, and keep them growing through winter. Some of the stronger seedlings may flower in their first year. Allow the plants to go dormant when the leaves yellow in late spring, and expect most of them to start flowering during the following year.

### GERBERA

Gerberas are brightly coloured South African daisies that are very popular as cut flowers, and can be grown without much difficulty in the greenhouse border. The plants form a rosette of grey-green leaves shaped rather like those of a dandelion, from the centre of which the flowers grow on long stalks.

**Varieties** Since plants are rarely available it is best to grow your own from seed. Choose *Gerbera jamesonii*, or one of the

Above and right: With their brightly coloured, highly scented flowers, freesias make a beautiful display in the greenhouse and are among the longest lasting of all cut flowers.
Below: Dwarf gerberas are available as pot plants, but you can also grow your own from seed.

tall stemmed hybrids. Dwarf gerberas are an innovation, and are often sold as pot plants, though they too can be grown from seed. Varieties such as 'Dwarf Frisbee' or 'Happipot' are suitable.

**Cultivation** Sow seed of gerbera in February in a heated propagator at 18·5°C (65°F) if possible, otherwise delay sowing until late April or May when the weather is warmer. (Late sown plants may not flower in their first year.) Prick the seedlings out when they are big enough, and then pot them into 9 cm ($3\frac{1}{2}$ in) pots. Dwarf varieties should be potted on into 13 cm (5 in) half pots. Full-sized types are best planted out into the border – 30–45 cm (12–18in) apart – when their original pots are filled with roots.

Gerberas need a warm sunny situation and dislike too much humidity. Water the plants sparingly, and feed regularly with a general-purpose liquid or soluble feed. Pot plants can be taken indoors when they come into flower, or left in the greenhouse for decoration.

Flowers of tall-stemmed varieties can be gathered as soon as they are fully open. Do not cut them in the usual way, instead pull the stems as you would rhubarb, taking care not to pull up the plant at the same time. In winter, keep gerberas almost dry, and cut off any dead leaves. If they are kept very dry they will survive in a greenhouse kept barely frost-free, but plants get through the winter in better condition if you maintain a minimum winter temperature of 4·5°C (40°F).

### LEMONS

Though growing lemon trees from pips is an interesting exercise, it is unlikely the trees will ever produce any fruit. Buying a grafted plant is a much better bet. This way, you will get lots of full-sized edible fruit from a plant of a manageable size, even in the first year. The flowers are delightful too – not only are they beautifully scented, but they are produced almost continuously. It is common to find flowers, and both green and ripe lemons, on the same plant virtually all the year round. This prolific nature, coupled with attractive camellia-like evergreen leaves, makes lemons amongst the most attractive of greenhouse plants to grow. They are surprisingly easy too.

Named varieties are occasionally available. 'Meyers Lemon' is probably the best to grow as it produces a reliable crop of large fruit, and only needs a minimum temperature of 4·5°C (40°F) in winter, whereas most other citrus plants need from 7·5–10°C (45–50°F).

**Cultivation** Repot lemon plants every spring into a larger sized pot and John Innes potting compost No. 3, until eventually they end up in 30–38 cm (12–15 in) pots. In subsequent years, top dress instead, replacing the top layer of compost with fresh John Innes compost No. 3.

Feed and water well during the growing season, but in winter keep the compost much drier. However, an occasional light watering will be needed to stop the leaves from shrivelling or falling off.

**Pruning and pests** Plants will need pruning in the autumn or spring to keep them in shape and prevent them from getting too big. Cut out entirely any branches that are dead or damaged, and shorten back any that are too long by half or one third their length. Always cut just above a leaf joint.

When the fruit appears, do not be in too much of a hurry to pick it. Let the fruit remain on the plants until fully ripe, when they will be coloured deep yellow, and taste much better than shop-bought lemons that are often picked when they are still bright green.

Lemon plants are not affected much by pests, such as greenfly, as their leaves are too tough for the insects to feed on. However, they are often attacked by scale insect, so look under the leaves regularly and spray as soon as any appear. If left unchecked the plant can be badly damaged, and the leaves will also be covered with black sooty mould.

It is not practical to propagate new lemon trees at home, as they have to be grafted. However, the original plant will be long lived if well looked after, and can be expected to produce a few lemons at a time almost all the year round.

### PASSION FLOWER

Climbing perennial pot plants best known for their extraordinary flowers, although many of the less well known varieties also produce edible passion fruit, just like those found in supermarkets.

Left: The passion flower that is most commonly available as a pot plant, *Passiflora caerulea*. Like other passion flowers, it can be trained up canes or wire netting to develop into a large and decorative climber in the greenhouse.

Opposite: *Passiflora quadrangularis* is one of the varieties of passion flower grown for its edible fruits.

Although poinsettias are a familiar sight at Christmas, they naturally produce their red bracts in the spring. If you propagate your own plants from cuttings expect them to flower around Easter.

Plants of the common passion flower (*Passiflora caerulea*) are readily available. This species is grown for its flowers, and rarely produces fruit, which would be egg-shaped, yellow, and not suitable for eating. If you do want fruits, grow *P. edulis* or *P. quadrangularis*. Both have large and fascinating flowers, followed by egg-sized fruit which start off green and slowly turn purple as they ripen. These plants are occasionally available, otherwise you will have to grow your own from seed.

**Cultivation** Passion flowers are easy plants to grow. They thrive best in a warm sunny spot. Grow them in large pots and train the stems up a framework of canes, or alternatively plant them in the border and let the stems ramble up wire netting on the side of the greenhouse. It is important to water and feed the plants well during the growing season.

The fruit start to swell almost as soon as the flowers are over, provided they have been pollinated (you need two flowers open at the same time for this to happen – they are not self-fertile). They are ready to eat some time after they have turned purple, when the skin wrinkles. The fruit will easily fall from the plant when it is ripe. Passion fruit are eaten rather like boiled eggs; just slice the top off and eat the contents with a spoon. Fruit are produced a few at a time throughout mid and late summer.

The plants will start shedding their leaves towards autumn. When this happens, gradually cut down the watering to prepare them for their winter rest. Once all the leaves have fallen, cut the old stems down to 15 cm (6 in) from the base of the plant, and remove all the dead leaves which could otherwise go mouldy. Keep the plants fairly dry in winter, though an occasional light watering may be needed to stop the remaining stems from shrivelling. When new shoots start to appear in spring, gradually begin watering again.

Plants can be grown from seed sown in the spring (these won't fruit until they are two to three years old). They can also be grown from cuttings taken in spring or summer, though they are not as easy to root as many greenhouse plants.

**POINSETTIA**

Poinsettias are popular, traditional Christmas pot plants, with bright red, pink or white bracts (the true flowers are the tiny yellow elements in the centre). The plants are not suited for growing permanently in the greenhouse as they need higher winter temperatures than would be economical. However, it is useful to keep plants in the greenhouse after they have finished flowering, when they have lost their looks. Poinsettias are not the easiest of plants to keep, and many people find it easier just to throw away the old plants and buy new ones each year. If you want to try keeping them, this is what to do.

**Cultivation** When the flowers are over, take the plants out to the greenhouse and cut the stems down to about 10 cm (4 in) above the top of the pot. Dab a little sharp sand on to the cut to stop the white sap bleeding out (wash your hands afterwards as the sap is an irritant). Repot if necessary, and water very sparingly until the plant starts making new growth. Then increase the watering, but always keep poinsettias rather drier than normal greenhouse plants. Feed them occasionally. Grow poinsettias shaded from the very brightest sun during the summer.

In the autumn, when the weather starts getting cold, it is advisable to move the plants back into the greenhouse as they need a minimum temperature of 13°C (55°F). Do not be surprised if they do not produce new red bracts for Christmas – they are specially treated at the nursery to make them flower out of season. They will probably flower again around Easter.

**Propagation** Poinsettias can be propagated by cuttings. It is most convenient to use the stems you cut off in late spring for cuttings, though you can take them from plants any time during the spring and summer. They root best in sharp sand.

Plants you raise yourself from cuttings will grow much bigger than those you have bought. This is because the bought plants will have been treated with a chemical dwarfing agent that is not available to amateur growers. However, plants can be stopped once or twice to give them a bushier appearance.

**PRIMULA**

Several different kinds of primula are grown as winter and early spring flowering pot plants – *Primula obconica, P. malacoides, P. sinensis,* and several good hybrids. You can buy the plants when they are in flower but for a wider choice of unusual kinds it is best to grow your own from seeds.

**Propagation** To have flowers for Christmas, sow *P. obconica* at the end of January, *P. sinensis* in March, and *P. malacoides* in April. If you want more plants to flower later in the spring, make another sowing of each of these a few weeks after the first.

**Cultivation** Greenhouse primulas need to be grown in permanent shade and moisture. Sow the seeds on the surface of the compost (don't cover it), and stand the pots in a shallow tray of water to keep

Primulas are available in hundreds of different colours and can be grown from seed for winter and spring flowering.

Above: *Primula obconica* is one of the most popular varieties for growing under glass, with colours ranging from white, pink and red to lilac, mauve and even blue.

Right: Although Streptocarpus, or Cape primrose, are often sold as pot plants for indoor display, they are easier to cultivate in a heated greenhouse, since they require a constantly humid atmosphere.

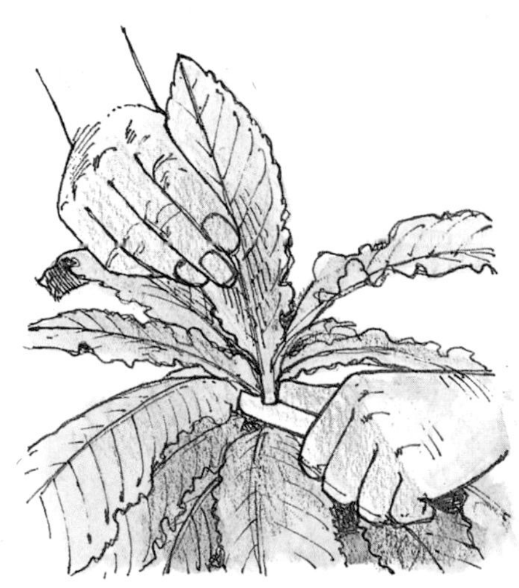

2. Fill a 5 cm (2 in) pot with general purpose compost and, using a small stick or the end of a pencil, make a hole 4 cm ($1\frac{1}{2}$ in) deep in the centre. Push the cut end of the leaf in and firm well. Water in well and keep constantly humid until the cutting is well rooted and a new plant has started to grow.

TAKING STREPTOCARPUS LEAF CUTTINGS

1. Cut a young but full size leaf from near the centre of an established plant. Use a sharp knife and cut the leaf as near to its base as possible.

3. Sometimes you will find more than one plant growing from a single cutting. When the plants are big enough to handle, pot each one individually. The leaf can be removed once the plants are growing well.

them damp. Seed can go into the propagator to germinate but it is not essential – what is vital is that the pots are kept shaded, and at a temperature below 16°C (60°F) or they will not be able to germinate until the temperature drops.

When the seedlings are big enough, prick them out into trays and then pot them into 9 cm ($3\frac{1}{2}$ in) pots. Use peat-based compost, and again keep the plants permanently moist and well shaded. In an all-glass greenhouse, the best place to grow them is on moist capillary matting underneath the staging.

**Display** Feed regularly, and when the flower stems appear take extra care the plants do not dry out at all. Plants in full flower can be taken indoors, or left in the greenhouse for winter display. After flowering, primula plants are thrown away and new plants are raised from seed each year.

**STREPTOCARPUS**

Cape primrose, or Streptocarpus, are pretty little plants with long strap-like leaves and large exotic looking flowers in a wide range of colours. They are much easier to grow in a slightly heated greenhouse than they are indoors, as the plants like a constantly humid atmosphere. They must also be kept well shaded from direct sun, and will grow particularly well under the staging of an all-glass greenhouse.

**Cultivation** Plants should be kept just moist during the growing season – spring to late summer – and fed regularly, especially when in flower. Old leaves which have become broken or damaged should be cut off, as should dead flower stems, to keep plants looking their best.

**Propagation** Streptocarpus can be propagated from seed in spring or from leaf cuttings taken in spring or late summer. They are not the easiest plants to propagate successfully, because the seedlings or cuttings must never be allowed to dry out. It helps to stand the pots on damp capillary matting to maintain the necessary moisture.

Young plants are very slow growing at first, and will probably only flower towards the end of their first year. Old plants can be split up in spring or autumn; plants produced this way are much easier to manage and also have the advantage of flowering sooner.

# A NURSERY FOR PLANTS AND VEGETABLES

Although tomatoes, peppers, aubergines, cucumbers, melons and many bedding plants and annuals can be raised on windowsills indoors, much better results will be obtained in the more controlled environment of a greenhouse.

## TOMATOES, PEPPERS AND AUBERGINES

If you want to raise your own tomato, pepper and aubergine plants, a heated greenhouse is almost essential. The plants are initially slow growing, and need to be sown early in spring and kept in high temperatures, otherwise they will not start cropping until very late in the summer. It is sometimes possible to raise reasonable plants by sowing seed on a warm, well-lit indoor windowsill, but results are not so reliable. Unless you have the proper facilities, it is normally better to buy plants when you are ready to plant them.

### SOWING AND PRICKING OUT

To raise greenhouse tomato, pepper and aubergine plants, sow the seeds thinly in pots in a temperature of 16°–21°C (60°–70°F) during February or early March. (An electrically heated, thermostatically controlled propagator is the most economical way of providing the temperature needed.) Keep the seed compost just moist but take care not to over-water as damping off is always a problem with early sowings. (Water with cheshunt compound or spray with liquid copper if damping off is a problem.)

When the seedlings have come through, wait until the first pair of leaves (seed leaves) have opened out fully before pricking them out. Handle the seedlings by their leaves, not by the stems. Prick out only the strongest seedlings, as you will probably only need a few plants, but do prick out half a dozen or so more seedlings than you need plants. This allows you to choose the pick of the bunch at planting time.

Put the seedlings into clean trays, filled with a good peat-based seed compost. When pricking out, plant the seedlings right up to their necks in the compost, so the seed leaves are almost resting on the surface. Do this even if the seedlings have become a little drawn up and leggy, as it produces better plants.

Return the pots of young seedlings to the propagator after watering them in, and grow them on at the same temperature, 16–21°C (60–70°F), for another few weeks.

### GENERAL CARE OF YOUNG PLANTS

Ventilate the propagator slightly on fine days (most kinds have vents in the lid), to prevent fungal disease, but shut the vents

**PRICKING OUT SEEDLINGS**

1. Prick out the seedlings, when the seed leaves have just opened out and they are large enough to handle. It helps if you loosen the roots gently with a plant tag.

2. Plant them in rows in another tray of fresh compost. Make small holes with a plant tag, setting the seedlings so their leaves are just above the surface of the compost.

3. After filling the tray with seedlings, water them in lightly, before returning them to the propagator for another few weeks.

again at night. Then start acclimatizing the young plants to cooler conditions very slowly.

Start when the young plants are several centimetres high, gradually reducing the temperature in the propagator to 10°C (50°F) when the plants are 10–13 cm (4–5 in) high. Then start hardening the plants off, by removing the lid of the propagator during the day, and replacing it at night. After a week or so, the plants should be ready to leave the propagator and take their place on the greenhouse staging. Keep the heating in the greenhouse set as high as you can, ideally at 10°C (50°F), but certainly no lower than 7·5°C (45°F).

During the entire propagation period keep a close watch on the plants and spray them as soon as you see the first signs of any fungal disease – some growers like to spray this group of plants fortnightly with benomyl as a precaution. Although the disease is normally the main problem, keep a watch out for greenfly or whitefly, too, and again spray if necessary.

Water the plants sparingly so as not to encourage over-lush growth, but when you do water – ideally once a week – give them a diluted liquid tomato feed made up to the usual strength. When the young plants fill their pots with roots, they are ready for planting.

By this time the tomato plants should have their first flowers just opening – if

Tomatoes, such as 'Gardener's Delight' can be raised from seed and then grown outdoors if you have a heated greenhouse. Sow in early spring, to ensure ripening before the end of the summer.

not, delay planting for a while as tomatoes tend to grow rather too leafy unless they are planted in flower. Do not wait for peppers and aubergines to flower, but plant as soon as the roots start coming out through the bottom of the pot. If you wait too long, they suffer a check in growth from which they never really recover, and the inevitable result is that cropping will also be jeopardized.

## CUCUMBERS AND MELONS

Cucumber and melon plants do not need sowing as early as tomatoes, since they are much faster growing plants.

### SOWING

If you have a cold greenhouse you can raise your own cucumber or melon plants by sowing them during May, or even as late as June. Or you can raise them on a warm indoor windowsill, sowing in late April or early May. If you have a heated greenhouse and propagator, though, sow the seeds in mid March at a temperature of 21°C (70°F).

To raise cucumber and melon plants, sow the seeds singly in 9 cm (3½ in) pots, half filled with a good peat-based seed compost. They germinate very quickly.

### GENERAL CARE

When the seed leaves open out, start to top up the pots with more seed compost, 13 mm (½ in) at a time. This has the same effect as pricking out seedlings up to their necks. This individual treatment avoids any damage to either the plants or their roots, and is advisable since cucumbers and melon plants are rather sensitive in their early stages.

Start gradually lowering the temperature in the propagator a few degrees at a time, until by the time the plants have three or four leaves the temperature is down to 10°C (50°F). The plants will need a little more watering than tomato plants. After three to four weeks, start to give them a well diluted feed once or twice a week using a general-purpose liquid or soluble feed.

Spray with fungicide if necessary, but cucumber plants are notorious for dying off very quickly if anything goes wrong with them, and it is easier to raise new plants than try and save sick ones. Harden the plants off as described for tomatoes, and plant them out as soon as the roots start to show through the holes in the bottom of the pot. As with peppers and aubergines, plants will not grow so successfully if they are allowed to become pot bound, so check to make sure that this does not happen.

Sweet pea seedlings in trays of seed compost. When they fill the tray, it's time to harden them off. Stand outside during the day, and bring them in at night, before planting outdoors permanently.

## BEDDING PLANTS

Annual bedding plants come in two basic types; hardy annuals and half-hardy annuals (HA or HHA). Hardy annuals include sweet peas, cornflowers, larkspur, pot marigolds (*Calendula*), alyssum, godetia, sunflowers, nasturtiums and love-in-a-mist (*Nigella*). Examples of half-hardy annuals are anthirrinums, bedding dahlias, morning glory (*Ipomoea*), salvia, French and African marigolds (*Tagetes*), tobacco plants (*Nicotiana*), lobelia, petunias and zinnias. Seed packets are always marked to show which are hardy and which half-hardy—an important

Above: Half-hardy annual seeds can only be successfully raised in a heated greenhouse. When the seed leaves have formed, making the seedlings large enough to handle, it's time to prick them out.

Being hardy annuals, nasturtium seeds can be usually sown outdoors. On wet, heavy soil, or during a cold spring, however, it's advisable to raise them in a greenhouse, and then plant out later.

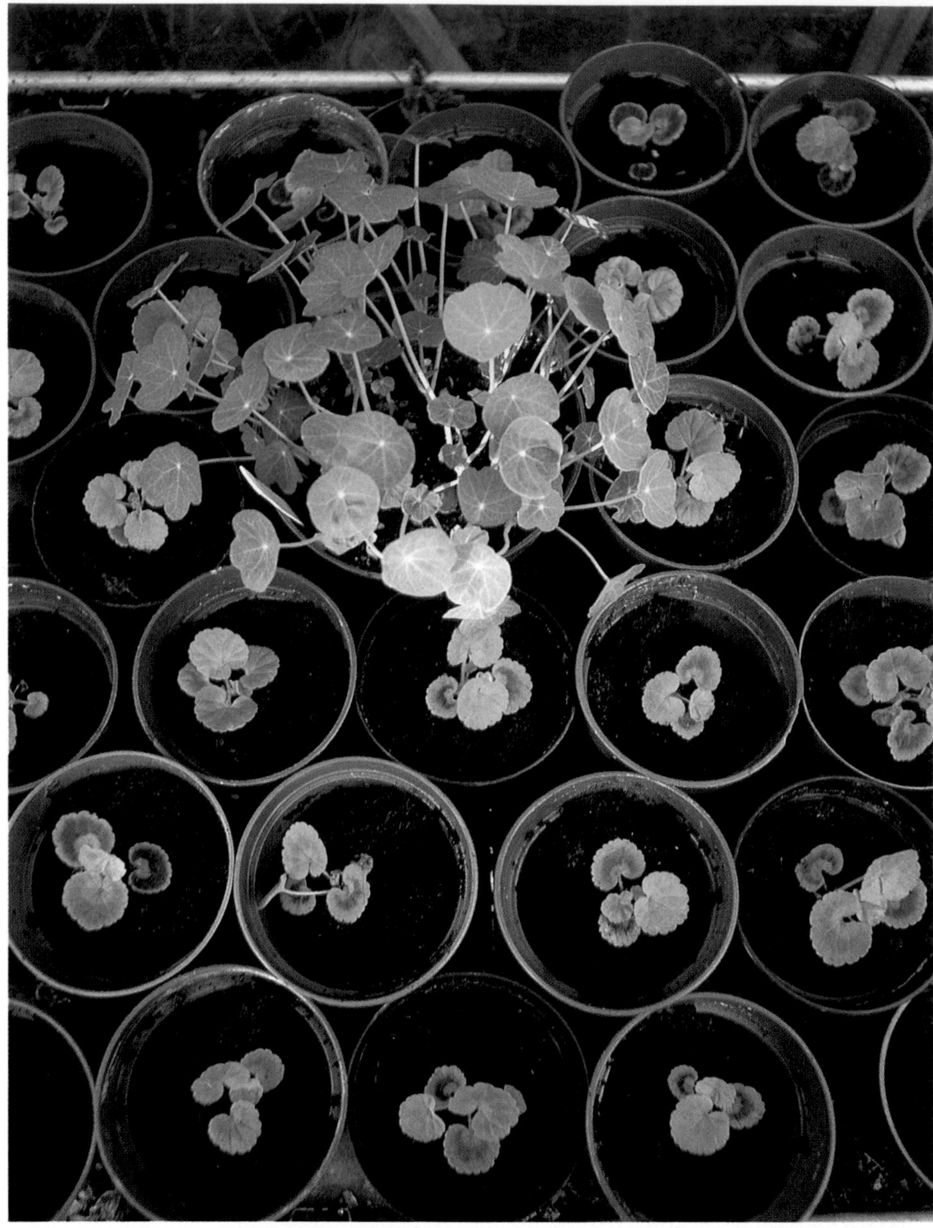

Zonal geraniums, distinguished by their green leaves with conspicuous darker markings, can be grown from seed (other types of geraniums are usually raised from cuttings).

distinction as the two are grown in slightly different ways.

What both types have in common is that they must be sown early in spring, during March, or they will not be big enough to start flowering at the beginning of the summer.

## HARDY ANNUALS

Hardy annuals do not mind the cold, and can be sown straight into the garden where they are to flower, provided growing conditions are good. But in a cold spring, on wet heavy soil, or if your garden soil is likely to be full of weed seeds which will quickly grow and smother young seedlings, it is best to grow hardy annuals in trays in the greenhouse, and plant them out later. So long as you only grow hardy annuals, you can raise bedding plants in an unheated greenhouse.

**Sowing** To raise hardy annuals under glass, sow the seeds in small pots of seed compost, and water them in. Keep them shaded from direct sun, and take care not to overwater whilst not letting the compost become completely dry either. Watch out for seedlings keeling over suddenly, which may indicate damping off. Remove affected seedlings immediately if it occurs, and spray the remainder with cheshunt compound or liquid copper.

**Pricking out and growing on** When the seedlings are big enough to handle, prick them out into trays of seed compost, spacing them 5 cm (2 in) apart. Handle them by the leaves, not the stems, to avoid bruising. Water them in, and water again whenever the compost starts to feel dryish; there is no need to feed for about four to six weeks after pricking out the seedlings. After that, water with liquid or soluble feed regularly, according to the manufacturer's instructions.

When the plants fill the tray, harden them off for a week or two by standing them outside during the day and bringing them back into the greenhouse at night. Then they are ready to plant out. You do not need to wait until after the risk of frost is over to plant out hardy annuals, though obviously it pays to choose good weather.

## HALF-HARDY ANNUALS

Half-hardy annuals need more warmth, and can only be propagated 100 per cent successfully in a heated greenhouse. An electrically heated propagator is a great help, as this is an economical way to provide the high temperatures they need early in life.

**Sowing** Sow the seed in the same way as for hardy annuals, but after watering them in, place the pots inside the propagator with the thermostat set at 18·5–21°C (65°–70°F).

Cover the lid of the propagator with a piece of old net curtain, or something similar, to shade the seedlings from the sun. Check them every day and when a good number of seedlings are through, gradually start lowering the temperature in the propagator a few degrees at a time.

**Pricking out and growing on** When the seedlings are big enough, prick them out into trays and then return the trays to the propagator for a week or two longer while you continue lowering the temperature slowly. By the time the seedlings are almost touching each other you should have hardened them off enough to stand them on the greenhouse staging, where the temperature will only be 4·5°–7·5°C (40°–45°F) at night.

From now on, grow them in exactly the same way as hardy annuals, but taking particular care to harden them off very thoroughly before planting them out. As they dislike cold weather, do not plant half-hardy annuals out until after the date of the last frost expected in your area – this is normally mid May in the south of the country, and early June in the north.

**Growing on the windowsill** If you do not have a propagator, it is possible to germinate half-hardy annual seeds on a warm indoor windowsill. This needs to be out of direct sunlight, but in good indirect light, or the seedlings will become 'leggy', making them particularly susceptible to fungal diseases.

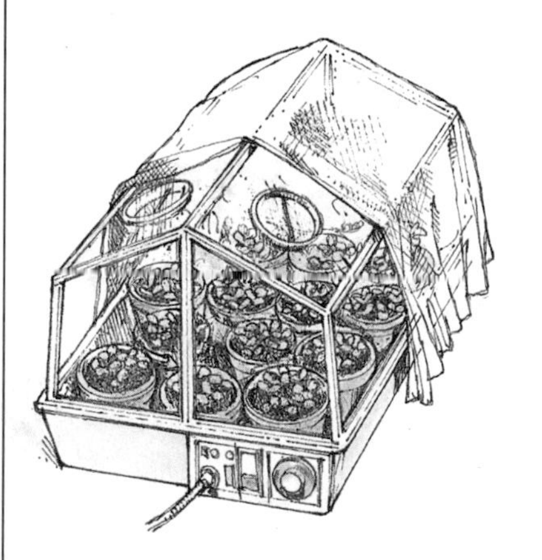

An electrically heated propagator with thermostatic control is ideal for propagating half-hardy annuals. On sunny days, shade the seedlings with fine netting to prevent scorching.

Sow the seeds as described before (see *Sowing*), but after watering them in, stand the pots inside large plastic bags to retain humidity until the seeds have germinated. When the seedlings come through, prick them out into trays – you can buy special kinds for use on windowsills, which have drip trays underneath and plastic covers on top. Once the weather is warm enough, move the trays out to the greenhouse with the heating set at a minimum of 7·5°C (45°F), and grow on as before.

## GROWING LATE PLANTS TO FILL GAPS

People sometimes deliberately sow a few bedding plants later, in May or even early June, to produce plants for filling odd gaps that sometimes appear in a border towards the end of the summer.

Mesembryanthemums are half-hardy annuals suitable for growing in sunny rockeries and on banks.

For high quality biennials, like these sweet William, sow seed under glass in summer, keep in a cold greenhouse over winter and plant out the following spring for a summer display.

If you want to do this, sow a few seeds thinly straight into 9 cm ($3\frac{1}{2}$ in) pots on the greenhouse staging, keep them shaded from strong sun, and do not prick them out. Instead, let the plants grow in a clump, and when they fill the pot with roots, transplant the entire group without splitting it up, to wherever more plants are needed in a border.

## HERBACEOUS AND BIENNIAL FLOWERS

Herbaceous plants are border plants such as delphinium, lupin and shasta daisy, that die down in winter and come up again every spring. Biennial flowers include wallflowers, sweet Williams and foxgloves that grow leaves in their first year, flower in their second and are then replaced with new plants. Both types of plants are commonly grown from seed, which is sown in mid summer, though many perennials can also be grown from cuttings taken in spring. It takes about 6 months to 1 year to have plants ready to go out in the garden. The plants are propagated in spring or summer, planted out in autumn or spring, and flower the year after.

## GROWING FROM SEED

You do not need a heated greenhouse or a propagator for growing perennial and biennial flowers from seed, as they are sown in mid summer.

Sow the seed thinly in pots in the greenhouse, following the same method as for hardy annual bedding plants. Because they are sown during the hottest part of the year, it is most important to keep the pots moist, shaded and as cool as possible all the time. When the seedlings are big enough, prick them out into trays and later pot them into 9 cm ($3\frac{1}{2}$ in) pots. They can then be placed outside for the summer, and the plants set out in their final garden positions in the autumn.

If you want really good quality plants,

TAKING CHRYSANTHEMUM CUTTINGS

1. In early spring, cut shoots growing from chrysanthemum stools just below leaf joints.

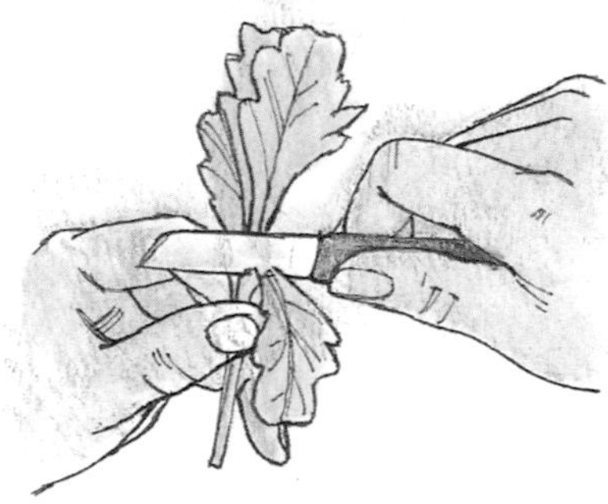

2. Remove the lower leaves of the shoot, using a sharp knife, and then push into pots or trays of compost.

3. Place the pots or trays of cuttings in a propagator. They should root quickly if kept at a temperature of 16°C (60°F).

however, it is a good idea to keep them in the greenhouse for the winter (either a cold or frost-free greenhouse is fine). The plants are then planted out in spring, around late March, during a spell of reasonably good weather. This is a particularly useful technique if you garden on wet heavy soil, for young plants that are put out in autumn often rot. They will certainly get off to a better start planted in the spring, unless the soil is excessively free draining. All perennial and biennial plants can be overwintered under glass in pots, except those that flower early in the spring, such as wallflowers. These are best planted in the autumn.

## GROWING FROM CUTTINGS

Many kinds of border plants can also be grown from cuttings. This is a useful way of propagating plants you already have growing well in the garden or where you can get cuttings from friends. These cuttings are best taken in early spring, when the first new shoots appear. You need a heated greenhouse, and ideally a heated propagator to guarantee success.

Dahlia and chrysanthemum cuttings are very easy to raise. Both plants are dug up from the garden in autumn and stored in a frost-free place over winter, so the bare roots can be forced to produce the cuttings you need.

Pot the roots in moist peat, and then put in a warm place such as the propagator. When they have grown a few shoots 10 cm (4 in) long, cut them off and use them as cuttings. These will root quickly in the propagator at 16°C (60°F). Old dahlia tubers can be replanted, but old chrysanthemum plants are normally thrown away after producing a good crop of cuttings.

Garden plants such as delphiniums and lupins produce shoots in the garden in early spring and these too can be used as cuttings. Growing such plants from cuttings is a good idea if you want a lot of them and don't mind waiting a year. If you only need one or two new plants, or want immediate results, it is better to dig up and split the old roots in autumn or early spring, giving an immediate supply of new flowering size plants. To take cuttings from these plants, there is no need to dig up the roots and force them. Just cut off a few shoots as soon as they are about

Cuttings are easy to grow from lupin and other herbaceous plants in early spring. When shoots are about 10 cm (4 in) long, cut them away from the stem of a plant just below a joint. For best results, grow the cuttings in a propagator in the greenhouse. Make a hole in the compost with a dibber or wooden stick and insert each cutting firmly. Grow the cuttings in a moist atmosphere at about 16°C (60°F). The roots should develop in about three to four weeks.

10 cm (4 in) long and root them as before. (Do not take more than about one third of the shoots from any plant or you will prevent it growing healthily.)

Pot the cuttings when they are well rooted and grow them on until the plants are large enough to plant out in the garden, which will probably be in the autumn. Again, if growing conditions are not very good or you want especially good plants, you could pot them into bigger pots and keep them in a cold or frost-free greenhouse over the winter.

## VEGETABLES

Many people sow their vegetable crops straight into the vegetable garden in rows. But if you have a greenhouse, it is worthwhile raising some – or all – of your vegetable plants under cover. Given protection from the weather you can get early crops off to an even earlier start than usual, as well as producing top quality young plants that will give bigger or better crops. A cold greenhouse is all you need for raising most vegetables, but a little heat is useful for producing extra early plants.

Vegetable plants can be divided into two main types, in much the same way as bedding plants. There are the hardy types, cabbages, leeks, etc, which don't mind the cold and can be planted out before the last expected frost, and half-hardy kinds, such as sweet corn, French beans, marrows and courgettes, which cannot be planted out until after the last frost. Like bedding plants, it is important to sow most kinds of vegetables at just the right time if they are to crop properly. With fast growing kinds, like lettuce, though, sowing dates are less precise. These crops can be sown little and often, producing a succession of crops. Full details of the sowing times for individual varieties of vegetables will be found in the instructions on the backs of the seed packets, but the following chart gives a general guide.

Although you can sow lettuce straight into the garden, the results will be better if the seedlings are raised in the greenhouse. Sow seeds every two or three weeks for a steady supply.

VEGETABLE SOWING UNDER GLASS

| Crop | Sow | Notes |
|---|---|---|
| Broad beans | Feb–Mar | |
| Broccoli – sprouting | April | |
| Brussels sprouts | Feb<br>Mar–April | early varieties<br>late varieties |
| Cabbage – spring | July–Aug | |
| Cabbage – summer | Feb–Mar | |
| Cabbage – winter | April–May | |
| Calabrese | Mar–May | |
| Cauliflower | Jan–Mar | |
| Courgettes | April | |
| Cucumbers – outdoor | April | |
| French beans | April | |
| Herbs | Feb–April<br>April | frost-hardy varieties<br>tender varieties |
| Leeks | Jan–Feb<br>Feb–Mar | early varieties<br>late varieties |
| Lettuce | Jan–July | |
| Marrows | April | |
| Onions | Feb–Mar | |
| Peas | Feb–June | |
| Runner beans | April | |
| Savoy cabbage | April–May | |
| Sweet corn | April | |
| Tomatoes – outdoor | Mar | |

French beans and other half-hardy vegetables will not survive a frost or cold weather, so raise seedlings in the greenhouse and plant outside in milder weather. 'Blue Lake' French beans, shown here, are ready for picking.

## HARDY VEGETABLES

Hardy vegetables, such as lettuce, cabbage, cauliflower, brussels sprouts, leeks and onions, all of which have small seeds, can be sown in the same way as hardy bedding plants – in pots, with the seedlings being pricked out into trays later.

Although they will germinate without any heat, the seeds do come up better if they are kept in a frost-free greenhouse, or a heated propagator. This is especially useful if you are making very early sowings.

A temperature of 16°C (60°F) is all that is needed; in fact lettuce may not germinate at higher temperatures than this. Large seeded hardy vegetables, such as peas and beans, are best space sown – that is the seeds should be spaced out about 2·5–5 cm (1–2 in) apart in rows in a seed tray. This way there is no need to prick out the seedlings. The young plants should be planted out in the garden as soon as you see roots beginning to grow through the holes in the bottom of their tray.

Globe artichokes have a better chance of surviving if you grow from seed in a greenhouse instead of sowing directly in the garden. When seedlings are large enough to handle, prick them out into pots. Transplant to the garden when danger of frost has passed.

For top quality Savoy cabbages, raise the seedlings in a frost-free greenhouse or, even better, an electric propagator. Sow the seed in spring and plant out in summer for harvesting during the winter.

To space sow, fill the tray with seed compost, space the seeds out over the surface, and press them lightly into the surface so that they are just covered with compost. Water them in, and treat as usual from then on. These seeds, too, germinate without extra heat, but if it is available, they will come up much faster and better. Again, the young plants need to be planted as soon as the tray is filled with roots. There is no need to wait until after the risk of frost, though as usual it pays to plant during a good spell of weather.

**HALF-HARDY VEGETABLES**

If you want to grow half-hardy vegetables, such as marrows, sweet corn or French beans, a frost-free greenhouse is necessary, and a heated propagator will come in very useful.

Because the plants will not withstand any frost, it is essential to sow at precisely the right time so that the plants are ready to be set out as soon as the weather is warm enough for them. They are generally quite fast growing plants – if

'Vegetable Spaghetti', a variety of squash, will thrive if grown under glass. To eat this intriguing vegetable you boil it whole for 25 minutes, then cut it in half and fork out the spaghetti-like strands.

Bush tomato plants grow without extra support, but it can be difficult to see the crop among the thick foliage.

you live in the south of the country and want plants to put out in mid May, sow from early to mid April. Further north, you should sow up to two weeks later.

As half-hardy vegetables mainly have large seeds, they can be space sown in trays, in the same way as peas and beans. But for even better results, sow two or three seeds in a 9 cm ($3\frac{1}{2}$ in) pot, and remove all but the strongest seedlings when they come up. This way, if the weather is too cold when the pots are filled with root, you can move them into larger pots, and continue growing them under glass for another week or two if need be, without them coming to harm.

## TREES AND SHRUBS

Raising your own trees and shrubs from scratch is a rewarding pastime, as well as an inexpensive way of stocking a garden or producing plants for a new hedge. Although young plants could be propagated outside in the vegetable garden or in a cold frame, they will grow much faster under glass.

They are also safer under glass, where there is less risk of them being overwhelmed by weeds, or destroyed by mice, rabbits or slips of the hoe. A cold greenhouse is all you need, plus a good deal of patience. Although some of the faster growing shrubs may be ready for planting after a year, many kinds take longer.

## TREES AND SHRUBS FROM SEED

A huge range of trees and shrubs can now be grown from seed, which is readily available to the amateur gardener. The majority of seed firms despatch seeds during the spring months, and this is the most suitable time to sow them.

**Germination** Sow them in pots in exactly the same way as usual, but cover the seeds with a thin layer of horticultural sand. Water in, and keep the pots moist, and in a shady spot. Some may germinate within a few weeks, but don't worry if they take longer – many trees and shrubs are notoriously slow to come through.

Many kinds won't germinate at all until after a prolonged cold spell. This is nature's way of ensuring that the young seedlings only come up in spring, and not just before the start of bad weather. There

'Tennessee Waltz', like other fuchsia hybrids, can be increased by taking cuttings of young shoots any time between spring and early autumn. Use only the best plants.

are two ways of tackling this delay. One is to be patient, and put the pots of seeds outside in the garden (keeping them watered in the meantime) until the following spring. Then if you bring them in around February or March, and put them into the heated propagator at 16°–21°C (60°–70°F) they should come up within a few weeks. In an unheated or frost-free greenhouse they'll take a bit longer.

The other alternative is to fool the seeds into thinking that winter has come and gone, by popping them into the fridge for four to six weeks. To work properly, the seed must be either sown in a pot or mixed with some sand, and kept moist during this treatment. Just putting the packet of seed into the fridge does not work. (To prevent domestic objections, you can always put the pots of seed inside polythene bags.)

When the seeds do come up, there is no need to prick them out straight away provided they are well spaced out. They normally do better left to grow on for a while without being disturbed.

**Potting up and potting on** The best time to pot seedlings is in the autumn, just after they stop growing, or early the following spring. Use 9 cm ($3\frac{1}{2}$ in) pots and John Innes potting compost No. 2, and grow them on in slight shade, keeping the young plants just moist all the time.

When the original containers are full of root, pot them on to 13 cm (5 in) pots. If you have a lot of plants and don't want to go to the expense of buying plastic pots, use the type that look like black polythene bags – these are sold in garden centres very cheaply.

**Cultivation** Feed and water the young plants well during the growing season, from spring to late autumn, but keep them almost dry in winter. If space permits, grow the young plants on in a well-shaded and well ventilated greenhouse in summer, and in winter – this will make them grow fast. But if you need the room, plunge rows of pots up to their rims in the soil in the vegetable garden. And don't forget they still need regular feeding and watering.

Different species will grow at different rates, but the first should be ready to plant out 18–24 months after sowing. It is fairly important not to plant young trees and shrubs out until they are about the same size as those you would buy from a garden centre. In your home 'nursery' young plants will automatically get regular attention, but out in the garden they are more likely to be left to fend for themselves, and unless they are reasonably big there is a high risk of losing them if you plant them out too soon.

### TREES AND SHRUBS FROM CUTTINGS

Although seeds are a cheap way of adding new trees and shrubs to the garden, cuttings will give you much faster results. In some cases you will have plants that are ready to put out within a year, provided you choose fast growing kinds. The drawback, however, is that you will need to find a suitable source of cuttings in the first place.

**Availability** You can use plants in your own garden, or those belonging to friends. Alternatively, join a horticultural society and arrange to make swaps with other members. You can sometimes buy tree and shrub cuttings that are already rooted. These just need potting and growing on, following the same method given below after rooting your own cuttings.

**Suitable varieties** Not all shrubs are easy to root from cuttings. As a rough guide, you can reckon plants that are expensive to buy are difficult to propagate. Trees and shrubs that grow particularly quickly and easily from cuttings include lavender, shrubby sages (*Salvia*), hardy fuchsias, rosemary, hydrangea, hebe, rue (*Ruta*) and cistus. Moderately easy, though a bit slower to root, are dogwood (*Cornus*), butterfly bush (*Buddleia*), Mexican orange blossom (*Choisya ternata*), smokebush (*Cotinus coggygria*), hypericum, mahonia, shrubby potentillas, flowering currants (*Ribes*), alder (*Sambucus*), escallonia, rose species, berberis, pyracantha, forsythia, weigela, willows (*Salix*) and poplars. (Always take more cuttings than you need, to allow for the inevitable losses.)

There are two seasons when shrub cuttings root particularly well – mid summer and early autumn. The techniques used are the same for both groups, but the first root and grow quicker, so they are best kept separate from the others for ease of working.

**MID SUMMER CUTTINGS**

In June and July the new growth is still soft, so take softwood cuttings in the same way as you would of a geranium or fuchsia. Use secateurs to cut 10 cm (4 in) lengths from the tips of strong, healthy looking shoots. Put them straight into a polythene bag to stop them wilting while you finish collecting your other cuttings.

Back at the greenhouse, prepare the cuttings using a very sharp knife to cut cleanly just beneath a leaf joint, and remove the leaves from the lower half of the stem. Dip the base of each cutting in hormone rooting powder, and push four to six of them around the edge of a 13 cm (5 in) pot filled with a mix of 50 per cent sharp horticultural sand and 50 per cent sedge peat. Water them in, and spray the foliage with fungicide solution immediately afterwards. From then on, keep the cuttings humid, shaded, and well ventilated so they don't get too hot.

**General care** A good place to root shrub cuttings in summer is under the staging, provided the greenhouse has glass down to ground level. They should

New growth and a healthy appearance indicate that fuchsia cuttings have rooted. Pot them on into individual pots immediately – a long delay may check their growth. Where cuttings have been taken from several varieties, make sure you label them.

### HARDWOOD CUTTINGS

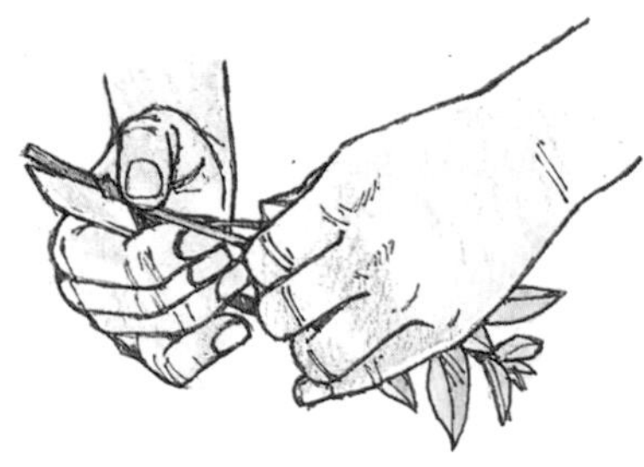

1. Take 15–20 cm (6–8 in) hardwood cuttings from shrubs in September. Trim the base of the shoot below a leaf joint.

2. Pinch out the soft growing tip, using your thumb and finger, and then remove most of the lower leaves.

3. Push the cuttings into a prepared bed in the greenhouse border, leaving 2·5–5 cm (1–2 in) showing above ground.

Increase your stock of herbs by taking semi-ripe cuttings from shrubby species – bay, sage, rosemary and rue – in summer. Pot in a peat and sand mix.

be kept constantly just moist. Check daily to see if watering is needed, but avoid over-watering or they may rot. To prevent the leaves from wilting, keep the air around the cuttings humid by spraying them with water every morning, or by damping down the floor of the greenhouse. An effective way of keeping shrub cuttings both moist and humid is by standing the pots on damp capillary matting. Also spray the cuttings fortnightly with fungicide as a precaution to stop grey mould and other fungal diseases developing. If any are seen remove affected leaves or cuttings at once.

The easier cuttings should be fairly well rooted in about six weeks; others may take a few weeks longer. You can easily tell when cuttings have rooted, as suddenly the leaves look plump and healthy, and the young plants start to grow. You will also see roots beginning to grow out through the hole in the base of the pot.

**Growing on** When the cuttings are well rooted, pot each one individually into a 9 cm ($3\frac{1}{2}$ in) pot filled with potting compost. Don't leave them too long in the original pot as the peat/sand mixture in which they were rooted does not contain any plant foods.

The staging of a well-ventilated and well-shaded greenhouse makes a good site for growing on shrub cuttings. In summer feed and water them well, but during the winter keep them almost dry.

Grow the young plants on in the same way as suggested for shrubs raised from seed (see page 81). Feed and water them well, and pot on to 13 cm (5 in) pots when they need it. Stop the new shoots once or twice to make the plants become bushy. Plant them out when they are as big as the ones you might buy commercially.

**EARLY AUTUMN CUTTINGS**

By September, the parent plants you take your cuttings from will not be growing as fast as in summer. The shoots will be woodier, deciduous plants will be about to shed their leaves, and there will not be enough time for cuttings to get well rooted before the winter rest starts. So it pays to make a few small modifications to the method, since these are hardwood shrub cuttings.

**Preparation** Instead of putting the cuttings into pots, it is far better to place them straight into a prepared bed in the border. To prepare the bed, fork plenty of peat and horticultural grit into the soil. This will turn it into a good rooting compost.

If the greenhouse can conveniently be emptied, now is a good time to give it a thorough cleaning. Drench the cuttings' bed with a garden disinfectant, such as Jeyes Fluid, to get rid of any diseased organisms. Leave it for a few days, then fork the soil over and wait until the smell of the disinfectant has completely cleared before taking cuttings.

**Method** Make the cuttings a little longer than before, about 15–45 cm (6–8 in) long. Use a sharp knife to cut the base of the cuttings neatly just below a leaf joint. Then pinch out the growing tip of each shoot, so you remove all the soft, half-grown leaves and only full size leaves remain. Next, remove the leaves from all but the top layer of each cutting.

Dip the base of the cuttings in rooting powder, and push them into the prepared bed, to within 2·5 cm (1 in) of their tops, in a row, spaced about 15 cm (6 in) apart. Water them in, and spray the tops with fungicide as before. Water only lightly in winter, just enough to stop them drying out completely. Don't disturb them until spring, when cuttings that start growing strongly can be dug up carefully and potted. Grow them on as for summer cuttings, leaving unrooted cuttings longer.

# PESTS AND DISEASES UNDER GLASS

When you put up a new greenhouse, you are unlikely to be troubled much by pests or diseases, as it takes time for the house to be colonized by them. But after a year or so, the odd problem will undoubtedly crop up. If you know what to expect, and are properly equipped to tackle these as soon as they arise, you will always be able to keep plants healthy – without using any more chemicals than necessary. One point to bear in mind is that not all greenhouse problems are caused by pests and diseases alone. Some are growing problems, that are best prevented by correct cultivation.

## PESTS

The majority of common greenhouse insect pests can be tackled effectively by spraying with any good systemic insecticide, but don't be afraid to take advice on individual brands from a professional. Some insect pests, such as whitefly and red spider mite, are persistent and need spraying at regular intervals.

**Natural control** Insects can also be controlled without chemicals, by encouraging natural insect predators, such as ladybirds, lacewings and hoverflies, to do the job for you. If you want to use natural pest control, the best plan is to stop using chemicals anywhere in the garden, and plant lots of brightly coloured flowers that provide a good nectar feed for the adult insects – French marigolds (*Tagetes*) are particularly good for encouraging beneficial insects.

Many of these beneficial insects will then find their way inside the greenhouse whenever the ventilators or door are open, but to encourage them in, try planting a few French marigolds in the greenhouse

A clump of French marigolds in a greenhouse will attract nectar-feeding insects whose larvae are predators of greenfly.

border too. Other useful natural predators to encourage are centipedes and black beetles – they remove many harmful insects at ground level.

Outside in the garden, encourage frogs, toads, hedgehogs and garden birds to visit. They will consume vast quantities of slugs and snails, cutting down the chances of these pests attacking plants in the greenhouse. Bluetits will clean large numbers of greenfly from roses and fruit trees, again making it less likely the insects will find their way into the greenhouse.

The biggest problem with natural pest control is that it takes a while for the numbers of beneficial insects to build up to a useful level. If you do have a serious outbreak of greenfly to contend with in the meantime, you may have to spray in order to save plants from being ruined. In this case, use a product based on pirimicarb that is harmless to beneficial insects.

### COMMON GREENHOUSE PESTS

**Ants** They can be a nuisance if they take up residence in a pot, when they remove much of the compost in the process of building a nest. Use ant powder, or if the nest is accessible try pouring boiling water into it.

**Birds** They can be a problem in summer when the greenhouse door and ventilators are open. They may peck ripening tomatoes or grapes, or uproot seedlings. Deter them by fixing netting over vents and door or by hanging a curtain of plastic strips over the doorway.

**Caterpillars** Rarely much of a problem under glass, though they can occasionally make holes in leaves or tomatoes. Culprits can often be found and removed by hand, without spraying.

**Greenfly** Tiny green, pink or brown insects which do not fly, and are found on the growing tips of shoots or under young leaves. Most plants are affected, especially those with soft leaves. Any systemic insecticide will control them, or use a product based on pirimicarb where you want to protect beneficial insects.

**Mice** More of a problem in winter and early spring, especially in country districts. Mice will remove any seeds large enough to eat, but especially peas and beans, which are often buried in the border for later germination. They will also eat small seedlings. Use poisonous bait, traditional traps, or the new humane mouse traps which catch mice, letting you later release them unharmed.

**Mushroom fly** Small black flies that gather in clouds round potted plants. The adults are harmless but lay their eggs in pots, particularly in peat-based composts. The larvae feed on young roots and can do much damage to small seedlings. Protect plants by watering the compost with a solution of malathion, made up to the same strength as you would use for spraying. This should also kill the larvae while they are small.

An infestation of whitefly has caused the edges of these geranium leaves to turn yellow. The plants will eventually be weakened but, except in severe cases, not killed.

Left: Scale insects, which attach themselves to the undersides of leaves, can be removed with a cloth.

Above: The mottling on the leaves of this busy Lizzy is the result of red spider mites.

**Red spider mite** Minute non-flying insects, almost invisible to the naked eye, cause leaves to turn yellow and drop off. In severe cases, small fine webs can be seen at the tips of shoots. They are particularly common on cucumbers, fuchsias and ivies, though most plants can be affected. Spray with a product containing pirimiphos-methyl.

**Scale insect** Less common in a mixed collection, this limpet-like insect about 3 mm ($\frac{1}{8}$ in) long attaches itself to stems and leaves of waxy leaved plants such as citrus. Spray with systemic insecticide.

**Slugs and snails** Among the worst pests under glass. They will make holes in the leaves of mature plants, and often eat

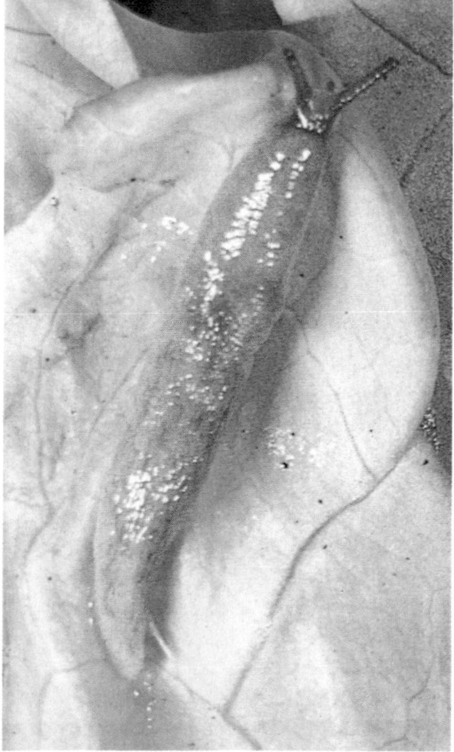

Left: If you see slugs on lettuce leaves, pick them off before they cause any damage.

Above: A colony of greenfly on a house plant can be sprayed with a systemic insecticide.

small seedlings entirely. To prevent slug damage, sprinkle slug pellets very thinly under staging and in the border between plants, or use one of the new products based on aluminium sulphate which are kinder to wildlife. You can also put out an old-fashioned slug trap: a saucer of beer in which slugs and snails will drown.

**Vine weevil** Adults are rarely seen. The larvae, however, are fat white C-shaped grubs often found in pots, especially of cyclamen and primula, though other plants may be affected too. They feed on roots; affected plants turn yellow and wilt rapidly. Protect vulnerable species by watering on a solution of a product containing heptenophos and permethrin in spring.

**Whitefly** Small white, moth-like flying insects found underneath young leaves, especially on fuchsias, though many other plants are affected too. Spray frequently with a product containing permethrin or pirimiphos-methyl.

**Woodlice** Small creatures, 6–13 mm ($\frac{1}{4}$–$\frac{1}{2}$ in) long, that roll up into balls when disturbed. It is said they do not harm plants, only feeding on decaying vegetation. However, it is best to play safe by clearing away rubbish where they can hide, and keeping the greenhouse as clean and tidy as possible to discourage them from taking up residence.

## DISEASES

Plant diseases are most common in early spring, autumn and winter, when the air is cold and damp and light levels are low. You can prevent many diseases by keeping the greenhouse clean and tidy, and removing dead leaves and flowers from

Powdery mildew is a white powder-like mould which appears on leaves when the weather is dull. It is very common in the autumn months.

plants as soon as they are seen. It is also a good idea to keep the greenhouse well ventilated, and to avoid watering plants except when absolutely necessary in winter. Much damping off in seedlings can be avoided by sowing later in spring rather than trying to make too early a start.

### COMMON PLANT DISEASES

**Damping off (seedlings)** This is commonest in early spring. Ensure seed trays, pots and propagators are kept scrupulously clean, and rinse before use with garden disinfectant such as Jeyes Fluid. Ventilate the propagators as soon as seedlings start germinating. Avoid keeping early sown seedlings too wet. If damping off starts, spray with copper fungicide or cheshunt compound.

**Grey mould** Light grey fluff found growing on leaves, fruit or flowers at any time of the year, but particularly when humidity is high and light levels are low. Spray with systemic fungicide such as benomyl or thiophanate-methyl.

**Neck rot** Commonest on young melons and cucumbers, and plants with soft fleshy stems such as cacti and succulents. It is often caused by keeping plants too wet when they are young, in winter when they are resting, or whenever growing conditions are not good. Avoid neck rot by not overwatering at these times. Plants such as cacti can often be treated by cutting away the top of the plant, and re-rooting it. With other kinds of plants cuttings can sometimes be taken to save them.

**Powdery mildew** Talcum-like powder on upper surfaces of leaves, especially cucumbers, though other plants can be affected too. It is mainly a problem in autumn. Spray with benomyl, thiophanate-methyl, carbendazin or liquid copper.

**Root rot** Again, this may be caused by overwatering. The fine root hairs that take water into the plant are killed, so the plant wilts although it has plenty of water. Affected plants may recover if you allow the compost to dry out and keep it drier than usual for a few weeks while new root hairs grow.

Root rot can also be caused by organisms in the soil if the same crops, such as tomatoes, are repeatedly grown in the same site. Avoid this problem by growing crops in a different place each year, by replacing the top 45 cm (18 in) of border soil every year, or by using growing bags for a few years.

## OTHER COMMON PROBLEMS

**Moss or algae** When growing on the compost it normally indicates overwatering – remove it by hand, and keep affected plants slightly drier in future. Make sure watering cans are not left full of water, as algae which develops inside can then spread into plant pots every time you water. Prevent it from forming by washing out the can periodically with garden disinfectant and rinse before use.

Algae and moss growing on the glass or structure of the greenhouse may indicate prolonged high humidity, but it is more usually a sign that the greenhouse is ready for its annual spring clean. Remove plants and scrub down the inside of the house (the glass panes and the frame) and staging with warm water and garden disinfectant, rinse well with clean water, and return the plants.

**Over/underwatering** In both cases plants are likely to show similar symptoms – poor growth and yellowing leaves which eventually drop off. Check the plants daily to see if they need watering, instead of guessing, and aim to keep the pots evenly moist in summer, and dryish in winter. Remember that overwatering, is a common cause of plant failure.

If incorrect watering is a frequent problem, it is a good idea to invest in a water meter to help you get it right, or to change the kind of compost you use. Note that soil-based composts, such as John Innes, dry out fast and need plenty of water, whereas the peat-based kinds hold water for longer and therefore should be watered more sparingly.

**Sun scorch** This can be fatal to young plants and seedlings, and causes unsightly beige marks on leaves of older plants where areas of tissue have been killed. To prevent scorch, always keep young seedlings and cuttings shaded from direct sun, and shade newly potted plants for a week or two until they are well established. Some plants, such as streptocarpus and ferns, need to be grown in slightly shaded

Plant diseases, like the fungal infection on this ivy, can be prevented by removing all dead leaves as soon as you see them.

Paint liquid shading over part of the greenhouse in summer to prevent the sun scorching young plants.

conditions throughout their lives.

Plants most at risk can be protected from scorch by growing them under the staging in summer (they will get enough light if in an all-glass greenhouse), by shading the glass with a liquid shading paint, or by shading part of the house with an old net curtain or sheet.

Badly scorched plants usually die, but those only slightly affected can often be treated by cutting off the most badly damaged leaves. Then put the plant in a cool, shady place, and water well until it starts growing again.

## TOMATO PROBLEMS

Unlike most greenhouse plants that are reasonably trouble free much of the time, tomatoes have a large collection of problems you can expect to come across sooner or later.

Flowers that open but do not set fruit may not have been properly pollinated. This is a common problem with early planted crops in heated greenhouses. You must spray the flowers with water from a hosepipe on fine days or use a hormone fruit setting spray.

Flowers that drop off without opening may be affected by grey mould – spray with benomyl.

Above: Erratic watering of tomato plants can cause fruits to split or crack when they ripen.

Right: Spray plants in the early morning or late afternoon when the sun is not too strong.

Tomato plants that grow lots of leaf but no flowers may have been planted too soon. Next time delay planting until the first truss (bunch) of flowers has opened.

Small pale coloured spots on ripe or unripe fruit is ghost spot, caused by grey mould. Affected fruit are perfectly all right to eat. You cannot treat spotted fruit, but prevent it by spraying with benomyl, particularly in warm, humid weather.

Split or cracked fruit are caused by uneven watering, where plants alternate between being too wet and too dry. The results do not show until some time later, so it is difficult to find out when it may have happened. Avoid the problem by keeping plants uniformly moist – if necessary use an automatic watering system.

Blotchy green patches on otherwise ripe fruit is blotchy ripening – this can be caused by insufficient potash, in which case increase the amount of feed you are giving and be sure to use a special high potash liquid tomato feed. It can also be caused by premature ripening if the plants have had their lower leaves removed – do not take off any leaves unless they have turned yellow.

## SPRAYING HINTS AND TIPS

If you have to spray, always follow the manufacturer's instructions on dilution rate and how often to apply the product. As a general rule, whenever you spray:

- Avoid spraying in bright sunlight/ when plants have been kept very dry, or they may scorch – early morning or late evening is the best time to spray.
- Always make sure you spray in good time; don't wait until damage is severe or it will take plants longer to recover, and they will be left with marked leaves which are unlikely to improve.
- Check the instructions on the bottle to ensure that the spray you are using is suitable for the plants you want to treat. If any plants are known to be sensitive to a particular product, these will be listed in the manufacturer's instructions.
- Always keep a separate sprayer for weedkillers – however well you wash the sprayer out afterwards, there is a risk that a trace may remain that will damage or kill greenhouse plants.

# INDEX

# ACKNOWLEDGEMENTS

The Publishers wish to thank the following for providing photographs in this book:
Baco Ltd/Tony Brabner 13; Eric Crichton 11t, 17, 31, 33b, 36, 38b, 54b, 55, 56, 57, 58, 61, 63tl&b, 65, 66, 67, 68t, 88, 89t, 93t; The Garden Picture Library/R Sutherland 6; Photos Horticultural 20, 27, 62, 71, 79t, 80b, 89b, 90; The Harry Smith Collection 46, 48; Peter Stiles 28, 29t, 38t, 54t, 63tr, 81; Suttons Seeds Ltd 50, 51r.

The following photographs were taken specially for the Octopus Publishing Group Picture Library:
7, 25, 51l, 91; M Boys 10, 15b, 32t, 41, 44, 49, 72, 74, 76, 78, 79b, 84, 85; M Crockett 15t, 16, 23, 26, 93b; J Harpur 11b, 37, 59b, 92; Neil Holmes 8, 12, 18, 21, 30, 34, 35, 39, 40, 42, 43, 47, 53, 60, 68b, 73t, 80t, 83, 86; John Moss 52; John Sims 87; George Wright 32b, 33t, 59t, 64, 73b, 75, 77, 82.